Project Management Professional (PMP)® Cert Guide

D1243894

Gregory Horine, Asad Haque

Pearson

Project Management Professional (PMP)® Cert Guide

ISBN-13: 978-0-13-791893-5

ISBN-10: 0-13-791893-3

Library of Congress Cataloging-in-Publication Data: 2023930985

1 2023

Trademarks

Warning and Disclaimer

Special Sales

For information about buying this title in bulk quantities, or for special sales opportunities (which may include electronic versions; custom cover designs; and content particular to your business, training goals, marketing focus, or branding interests), please contact our corporate sales department at corpsales@pearsoned.com or (800) 382-3419.

For government sales inquiries, please contact governmentsales@pearsoned.com.

For questions about sales outside the U.S., please contact intlcs@pearson.com.

Vice President, IT Professional
Mark Taub

Product Line Manager
Brett Bartow

Executive Editor
Laura Norman

Development Editor
Christopher A. Cleveland

Managing Editor
Sandra Schroeder

Senior Project Editor
Tonya Simpson

Copy Editor
Chuck Hutchinson

Indexer
Timothy Wright

Proofreader
Charlotte Kughen

Publishing Coordinator
Cindy Teeters

Cover Designer
Chuti Prasertsith

Compositor
codeMantra

Pearson's Commitment to Diversity, Equity, and Inclusion

Pearson is dedicated to creating bias-free content that reflects the diversity of all learners. We embrace the many dimensions of diversity, including but not limited to race, ethnicity, gender, socioeconomic status, ability, age, sexual orientation, and religious or political beliefs.

Education is a powerful force for equity and change in our world. It has the potential to deliver opportunities that improve lives and enable economic mobility. As we work with authors to create content for every product and service, we acknowledge our responsibility to demonstrate inclusivity and incorporate diverse scholarship so that everyone can achieve their potential through learning. As the world's leading learning company, we have a duty to help drive change and live up to our purpose to help more people create a better life for themselves and to create a better world.

Our ambition is to purposefully contribute to a world where

- Everyone has an equitable and lifelong opportunity to succeed through learning.

- Our educational products and services are inclusive and represent the rich diversity of learners.

- Our educational content accurately reflects the histories and experiences of the learners we serve.

- Our educational content prompts deeper discussions with learners and motivates them to expand their own learning (and worldview).

While we work hard to present unbiased content, we want to hear from you about any concerns or needs with this Pearson product so that we can investigate and address them.

Please contact us with concerns about any potential bias at https://www.pearson.com/report-bias.html.

Contents at a Glance

Table of Contents

About the Authors

Gregory M. Horine is a certified (PMP, CCP, CSM, SAFe POPM, SAFe RTE, Six Sigma Green Belt) business technology and IT professional with a track record of successful results using servant leadership principles and a focused customer orientation. Gregory has been consistently recognized for excellence in "people" management, leadership maturity, communication skills, problem-solving skills, and in establishing long-term client relationships. Primary areas of expertise and strength include project management and leadership; complete project life cycle experience across multiple industries; agile, waterfall, and hybrid application development; package implementation and integration; enterprise solution development; effective use of project management tools; Microsoft Project; application release management; application development team management; product and product line management; project and portfolio management tools; data analysis and transformation; business process analysis and improvement; vendor and procurement management; mind mapping tools; testing, quality, and risk management; regulatory and process compliance; security and privacy compliance; IT infrastructure upgrades and rollouts; IT Service Management (ITSM) processes; PMO setup and implementation; and remote team management.

In addition, Gregory holds a master's degree in computer science from Ball State University and a bachelor's degree in both marketing and computer science from Anderson University (Anderson, Indiana).

Through his servant leadership approach, Gregory has established a track record of empowering his teammates, improving project communications, overcoming technical and political obstacles, and successfully completing projects that meet the targeted objectives.

Gregory is grateful for the guidance and the opportunities that he has received from many mentors throughout his career. Their patience and influence have helped form a rewarding career marked by continuous learning and improvement.

Asad E. Haque, PMP®, PMI-ACP®, is a well-renowned project management trainer, consultant, and PMP® instructor with more than 30 years of industry experience. He is a PMI Authorized Training Partner (ATP) Instructor and developed the *PMP Certification Complete Video Course and Practice Test* for Pearson/O'Reilly. He is the host of Pearson's two-day PMP Certification Crash Course.

Asad earned his PMP® certification in 2010 and soon afterward began teaching the PMP syllabus for some of the top project management training companies in the USA. He still teaches for them. He has helped thousands of students achieve high first-time pass rates on the PMP exam, and he consistently receives excellent ratings from students. In addition, Asad has taught for universities, the military, corporations, and PMI Authorized Training Providers (ATPs).

After graduating from the University of Salford, UK, with a bachelor's degree in computer science and economics, Asad began a short-lived career in accounting and finance before switching gears to information technology. For 20+ years he managed and led functional IT projects, including human resource information systems (HRIS), business intelligence (BI), and enterprise resource planning (ERP). Asad has led both technical and business teams in implementing solutions for 401K defined contribution plans, health and welfare, and other employee benefits for several Fortune 500 clients. He has managed cross-functional teams globally and has always been recognized for his excellent communication skills among team members, clients, and vendors, and this is truly reflected in the quality of his instruction. Companies that Asad has worked for in the past include Hewitt Associates, IBM, HSBC, First Industrial Realty Trust, and the Northern Trust Bank.

Asad is the cofounder and instructor of 1st Choice Project Management Training based in Chicago, Illinois, and he travels extensively both nationally and internationally to lead such training. Through 1st Choice, he has developed management training materials for clients and teaches several PDU classes on leadership, strategic and business management, and the PMI-ACP exam preparation. He has also partnered in developing a PMP exam simulator.

You can connect with Asad via LinkedIn: https://www.linkedin.com/in/asadehaque/.

Dedications

This book is dedicated to the "students" that I constantly visualized in my mind as I developed this book. The bright and caring family that surrounds my life, including my wife, parents, siblings, in-laws, aunts, uncles, cousins, and grandparents.

This book is dedicated to my father, Nelson "Bud" Horine, who passed away in 2020. My "best man" who is and will be missed.

This book is also dedicated to the parents, families, practitioners, and researchers who are diligently fighting to rescue children from autism spectrum and bipolar disorders.

This book is dedicated to the brave individuals fighting for freedom and against the forces of censorship and tyranny.

This book is dedicated to my key inspirational sources: my incredible wife, Mayme (I still wake up every day with a smile in my heart knowing I am married to her), and my "fabulous five" children: Michael, Victoria, Alex, Luke, and Elayna (each one is a hero to me).

—Greg

I would like to dedicate this book to my amazing wife, Rashida, my partner in life, my partner in business, and my best friend, without whose unwavering support and encouragement this would not have happened. To our eldest daughter, Aleema, who has been pushing me for several years to write a project management book. Her drive and enthusiasm have shown me what can be achieved. To our daughter, Alisha, whose hard work and dedication are an example of how never to give up even when things are not going according to plan. And finally, to our youngest daughter, Sabeen, who has no idea what project management is but has promised to read this book.

—Asad

Acknowledgments

Writing *Project Management Professional (PMP) Cert Guide* is a project in itself! With this Cert Guide, just like any project, you need the involvement of many outstanding team members to make it happen and ensure success. We are grateful for the patience, support, and teamwork demonstrated by our editing team: Laura Norman, who always kept the project on track; Chris Cleveland and Tonya Simpson, who ensured our writing was always the best; and the rest of the Pearson publishing team.

We Want to Hear from You!

As the reader of this book, *you* are our most important critic and commentator. We value your opinion and want to know what we're doing right, what we could do better, what areas you'd like to see us publish in, and any other words of wisdom you're willing to pass our way.

We welcome your comments. You can email or write to let us know what you did or didn't like about this book—as well as what we can do to make our books better.

Please note that we cannot help you with technical problems related to the topic of this book.

When you write, please be sure to include this book's title and author as well as your name and email address. We will carefully review your comments and share them with the author and editors who worked on the book.

Email: community@informit.com

Reader Services

Register your copy of *Project Management Professional (PMP) Cert Guide* at www.pearsonitcertification.com for convenient access to downloads, updates, and corrections as they become available. To start the registration process, go to www.pearsonitcertification.com/register and log in or create an account*. Enter the product ISBN 9780137918935 and click Submit. When the process is complete, you will find any available bonus content under Registered Products.

*Be sure to check the box that you would like to hear from us to receive exclusive discounts on future editions of this product.

Introduction

The Project Management Professional (PMP) certification is a credential that is internationally recognized in the project management discipline. It signifies an individual has the process knowledge, experience, and training that is required to practice the methodologies prescribed by the Project Management Institute (PMI). It has become a professional standard and prerequisite for countless organizations and companies. As of the time of writing, according to PMI, there are currently more than 1 million PMP certification holders in more than 120 countries, and the numbers continue to grow.

Industries that rely on PMP certification include information technology, telecommunications, construction, health care, government, and many other professions. Because project management applies to all industries, the PMP certification is applicable to all projects in all industries, in all locations, regardless of the size and nature. Many corporations are requesting PMP certification as a requirement for career development or as a prerequisite to employment. The requirements for PMP certification are extensive. PMI requires specific educational and experience attributes before an application can be submitted. Upon completion of the requirements and passing of the exam, additional continuing certification requirements have to be fulfilled to maintain certification.

These requirements, along with a detailed discussion about what to expect on the PMP exam, are discussed in detail in Chapter 1.

If you plan to be a PMP certified project manager, we recommend that you acquaint yourself with the Project Management Institute (PMI). This is the organization that will provide support and educational opportunities to you. Being part of this body of dedicated and learned professionals will greatly assist and support your efforts as a project manager.

We also recommend that you seek out the local PMI chapter in your area. Many of the local chapters provide study groups and seasoned professionals who can provide assistance and encouragement as you go through the certification process. The local chapters generally host monthly or bimonthly meetings with guest speakers who can also enhance your project management knowledge. Although our book is an excellent resource guide, study groups and partners can provide you with reinforcement of the information.

Goals and Methods

The number one goal of this book is to help you pass the PMP® Certification exam, and we have arranged this book in a logical way to ensure you understand the topics needed to pass the exam. The materials in this book are based on the *Project Management Body of Knowledge (PMBOK® Guide)*, Sixth Edition, the *Project Management Body of Knowledge (PMBOK® Guide)*, Seventh Edition, and the Project Management Professional (PMP)® Examination Content Outline (ECO)—January 2021. PMI states that the PMP exam is based on multiple resources that constitute the Authorized Training Partner (ATP) materials, and we have covered all of these topics in a way that is easy and logical to follow.

We have also provided many exam tips and pointers along the way to ensure you get the most out of your studying.

At the beginning of each chapter, we have listed the ECO tasks that apply to that chapter. These ECO tasks could apply either directly or indirectly to the chapter in question. The nature of the ECO tasks is such that they overlap many topics.

In addition, we have filled this book and practice exams with more than 290 questions/answers and explanations in total, including two 180-question practice exams. All exams are located in the Pearson Test Prep practice test software in a custom test environment. These tests are geared to check your knowledge and ready you for the real exam.

How to Use This Book

This book uses several key methodologies to help you discover the exam topics on which you need more review, to help you fully understand and remember those details, and to help you prove to yourself that you have retained your knowledge of those topics. Therefore, this book does not try to help you pass the exams only by memorization; instead, it is designed to help you truly learn and understand the topics.

The book includes many features that provide different ways to study so you can be ready for the exam. If you understand a topic when you read it but do not study it any further, you probably will not be ready to pass the exam with confidence. The features included in this book give you tools that help you determine what you know, review what you know, better learn what you don't know, and be well prepared for the exam. These tools include the following:

- **"Do I Know This Already?" Quizzes:** Each chapter begins with a quiz that helps you determine the amount of time you need to spend studying that chapter. The answers are provided in Appendix A, "Answers to the 'Do I Know This Already?' Quizzes and Review Questions."

- **Foundation Topics:** These are the core sections of each chapter. They explain the tools and hacking concepts, and explain the configuration of both for the topics in that chapter.

- **Exam Preparation Tasks:** This section lists a series of study activities that you should complete after reading the "Foundation Topics" section. Each chapter includes the activities that make the most sense for studying the topics in that chapter. The activities include the following:

  - **Review All Key Topics:** The Key Topic icon appears next to the most important items in the "Foundation Topics" section of the chapter. The Review All Key Topics activity lists the key topics from the chapter and their page numbers. Although the contents of the entire chapter could be on the exam, you should definitely know the information listed in each key topic. Review these topics carefully.

  - **Define Key Terms:** Although certification exams might be unlikely to ask a question such as "Define this term," the PMP exam requires you to learn and know a lot of tools and how they are used. This section lists some of the most important terms from the chapter, asking you to write a short definition and compare your answer to the Glossary.

  - **Review Questions:** Each chapter includes review questions to help you confirm that you understand the content you just covered. The answers are provided in Appendix A, "Answers to the 'Do I Know This Already?' Quizzes and Review Questions."

Who Should Read This Book?

The *Project Management Professional (PMP) Cert Guide* is a must-have for anyone who fits into any of the following categories:

- Anyone who wants to pass the PMP® Certification exam and advance their career in project management.

- Anyone who was previously unsuccessful in passing the exam and wants a review of the PMP® materials and exam techniques to be successful the next time around.

- Those who are starting their PMP® journey and want a "one-stop shop" book that leads them through the application process, study materials, exam techniques, and all the knowledge needed to pass the exam.

- Anyone who wants to understand the PMI® principles and standards for project management and apply those principles into their project.

The prerequisites for the exam are as follows. Candidates with a four-year bachelor's degree (or global equivalent) need to be able to illustrate 36 months of project management or lead experience in the past eight years. Those without a bachelor's degree need to show 60 months of project management or lead experience within the past eight years.

Even if you do not meet these requirements, this book still provides insight into the terminology and processes of project management and a great starting point to focus your studying for when you do meet the requirements and are ready to take the exam. It is never too early to start your PMP® journey and prepare for the road ahead.

PMP® Certification Exam Topics

If you haven't downloaded the Project Management Professional (PMP)® Examination Content Outline and Specifications, do it now from the bottom of the PMI website: https://www.pmi.org/certifications/project-management-pmp. Review this document and make sure you are familiar with every item that is listed. Use the information found in this document to aid in your studies while you use this book.

The following two tables are excerpts from the Examination Content Outline and Specifications document. Table I-1 lists the PMI-PMP® domains and each domain's percentage of the exam.

Table I-1   PMI-RMP® Exam Domains

Domain	% of Exam
People	42%
Process	50%
Business Environment	8%

The PMI-PMP® domains are then further broken down into individual tasks with some enablers, which are illustrative examples of the work associated with the task.

Table I-2 lists the PMI-PMP® domains and tasks and their related chapters in this book. It does not list the enablers for each task. Please refer to the PMI Project Management Professional (PMI-PMP)® Examination Content Outline and Specifications for full details.

Table I-2 PMI-PMP® Exam Domains, Tasks, and Chapter Mapping

Domain I: People

Task	Chapter(s)
1 Manage conflict	3, 5, 9
2 Lead a team	4, 6, 7, 8, 9, 13
3 Support team performance	4, 7, 9, 10, 13, 15
4 Empower team members and stakeholders	6, 9, 11
5 Ensure team members/stakeholders are adequately trained	9
6 Build a team	4, 9
7 Address and remove impediments, obstacles, and blockers for the team	4, 9, 11, 13
8 Negotiate project agreements	8, 9, 12, 13
9 Collaborate with stakeholders	4, 5, 6, 8, 9, 10, 12, 13, 14, 15
10 Build shared understanding	4, 5, 6, 7, 8, 10, 11, 12, 14, 15
11 Engage and support virtual teams	4, 9, 10
12 Define team ground rules	9
13 Mentor relevant stakeholders	5, 9, 13
14 Promote team performance through the application of emotional intelligence	9, 13

Domain II: Process

Task	Chapter(s)
1 Execute project with the urgency required to deliver business value	3, 4, 6, 7, 8, 11, 14, 15
2 Manage communications	10, 12, 14, 15
3 Assess and manage risks	7, 12, 13, 14
4 Engage stakeholders	4, 5, 6, 9, 10, 13, 14, 15
5 Plan and manage budget and resources	8, 9, 12, 13, 14
6 Plan and manage schedule	7, 8, 12, 13, 14
7 Plan and manage quality of products/deliverables	4, 6, 8, 11, 12, 13, 14
8 Plan and manage scope	6, 8, 12, 13, 14
9 Integrate project planning activities	3, 4, 7, 8, 9, 11, 12, 13, 14, 15
10 Manage project changes	4, 6, 8, 11, 12, 13, 14

Domain I: People

Task	Chapter(s)
11 Plan and manage procurement	8, 12, 11, 12, 14
12 Manage project artifacts	4, 14, 12, 14, 15
13 Determine appropriate project methodology/methods and practices	3, 7, 13
14 Establish project governance structure	2
15 Manage project issues	4, 11, 12, 13, 14
16 Ensure knowledge transfer for project continuity	4, 9, 10, 11, 12, 14, 15
17 Plan and manage project/phase closure or transitions	6, 15, 14, 15

Domain III: Business Environment

Task	Chapter(s)
1 Plan and manage project compliance	6, 11, 13
2 Evaluate and deliver project benefits and value	4, 6, 7, 8, 11, 13, 14, 15
3 Evaluate and address external business environment changes for impact on scope	11, 16, 13, 14
4 Support organizational change	9, 16

Companion Website

Register this book to get access to the Pearson Test Prep practice test software and other study materials plus additional bonus content. Check this site regularly for new and updated postings written by the authors that provide further insight into the more troublesome topics on the exam. Be sure to check the box that you would like to hear from us to receive updates and exclusive discounts on future editions of this product or related products.

To access this companion website, follow these steps:

1. Go to www.pearsonitcertification.com/register and log in or create a new account.

2. On your Account page, tap or click the **Registered Products** tab, and then tap or click the **Register Another Product** link.

3. Enter this book's ISBN: **9780137918935**.

4. Answer the challenge question as proof of book ownership.

5. Tap or click the **Access Bonus Content** link for this book to go to the page where your downloadable content is available.

Please note that many of our companion content files can be very large, especially image and video files.

If you are unable to locate the files for this title by following the preceding steps, please visit http://www.pearsonitcertification.com/contact and select the Site Problems/Comments option. Our customer service representatives will assist you.

Pearson Test Prep Practice Test Software

As noted previously, this book comes complete with the Pearson Test Prep practice test software containing two full exams. These practice tests are available to you either online or as an offline Windows application. To access the practice exams that were developed with this book, please see the instructions in the card inserted in the sleeve in the back of the book. This card includes a unique access code that enables you to activate your exams in the Pearson Test Prep software.

NOTE   The cardboard sleeve in the back of this book includes a piece of paper. The paper lists the activation code for the practice exams associated with this book. Do not lose the activation code. On the opposite side of the paper from the activation code is a unique, one-time-use coupon code for the purchase of the Premium Edition eBook and Practice Test.

Accessing the Pearson Test Prep Software Online

The online version of this software can be used on any device with a browser and connectivity to the Internet, including desktop machines, tablets, and smartphones. To start using your practice exams online, simply follow these steps:

1. Go to www.PearsonTestPrep.com and select **Pearson IT Certification** as your product group.

2. Enter your email/password for your account. If you do not have an account on PearsonITCertification.com or CiscoPress.com, you will need to establish one by going to PearsonITCertification.com/join.

3. On the My Products tab, tap or click the **Activate New Product** button.

4. Enter this book's activation code and click **Activate**.

5. The product will now be listed on your My Products tab. Tap or click the **Exams** button to launch the exam settings screen and start your exam.

Accessing the Pearson Test Prep Software Offline

If you want to study offline, you can download and install the Windows version of the Pearson Test Prep software. There is a download link for this software on the book's companion website, or you can just enter this link in your browser:

http://www.pearsonitcertification.com/content/downloads/pcpt/engine.zip

To access the book's companion website and the software, simply follow these steps:

1. Register your book by going to http://www.pearsonitcertification.com/register and entering the ISBN: **9780137918935**.

2. Respond to the challenge questions.

3. Go to your account page and select the **Registered Products** tab.

4. Click the **Access Bonus Content** link under the product listing.

5. Click the **Install Pearson Test Prep Desktop Version** link under the Practice Exams section of the page to download the software.

6. After the software finishes downloading, unzip all the files on your computer.

7. Double-click the application file to start the installation, and follow the on-screen instructions to complete the registration.

8. When the installation is complete, launch the application and click the **Activate Exam** button on the My Products tab.

9. Click the **Activate a Product** button in the Activate Product Wizard.

10. Enter the unique access code found on the card in the sleeve in the back of your book and click the **Activate** button.

11. Click **Next** and then the **Finish** button to download the exam data to your application.

12. You can now start using the practice exams by selecting the product and clicking the **Open Exam** button to open the exam settings screen.

Note that the offline and online versions will sync together, so saved exams and grade results recorded on one version will be available to you on the other as well.

Customizing Your Exams

When you are in the exam settings screen, you can choose to take exams in one of three modes:

- Study Mode
- Practice Exam Mode
- Flash Card Mode

Study Mode allows you to fully customize your exams and review answers as you are taking the exam. This is typically the mode you would use first to assess your knowledge and identify information gaps. Practice Exam Mode locks certain customization options, as it is presenting a realistic exam experience. Use this mode when you are preparing to test your exam readiness. Flash Card Mode strips out the answers and presents you with only the question stem. This mode is great for late-stage preparation when you really want to challenge yourself to provide answers without the benefit of seeing multiple-choice options. This mode will not provide the detailed score reports that the other two modes will, so it should not be used if you are trying to identify knowledge gaps.

In addition to these three modes, you will be able to select the source of your questions. You can choose to take exams that cover all the chapters, or you can narrow your selection to just a single chapter or the chapters that make up specific parts in the book. All chapters are selected by default. If you want to narrow your focus to individual chapters, simply deselect all the chapters and then select only those on which you want to focus in the Objectives area.

You can also select the exam banks on which to focus. Each exam bank comes complete with a full exam of questions that cover topics in every chapter. The exam printed in the book is available to you as well as two additional exams of unique questions. You can have the test engine serve up exams from all banks or just from one individual bank by selecting the desired banks in the exam bank area.

There are several other customizations you can make to your exam from the exam settings screen, such as the time of the exam, the number of questions served up, whether to randomize questions and answers, whether to show the number of correct answers for multiple-answer questions, or whether to serve up only specific types of questions. You can also create custom test banks by selecting only questions that you have marked or questions on which you have added notes.

Updating Your Exams

If you are using the online version of the Pearson Test Prep software, you should always have access to the latest version of the software as well as the exam data. If you are using the Windows desktop version, every time you launch the software, it will check to see whether there are any updates to your exam data and automatically download any changes that were made since the last time you used the software. This requires that you are connected to the Internet at the time you launch the software.

Sometimes, due to many factors, the exam data may not fully download when you activate your exam. If you find that figures or exhibits are missing, you may need to manually update your exams.

To update a particular exam you have already activated and downloaded, simply select the **Tools** tab and click the **Update Products** button. Again, this is an issue only with the desktop Windows application.

If you want to check for updates to the Pearson Test Prep exam engine software, Windows desktop version, simply select the **Tools** tab and click the **Update Application** button. This will ensure you are running the latest version of the software engine.

Premium Edition eBook and Practice Tests

This book also includes an exclusive offer for 80 percent off the Premium Edition eBook and Practice Tests edition of this title. Please see the coupon code included with the cardboard sleeve for information on how to purchase the Premium Edition.

## CHAPTER 1

The PMP Exam: How to Prepare and Pass

The *Project Management Professional (PMP)* certification is the premier credential recognized internationally in the project management discipline. It signifies an individual has the process knowledge, experience, and training required to practice the principles and standards prescribed by the Project Management Institute (PMI). It has become a professional standard and prerequisite for many organizations and companies globally.

According to PMI, there are currently more than 1 million PMP certifications in more than 120 countries, and the numbers continue to grow.

Industries that rely on PMP certification include information technology, telecommunications, construction, healthcare, government, and numerous other professions. Because project management is not specific to any industry or process, the PMP certification applies to all types of projects regardless of size, location, nature, and industry. Many corporations request the PMP certification as a requirement for career development or as a prerequisite to employment.

The requirements for PMP certification are extensive. PMI requires specific educational and experience attributes before an application can be submitted. The *PMP Certification Handbook* is a good source for explanation of the required educational and work background.

After completing the requirements and passing the exam, you must fulfill additional continuing certification requirements to maintain certification. The Continuing Certification Requirements (CCRs) mandate that you accumulate at least 60 Professional Development Units (PDUs) every three years after achieving your PMP certification. PDUs can be accumulated by attending various PMI programs, seminars, and educational opportunities.

This chapter provides you with an understanding of the approach to the PMP exam; it covers the following learning objectives:

- Identify who PMI is and what its vision is

- Understand the contents of the PMP exam

- Identify changes to the new exam and changes to the *PMBOK® Guide*, Seventh Edition, and how this relates to the *PMBOK® Guide*, Sixth Edition

- Understand how to approach your studying for the PMP exam

- Understand the common gaps you may have in your experience and terminology and how to fill those gaps for PMP exam purposes

Who Is PMI?

The Project Management Institute is the globally recognized body for creating and updating the standards and principles of project management. The institute was founded in 1969.

PMI creates the standards and framework for project management; it does not tell you how to manage a project. It is not creating a methodology for project management—and this is something very important to understand when studying for the PMP exam.

Why does PMI not tell you how to manage a project? Because every industry manages projects differently. An IT project is managed differently from a construction project, which is managed differently from a pharmaceutical project developing a vaccine. Many factors go into managing a project (factors that we discuss in this book), such as geographical location (you will manage a project in the Arctic very differently to the same project in the Sahara Desert). PMI has taken all these factors into consideration and created a universal standard/framework for project management that could be applied to any industry in any situation. These standards or framework for project management are documented in the *Project Management Body of Knowledge (PMBOK® Guide)*, and organizations tailor the PMI standards/framework to match what is relevant for their situation. PMI regularly updates the *PMBOK® Guide* and, as of this writing, the latest version is the *PMBOK® Guide*, Seventh Edition.

Thus, the PMP certification is not based on any industry, process, or organization. PMP certification is relevant for construction engineers as well as those who work in IT, healthcare, and manufacturing. It applies to small projects and large projects. It applies to projects on the North Pole as well as the equator. PMI's standards apply to all projects.

For the exam, it is important to answer questions based on the PMI framework (not necessarily based on practices from your organization or industry). As you are studying, it is important to understand PMI terminology and PMI practices regarding project management. Always remember that exact project management procedures are different from industry to industry and organization to organization. Even within the same organization, different teams may be managing projects differently. When answering questions, you should refrain from thinking in terms of your industry or organization.

Changes to the *PMBOK® Guide*, Seventh Edition

Although this section discusses the changes to the *PMBOK® Guide* from the sixth to the seventh editions, the PMP exam itself is not based on a particular *PMBOK® Guide*. PMI uses multiple sources to develop its syllabus and, ultimately, PMP exam questions. However, the new exam utilizes these concepts significantly and mirrors a lot of these similar changes. You can find the list of latest books that PMI refers to on the PMI.org website.

Earlier versions of the *PMBOK® Guide* were focused on Inputs, Tools & Techniques and Outputs (ITTOs), which represented a process-driven approach to project management.

The *PMBOK® Guide*, Seventh Edition, is now focused on delivering value and outcome to the stakeholder, and as such, PMI has created the *PMIstandards+*. Per PMI, this is the first interactive digital platform that incorporates current, emerging, and future practices, methods, artifacts, and other useful information. Figure 1-1 summarizes the changes between the sixth and seventh editions of the *PMBOK® Guide*, along with the connection to the PMIstandards+ digital platform.

The *PMBOK® Guide*, Seventh Edition, Standard for Project Management introduces the System for Value Delivery and Twelve Project Management Principles.

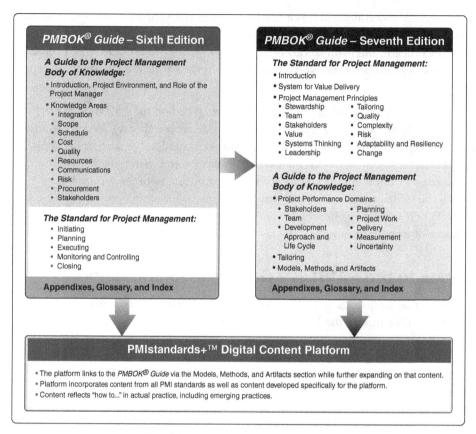

Figure 1-1 Mapping of *PMBOK® Guide*, Sixth Edition, to *PMBOK® Guide*, Seventh Edition (Used with Permission of Project Management Institute)

The System for Value Delivery

The System for Value Delivery is focused on creating value for stakeholders and customers. Value can be in many forms, such as creating a new product or service, improving efficiency, making environmental improvements and organizational changes, to name but a few. Every organization will determine the value that it is trying to achieve from the business venture and what success or failure means on the project.

The System for Value Delivery covers the following topics:

- **Creating Value:** Value is the net quantifiable benefit derived from a business endeavor and can be in many forms, such as financial benefits, market share, first to market, and new customers, to name but a few.

- **Organization Governance Systems:** Project governance refers to the framework of policies, functions, processes, procedures, and responsibilities to ensure projects are running smoothly and consistently.

- **Functions Associated with Projects:**

  - Functions refer to the many roles and activities on a project that need to be coordinated to successfully complete a project.

  - Various functions within an organization or a project provide oversight and coordination of the work; present objectives and feedback; facilitate and support the work; provide knowledge, skills, and experiences; and provide resources for the project.

The Twelve Project Management Principles

The Twelve Project Management Principles, which are discussed in more detail in future chapters, are described here. These principles provide a foundation for effective project management; they are not prescriptive in nature. The way they are applied will vary depending on the organization, project, team, stakeholders, and so on. These principles are interwoven in the performance domains that are explored in more detail later in the book. In part, they are also influenced by the PMI Code of Ethics and Agile Manifesto.

- **Stewardship:** This principle encompasses responsibilities within and external to the organization and includes integrity, care, trustworthiness, and compliance.

- **Team:** The team is made up of individuals with diverse skills, knowledge, and experience who work collaboratively to share a common objective and goal to achieve project success.

- **Stakeholders:** A stakeholder is any individual, group, or organization that may impact or be impacted, or perceive themselves to be impacted, by a project, program, portfolio, or any activity or decision.

- **Value:** Value is the ultimate indicator of project success or failure and can be realized at various points along the project or at the end of the project, depending on the type, nature, and size of the project.

- **Systems Thinking:** This principle entails taking a holistic view of how all the components of a project interact with one another and external factors.

- **Leadership:** Project managers (PMs) and leaders bring individuals and teams together to accomplish project objectives. Leadership skills are paramount to achieving success and contribute to positive outcomes. Any team member can exhibit leadership behavior.

- **Tailoring:** Tailoring is adapting the approach, governance, and processes of project management to the given situation, location, or circumstance.

- **Quality:** Quality is the degree to which a set of inherent characteristics fulfills requirements (ISO 9000).

- **Complexity:** Complexity is the result of the human behavior, systems interaction, uncertainty (risks), and ambiguity, and can emerge at any time throughout the project.

- **Risk:** A risk is a future uncertain event which, if it occurs, can have a positive or negative impact.

- **Adaptability and Resiliency:** Adaptability is the ability to respond to the changing environment. Resilience is the ability to recover from challenges and setbacks.

- **Change:** Organizations must adapt to change to remain relevant in the business world. Having a structured change management approach is vital to the success of any organization due to the rapid nature of the changing business environment today. Not all stakeholders embrace change; thus, this is a challenge for many organizations.

Project Performance Domains

The *PMBOK® Guide*, Seventh Edition, identifies the following eight performance domains that form an integrated system to enable successful delivery of the project:

- **Stakeholder Performance Domain:** This domain refers to the activities and functions related to identifying and engaging stakeholders throughout the project.

- **Team Performance Domain:**

  - This domain refers to the activities and functions related to the team members who are responsible for producing the end result of the project and making decisions throughout the project.

  - There are many roles on a project that all need to collaboratively work together.

- **Development Approach and Life Cycle:**

  - There are many project management methodologies, such as predictive (often referred to as traditional or waterfall), agile, incremental, iterative, and hybrid.

- Each approach is suitable for particular projects based on the size, complexity, industry, and situation. There is no "one-size-fits-all" methodology that can be used for every project.

- **Planning Performance Domain:** This domain is focused on planning the activities, work packages, and coordination of the work before it is executed.

- **Project Work:** This domain addresses the execution of the work according to the plan and managing the resources required to successfully execute the work.

- **Delivery:** This domain refers to the functions and activities required to deliver the scope and quality of the project.

- **Measurement:** This domain refers to comparing the actual results with the plan to assess the performance of the project. This is often referred to as "monitoring and controlling."

- **Uncertainty:** This domain refers to risk management. A risk is a future uncertain event and can impact every activity of a project.

Tailoring

Tailoring refers to the adaptation of PMI's standards, project management approach, governance, and processes to match what is relevant for the particular industry, organization, and nature of the project. For example, a construction project to build a road through a desert will be managed very differently from an IT project in a well-populated major city. Both projects will utilize different processes and methodologies and so will tailor the PMI's standards differently.

Any of the 8 performance domains and 12 performance principles can be tailored according to the size, nature, and circumstances of the project. The goal should always be delivering value.

Models, Methods, and Artifacts

The team will build a framework for structuring projects to deliver value and outcome to the customer. In doing so, they will need to utilize various models, methods, and artifacts defined as follows:

- **Model:** Thinking strategy to explain processes and framework

- **Method:** Means for achieving an outcome, output, result, or deliverable

- **Artifact:** Project documentation that can be a template, output, or deliverable

The project practitioner needs to be familiar with and tailor the common set of models, methods, and artifacts outlined in *PMBOK® Guide*, Sixth and Seventh Editions. The Process Group and Knowledge Area approach of *PMBOK® Guide*, Sixth Edition, is one of several valid and reliable models that many practitioners refer to. This book covers the core models that you need to know for the exam.

The PMP Application Process

Eligibility for the test is based on whether you have a four-year bachelor's degree or global equivalent. Table 1-1 outlines the PMP exam eligibility requirements.

Table 1-1   Eligibility to Take the PMP Exam

	Four-Year Bachelor's Degree (or Global Equivalent)	**No Bachelor's Degree (High School, Associate Degree, or Global Equivalent)**
Required Work Experience	Thirty-six months of experience leading or directing projects	Sixty months of leading or directing projects
Required Education	Thirty-five hours of project management education, or CAPM® certification	Thirty-five hours of project management education, or CAPM® certification

Over the years, PMI has made several changes to the application process as well as the contents of the PMP application as it adjusts to changes in the market, so the following application process is a broad outline based on the current process at the time of writing:

1. Create an account at www.pmi.org.

2. Become a member of PMI® (optional).

   Table 1-2 provides a summary of the membership and exam fees.

3. Fill out the application.

   Use high-level project descriptions using PMI terminology, not industry-specific or company-specific language, jargon, or acronyms.

4. You may receive notice that you are being audited.

   ■ Audit selection is purely random and not based on anything written on your application.

   ■ If you are selected for an audit, you must follow the procedures given in the instructions.

- The audit process generally requires you to provide evidence of your work experience (usually a signature from a stakeholder familiar with the work that you performed on the project) and your highest level of education.

5. PMI will take up to one week (five business days) to review your application.

6. Pay for the exam. Table 1-2 provides a summary of the exam fees.

7. You will receive an eligibility ID to take the test.

8. You can then schedule the test at www.pearsonvue.com. The options include either of the following:

    - Online Proctored Testing

    - Testing Center

9. You will receive your results immediately after you complete your exam, and when you pass, you are PMP certified!

Table 1-2   Fee Comparison Between PMI Members and Nonmembers

	PMI Member	Nonmember
Membership Fee	$139*	—
Exam Fee	$405	$555
Savings	$11	
Retake Fee	$275	$375

*All values based on US$

What Is the PMP Exam Like?

The PMP exam is a computer-based exam with 180 random questions to answer in 3 hours and 50 minutes, or 230 minutes (that's 76 seconds per question).

You do not have a lot of time in which to answer questions, so time management is of utmost importance here. Some questions might take only a few seconds to answer, but some may take a couple of minutes or a few minutes. It is important to not spend too much time on a particular question.

Out of the 180 questions, 5 are experimental questions, which are not marked and are not used to determine whether you passed or failed. The exam is therefore marked out of 175 questions. The experimental questions represent questions that PMI has added to the databank to observe how students are answering them before deciding to add them as actual questions, modify, or remove. You will not be able to identify which of the questions are experimental.

Questions may be marked for review and answered later. You can answer a question and then change your answer later if you want (however, only within a 60-question segment, as outlined later). You also can skip questions and return to them later. You can also view which questions you have answered, marked for review, or not answered yet, and use that page to jump to other question.

Questions are based on the Exam Content Outline (ECO) and are based on the following three domains:

- **People:** 42 percent

- **Process:** 50 percent

- **Business Environment:** 8 percent

Approximately half of the exam represents the predictive approach to project management, and the other half represents agile and hybrid approaches. Predictive, agile, and hybrid approaches are relevant to all three domains and do not pertain to any domain.

NOTE The term *predictive* refers to the traditional style of project management (also referred to as *waterfall*). Here, the project manager plans all the work at the beginning of the project, delegates the work to the appropriate teams, and delivers the final product to the customer at the end of the project. On an agile project, the team members themselves make decisions about the project and deliver value to the customer at regular iterations known as *sprints*. A hybrid methodology is a mixture of predictive and agile.

Each domain consists of tasks and enablers. The definitions of these terms are as follows:

- **Domain:** A domain is a high-level area of knowledge needed to effectively manage projects.

- **Tasks:** These represent the responsibilities of the project manager within each domain area.

- **Enablers:** Enablers are the work associated with each task. In the ECO, these are given as examples rather than being an exhaustive list.

Table 1-7 at the end of the chapter provides the full exam content outline.

After you have submitted your exam, you will get your results immediately. PMI does not release the passing score because there is no set pass mark and the score is dependent on the actual questions asked during the exam. The final result earned is either a pass or fail, with the following classification for each of the three domains:

- Above Target

- Target

- Below Target

- Needs Improvement

You will need to be Above Target or Target in each domain to pass the PMP exam.

Types of Questions

You should expect to see some of the following question types on the exam:

- **Scenario/Situational Questions:** You will need to apply PMI's principles and standards to a given scenario. For example, you may get a situation in which something has gone wrong and you are asked what you could have done to prevent that situation; or you could be asked what you should do next. These questions often ask about how to deal with stakeholders and team members.

EXAM TIP   When dealing with stakeholders and team members, look for option choices that engage and collaborate stakeholders and team members, and option choices where the project manager is being proactive rather than reactive. If the question refers to some sort of process ("What should you do next?"), look for updating a plan document.

- **Extraneous Information, Irrelevant Scenarios, Long-Winded Verbiage:** Some scenario questions may contain irrelevant information. You must be able to navigate through these ambiguities and be able to pick out key words and phrases to answer the questions. Sometimes the entire question may be irrelevant to the scenario; I refer to these as "bait-and-switch" questions.

EXAM TIP   Read the last sentence first because that often is the question. Understand the question before you start reading the scenario.

- **More Than One Possible Option:** Many times, all given options may seem like good options. But there is only correct answer. You need to learn to pick the best option. For example, after the scenario, the question might ask, "What document should you refer to?" and all four option choices look like good options. You think they would all be documents that you would refer to, but there is only one correct option.

EXAM TIP   One key word or phrase could lead you to the correct answer. Learn to pick out key words and phrases in a question.

- **None of the Options Are Any Good!:** Many times, none of the options given seem to be good answers, so you might not see the perfect option. Again, you have to learn to choose the best of these "no good" answers.

- **Choose Two or Three:** This is a new style of question for the PMP exam introduced in the 2021 ECO. There may be four or more option choices, of which there are two (or three) correct answers. You must choose all the correct answers to get credit for the question. The question will always state how many you must select. If it does not, there is only one correct answer. There is no partial credit for any question. If you get one of the option choices incorrect, the whole question is marked as incorrect.

- **Drag and Drop:** This is a new style of question for the PMP exam introduced in the 2021 ECO. Here, you have to match definitions with terminology. You may see the definition on one side and the terminology on the other, so you must drag the definition to the terminology. There is no partial credit for these questions. If you mismatch one definition, the whole question is marked as incorrect.

- **True/False:** This is a new style of question for the PMP exam introduced in the 2021 ECO. A statement is given, and you have to determine whether that statement is correct or incorrect. There are only two option choices here.

- **Hot Spot:** This is a new style of question for the PMP exam introduced in the 2021 ECO. You may be given a graph or a chart to interpret, and the option choices are shown on the chart or graph itself.

- **Correct Answer to a Different Question:** You must answer the question given, which is usually the last sentence. If you do not read the last sentence carefully, sometimes you can make an assumption on what you think the question is rather than what the question actually is and consequently get the answer wrong. The option choices may be true statements based on the scenario but do not answer the question being posed.

- **Mathematical:** There are a few mathematical questions, but since the start of the 2021 ECO exam, most of the math questions have been interpretation of data, with just a few calculations. However, you must still understand the formulae to be able to answer these questions.

- **Memory Test:** As with all exams, there may be some element of memorization of facts, but this is minimal. Most questions are about applying your knowledge, not what you have memorized.

- **Questions That Just Don't Seem to Make Sense or Are Vague:** You might need to read a question multiple times to even understand what the question is asking.

- **Real World vs. PMI®:** If there is a discrepancy between the real world and PMI's principles and standards, PMI's principles and standards will always prevail when you are answering a PMP exam question. Many organizations and industries manage projects differently and follow their own procedures and guidelines that may not be in line with PMI's standards. You must answer the question based on PMI's principles, not based on your industry's or organization's procedures.

PMP Exam Content Outline

The PMP exam syllabus is detailed in the 2021 PMP Exam Content Outline (ECO), and the extract in Table 1-3 represents topics that are either new to the syllabus or more heavily emphasized than before. The full ECO is listed at the end of this chapter.

Table 1-3   Newly Added or Higher-Emphasis ECO Topics

Domain I	People
Task 2	**Lead a team:**
	■ Set a clear vision and mission.
	■ Support diversity and inclusion (e.g., behavior types, thought process).
	■ Value servant leadership (e.g., relate the tenets of servant leadership to the team).
	■ Determine an appropriate leadership style (e.g., directive, collaborative).
	■ Inspire, motivate, and influence team members/stakeholders (e.g., team contract, social contract, reward system).
	■ Analyze team members and stakeholders' influence.
	■ Distinguish various options to lead various team members and stakeholders.

Domain I	People
Task 4	**Empower team members and stakeholders:** ■ Organize around team strengths. ■ Support team task accountability. ■ Evaluate demonstration of task accountability. ■ Determine and bestow level(s) of decision-making authority.
Task 5	**Ensure team members/stakeholders are adequately trained:** ■ Determine required competencies and elements of training. ■ Determine training options based on training needs. ■ Allocate resources for training. ■ Measure training outcomes.
Task 7	**Address and remove impediments, obstacles, and blockers for the team:** ■ Determine critical impediments, obstacles, and blockers for the team. ■ Prioritize critical impediments, obstacles, and blockers for the team. ■ Use network to implement solutions to remove impediments, obstacles, and blockers for the team. ■ Re-assess continually to ensure impediments, obstacles, and blockers for the team are being addressed.
Task 14	**Promote team performance through the application of emotional intelligence:** ■ Assess behavior through the use of personality indicators. ■ Analyze personality indicators and adjust to the emotional needs of key project stakeholders.
Domain II	Process
Task 1	**Execute project with the urgency required to deliver business value:** ■ Assess opportunities to deliver value incrementally. ■ Examine the business value throughout the project. ■ Support the team to subdivide project tasks as necessary to find the minimum viable product.
Task 13	**Determine appropriate project methodology/methods and practices:** ■ Assess project needs, complexity, and magnitude. ■ Recommend project execution strategy (e.g., contracting, finance). ■ Recommend a project methodology/approach (i.e., predictive, agile, hybrid). ■ Use iterative, incremental practices throughout the project life cycle (e.g., lessons learned, stakeholder engagement, risk).

Domain II	Process
Task 14	**Establish project governance structure:** ■ Determine appropriate governance for a project (e.g., replicate organizational governance). ■ Define escalation paths and thresholds.
Task 15	**Manage project issues:** ■ Recognize when a risk becomes an issue. ■ Attack the issue with the optimal action to achieve project success. ■ Collaborate with relevant stakeholders on the approach to resolve the issues.
Task 16	**Ensure knowledge transfer for project continuity:** ■ Discuss project responsibilities within team. ■ Outline expectations for working environment. ■ Confirm approach for knowledge transfers.
Domain III	**Business Environment**
Task 1	**Plan and manage project compliance:** ■ Confirm project compliance requirements (e.g., security, health and safety, regulatory compliance). ■ Classify compliance categories. ■ Determine potential threats to compliance. ■ Use methods to support compliance. ■ Analyze the consequences of noncompliance. ■ Determine necessary approach and action to address compliance needs (e.g., risk, legal). ■ Measure the extent to which the project is in compliance.
Task 2	**Evaluate and deliver project benefits and value:** ■ Investigate that benefits are identified. ■ Document agreement on ownership for ongoing benefit realization. ■ Verify measurement system is in place to track benefits. ■ Evaluate delivery options to demonstrate value. ■ Appraise stakeholders of value gain progress.
Task 4	**Support organizational change:** ■ Assess organizational culture. ■ Evaluate impact of organizational change to project and determine required actions. ■ Evaluate impact of the project to the organization and determine required actions.

Changes to the New Exam

The PMP exam is not based primarily on any *PMBOK® Guide* version anymore. The PMP exam is based on several books that are listed on the PMI.org website; however, you do not need to purchase all of these books to study for the PMP exam.

Until December 31, 2020, the PMP exam was based mostly on *PMBOK® Guide*, Sixth Edition, and the questions were randomized based on process groups (also known as domains). The five domains and the percentage breakdown were as follows:

- **Initiating:** 13 percent
- **Planning:** 24 percent
- **Executing:** 31 percent
- **Monitoring and Controlling:** 25 percent
- **Closing:** 7 percent

Most questions (95+ percent) were based on the traditional (predictive) style of project management. There were only a few questions on agile. Every single question was multiple choice containing four option choices, of which there would be only one correct answer.

On January 4, 2021, PMI introduced major changes to the exam that included the *PMBOK® Guide*, Sixth Edition, not being the main source of test questions. Moreover, PMI released 10 books that would be the inspiration for PMP exam questions. The syllabus is now documented in the PMP Exam Content Outline (ECO) that is available from the PMI.org website.

The 2021 ECO adds a lot more agile concepts than ever before as well as leadership topics that were not on the exam before. As noted earlier, the exam is now broken into three domains with 50 percent of the exam tests being predictive concepts and 50 percent being agile and hybrid concepts. Hybrid is considered a mix of predictive and agile for the PMP exam purposes.

Prior to January 2021, the focus of the exam was understanding the process groups and knowledge areas that made up PMI's principles of project management. It was important to understand the Inputs, Tools & Techniques and Outputs (ITTOs) of each process, and there were specific questions about ITTOs within each process. You needed to know which ITTO belonged to which of the 49 processes, and it was recommended for students to memorize the *process map*, the grid that shows the relationship between process groups, knowledge areas, and processes.

For the current exam, the concentration is now on the purpose of these ITTOs—when to use them and how to use them, not necessarily which of the individual processes they belong to. You now need to concentrate on knowing which tools and documents would be appropriate in a given situation, rather than which individual process a document is an input or output of. You will need to apply your knowledge of the 12 principles and the performance domains on the situational questions.

Moreover, project documents that were previously referred to as *inputs* and *outputs* are now referred to as *artifacts*.

The format of the PMP exam has also changed several times in recent years as PMI has responded to the changing COVID-19 situation.

Until March 2020, the exam consisted of 200 multiple-choice questions for candidates to answer in four hours, with no scheduled breaks. The exam had to be taken at an authorized testing center.

In April 2020, PMI allowed the exam to be administered as an online proctored exam. The format changed to 200 multiple-choice questions to answer in four hours, with a mandatory 10-minute break around the halfway point. Students had a choice of taking the exam at a testing center or as an online proctored exam.

In January 2021, at the start of the new 2021 ECO, the exam format changed again to what is now the current format. The PMP exam now consists of 180 questions to answer in 3 hours and 50 minutes (230 minutes). The exam is broken up into three sections of 60 questions each, with a 10-minute break in between sections one and two and sections two and three, respectively. The break is optional but recommended. The questions in each 60-question section are random, and questions do not pertain to any particular topic in the ECO. The next question can be from any area of the syllabus.

After you start the exam, you will initially have access to the first set of 60 questions only. You can answer these questions in any sequence and change answers as you want. Questions can be marked for review and returned to later, or you can skip questions and come back to them later. When you get to question 60, you can go back and check your answers.

When you are confident of your answers to the first section, then you can start the 10-minute break. After the break starts, there is now no access to those first set of 60 questions again. They are submitted, and it is not even possible to view them.

As the break starts, you can either

- Take the full 10 minutes.
- Take a few minutes (no more than 10).
- Not take a break at all and start the next set of 60 questions.

Do not break for longer than 10 minutes because that is the maximum allotted time, and taking more can result in failure of the exam.

Upon your return, you will now have access to questions 61 through 120, and the same procedure as mentioned applies.

The break starts when you start the break. It does not start automatically after question 60 or 120, nor does it start after a particular time. If you spend too long in the first section, you will use up time for the second section.

You now have a choice of scheduling the exam at a Pearson Vue testing center, or you may schedule an online proctored exam. You will select this after you have paid the exam fees and received an eligibility ID to schedule the test.

Table 1-4 outlines a summary of changes to the new exam.

Table 1-4   Summary of Changes to the New Exam

Category	Prior to 2021 Exam	2021 Exam
Domains	Initiating (13%)	Process (50%)
	Planning (24%)	People (42%)
	Executing (31%)	Business Environment (8%)
	Monitoring and Controlling (25%)	
	Closing (7%)	
Life Cycle	Predictive	Predictive (50%)
	(One or two questions on agile)	Agile and hybrid (50%)
Number of Questions	200	180
Numbers Scores	175	175
Length of Exam	4 hours (240 minutes)	3 hours 50 minutes (230 minutes)
Types of questions	Multiple choice with one correct answer	Multiple choice with one correct answer
		Multiple choice with multiple correct answers
		True/False
		Drag and Drop (Matching)
		Hot Spot
Location	Testing Center only	Testing Center
		Online Proctored

Scheduling at a Pearson Vue Testing Center

You can schedule the exam at any Pearson Vue testing center that administers the PMP exam worldwide; you are not restricted to scheduling at only the ones closest to you.

Pearson Vue administers many exams from many industries and professions, so you are competing for seats based on availability. After you receive your eligibility ID to schedule the test, it is advisable to check availability to sit the exam and schedule a date as you see fit before that date is taken. If other candidates (taking other exams) cancel their exam, spots can randomly open up.

It is recommended you arrive at the testing center early so you can get settled in and relaxed and have time to fill out any necessary paperwork. Your confirmation email will detail the items that you need to take to the testing center with you and will include the forms of identification that you need to take.

You will not be allowed to take any personal items with you into the exam room but will usually be given a locker or other space to store your personal items, such as cellphones, watches, snacks, water bottle, purses, and wallets.

Some testing centers will provide pen and paper (or a dry erase board and marker), but this varies by testing center. An electronic whiteboard will be provided on the exam screen.

Table 1-5 outlines some of the pros and cons of taking the exam at the testing center.

Table 1-5 Pros and Cons of Taking the Exam at the Testing Center

Pros	Cons
The testing center is specifically designed for candidates taking an exam.	Availability may be restricted due to the center's opening hours and candidates taking other certification exams.
You will not need to worry about people walking into the room by accident or the proctor hearing voices from another room (as per the online proctored exam).	You must physically go to the testing center, which can add significant time depending on how far it is.
The Internet connection will generally be more stable than at your home.	
In the unlikely event of the center's computer crashing, or its Internet service goes down, then the testing center will either provide an alternative or ask you to reschedule at no additional cost.	
Many testing centers still provide paper and pen or dry erase board and markers.	

Scheduling an Online Proctored Exam

You can select to take the exam as an online proctored exam from the comfort of your home, office, or any other location that has a stable Wi-Fi connection. You must leave your web cam on the entire time. If you do not have a web cam, you will not be able to take an online proctored exam.

Before you start the exam, you will be required to show your ID to the proctor, who may take a picture of it. You will need to move the web cam around to show the proctor your room. You will communicate with the proctor via VoIP, but a phone number will be provided in case you have technical issues.

The restrictions for taking the exam as an online proctored exam are as follows:

- Your web cam must be on the entire time, and your face must be within the frame for each 60-question segment.

- You must be in an enclosed room with the door closed, and no one is allowed to be in the same room as you. You cannot take the exam in a public area such as a kitchen or living room. If you are in your company's office, it must be in an enclosed office, not an open cube.

- If someone accidentally walks into the room, the proctor will cancel your exam.

- If the proctor hears any voices (such as a loud TV in the room next door or someone talking loud enough for the proctor to hear), they can cancel your exam.

- You will not be allowed to talk, stand, or leave the room during the exam. Again, the proctor may cancel the exam for these reasons.

- Your desk must be free of all materials, including books, paper, pens, and calculator. Your desk must be completely clear.

- You cannot use additional monitors or devices, and they must be unplugged and switched off.

- You cannot use any writing implements such as pens, pencils, or markers; you are not allowed any paper or calculators. You will have access to an electronic calculator and an electronic whiteboard.

- During the entire exam you will not be allowed access to mobile phones, headphones, other computers or tablets, watches, wallets, purses, bags, or coats.

- If your Internet goes down during the exam or your computer crashes, if you do not log back in within a certain allotted time period, your exam may be forfeited.

Table 1-6 outlines some of the pros and cons of taking an online proctored exam.

Table 1-6   Pros and Cons of Taking an Online Proctored Exam

Pros	Cons
There is a lot more availability for scheduling the exam because the exam is worldwide and proctors will be available 24/7.	There are many restrictions, as noted in the preceding list.
You don't have to physically go to a testing center, which is very convenient if a testing center is not located nearby.	Failure to comply with these restrictions (even if they are beyond your control) can result in failure of the exam.

Study Tips and Exam-Taking Strategies

In addition to knowing and understanding the course material, you also need to understand exam technique and test-taking strategies for successful completion of the PMP exam.

Because the PMP exam now consists of 180 questions to answer in 230 minutes, you have an average of 1 minute and 16 seconds per question (76 seconds) on average; therefore, time management is vital on such an exam. If you spend too long on one question, it can eat into your time for other questions. Many challenges might be thrown at you in the exam, so it is important to be able to navigate through all the nuances and ambiguities that may be present on the exam.

Sometimes the scenario might contain irrelevant information. Sometimes terminology might be used incorrectly or mismatched. Many times, all options look correct, but there is only one correct answer. Likewise, many times all options might look incorrect, but you must pick the best of the options given. There may be occasions when you don't even understand the question being asked, or one keyword or phrase might lead you to the correct option.

It is important to be able to navigate through the PMP exam questions and be able to identify keywords, distractors, irrelevant information, and relevant information. Consider the following strategies for navigating these question components:

- The entire question may hinge on one keyword or phrase. Learn to pick out keywords, phrases, distractors, and irrelevant information.

- Be aware of keywords such as *not*, *next*, *least likely*, *most likely*, *best*, *first*, *except*. These are often overlooked when reading a question.

- Beware of nonsubstantive options: "quality is really important." Such options may be true, but what does that statement actually mean? Those options are usually incorrect.

- Unlearn your real-world experiences! Learn to think the PMI way.

- Always think in terms of PMI principles. PMI standards are meant to support all projects in all industries, no matter how simple or complex. Some standards may or may not apply to your industry.

- Eliminate incorrect answers. Sometimes you need to choose the best out of the "no good" options!

- Change your answer only when you are absolutely sure.

- For "What should you do next?" questions, look for things such as updating a document, evaluating or analyzing a process, communicating to a stakeholder, engaging a stakeholder, or performing the next process on the process grid.

- Do not leave a question blank. There is no negative marking. A blank answer will always be marked incorrect.

Common Conceptual Gaps

PMI is setting a framework and standard that can be applied to any project of any size in any industry in any location. But projects are managed very differently based on industry, location, size, and many other factors. An IT development project is managed differently from a house construction project. A project to build a road in a sparsely populated Arctic village will be managed very differently from a project to build a road in a well-populated central Asian city.

Thus, depending on your industry and your experience, many of the concepts that you need to understand and master for the PMP exam may not apply to your line of work. If you work in construction, agile concepts will not apply to you, yet you will still need to master the agile concepts to be able to answer those questions and pass the exam.

Even if you are familiar with certain PMI concepts, your experience might differ from what is advocated by the PMI standards and principles. For example, you might be accustomed to including project activities in the work breakdown structure (WBS), but, for the PMP exam, activities are not part of the WBS. A rough order of magnitude (ROM) range estimate for PMI's purposes is defined as a range of –25 percent to +75 percent. In your experience, a ROM may be a different range. Certainly, in my experience, my stakeholders would never accept such a wide estimate range.

When you're studying for the exam and when you're answering PMP exam questions, it is of utmost importance to base your answers according to PMI's principles and standards and not to think in terms of your organization's procedures or your company or industry's best practices.

The following are a few examples of common conceptual gaps between real-world experiences and PMI concepts:

- **Culture Clash:** Nearly every organization implements project management differently, and many projects might not be consistent with PMI's view of the world. You will want to identify those differences for your own situation.

- **The Title of "Project Manager":** This is a very broad title in most organizations, and there may be many layers of project managers for a given project. For example, in the IT industry, a technical team lead, project administrator, lead analyst, project leader, project coordinator, and systems consultant may all be considered project managers. Yet they have different responsibilities. For PMI's exam purposes, a project manager on a predictive project is accountable for the project and so will have a high level of authority regarding decision-making on the project. However, on an agile project, the team members themselves are responsible for making project decisions; the team facilitator (or Scrum master—the closest equivalent to the project manager) is a servant leader. You need to be able to distinguish between the project manager role and the team facilitator role on exam questions. For PMI's purposes, a pure agile project does not have a project manager per se, but the responsibilities are divided between the agile team, the team facilitator, and the product owner.

- **Unapproved Practices:** On many projects in many organizations, project management practices and techniques used routinely may be considered "inappropriate" by PMI (for example, senior management forcing their own estimates to the team). These will appear on the exam as incorrect options.

- **Bigger Ballpark:** For many industries, the PMI principles and standards describe a field of project management that is much broader and complex than what you may have experienced in real life.

- **The Whole Story:** Many project managers lack experience in the complete life cycle of project management. Generally, there is minimal exposure to the Initiating and Closing phases. Project managers in some industries might not be familiar with agile principles. For someone who has worked only in agile, you might not be familiar with predictive concepts. You must understand the complete project management process as described by PMI, for both predictive and agile.

Common Experience Gaps

The role of the project manager is very wide and varied across different organizations and industries. In some cases, a team lead can be called a project manager, who reports to a senior person, who can also be considered a project manager, and so on.

In addition, a project manager's role in a predictive project is very different to the team facilitator's role on an agile project.

The assumption for the PMP exam is that if the question relates to predictive projects, then, unless the question states otherwise, the project manager has a "command and control" authority in a strong matrix organization. In other words, the PM has high authority and is responsible for making day-to-day decisions on projects.

Whereas the project manager has ultimate accountability on a predictive project, the product owner is ultimately accountable for the business solution on a pure agile project.

Regardless of your role on your projects in your organization, for the PMP exam, you must think in terms of PMI's principles regarding the authority and responsibilities of the project manager and all other team members, whether predictive or agile. Your own personal experience may not encompass the full range of experiences and skill sets that are assumed for the project manager role discussed by PMI. You need to properly understand the role of the project manager in order to pass the PMP exam.

Your role may differ from the PMI assumptions in the following ways. This list is not exhaustive by any means.

- **Project Processes:** There are 49 processes listed in the *PMBOK® Guide*, Sixth Edition (page 25). You may not perform all of those processes on your real-world projects. For example, if a project does not require you to reach out to vendors or external organizations to supply you with resources, you will not need to perform any of the procurement management processes. However, an assumption to make for any predictive question is that all of these 49 processes could be relevant to the predictive scenario. Likewise, all of PMI's concepts for agile will be relevant for any agile question, despite the fact that your agile experience may differ.

- **Project Management Plans:** For PMP exam purposes, it is assumed that all the components of the project management plan will be documented and progressively elaborated throughout the predictive project. In reality, many organizations may treat some of the management plans as standard operating procedures (SOPs) to be used as a best practice for all their projects. For example, your procedures for collecting requirements may be the same across all your projects, so you will not need to create a separate requirements management plan for each project. However, on many external consulting projects, this document will need to be created from scratch because the procedures may be different for every assignment. However, for tailoring purposes, PMI recognizes both approaches and refers to these SOPs as organizational process assets (OPAs), which are an input to every single planning process in predictive projects. Most of these components of the project management plan will not be relevant on agile projects.

- **Project Schedule:** Some organizations simply refer to the project schedule or a Gantt chart as "the project plan." This is an incorrect approach. A project plan goes well beyond the schedule and should include a plan for all the knowledge areas listed in the *PMBOK® Guide*, Sixth Edition (page 25). There are many ways of developing a schedule, but the approach discussed for the PMP exam is the critical path method. You must understand this approach using both the zero-day method and the one-day method. Both are discussed in detail in Chapter 7, "Project Schedule." Agile projects do not use a true schedule but use a product roadmap instead.

- **Project Performance Tracking:** PMI's recommended approach for tracking the budget and performance is earned value management (EVM), also known as earned value analysis (EVA). This is not used in all industries, and you may not be familiar with this concept. In addition, depending on your role, you may have only limited experience in managing costs and the budget on your project. Regardless, you need to be accustomed to the EVM principles and formulae for the exam.

- **Risk Management:** Projects vary greatly by size, nature, and purpose. Depending on your experience, you may or may not have been involved in managing and controlling risks on your projects. Risk management is a major knowledge area for the PMP exam, so you must master these concepts for the PMP exam.

Common Terminology Gaps

It is important for you to answer questions based on PMI terminology and use the right terminology in the right context. You may find that

- You are not familiar with a term, artifact, or tool.

  or

- You might have a different definition or understanding of that term, artifact, or tool.

When you're studying for the exam, and when you're using this book, it is important for you to concentrate on the purpose of documents, artifacts, tools, and procedures and to understand how and when to use them.

The following are a few examples of how some organizations in the real world may use certain terms differently from PMI:

- **Project Charter:** For PMI purposes, a project charter is simply a high-level document that authorizes the project to begin. Not much information is known about the project at this point, so no project details are documented here. In some organizations the project charter contains the baseline budget and the schedule/deadline for the project. This would be an incorrect answer for the PMP exam. Plus, in many organizations, this document may be given other names (for example, project initiation form, project authorization).

- **Project Management Plan:** The *PMBOK® Guide* explains that the project management plan is a combination of many documents that span across all the knowledge areas and includes the subsidiary plans, baselines, and additional components. However, many organizations consider the project management plan to be a Gantt chart or a schedule. This should be regarded as an incorrect view because project managers need to plan all aspects of a project, not just the schedule. Agile projects do not have a baseline, nor many of the components that comprise the project management plan.

- **Work Breakdown Structure (WBS):** For PMI's purposes, the lowest level of the WBS is the work package (not activities, as is often the practice in many organizations).

- **Risk Mitigation:** Several risk response strategies are mentioned in Chapter 13, "Uncertainty"; all these terms correspond with the PMI terms. In reality, many organizations simply use the term *mitigate* to mean the combination of all these risk response strategies. You must be able to clearly identify and understand when to use all the various risk response strategies discussed by PMI.

- **Rough Order of Magnitude:** Every organization has its own definition of a high-level ball-park figure. The *PMBOK® Guide* defines this as –25 percent to +75 percent.

A glossary of PMP terms is included in this book and can be found in the *PMBOK® Guide*, Sixth and Seventh Editions. Make sure you understand these terms.

What Is Important to PMI?

To better appreciate why these common gaps exist and to better prepare for the exam, let's review some of the underlying principles guiding PMI's vision of project management:

- The project manager "makes it happen" and "brings it all together." A project manager is someone who can get work done and get teams working together.

The PM can bring team members together to work through issues, challenges, and conflicts to ensure work is getting complete and meeting the scope of the project. The project manager is assumed not to have the role of a technical expert but will bring technical experts to work together to fulfill the goals of the project. The project manager on a predictive project has a somewhat "command and control" authority and is accountable for all the constraints on the project.

A team facilitator on an agile project, on the other hand, is a servant leader who brings the agile team together and creates an environment for the agile team to make project decisions. The facilitator ensures the team has all the tools and information necessary to make decisions and start the work. This role also removes any impediments or blockers that may be impacting team progress.

- Planning is of paramount importance on predictive projects. In fact, 24 of the 49 *PMBOK® Guide*, Sixth Edition, processes are under the Planning process group. Every aspect of the project must be planned and then executed accordingly (the executing process group). Throughout the project, the actual results from executing are compared to the plan to determine variances, and decisions must be made on how to move forward (the monitoring and controlling process group).

Even in agile, planning is of paramount importance although new requirements can be continuously added throughout the agile release. For instance, the team must plan how many sprints there should be in a release, the length of each sprint, and how many user stories or story points they can accomplish in a sprint.

- Agile projects must follow the Agile Manifesto, including the 4 paired values and 12 principles discussed in Chapter 3, "Development Approach and Life Cycle Performance."

- Project documents are now known as artifacts, and you must know the purpose of each artifact and when to use them.

- The project management plan describes how the project is going to be planned, executed, monitored and controlled, and closed, and it includes plans for all the knowledge areas. Each subsidiary plan plus the baselines and additional artifacts collectively make up the project management plan.

- The work breakdown structure is an important planning tool for predictive projects and used as a starting point for progressive elaboration.

- Communication is the most important job skill for a project manager (90 percent of the PM's time is spent here). A project manager brings stakeholders together to make important decisions about the project and brings teams together to successfully complete project deliverables. Consequently, project managers must have leadership skills and other interpersonal and management skills, all of which are discussed in detail in later chapters.

- The risk management process is very important and is a continuous project management activity.

- Likewise, quality should be built into the project management process. The focus should be preventing an issue from occurring, but if an issue does occur, you need to fix the issue and ensure it doesn't reoccur.

- All estimating should be completed by the people who will actually perform the work. Estimates should come from subject matter experts, not senior management.

- All projects, regardless of outcome, should complete the closing process. The emphasized outputs from this are as follows:

  - Capturing lessons learned

  - Executing proper administrative closure

Key PMI Assumptions

When answering PMP exam questions, you can make certain assumptions that can sometimes help in choosing the correct answer. The following is not an exhaustive list but represents many of the common assumptions for the PMP exam:

- Project managers are proactive and always taking some sort of action. You should always choose the proactive approach over a reactive approach.

- The project manager is selected when the project is authorized, before any estimating or preliminary requirements gathering is done. Project managers are heavily involved in preliminary estimates and assist in writing the project charter.

- The project manager is ultimately accountable in predictive projects, but the product owner has ultimate accountability for the business solution in pure agile projects.

- Project managers always engage and collaborate with stakeholders. Look for option choices that involve collaboration and engagement.

- Project managers do what is best for the project (not what's best for them). Project managers make decisions and influence stakeholders for the good of the project, not because they are gaining something personally.

- Unless the question states otherwise, adequate documentation is being performed. Project documents are regularly updated with current information and status.

- Unless the question states otherwise, historical information is always available. Project managers can leverage historical project files to make decisions about the current project.

- Unless the question states otherwise, for predictive projects, a change control process is in place *and* the team is following. Project managers are properly controlling all changes to a project and preventing unnecessary changes. If a change has been identified that can affect the baseline, it will always go through a change control process.

- Procurement questions are usually from the buyer's perspective. Unless the question states otherwise, you are the buyer, and the seller is selling you goods or services. Therefore, you are now the customer, a key stakeholder.

- The project baselines are used to monitor and control predictive projects. Any deviations from the baseline must go through the change control process. Agile projects do not have a baseline.

- Generally, a "negative" tone in an option choice signifies an incorrect approach. For example, if you see option choices that point fingers toward another team due to an issue that occurred, that will be the wrong approach. If you see an option choice that recommends ignoring a stakeholder, that will be the wrong approach.

PMP Exam Content Outline

The 2021 Exam Content Outline (ECO) represents the PMP exam syllabus and is divided into three domains:

- People Domain
- Process Domain
- Business Environment Domain

Each domain comprises a number of tasks, which contains enablers to perform those tasks. Table 1-7 shows the domains, tasks, and enablers of the 2021 ECO.

Table 1-7   The 2021 Exam Content Outline (ECO)

Domain I	People—42%
Task 1	**Manage conflict:** ■ Interpret the source and stage of the conflict. ■ Analyze the context for the conflict. ■ Evaluate/recommend/reconcile the appropriate conflict resolution solution.
Task 2	**Lead a team:** ■ Set a clear vision and mission. ■ Support diversity and inclusion (e.g., behavior types, thought process). ■ Value servant leadership (e.g., relate the tenets of servant leadership to the team). ■ Determine an appropriate leadership style (e.g., directive, collaborative). ■ Inspire, motivate, and influence team members/stakeholders (e.g., team contract, social contract, reward system). ■ Analyze team members and stakeholders' influence. ■ Distinguish various options to lead various team members and stakeholders.
Task 3	**Support team performance:** ■ Appraise team member performance against key performance indicators. ■ Support and recognize team member growth and development. ■ Determine appropriate feedback approach. ■ Verify performance improvements.
Task 4	**Empower team members and stakeholders:** ■ Organize around team strengths. ■ Support team task accountability. ■ Evaluate demonstration of task accountability. ■ Determine and bestow level(s) of decision-making authority.
Task 5	**Ensure team members/stakeholders are adequately trained:** ■ Determine required competencies and elements of training. ■ Determine training options based on training needs. ■ Allocate resources for training. ■ Measure training outcomes.

Domain I	People—42%
Task 6	**Build a team:**
	■ Appraise stakeholder skills.
	■ Deduce project resource requirements.
	■ Continuously assess and refresh team skills to meet project needs.
	■ Maintain team and knowledge transfer.
Task 7	**Address and remove impediments, obstacles, and blockers for the team:**
	■ Determine critical impediments, obstacles, and blockers for the team.
	■ Prioritize critical impediments, obstacles, and blockers for the team.
	■ Use network to implement solutions to remove impediments, obstacles, and blockers for the team.
	■ Reassess continually to ensure impediments, obstacles, and blockers for the team are being addressed.
Task 8	**Negotiate project agreements:**
	■ Analyze the bounds of the negotiations for agreement.
	■ Assess priorities and determine ultimate objective(s).
	■ Verify objective(s) of the project agreement is met.
	■ Participate in agreement negotiations.
	■ Determine a negotiation strategy.
Task 9	**Collaborate with stakeholders:**
	■ Evaluate engagement needs for stakeholders.
	■ Optimize alignment between stakeholder needs, expectations, and project objectives.
	■ Build trust and influence stakeholders to accomplish project objectives.
Task 10	**Build shared understanding:**
	■ Break down situation to identify the root cause of a misunderstanding.
	■ Survey all necessary parties to reach consensus.
	■ Support outcome of parties' agreement.
	■ Investigate potential misunderstandings.

Domain I	People—42%
Task 11	**Engage and support virtual teams:**
	■ Examine virtual team member needs (e.g., environment, geography, culture, global, etc.).
	■ Investigate alternatives (e.g., communication tools, colocation) for virtual team member engagement.
	■ Implement options for virtual team member engagement.
	■ Continually evaluate effectiveness of virtual team member engagement.
Task 12	**Define team ground rules:**
	■ Communicate organizational principles with team and external stakeholders.
	■ Establish an environment that fosters adherence to the ground rules.
	■ Manage and rectify ground rule violations.
Task 13	**Mentor relevant stakeholders:**
	■ Allocate the time to mentoring.
	■ Recognize and act on mentoring opportunities.
Task 14	**Promote team performance through the application of emotional intelligence:**
	■ Assess behavior through the use of personality indicators.
	■ Analyze personality indicators and adjust to the emotional needs of key project stakeholders.
Domain II	Process—50%
Task 1	**Execute project with the urgency required to deliver business value:**
	■ Assess opportunities to deliver value incrementally.
	■ Examine the business value throughout the project.
	■ Support the team to subdivide project tasks as necessary to find the minimum viable product.
Task 2	**Manage communications:**
	■ Analyze communication needs of all stakeholders.
	■ Determine communication methods, channels, frequency, and level of detail for all stakeholders.
	■ Communicate project information and updates effectively.
	■ Confirm communication is understood and feedback is received.

Domain II	Process—50%
Task 3	**Assess and manage risks:**
	■ Determine risk management options.
	■ Iteratively assess and prioritize risks.
Task 4	**Engage stakeholders:**
	■ Analyze stakeholders (e.g., power interest grid, influence, impact).
	■ Categorize stakeholders.
	■ Engage stakeholders by category.
	■ Develop, execute, and validate a strategy for stakeholder engagement.
Task 5	**Plan and manage budget and resources:**
	■ Estimate budgetary needs based on the scope of the project and lessons learned from past projects.
	■ Anticipate future budget challenges.
	■ Monitor budget variations and work with governance process to adjust as necessary.
	■ Plan and manage resources.
Task 6	**Plan and manage schedule:**
	■ Estimate project tasks (milestones, dependencies, story points).
	■ Utilize benchmarks and historical data.
	■ Prepare schedule based on methodology.
	■ Measure ongoing progress based on methodology.
	■ Modify schedule, as needed, based on methodology.
	■ Coordinate with other projects and other operations.
Task 7	**Plan and manage quality of products/deliverables:**
	■ Determine quality standard required for project deliverables.
	■ Recommend options for improvement based on quality gaps.
	■ Continually survey project deliverable quality.
Task 8	**Plan and manage scope:**
	■ Determine and prioritize requirements.
	■ Break down scope (e.g., WBS, backlog).
	■ Monitor and validate scope.

Domain II	Process—50%
Task 9	**Integrate project planning activities:**
	■ Consolidate the project/phase plans.
	■ Assess consolidated project plans for dependencies, gaps, and continued business value.
	■ Analyze the data collected.
	■ Collect and analyze data to make informed project decisions.
	■ Determine critical information requirements.
Task 10	**Manage project changes:**
	■ Anticipate and embrace the need for change (e.g., follow change management practices).
	■ Determine strategy to handle change.
	■ Execute change management strategy according to the methodology.
	■ Determine a change response to move the project forward.
Task 11	**Plan and manage procurement:**
	■ Define resource requirements and needs.
	■ Communicate resource requirements.
	■ Manage suppliers/contracts.
	■ Plan and manage procurement strategy.
	■ Develop a delivery solution.
Task 12	**Manage project artifacts:**
	■ Determine the requirements (what, when, where, who, etc.) for managing the project artifacts.
	■ Validate that the project information is kept up to date (i.e., version control) and accessible to all stakeholders.
	■ Continually assess the effectiveness of the management of the project artifacts.
Task 13	**Determine appropriate project methodology/methods and practices:**
	■ Assess project needs, complexity, and magnitude.
	■ Recommend project execution strategy (e.g., contracting, finance).
	■ Recommend a project methodology/approach (i.e., predictive, agile, hybrid).
	■ Use iterative, incremental practices throughout the project life cycle (e.g., lessons learned, stakeholder engagement, risk).

Domain II	Process—50%
Task 14	**Establish project governance structure:**
	■ Determine appropriate governance for a project (e.g., replicate organizational governance).
	■ Define escalation paths and thresholds.
Task 15	**Manage project issues:**
	■ Recognize when a risk becomes an issue.
	■ Attack the issue with the optimal action to achieve project success.
	■ Collaborate with relevant stakeholders on the approach to resolve the issues.
Task 16	**Ensure knowledge transfer for project continuity:**
	■ Discuss project responsibilities within team.
	■ Outline expectations for working environment.
	■ Confirm approach for knowledge transfers.
Task 17	**Plan and manage project/phase closure or transitions:**
	■ Determine criteria to successfully close the project or phase.
	■ Validate readiness for transition (e.g., to operations team or next phase).
	■ Conclude activities to close out project or phase (e.g., final lessons learned, retrospective, procurement, financials, resources).
Domain III	Business Environment—8%
Task 1	**Plan and manage project compliance:**
	■ Confirm project compliance requirements (e.g., security, health and safety, regulatory compliance).
	■ Classify compliance categories.
	■ Determine potential threats to compliance.
	■ Use methods to support compliance.
	■ Analyze the consequences of noncompliance.
	■ Determine necessary approach and action to address compliance needs (e.g., risk, legal).
	■ Measure the extent to which the project is in compliance.

Domain III	Business Environment—8%
Task 2	**Evaluate and deliver project benefits and value:**
	■ Investigate that benefits are identified.
	■ Document agreement on ownership for ongoing benefit realization.
	■ Verify measurement system is in place to track benefits.
	■ Evaluate delivery options to demonstrate value.
	■ Apprise stakeholders of value gain progress.
Task 3	**Evaluate and address external business environment changes for impact on scope:**
	■ Survey changes to external business environment (e.g., regulations, technology, geopolitical, market).
	■ Assess and prioritize impact on project scope/backlog based on changes in external business environment.
	■ Recommend options for scope/backlog changes (e.g., schedule, cost changes).
	■ Continually review external business environment for impacts on project scope/backlog.
Task 4	**Support organizational change:**
	■ Assess organizational culture.
	■ Evaluate impact of organizational change to project and determine required actions.
	■ Evaluate impact of the project to the organization and determine required actions.

This chapter covers the following topics that are foundational to preparing for the PMP exam questions and to getting the most out of the subsequent chapters in this book.

- **Core Project Management Concepts:** Review and clarify what projects are, what project management is, common functions associated with a project, and the role of the project manager.

- **Project Management Fundamentals:** Review the academic aspects of the project management domain, including process groups, knowledge areas, principles, performance domains, and project life cycle.

- **Project Environment:** Review the key aspects of the project environment and how they impact a project, including the system of value delivery, stakeholders, organizational structure, PMO types, and other internal and external factors.

## CHAPTER 2

Project Management 101

This chapter reviews the key concepts, fundamentals, and terms that provide the foundation for the PMP exam questions and the foundation for the deeper dive we take throughout the rest of the book. Although the PMP Exam Content Outline does not address these topics specifically, you need to have a firm understanding of the material in this chapter to better understand the context the exam questions will address.

While some of the material in this chapter is covered in the "Standard for Project Management" section of the *PMBOK® Guide*, Seventh Edition, we want to review all the key Project Management 101 elements that will better prepare you for the exam.

"Do I Know This Already?" Quiz

The "Do I Know This Already?" quiz allows you to assess whether you should read this entire chapter thoroughly or jump to the "Exam Preparation Tasks" section. If you are in doubt about your answers to these questions or your own assessment of your knowledge of the topics, read the entire chapter. Table 2-1 lists the major headings in this chapter and their corresponding "Do I Know This Already?" quiz questions. You can find the answers in Appendix A, "Answers to the 'Do I Know This Already?' Quizzes and Review Questions."

Table 2-1 "Do I Know This Already?" Section-to-Question Mapping

Foundation Topics Section	Questions
Core Concepts	1–7
Project Management Fundamentals	8–12
Project Environment	13–18

CAUTION The goal of self-assessment is to gauge your mastery of the topics in this chapter. If you do not know the answer to a question or are only partially sure of the answer, you should mark that question as wrong for purposes of the self-assessment. Giving yourself credit for an answer you correctly guess skews your self-assessment results and might provide you with a false sense of security.

1. What are the two most important attributes that describe a project according to the Project Management Institute (PMI)?

    a. Must have a project charter and a project manager

    b. Produces a unique product, service, or result and is a temporary endeavor

    c. Produces a product and has dedicated resources

    d. Must be approved by an executive sponsor and have a measurable ROI

2. What is project management per PMI?

    a. The application of servant leadership to meet project goals

    b. Being an effective communicator and producing timing status reports

    c. The application of knowledge, skills, tools, and techniques to project activities to meet project requirements

    d. Following a rigorous methodology to ensure a project is completed on time and under budget

3. Which of the following are common functions associated with projects?

    a. Maintain governance, present objectives and feedback, produce earned value analysis reports

    b. Provide resources and direction, facilitate and support, generate detailed schedules

    c. Apply expertise, provide oversight and coordination, agile development

    d. Perform work and contribute insights, provide business direction and insight, maintain governance

4. What are the key skills a project manager needs to be successful?

    a. Leadership, technical project management, communication

    b. Leadership, technical project management, business acumen

    c. Status reporting, communication, schedule development

    d. Strategic and business management, schedule development, facilitating meetings

5. What is the relationship between a project and a product?

    a. There is no difference between them.

    b. A project creates a product.

    c. A product generates revenue and value to customers on an ongoing basis.

    d. Both are part of portfolio and program management.

6. What are some common project constraints that a project manager must balance?

    a. Scope, schedule, documentation

    b. Scope, schedule, executive sponsorship

    c. Budget, quality, PMO oversight

    d. Resources, scope, schedule

7. How does a project manager role differ from a Scrum master and product owner on hybrid agile projects?

    a. They are not different. The roles are interchangeable.

    b. The project manager and Scrum master roles are interchangeable. The product owner is focused on the product being delivered.

    c. The project manager and product owner roles are interchangeable. The Scrum master is focused on guiding the core team through the Scrum process.

    d. The project manager is focused on the overall project performance. The Scrum master is focused on guiding the core team through the Scrum process. The product owner is focused on the product being delivered.

8. Which of the following are some of the Twelve Project Management Principles per PMI?

    a. Effectively engage with stakeholders; focus on value; enable change to achieve the envisioned future state

    b. Create a collaborative project team environment; embrace adaptability and resiliency; always prioritize schedule and budget over any other stakeholder concerns

    c. Demonstrate leadership behaviors; build quality into processes and deliverables; customize status reports for each stakeholder group

    d. Tailor project approach based on context; navigate complexity; address high-risk items first in the project work plan

9. What are the process groups of project management?

    a. Initiating, planning, development, testing, and deployment

    b. Planning, implementation, monitoring and controlling, and closing

    c. Initiating, planning, executing, monitoring and controlling, and closing

    d. Business case development, planning, executing, controlling, and closing

10. Which of the following are some of the 10 knowledge areas of project management?

    a. Scope management, schedule management, status report management

    b. Integration management, cost management, stakeholder management

    c. Quality management, procurement management, issue management

    d. Communications management, risk management, team management

11. Which of the following are some of the eight performance domains of project management?

    a. Planning, project work, integration management

    b. Approach and life cycle, delivery, closing

    c. Team, measurement, uncertainty

    d. Stakeholders, uncertainty, leadership

12. At what point in a project's life cycle is the level of uncertainty and risk the highest?

    a. During development

    b. At the beginning

    c. Right before deployment

    d. During testing

13. What is a System for Value Delivery?

    a. A project management system focused on achieving the project goals

    b. A financial approach to projects to ensure the project's ROI is achieved

    c. A collection of projects and products focused on maximizing customer satisfaction

    d. A collection of strategic business activities aimed at building, sustaining, and/or advancing an organization

14. What is the relationship between a project, a program, and a portfolio?

    a. The only difference is size of their scope.

    b. A portfolio is focused on the financial aspects of programs and projects.

    c. A portfolio can consist of programs and projects; a program is a group of related projects.

    d. A portfolio consists of programs, and a program consists of related projects.

15. What are the three main types of organizational structures?

    a. Functional, matrix, and project-oriented

    b. Hierarchical, flat, and team-oriented

    c. Projectized, balanced matrix, and hierarchical

    d. Functional, decentralized, and centralized

16. What are some of the resources often included in the organizational process assets?

    a. Process assets, organizational culture, infrastructure

    b. Process assets, data assets, market conditions

    c. Methodologies, templates, document libraries, policies, and procedures

    d. Templates, document libraries, governance system, and regulatory environment

17. What are three different types of PMOs?

    a. Monitoring, executing, reporting

    b. Supportive, controlling, directive

    c. Low-level control, medium-level control, and high-level control

    d. Functional, integrated, supportive

18. Who are considered some of the stakeholders on a project?

    a. Just customers and end users

    b. Project leadership team, end users, project sponsor, competitor organizations

    c. Only the people who either purchase the project work or use the product/service resulting from the project

    d. Project manager, customers, end users, operations

Foundation Topics

Core Project Management Concepts

Let's review the key core concepts of projects, project management, functions associated with a project, and the role of the project manager (PM). Clarity on these subjects and a better understanding of the project manager mindset expected from PMI will help you answer more questions correctly on the exam.

If you are like most people, you are "pretty sure" you know what projects are, and you "think" you know what project management is (and what a project manager does), but there's always a varying amount of uncertainty in those perceptions. So, let's start off by clarifying some key concepts.

Project management is simply the process of managing projects (and you thought this was going to be difficult). Although this definition is not particularly helpful, it does illustrate three key points:

- Project management is not "brain surgery." Yes, it covers a vast array of subjects, processes, skills, and tools, but the key fundamentals of project management are straightforward and are consistent across industries.

- To better understand project management, you need to understand what a project is. The nature of a project provides insights into the scope and challenges of project management.

- To better understand project management, you need to understand what is implied by the term *managing* and how this compares against traditional business management.

And before we delve into these three points, let's look at how PMI defines project management.

The PMI definition of *project management* is the application of knowledge, skills, tools, and techniques to project activities to meet project requirements. Project management refers to guiding the project work to deliver the intended *outcomes*. *Project teams* can achieve the outcomes using a broad range of approaches (e.g., predictive, hybrid, and adaptive).

What Is a Project Exactly?

Per PMI, a *project* is a temporary endeavor to produce a unique product, service, or result. The temporary nature of projects indicates a beginning and an end to the project work or a phase of project work. Projects can stand alone or be part of a program or portfolio.

In other words, a ***project*** is the work performed by an organization one time to produce a unique outcome. By *one time*, we mean the work has a definite beginning and a definite end, and by *unique*, we mean the work result is different in one or more ways from anything the organization has produced before. Examples of projects include the following:

- Building a new house

- Developing a new software application

- Performing an assessment of current manufacturing processes

- Improving an organizational business process

- Writing a book

- Relocating a company's technology infrastructure to a new location or to a cloud platform

- Merging two organizations

- Developing a new medical device

This definition is in contrast to the operations of an organization. The operational work is the ongoing, repetitive set of activities that sustain the organization. Examples of ongoing operations include the following:

- Processing customer orders

- Performing accounts receivable and accounts payable activities

- Executing daily manufacturing orders

- Performing recommended equipment maintenance procedures

- Conducting customer account maintenance

To further explain the nature of projects (and project management) and how they compare to the ongoing operations of an organization, please review the summary in Table 2-2.

Table 2-2 Comparing Projects and Operations

Feature	Projects	Operations
Key Similarities	Planned, executed, and controlled	Planned, executed, and controlled
	Performed by people	Performed by people
	Resource constrained	Resource constrained
Purpose	Attain objectives	Sustain the organization
Time	Temporary	Ongoing
	Definite beginning and end points	

Feature	Projects	Operations
Outcome	Unique product, service, or result	Repetitive product, service, or result
People	Dynamic, temporary teams formed to meet project needs Generally not aligned with organizational structure	Functional teams generally aligned with organizational structure
Authority of Manager	Varies by organizational structure Generally minimal, if any, direct line authority	Generally formal, direct line authority

NOTE The Project Management Institute (PMI) definition of *project* is a temporary endeavor to produce a unique product, service, or result. The temporary nature of projects indicates a beginning and an end to the project work or a phase of project work. Projects can stand alone or be part of a program or portfolio.

Comparing Projects and Products

To better clarify what projects are, another aspect to review is how projects compare to **products**. With the increasing focus and adoption by organizations on product management, there is often some confusion on how projects and products differ. We touch on this issue throughout the book, but to jump-start this understanding, please review the summary in Table 2-3.

Table 2-3 Comparing Projects and Products

Feature	Projects	Products
Relationship to Each Other	Creates a product Can be used to update or improve a product	Result of a project
Purpose	Attain objectives	Generate revenue for organization and value to customers on an ongoing basis
Focus	Executing the process to achieve objectives while managing constraints	Maximizing value of the product
Time	Temporary Definite beginning and end points	Ongoing until product is retired

Feature	Projects	Products
Key Similarities	Delivering value to customer	Delivering value to customer
	Quality focus	Quality focus
	Resource and budget constraints	Resource and budget constraints
Teams	Dynamic, temporary teams formed to meet project needs	Functional permanent team members
		Initial project team members may become part of a permanent product team

Functions Associated with Projects

Before we get into managing projects and the role of the project manager, it is worth noting that PMI highlights a set of common functions associated with projects. The significant points from this list are that it takes a project team working efficiently and effectively together to deliver the value of a project and that the project manager is not the one who performs all of these functions. The project manager cannot do the work alone. This is not a new revelation. But this list is an acknowledgment from PMI that the team members responsible for key project functions will vary depending on the context of the project and the project approach exercised. Table 2-4 summarizes these project functions from the *PMBOK® Guide*, Seventh Edition, and provides examples of common project roles that fulfill the function.

Table 2-4   Summary Description of *PMBOK® Guide*, Seventh Edition, Functions Associated with Projects

#	Function	Common Activities	Role(s) That Typically Perform(s) Function
1	Provide Oversight and Coordination	Orchestrating work of the project	Project Manager
		Leading the planning, controlling, and monitoring activities	
		Consulting with executives and business unit leaders to advance project objectives, improve project performance, and meet customer needs	
		Benefits realization and sustainment	
		Support programs and portfolios that the project is a part of	
2	Present Objectives and Feedback	Provide perspectives, insights, and clear direction from customers and end users regarding requirements, outcomes, and expectations	Project Sponsor
			Project Manager
		In adaptive and hybrid environments, the need for ongoing feedback is greater	Business Analyst
			Product Owner
			Business SMEs

#	Function	Common Activities	Role(s) That Typically Perform(s) Function
3	Facilitate and Support	Encouraging team participation, collaboration, and a sense of shared responsibility for the work results	Project Manager
		Help team create consensus around solutions, make decisions, and resolve conflicts	
		Coordinate meetings	
		Support people through change	
		Proactively address obstacles	
4	Perform Work and Contribute Insights	Provide the knowledge, skills, and experience to generate the project deliverables and outcomes	Project Team
			SMEs
			Consultants
5	Apply Expertise	Provide the knowledge, vision, and expertise in a specific subject for the project	Technical SMEs
		Offer advice and support and contribute to the project team's learning process and work quality	Consultants
			Team Leaders
		Can be internal or external to the organization	
		Can be full or part time	
6	Provide Business Direction and Insight	Guide and clarify the direction of the project and/or product outcome	Product Owner
		Prioritize requirements based on business value, dependencies, and risk	Business Leads
			Business Analysts
		Provide feedback to project team on next work increment, especially on hybrid and adaptive projects	Project Manager
			Steering Committee
		Solicit feedback from other stakeholders, customers, and project team to maximize value of product outcome	
7	Provide Resources and Direction	Promote the project and communicate organization's vision, goals, and expectations to the project team and the broader stakeholder community	Business Relationship Manager
		Advocate for the project team by helping to secure decisions, resources, and authority that allows the project to progress	Program Manager
			Steering Committee
			Project Sponsor
		Serve as liaison between senior management and project team and help to keep project aligned with business objectives, remove obstacles, resolve issues, and address risks outside the bounds of the project team's authority	Account Executive

#	Function	Common Activities	Role(s) That Typically Perform(s) Function
8	Maintain Governance	Approve and support recommendations made by project team Monitor project progress toward achieving targeted outcomes Maintain linkages between project team and the strategic/business objectives which can change over time	Steering Committee PMO Project Sponsor

Managing Projects

What do we mean when we say "managing projects"?

- We mean applying both the science and the art of planning, organizing, implementing, leading, and guiding the work of a project to deliver the intended outcomes.

- We mean the process of defining a project, developing a plan, executing the plan, monitoring progress against the plan, overcoming obstacles, managing risks, and taking corrective actions.

- We mean the process of managing the competing demands and trade-offs between the desired results of the project (scope, performance, quality) and the natural constraints of the project (time and cost).

- We mean the process of leading a team that has never worked together before to accomplish something that has never been done before in a given amount of time with a limited amount of money.

> **NOTE** The PMI definition of *project management* is the application of knowledge, skills, tools, and techniques to project activities to meet project requirements. Project management refers to guiding the project work to deliver the intended outcomes. Project teams can achieve the outcomes using a broad range of approaches (e.g., predictive, hybrid, and adaptive).

Sounds like fun, doesn't it? We explain each of these key aspects of project management throughout the book, and we discuss many of the specific tasks and responsibilities performed by the project manager later in this chapter.

What Is the Value of Project Management?

As the organizational operating environment continues to become more global, more competitive, and more demanding, organizations must adapt. They must become more efficient and more productive; they must do more with less. They must continually innovate. They must respond rapidly to a fast-changing environment. *How can they do this? How can they do this in a strategic manner? How can they do this and still have the proper management controls?* They can do this with effective project management. The strategic *value* points that effective project management can offer an organization include, but are not limited to, the following:

- Provide a controlled way to rapidly respond to changing market conditions and new strategic opportunities

- Maximize the innovative and creative capabilities of the organization by creating environments of focus and open communication

- Enable organizations to accomplish more with less cost

- Enable better leverage of both internal and external expertise

- Provide key information and visibility on project metrics to enable better decision-making management

- Increase the pace and level of stakeholder acceptance for any strategic change

- Reduce financial losses by "killing off" poor project investments early in their life cycles

NOTE *Stakeholder* is the term used to describe individuals and organizations who are actively involved in the project or whose interests might be impacted by the execution or completion of the project.

In addition to providing apparent value to any organization, project management also offers tremendous value to each of us as individuals. At a personal level, the value of effective project management

- Ensures that your work is put to the best use for the organization and is properly recognized

- Provides a career path that offers unique, challenging opportunities on each new project

- Provides a career path that requires all your abilities and knowledge, including your management, business, people, and technical skills

- Provides a career path that is high in demand and, generally, offers an increase in income

- Provides a career path that prepares you for organizational leadership positions

- Provides a career path that is recognized more each year as excellent preparation for C-level executive positions as more of these positions are filled by individuals with project management experience

- Provides a career path that enables you to be on the front lines of strategic organizational initiatives and have major impact on the organization's future

Why Are Projects Challenging?

From what we've covered so far, from your own experiences, or from your reading trade publications, you likely have some appreciation for the difficulty of completing a successful project. Let's review the key reasons why projects are challenging to manage:

- **Uncharted Territory:** Each project is unique. The work to be done has likely never been done before by this group of people in this particular environment.

- **Multiple Expectations:** Each project has multiple stakeholders that each has their own needs and expectations for the project.

- **Communication Obstacles:** Due to natural organizational boundaries, communication channels, and team development stages, communication of project information must be proactively managed to ensure proper flow.

- **Balancing the Competing Demands:** Every project is defined to produce one or more deliverables (scope) within a defined time period (time) under an approved budget (cost) with a specified set of resources. In addition, the deliverables must achieve a certain performance level (quality) and meet the approval of the key stakeholders (expectations). Each of these factors can affect the others, as Figure 2-1 illustrates. For example, if additional functionality (scope, quality) is desired, the time and cost (resources needed) of the project will increase. This is a key focus of an effective project manager.

NOTE The competing project demands are often referred to as the *triple constraint of project management*. Time and cost (or resources) are always two sides of the triangle. Depending on where you look, the third side is either scope, performance, or quality. In either case, it's the "output" of the project. Additionally, many recent variations of this model have included the additional demand of client expectations.

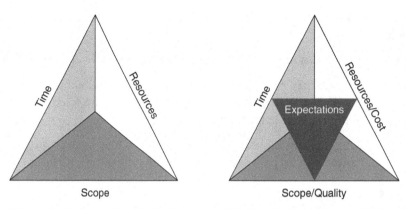

Figure 2-1   Competing Project Demands (Traditional Model on Left, Modern Model on Right), Summarizing the Relationships Between the Natural Competing Demands of Projects

To elaborate on the challenge of balancing the common project demands and constraints, this is one of the primary focuses of a project manager. Any change in any one of them will likely have an effect or impact on the others and the potential outcomes of the project. In addition, the project manager must communicate the importance of balancing these constraints in conjunction with stakeholder expectations and understand which aspects have the higher priority to them. The common project constraints include but are not limited to

- **Scope:** The work to be done on the project. Increasing the scope causes more work to be done and generally results in more cost and time needed and often more resources.

- **Quality:** The quality standards that the project must fulfill. Higher quality standards often require more work effort, which generally translates into more cost and time…and often more resources.

- **Schedule:** The calendar time required to complete the project. Changes here generally have an impact on the scope, quality, budget, resources, or risks.

- **Budget:** The cost required to accomplish the project's objectives. Changes here generally have an impact on the scope, schedule, or quality of the project.

- **Resources:** The resources that are needed to complete the work of the project. Each resource has an associated cost, along with the associated skill or quality level of the resource.

- **Risk:** The trade-off that comes with each decision made in the planning and execution of a project. The risk management decisions might have consequences that affect other constraints.

- **Cutting Edge:** Often, projects have a strategic, innovative focus. As a result, they often deal with new, leading-edge technologies. In these cases, the project has more risks, more unknowns, and is much more difficult to estimate accurately.

- **Organizational Impacts:** In addition to overcoming natural communication obstacles created by the project structure, the project manager must also manage overlaps in organizational approval and authority domains, contend with competing priorities for shared resources, deal with annual budget cycles that might not be aligned with the project's funding needs, and ensure that the project is aligned with the focus of the organization.

- **Collaboration:** Depending on the strategic level and scope of a project, the project team will consist of stakeholders across the organization from different functional areas that are likely not accustomed to working together. For project success, these different stakeholders must learn to work together and to understand the others' perspectives to make the best decisions for the project. Often, the project manager plays a key facilitating role in this collaboration process.

- **Estimating the Work:** Estimating project work is difficult, yet the time and cost dimensions of the project are built on these work effort estimates. Given the facts that the work of the project is often unique (never been done before at all, never been done with these tools, and never been done by these people), and most organizations do not maintain accurate historical records on previous projects (that might have similar work components), it is difficult to accurately estimate the effort for individual work items, not to mention the entire project as well as the challenges of needing to deliver a solution when the full requirements are undetermined. This challenge in particular is why agile management has grown in popularity and use throughout many organizations.

The Project Manager

The *project manager* has many activities to perform, challenges to overcome, and responsibilities to uphold over the life of a project. Depending on your individual experiences, your industry background, and the manner in which project management has been implemented in your organization, this full picture perspective may be quite enlightening to you.

To ensure that we have a common understanding of what a project manager does, let's review the different roles a project manager plays over the life of a project and discuss the prerequisite skills that you need to perform those roles. Most importantly, we accelerate your learning curve for the exam by sharing the characteristics of successful project managers and the common mistakes made by many others.

One Title, Many Roles

You've likely heard many of the analogies before to describe the role of project manager—the captain of the ship, the conductor of the orchestra, the coach of the team, the catalyst of the engine, and so on. There's truth and insight in each of the analogies, but each can be incomplete as well. To gain better understanding of what a project manager does, let's briefly discuss each of the key roles played by the project manager. And to clarify, these are not terms you need to know for the PMP exam, but they are used here to clarify the role and mindset of the project manager.

- **Planner:** Ensures that the project is defined properly and completely for success, all stakeholders are engaged, work effort approach is determined, required resources are available when needed, and processes are in place to properly execute and control the project.

- **Organizer:** Using work breakdown, estimating, and scheduling techniques, determines the complete work effort for the project, the proper sequence of the work activities, when the work will be accomplished, who will do the work, and how much the work will cost.

- **Point Person:** Serves as the central point of contact for all oral and written project communications.

- **Quartermaster:** Ensures the project has the resources, materials, and facilities it needs when it needs it.

- **Facilitator:** Ensures that stakeholders and team members who come from different perspectives understand each other and work together to accomplish the project goals.

- **Persuader:** Gains agreement from the stakeholders on project definition, success criteria, and approach; manages stakeholder expectations throughout the project while managing the competing demands of time, cost, and quality; and gains agreement on resource decisions and issue resolution action steps.

- **Problem Solver:** Utilizes root-cause analysis process experience, prior project experience, and technical knowledge to resolve unforeseen technical issues and take any necessary corrective actions.

- **Umbrella:** Works to shield the project team from the politics and "noise" surrounding the project, so they can stay focused and productive.

- **Coach:** Determines and communicates the role each team member plays and the importance of that role to the project's success, finds ways to motivate each team member, looks for ways to improve the skills of each team member, and provides constructive and timely feedback on individual performances.

- **Bulldog:** Performs the follow-up to ensure that commitments are maintained, issues are resolved, and action items are completed.

- **Librarian:** Manages all information, communications, and documentation involved in the project.

- **Insurance Agent:** Continuously works to identify risks and develop responses to those risk events in advance.

- **Police Officer:** Consistently measures progress against the plan, develops corrective actions, and reviews the quality of both project processes and project deliverables.

- **Salesperson:** An extension of the persuader and coach roles, but this role is focused on "selling" the benefits of the project to the organization, serving as a change agent, and inspiring team members to meet project goals and overcome project challenges.

 ## Key Skills of Project Managers

Although a broad range of skills is needed to effectively manage the people, process, and technical aspects of any project, it becomes clear there is a set of key skills that each project manager should have. Although these skill categories are not necessarily exclusive of each other, let's group them into five categories to streamline our review and discussion:

1. **Project Management Fundamentals:** The "science" part of project management, covered in this book, including office productivity suite (such as Microsoft Office, email, and so on), project management software, project collaboration tool, and work management tool skills.

2. **Business Management Skills:** Those skills that would be equally valuable to an operations or line-of-business manager, such as budgeting, finance, procurement, organizational dynamics, team development, performance management, coaching, and motivation.

3. **Technical Knowledge:** The knowledge gained from experience and competence in the focal area of the project. With it, you greatly increase your effectiveness as a project manager. You have more credibility, and you can ask

better questions, validate the estimates and detail plans of team members, help solve technical issues, develop better solutions, and serve more of a leadership role. Note this does not mean the project manager is the technical expert. It just means this knowledge makes them more effective in working with the technical experts to accomplish the project objectives.

4. **Communication Skills:** Because communication is regarded as the most important project management skill by the Project Management Institute, we feel it is important to separate them out. Skills included in this category include all written communication skills (correspondence, emails, documents), oral communication skills, facilitation skills, presentation skills, and—the most valuable—active listening. *Active listening* can be defined as "really listening" and the ability to listen with focus, empathy, and the desire to connect with the speaker.

TIP   Active listening is one of the secret weapons of effective project managers, and we cover this in more detail in Chapter 10, "Project Communications."

5. **Leadership Skills:** This category overlaps with some of the others and focuses on the attitude and mindset required for project management. However, it also includes key skills such as interpersonal and general people relationship-building skills, adaptability, flexibility, people management, degree of customer orientation, analytical skills, problem-solving skills, and the ability to keep the big picture in mind.

NOTE   The specific combination of skills that are required for a project manager to be successful on a given project vary depending on the size and nature of the project. For example, as a general rule, on larger projects, technical knowledge is less important than competence in the other skill categories.

As of 2022, PMI combines these key skill sets into three groups in the PMI Talent Triangle, as shown in Figure 2-2.

- **Ways of Working:** The knowledge, skills, and behaviors related to specific domains of project, program, and portfolio management. The technical aspects of performing one's role. This category was previously referred to as Technical Project Management.

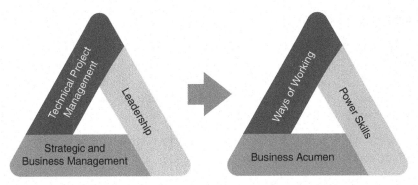

Figure 2-2 PMI Talent Triangle (Used with Permission of Project Management Institute)

- **Power Skills:** The knowledge, skills, and behaviors needed to guide, motivate, and direct a team to help an organization achieve its business goals. This category was previously referred to as Leadership.

- **Business Acumen:** The knowledge of and expertise in the industry and organization that enhances performance and better delivers business outcomes. This category was previously referred to as Strategic and Business Management.

I know, I know…after reading this, you are probably thinking either one or more of the following:

- "You must be kidding! I need to be good in all those areas to manage a project?"

- "Wait! I've been on projects before, and I've yet to see a project manager who could do all that."

- "Wait, you must be kidding! If anyone was excellent in all those areas, they would be a C-level executive of our company."

To help answer all these questions, please understand two important observations:

1. Many projects are not successful.

2. You do not need to get an "A" in all these categories to be successful as a project manager.

The key is that the project manager has the right mix of skills to meet the needs of the given project. In addition, a self-assessment against these skill categories enables you to leverage your strengths, compensate for your deficiencies, and focus your self-improvement program.

Qualities of Successful Project Managers

Given the many roles played by a project manager, the broad range of skills needed, and the inherent challenges in successfully delivering a project, we need to find ways to accelerate the learning process. Two key ways to accelerate this learning is to understand the qualities of successful project managers and to understand the common mistakes made by project managers.

Successful project managers do not share personality types, appearances, or sizes, but they do share four important features:

1. They focus on communication, collaboration, and engagement throughout the project.

2. They compensate for any skill deficiencies by staffing their teams accordingly.

3. They avoid the common mistakes described in the next section.

4. They bring a mindset and approach to project management that is best characterized by one or more of the following qualities:

   - **Take ownership:** Take responsibility and accountability for the project, lead by example, and bring energy and drive to the project. Without this attitude, all the skills and techniques in the world will only get you so far.

   - **Savvy:** Understand people and the dynamics of the organization; navigate tricky politics; have the ability to quickly read and diffuse emotionally charged situations; think fast; build relationships; leverage personal power for benefit of the project.

   - **Intensity with a smile:** Balance an assertive, resilient, tenacious, results-oriented focus with a style that makes people want to help; consistently follow up on everything and their resolutions without annoying everyone.

   - **Eye of the storm:** Demonstrate an ability to be the calm eye of the project hurricane; high tolerance for ambiguity; take the heat from key stakeholders (C-level executives, business managers, and project team); exhibit a calm, confident aura when others are showing signs of issue or project stress.

   - **Strong customer-service orientation:** Demonstrate the ability to see each stakeholder's perspective; are able to provide a voice for all key stakeholders (especially the sponsor) to the project team; have strong facilitation and collaboration skills; and have excellent active listening skills.

   - **People focused:** Take a team-oriented approach; understand that methodology, process, and tools are important, but without quality people it's very difficult to complete a project successfully.

- **Always keep "eye on the ball":** Stay focused on the project goals and objectives. There are many ways to accomplish a given objective, which is especially important to remember when things don't go as planned.

- **Controlled passion:** Balance passion for completing the project objectives with a healthy detached perspective, which enables them to make better decisions, continue to see all points of view, better anticipate risks, and better respond to project issues.

- **Healthy paranoia:** Balance a confident, positive outlook with a realism that assumes nothing, constantly questions, and verifies everything.

- **Context understanding:** Understand the context of the project—the priority that the project has among the organization's portfolio of projects and how it aligns with the overall goals of the organization.

- **Look for trouble:** Are constantly looking and listening for potential risks, issues, or obstacles; confront doubt head-on; deal with disgruntled users right away; understand that most of these situations are opportunities and can be resolved up front before they become full-scale crisis points.

15 Common Mistakes of Project Managers

Understanding the most common project management mistakes will help you focus your efforts and help you to avoid the same mistakes on your projects and avoid incorrect answers on the exam. The following are some of the most common mistakes made by project managers:

1. Not clearly understanding how or ensuring that the project is aligned with organizational objectives

2. Not properly managing stakeholder expectations throughout the project

3. Not gaining agreement and buy-in on project goals and success criteria from key stakeholders

4. Not developing a realistic schedule that includes all work efforts, task dependencies, bottom-up estimates, and assigned leveled resources

5. Not getting buy-in and acceptance on the project schedule

6. Not clearly deciding and communicating who is responsible for what

7. Not utilizing change control procedures to manage the scope of the project

8. Not communicating consistently and effectively with all key stakeholders

9. Not executing the project plan

10. Not tackling key risks early in the project

11. Not proactively identifying risks and developing contingency plans (responses) for those risks

12. Not obtaining the right resources with the right skills at the right time

13. Not aggressively pursuing issue resolution

14. Inadequately defining and managing requirements

15. Insufficiently managing and leading the project team

Project Manager vs. Scrum Master vs. Product Owner

To further clarify the role of the project manager, let's do a quick review on how the role differs on agile projects, and specifically how it differs from two prominent roles in the agile process: Scrum master and product owner. With the increasing adoption of agile project approaches, and the Scrum agile methodology, there is often some initial confusion about how a project manager fits in this environment because the Scrum methodology does not define a project manager role. And frankly, many organizations struggle to figure out how to leverage their existing project manager as they transition to agile and Scrum project approaches. As a result, it is this struggle that leads to confusion and uncertainty surrounding the project manager role on agile projects.

In summary, when you understand the roles of the Scrum master, the product owner, and the project manager, it's much easier to see the importance of each role and why they are all needed for a successful project.

As a reminder from Chapter 1, "The PMP Exam: How to Prepare and Pass," PMI uses the term *team facilitator* for the Scrum master role on pure agile projects and does not define a traditional PM role for a pure agile project. So this discussion technically applies to hybrid projects per PMI, and most real-world agile/adaptive projects are not pure in their implementation.

With that stated, let's briefly discuss each role to jumpstart this understanding:

- **Scrum Master:** A defined Scrum guide role that is focused on the core team and guiding them through the Scrum process. The Scrum master is a coach and a facilitator for both the development team and the product owner, and often the organization. They are focused on the work process, alleviating bottlenecks and continuously striving for process improvement. PMI calls this role team facilitator.

- **Product Owner:** A defined Scrum guide role that is focused on maximizing the value of the product being delivered. The product owner represents the customer and is responsible for defining the backlog items (e.g., requirements and features), setting priorities, and providing feedback to the core development team after each sprint (work increment)

- **Project Manager:** This role serves as overall leader and manager of the project itself. The project manager works with the Scrum master and product owner to ensure needs of the organization and business are being met. This role is responsible for delivering the project on time, in budget, and with the agreed-upon scope. In addition, the project manager handles building the team, securing the budget, developing and maintaining project schedules, delivering project communications, managing project issues and risks, and coordinating release deployments.

Seems fairly straightforward, right? So where does the confusion come into play? In my experience, the confusion stems from one, if not all, of these factors:

- Some of the traditional project manager functions are shared by the Scrum master, the product owner, and the core agile team.

- The Scrum master and/or product owner roles have not been properly staffed and/or individuals lack the requisite Scrum training.

- A single individual is serving a combination of these roles.

Now is it possible for a single person to serve a combination of these roles on hybrid projects? Sure, but it does run the risk of highly compromising the Scrum process. The most common scenario that can be successful is the project manager also serving as the Scrum master, but it does assume the project manager has the appropriate skills, training, and time to serve both roles properly. In general, the more aligned the organization is with the Scrum agile roles, and the more mature an organization becomes with successfully leveraging the Scrum approach, the clearer the differences and the importance of each of these roles become.

Project Management Fundamentals

Okay, now that we have covered the core key concepts of projects, project management, and the project manager role, let's take a more academic look at the breadth of the project management domain. These are the fundamentals of project management that you need to understand for better success on the exam.

PMI had defined project management as a set of 5 process groups (see Table 2-5), 10 knowledge areas (see Table 2-6), and a matrix chart that mapped all the distinct processes to the process groups and knowledge areas in its first six editions of their standards. These references are taken from the PMI's *A Guide to the Project Management Body of Knowledge*, Sixth Edition (*PMBOK® Guide*, Sixth Edition).

However, with the latest edition, the *A Guide to the Project Management Body of Knowledge*, Seventh Edition (*PMBOK® Guide*, Seventh Edition), PMI made a significant update to respond to the changing landscape, to emphasize project value and outcomes, and to capture how successful practitioners were actually applying these processes and knowledge areas to deliver successful projects for their organizations. So although they are not part of the latest PMBOK, it does not change the fact these are basic fundamentals of project management that a competent practitioner needs to be familiar with and know when and how to apply.

Table 2-5   Description of Project Management Process Groups

#	Process Group	Description per *PMBOK® Guide*, Sixth Edition	Common Terms
1	Initiating	Those processes performed to define a new project or a new phase of an existing project by obtaining authorization to start the project or phase.	*preliminary planning* *kicking off*
2	Planning	Those processes required to establish the scope of the project or project phase, refine the objectives, and define the course of action required to attain the objectives that the project was undertaken to achieve.	*defining* *developing the plan* *setting the stage*
3	Executing	Those processes required to coordinate the people and resources needed to implement the plan for the project or project phase.	*making it happen* *getting it done* *coordinating*
4	Monitoring and Controlling	Those processes required to track, review, and regulate the progress and performance of the project or project phase; identify any areas in which changes to the plan are required; and initiate the corresponding changes.	*tracking progress* *keeping on course* *measuring actual versus planned performance*
5	Closing	Those processes performed to formally complete or close the project, phase, or contract.	*transition* *closeout*

Figure 2-3 summarizes the relationships among the project management process groups, based on *PMBOK® Guide*, Sixth Edition.

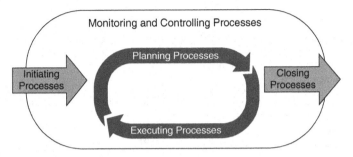

Figure 2-3   Project Management Process Relationships

Table 2-6   Project Management Knowledge Areas

#	Knowledge Area	Description per *PMBOK® Guide*, Sixth Edition	Common Deliverables
1	Project Integration Management	Processes and activities to identify, define, combine, unify, and coordinate the various processes and project management activities within the project management process groups.	Project Charter
			Project Management Plan
			Change Requests
			Work Results
2	Project Scope Management	Processes required to ensure that project includes all the work that is required and only the work that is required to complete the project successfully.	Scope Statement
			Work Breakdown Structure
			Formal Acceptance
3	Project Schedule Management	Processes required to ensure timely completion of the project.	Network Diagram
			Task Estimates
			Project Schedule
4	Project Cost Management	Processes involved in planning, estimating, budgeting, financing, funding, managing, and controlling costs so the project can be completed within the approved budget.	Cost Estimates
			Project Budget

#	Knowledge Area	Description per *PMBOK® Guide*, Sixth Edition	Common Deliverables
5	Project Quality Management	Processes for incorporating the organization's quality policy regarding planning, managing, and controlling project and product quality requirements to meet stakeholders' expectations.	Quality Management Plan Checklists Quality Reviews
6	Project Resources Management	Processes required to make the most effective use of the people, equipment, supplies, raw materials, facilities, and so on involved with the project.	Resource Requirements Role and Responsibility Matrix Organization Chart Performance Evaluations
7	Project Communications Management	Processes required to ensure timely and appropriate planning, collection, creation, distribution, storage, retrieval, management, control, monitoring, and ultimate disposition of project information.	Communication Management Plan Status Reports Presentations Lessons Learned Knowledge Repositories
8	Project Risk Management	Processes of conducting risk management planning, identification, analysis, response planning, response implementation, and monitoring risk on a project.	Risk Management Plan Risk Response Plan Risk Log
9	Project Procurement Management	Processes necessary to purchase or acquire products, services, or results needed from outside the project team.	Procurement Management Plan Statement of Work Proposals Contracts
10	Project Stakeholder Management	Processes required to identify the people, groups, or organizations that could impact or be impacted by the project, to analyze stakeholder expectations and their impact on the project, and to develop appropriate management strategies for effectively engaging stakeholders in project decisions and execution.	Stakeholder Register Stakeholder Engagement Plan Project Schedule Issue Log Change Requests

NOTE   The *PMBOK® Guide*, Sixth Edition, was released in 2017. The *PMBOK® Guide*, Seventh Edition, was officially released in August 2021. PMI targets an update to the PMBOK every four years.

As mentioned in Chapter 1, the latest edition—*PMBOK® Guide*, Seventh Edition— provides a foundation that is designed to be tailored to best meet the needs of the organization and individual project. PMI now defines project management as a set of 12 principles (see Table 2-7) and 8 performance domains (see Table 2-8). The principles are interwoven into how PMI expects each performance domain to be executed, and we review them throughout the remainder of the book.

Table 2-7   Description of the *PMBOK® Guide*, Seventh Edition, Twelve Project Management Principles

#	Category	Principle Label	Principle Statement
1	Stewardship	Be a diligent, respectful, and caring steward.	Stewards act responsibly to carry out activities with integrity, care, and trustworthiness while maintaining compliance with internal and external guidelines.
2	Team	Create a collaborative project team environment.	Project teams that work collaboratively can accomplish a shared objective more effectively and efficiently than individuals working on their own.
3	Stakeholders	Effectively engage with stakeholder.	Engage stakeholders proactively and to the degree needed to contribute to project success and customer satisfaction.
4	Value	Focus on value.	Continually evaluate and adjust project alignment to business objectives and intended benefits and value.
5	Systems Thinking	Recognize, evaluate, and respond to system interactions.	Recognize, evaluate, and respond to the dynamic circumstances within and surrounding the project in a holistic way to positively affect project performance.
6	Leadership	Demonstrate leadership behaviors.	Demonstrate and adapt leadership behaviors to support individual and team needs and to promote project success.
7	Tailoring	Tailor based on context.	Design the project approach based on the context, objectives, stakeholders, governance, and environment using "just enough" process to achieve the desired outcome while maximizing value, managing cost, and enhancing speed.

#	Category	Principle Label	Principle Statement
8	Quality	Build quality into processes and deliverables.	Maintain a focus on quality that produces deliverables that meet project objectives and align to the needs, uses, and acceptance requirements set by relevant stakeholders.
9	Complexity	Navigate complexity.	Continually evaluate and navigate project complexity so that approaches and plans enable the project teams to successfully navigate the project life cycle.
10	Risk	Optimize risk responses.	Continually evaluate exposure to risk to maximize positive impacts and minimize negative impacts to the project and its outcomes.
11	Adaptability and Resiliency	Embrace adaptability and resiliency.	Build adaptability and resiliency into the organization's and project team's approaches to help the project accommodate change, recover from setbacks, and advance the work of the project.
12	Change	Enable change to achieve the envisioned future state.	Prepare those impacted for the adoption and sustainment of new and different behaviors and processes required for the transition from the current state to the intended future state created by the project outcomes.

NOTE The PMBOK Principles of Project Management reflect the influence of the values and principles captured in the Agile Manifesto.

Table 2-8 Description of *PMBOK® Guide*, Seventh Edition, Eight Performance Domains of Project Management

#	Performance Domain	Focus	Desired Outcomes
1	Stakeholders	Activities and functions associated with stakeholders.	Productive working relationship with stakeholders. Stakeholder agreement with project objectives.
2	Team	Activities and functions associated with the people responsible for producing project deliverables.	Shared ownership. High-performing team. Applicable leadership and interpersonal skills demonstrated by all team members.

#	Performance Domain	Focus	Desired Outcomes
3	Approach and Life Cycle	Activities and functions associated with the approach, cadence, and life cycle phases of the project.	Approaches consistent with project deliverables. Project life cycle that connects delivery of value from beginning to end of project. Project life cycle that facilitates delivery cadence and approach required to produce the deliverables.
4	Planning	Activities and functions associated with the initial, ongoing, and evolving organization and coordination necessary to deliver project deliverables and outcomes.	Project progresses in an organized, coordinated, and deliberate manner. A holistic approach to delivering project outcomes. Evolving information is elaborated to produce the deliverables and outcomes. Time spent planning is appropriate for situation. Planning information is sufficient to manage expectations. There is a process to adapt plans based on emerging and changing needs or conditions.
5	Project Work	Activities and functions associated with establishing project processes, managing physical resources, and fostering a learning environment.	Efficient and effective project performance. Processes appropriate for the project and environment. Appropriate communication with stakeholders. Efficient management of physical resources. Effective management of procurements. Improved team capability due to continuous learning and process improvement.
6	Delivery	Activities and functions associated with delivering targeted scope and quality.	Project contributes to business objectives. Project realizes intended outcomes. Project benefits are realized in the timeframe planned. Project team has clear understanding of requirements. Stakeholders satisfied with project deliverables.

#	Performance Domain	Focus	Desired Outcomes
7	Measurement	Activities and functions associated with assessing project performance and taking appropriate actions to maintain acceptable performance.	Reliable understanding of project status.
			Actionable data to facilitate decision-making.
			Timely and appropriate actions to keep project performance on track.
			Achieving targets and business value by making informed and timely decisions based on reliable forecasts and evaluations.
8	Uncertainty	Activities and functions associated with risk and uncertainty.	Awareness of the holistic environment in which the project occurs.
			Proactively exploring and responding to uncertainty.
			Awareness of the interdependence of all project variables.
			Capacity to anticipate threats and opportunities and understand the consequences.
			Project delivery with minimal impact from unforeseen events or conditions.
			Opportunities are realized to improve project performance and outcomes.
			Cost and schedule reserves are leveraged to maintain alignment with project objectives.

NOTE   Project management is a broad field with great potential for specialized and in-depth study. There are entire books and training classes focused solely on advanced analysis of individual process groups, knowledge areas, principles, and performance domains.

Again, depending on your experiences, you might not have realized that project management consisted of all these elements, and you might not actually perform all these activities as a project manager in your organization. However, it is important to understand how big your playing field is for this exam. This book will not completely educate you on each of these project fundamental areas—process groups, knowledge areas, principles and performance domains—but it will provide you with the guidance and insights on all these aspects to improve your effectiveness on the exam.

Project Life Cycle

Before we move on to review the key aspects of the project environment, let's touch on a few key fundamentals related to the project life cycle that you'll need to know for the exam. The *project life cycle* encompasses the entire process from the project inception to project close. The specific life cycle of any given project will vary depending on industry, organization, level of project risk, and nature of the project goals, and we dive into this topic in more detail in Chapter 3, "Development Approach and Life Cycle Performance."

At a high level, three different approaches to projects can impact the specific nature of the project life cycle, and we alluded to them in Chapter 1. They are predictive, hybrid, and adaptive. A predictive approach is the traditional, waterfall style that is used when requirements are fixed up front and detailed planning can be done with confidence from the start. An adaptive approach, commonly referred to as *agile*, is used when requirements are uncertain and/or subject to change. In this approach, work is broken down into short iterations with heavy customer interaction and feedback with the intent of generating viable products and flushing out prioritized requirements as soon as possible. In a hybrid approach, a project is leveraging elements of both predictive and adaptive. Hybrid projects typically use aspects of incremental and iterative approaches, and a wide range of implementations is possible. The key is to use the right approach for each targeted outcome within the project. As mentioned, we cover all of this in much more detail in Chapter 3.

With the different high-level approaches acknowledged, there are a few characteristics shared by nearly all projects, and you may see questions on the exam that check your understanding of them.

- **The level of uncertainty and risk is the highest at the beginning of a project:** As the project matures, more is learned about the project and the product it produces. This process is called *progressive elaboration*. As you learn more about the project, all plans and projections become more accurate, and the level of risk and uncertainty decrease. This is one of the reasons agile and hybrid approaches have grown in popularity and acceptance, and why you will see early project phases include techniques like feasibility studies, prototypes, and proof of concepts to address this risk before significant investments are made.

- **Stakeholders assert the greatest influence on the outcome of a project at the beginning:** In general, after the project starts, the stakeholders' influence continually declines. Their influence to affect the project's outcome is at its lowest point at the end of the project. This is also another reason that agile and hybrid approaches are used more commonly now because, by design, they keep the stakeholder influence higher for a longer period of time.

- **Costs and activity vary throughout a project:** Costs and activity are both low at the beginning of a project, increase during the execution of project work, and tend to taper off to a low level as the project nears completion.

- **The earlier a change is identified, the cheaper it is:** The cost associated with any project changes are at that their lowest point at the project's beginning. No work has been done, so changing is easy. As more work is completed, the cost of any changes rises. With agile and hybrid approaches, which by nature anticipate changes, you are still attempting to identify the need for any significant changes as early as possible.

See Figure 2-4 for an illustration of these key project life cycle characteristics.

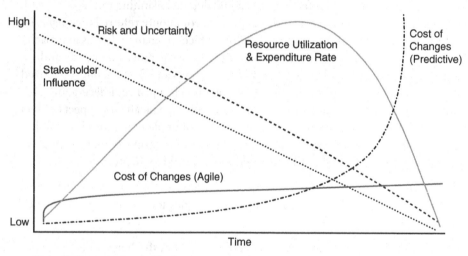

Note: Not to scale, for clarification purposes only

Figure 2-4 Project Life Cycle Characteristics

Project Environment

Now that we've reviewed the key core concepts and project management academic fundamentals, let's discuss the environment that a project exists within, and the important aspects related to this that you'll need to know for the exam.

For starters, let's acknowledge the obvious: Projects do not exist within a vacuum. They operate within an organization for the purpose of creating value for stakeholders of that organization. Given that, there are going to be obvious influences on the project from both within the organization and external to the organization.

System for Value Delivery

Let's begin with a concept mentioned in Chapter 1: a System for Value Delivery. I would argue this concept is not really new from PMI; it was just spoken about differently in the past. PMI has always acknowledged most organizations have multiple projects in motion at any one time and that projects can operate standalone, as part of a program, or as part of a portfolio. And to clarify here, PMI defines a **program** to be a group of related projects and activities that are managed in a coordinated manner to obtain benefits not available from managing them individually. An example of a program would be a home construction company developing a new neighborhood. The neighborhood development is the program, and each home being built is its own project. In addition, PMI defines a **portfolio** to be a group of projects, programs, subsidiary programs, and operations managed together to achieve strategic objectives. Following our same home construction example, a portfolio would be all the new neighborhood developments the company has planned or underway for the next several years, and each neighborhood development is a program.

With the System for Value Delivery in the *PMBOK® Guide*, Seventh Edition, PMI is recommending that organizations should systematically ensure the strategic goals and objectives are focused on stakeholder value and that the management of organizational activities and resources, including operations, are aligned and focused on delivering these values. Specifically, PMI defines a System for Value Delivery as a collection of strategic business activities aimed at building, sustaining, and/or advancing an organization. Portfolios, programs, projects, products, and operations can all be part of an organization's System for Value Delivery.

As mentioned previously, PMI now has the proper priority in its guidance to practitioners that the focus is on the outcome and the value the project delivers. This is the ultimate measure of project success. And by *value*, PMI means the worth, importance, or usefulness of something. Different stakeholders perceive value in different ways. Customers can define value as the ability to use specific features or functions of a product. Organizations can focus on business value as determined by financial metrics, such as return on investment (ROI) or customer acquisition metrics. There can also be societal value, which can include contributions to groups of people, communities, or the environment.

NOTE   PMI defines a ***System for Value Delivery*** as a collection of strategic business activities aimed at building, sustaining, and/or advancing an organization. Portfolios, programs, projects, products, and operations can all be part of an organization's System for Value Delivery.

While a System for Value Delivery involves both portfolio and program management disciplines, they are not part of the PMP exam. However, it is important to understand the different operating scenarios for a given project and where they fit in the organization delivery system. Figure 2-5 illustrates the three possibilities: stand-alone, part of a program, and part of a portfolio.

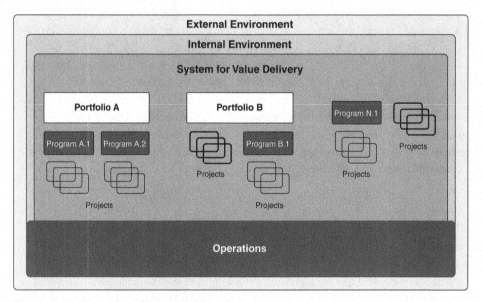

Figure 2-5   Example of System for Value Delivery

Stakeholders

As we mentioned in the previous section, projects exist to deliver value, and this value can be different for the various stakeholders impacted by the project. Although PMI now has an entire performance domain on stakeholder management, and we cover it in great detail in Chapter 5, "Stakeholder Engagement," as part of this chapter, we want to ensure there is baseline understanding of who the stakeholders are. In some work environments, there may be limited view on the stakeholder audience (it's not just the customers). In addition, your stakeholder audience can change and evolve as the project progresses through the life cycle. To help set this baseline, here's a list of typical stakeholders on a project:

- **Project Manager:** The person responsible for managing the project.

- **Customers:** The person or organization that purchases the work of the project. This can be the same as the project sponsor, but not always.

- **End User:** The person or organization that will receive and use the project's product or service.

- **Performing Organization:** The organization that performs the work of the project.

- **Project Team Members:** The members of the team who are directly involved in performing the work of the project.

- **Sponsor:** The person or organization that provides the authority and financial resources for the project.

- **Project Leadership Team (PMO, Steering Committee, Governing Bodies):** Project team members who are directly involved in managing or providing direction or governance to the project.

- **Suppliers:** The people or organizations that provide goods or services to the performing organization to help complete the work of the project.

- **Regulatory Bodies:** Public organizations or government agencies that are responsible for legally regulating aspects of a targeted activity. For projects, these regulatory bodies can require standards that must be adhered to for the project to complete successfully.

- **Operations:** The groups and activities within the organization needed to perform the functions of the organization on a daily basis.

Organizational Environment

As mentioned previously, projects operate within an organizational environment. The structure of the organization and project organizational maturity level of the organization will greatly impact how project managers will perform their responsibilities and what types of assets will be available to help them execute the project. Let's first look at the various organizational structures that exist and their impact on a project. The organizational structure impacts the relationship between operations and projects and, at a minimum, affects the following aspects of a project:

- The project manager's authority

- Resource availability

- Control of the project budget

- The project manager and administrative staff roles

Functional Organizational Structure

A *functional* organizational structure is a classical hierarchy in which each employee has a single superior. Employees are then organized by specialty, and work accomplished is generally specific to that specialty. Communication with other groups generally occurs by passing information requests up the hierarchy and over to the desired group or manager. Of all the organizational structures, this one tends to be the most difficult for the project manager because resources are not fully assigned to the projects, the project manager lacks authority to control work assignments and personnel and usually has to work with multiple functional managers (FMs) to acquire resources. They are often more of a project expeditor in these environments.

Matrix Organizational Structure (Weak, Balanced, Strong)

A *matrix* organization is a hybrid organizational structure between functional and project-oriented organizational structures. Matrix organization types are further divided into weak, balanced, and strong matrix organizations. The difference among the three is the level of authority given to the project manager versus the functional manager to allocate and manage team personnel. A *weak* matrix gives more authority to the FM, whereas the *strong* matrix gives more power to the PM. As the name suggests, the *balanced* matrix balances power between the FM and the PM. In a *weak* matrix environment, the PM is more of a project coordinator.

Project-Oriented Organizational Structure

In a *project-oriented* organization, there is no defined hierarchy, and the work is project based. The PM has full authority to acquire resources, manage the project, and accomplish the goals and objectives of the project. This includes the ability to escalate problems and issues to the highest levels of the organization as necessary. This is the most idealistic working environment for a project manager, although the PM is also held fully responsible for the outcome of the project, whether positive or negative.

Table 2-9 summarizes the types of organizations, their project management attributes, and their advantages and disadvantages.

Table 2-9   Summary of Organizational Structure Influences on Projects

	Functional	**Weak Matrix**	**Balanced Matrix**	**Strong Matrix**	**Project-oriented**
Description	Traditional. The staff reports to functional managers.	The PM and FM share responsibility, with the FM having more authority.	The PM and FM share responsibility with each having equal authority.	The PM and FM share responsibility, with the PM having more authority.	Projects do not exist under functional departments. The PM generally has sole management authority.
Project Manager Role	Project Expeditor. Part time or limited.	Project Coordinator. Part time with increased involvement.	Project Manager. Full time.	Project Manager. Full time.	Project Manager. Full time.
Authority Level of Project Manager	Very low.	Low.	Low to moderate.	Moderate to high.	High.
Team Member Allocation	Part time.	Part time.	Part time.	Full time.	Full time.
Resource Availability	Very low.	Low.	Low to moderate.	Moderate to high.	High.
Advantages	The FM is held accountable for the staff and project.	The PM has some level of authority to manage the project.	The PM has increased authority to assign resources and manage the project.	The PM has further authority to assign resources and manage the project.	The PM has full authority to assign resources and manage the project.
Disadvantages	The PM has little or no authority.	Conflicts between the FM and PM can occur.	Confusion about who is actually responsible for what parts of the project may develop.	The FM may feel left out of the process unless the project manager keeps the FM informed.	The PM holds sole accountability.

Other Organizational Factors

In addition to the organizational structure, other organizational factors influence a project. Each factor can be favorable, unfavorable, or neutral. A project manager needs to take inventory of these factors, especially when planning a project. The common organizational factors that can influence a project include the following:

- **Process Assets:** The tools, methodologies, approaches, templates, frameworks, patterns, and other PMO resources that exist within the organization; part of the organizational process assets (OPAs).

- **Data Assets:** The databases, document libraries, historical metrics, and artifacts from previous projects; part of the organizational process assets.

- **Knowledge Assets:** The tacit knowledge existing within the project team members and other members of the organization.

- **Governance Systems and Documentation:** The organizational structures, systems, processes, policies, and procedures dictating how projects are established, managed, monitored, and controlled throughout the project life cycle; part of the organizational process assets.

- **Organizational Culture:** The vision, mission, values, cultural norms, leadership style, ethics, risk tolerance, and code of conduct that exist within the organization.

- **Security and Safety:** The policies and procedures pertaining to facility access, data protection, levels of confidentiality, and proprietary information.

- **Infrastructure:** The existing facilities, equipment, organizational and telecommunications channels, information technology hardware, software, and capacity within an organization.

- **Information Technology:** The software systems used to facilitate the work of the project, such as Project Management Information Systems (PMIS), scheduling software, team collaboration tools, configuration management systems, work authorization systems, and interfaces to existing systems.

- **Geographic Distribution of Facilities and Resources:** The physical locations of work facilities, team members, and shared systems.

- **Procurement Procedures:** The organization's approved suppliers and contractors, collaboration agreements, any constraints pertaining to procurement of resources, and expected timeline for procuring resources.

- **Employee Capabilities:** The general and specialized knowledge, skills, expertise, and competencies that exist within the organization's employees.

It is worth noting that PMI modified the way it covered the various internal and external factors within the project environment in the *PMBOK® Guide*, Seventh Edition, versus the way it had previously. In the *PMBOK® Guide*, Sixth Edition, the breakdown focused on organizational process assets (OPAs) and ***enterprise environmental factors (EEFs)***. OPAs included the process, data, and governance procedure assets included in the previous list, and EEFs included the other items in the previous list plus all the external factors covered later in this chapter.

NOTE   In the *PMBOK® Guide*, Sixth Edition, PMI categorized internal and external factors in the project environment as either organizational process assets (OPAs) or enterprise environmental factors (EEFs).

OPAs include the process assets, data assets, and governance procedures mentioned earlier. EEFs include all external factors listed later in this chapter plus the other internal factors that are not part of OPA.

 PMO

One aspect of the internal organizational environment that we want to highlight is the ***Project Management Office (PMO)*** because you are likely to see a question on the exam about it. Many organizations have found that project management is so effective that they maintain an organizational unit with the primary responsibility of managing projects and programs. The unit is commonly called the PMO. The PMO is responsible for coordinating projects and, in some cases, providing resources for managing projects. A PMO can make the project manager's job easier by maintaining project management standards and implementing policies and procedures that are common within the organization. A PMO can support project managers by

- Managing shared resources across all projects administered by the PMO

- Identifying and developing project management methodology, best practices, and standards

- Providing coaching, mentoring, training, and oversight

- Monitoring compliance with project management standards policies, procedures, and templates via project audits

- Developing and managing project policies, procedures, templates, and other shared documentation (organizational process assets)

- Coordinating communication across projects

There are three types of PMO structures, depending on the amount of influence and control the PMO has over projects:

- **Supportive:** The PMO supplies technical and administrative support and provides input to project managers, as needed. This type of PMO provides low control.

- **Controlling:** The PMO does not directly manage projects but does require compliance with organizational methodologies, frameworks, and tools. This type of PMO provides medium control.

- **Directive:** The PMO manages projects. This type of PMO provides a high level of control.

External Factors

In addition to the factors within an organization that can influence a project, factors external to the organization can also impact a project. As before, each factor can enhance, constrain, or be neutral to the project. Here are some common external factors to be aware of:

- **Market Conditions:** This group includes factors such as market competition, market share, brand recognitions, key seasonal sales periods, technology trends, and trademarks.

- **Social and Cultural Influences:** This group includes the political climate, customs, ethics, perceptions, traditions, public holidays, and events that are specific to the regions and cultures the project exists within.

- **Regulatory Environment:** This group includes national or regional level laws and regulations that impact data protection, security, business conduct, employment, licensing, or procurement.

- **Industry Standards:** This group includes applicable standards that impact the product features, quality, or workmanship. These standards also impact the production of the product and to the environment.

- **Physical Environment:** This group includes any factor impacting the working conditions, including the weather.

- **Financial Considerations:** This group includes currency exchange rates, interest rates, taxes, tariffs, and inflation.

- **Commercial Databases:** This group includes standard cost estimating and industry risk analysis databases.

- **Academic Research:** This group includes industry studies, publications, and benchmarking results.

Exam Preparation Tasks

As mentioned in the section "How to Use This Book" in the Introduction, you have a couple of choices for exam preparation: the exercises here, Chapter 18, "Final Preparation," and the exam simulation questions in the Pearson Test Prep practice test software.

Review All Key Topics

Review the most important topics in this chapter, noted with the Key Topic icon in the outer margin of the page. Table 2-10 lists a reference of these key topics and the page numbers on which each is found.

Table 2-10   Key Topics for Chapter 10

Key Topic Element	Description	Page Number
Paragraph	Definition of project management	46
Paragraph	Definition of project	46
Table 2-2	Comparing Projects and Operations	47
Table 2-3	Comparing Projects and Products	48
Table 2-4	Summary Description of *PMBOK® Guide*, Seventh Edition, Functions Associated with Projects	49
Paragraph	Balancing competing project demands	54
Section	Key Skills of Project Managers	57
Table 2-5	Description of Project Management Process Groups	64
Table 2-7	Description of the *PMBOK® Guide*, Seventh Edition, Twelve Project Management Principles	67
Section	Project Life Cycle	71
Section	System for Value Delivery	73
Section	Stakeholders	74
Table 2-9	Summary of Organizational Structure Influences on Projects	77
Paragraph	OPA and EEF	79
Section	PMO	79

Define Key Terms

Define the following key terms from this chapter and check your answers in the glossary:

project management, outcome, project team, project, product, value, stakeholder, project manager, project life cycle, program, portfolio, System for Value Delivery, enterprise environmental factors (EEFs), Project Management Office (PMO)

Review Questions

1. Which of the following would not be considered an enterprise environmental factor (EEF)?

   a. Market conditions

   b. Your company's policies

   c. Government regulations

   d. Culture

2. Which of the following would be considered an OPA?

   a. Regulatory requirements

   b. Lessons Learned register for your current project

   c. Corporate culture

   d. Standard operating procedures for your organization

3. Which of the following would be considered project constraints?

   a. Budget

   b. Resources and schedule

   c. Budget, schedule, and quality

   d. Quality, resources, schedule, and budget

4. Your functional manager has told you that she will be responsible for making all key decisions on the project, but you will have the authority to delegate tasks to team members. What is your role?

   a. Project manager

   b. Project coordinator

   c. Team facilitator

   d. Project expeditor

5. A project manager for a life insurance company is trying to complete a package application implementation project but is unable to get the planned amount of time from key resources to complete some of the critical path tasks. The key resources are focused on completing their day-to-day tasks, and the project manager does not control the work assignments for these people. This scenario is an example of what type of organization?

   a. Project-oriented

   b. Tight matrix

   c. Functional

   d. Balanced matrix

6. Regarding the importance of management and leadership in projects, all the following statements are false except which one?

   a. Technical leadership is of primary importance in project management.

   b. A project can have only one leader.

   c. On a large project, the project manager is not expected to be the project's leader.

   d. Managing is primarily concerned with consistently producing key results expected by stakeholders.

7. Project managers need solid communication, leadership, and negotiation skills primarily because

   a. They must give presentations and briefings to senior management.

   b. They may be leading a team with no direct control over the individual team members.

   c. They must be able to effectively share their technical expertise.

   d. These skills are needed in locking down the best deals with vendors and suppliers.

8. Which of the following statements best describes the relationship between project life cycle phases and project management processes?

   a. Project management processes correspond one to one with project life cycle phases.

   b. Project life cycle phases can repeat within a project management process.

   c. Project management processes can repeat within a project life cycle.

   d. Project management processes are completely independent of project life cycle phases.

9. You are a project manager working for a regional hospital company. You have been assigned the responsibility to manage a project that performs monthly security vulnerability assessments and addresses any identified vulnerabilities. You question the assignment because

   a. Security vulnerability assessments do not materially contribute to your organization's System for Value Delivery and should not be considered important enough to be classified as a project.

   b. A security vulnerability assessment produces no specific product, so it is not a project.

   c. This endeavor cannot be considered a project because no start date is specified.

   d. The recurring nature of the assessment in addition to the lack of a target end date means that this endeavor is not a project at all.

10. During your HR software implementation project, two project team members are have difficulty working together. They come to you, the project manager, for help with resolving the issues. You immediately set up a meeting that includes the functional manager. After the meeting, you and the functional manager discuss the issues and agree on a solution. This type of management probably indicates you are working in what type of organizational structure?

   a. Balanced matrix

   b. Functional

   c. Weak matrix

   d. Project-oriented

11. Which of the following statements best describes the influence of stakeholders over the life of a predictive project?

   a. Stakeholders do not directly influence the project's outcome; they only provide authority and resources.

   b. Stakeholders ultimately direct all project activities.

   c. Stakeholder influence is the highest at the beginning and tends to decrease throughout the project.

   d. Stakeholder influence is low at the beginning and tends to grow throughout the project.

12. During your assembly line software implementation project, you find that training is not progressing as quickly as the schedule requires and the users are not able to do their work after completing the sessions. After investigating the situation, you discover the trainers do not have the proper experience and knowledge to effectively train your users. Which statement best describes the impact this situation has on the project and the effect your needed actions to rectify the situation will have?

   a. The schedule is suffering. To fix the situation, you have to hire more experienced trainers and schedule extra training sessions. Your schedule returns to planned values while cost increases.

   b. The quality and schedule are being negatively impacted. To fix the situation, you likely have to hire more experienced trainers at a higher rate and schedule extra training sessions. Quality and schedule return to planned values while cost increases.

   c. This problem is the responsibility of the organization that provided the trainers. The organization provides replacement trainers who are qualified at the same price to continue the training required.

   d. Although your training looks as though it is behind schedule, you wisely built in enough slack time to cover such a problem. You simply find replacement trainers and continue the training.

This chapter covers the following topics regarding the Development Approach and Life Cycle Performance domain.

- **Development Approach and Project Life Cycle Fundamentals:** Review and clarify the key fundamental concepts and terms associated with development approach and the project life cycle.

- **Development Approach Selection:** Review the various variables that must be considered when determining the development approach for a deliverable.

- **Relationship Between Project Deliverables, Delivery Cadence, Development Approach, and Project Life Cycle:** Review and clarify how the nature of the project deliverables, the delivery cadence needed, the development approach, and the project life cycle are related and how they impact each other.

- **Impact on Other Project Factors:** Review and clarify how determining the development approach and project life cycle interrelates with other project performance domains.

## CHAPTER 3

Development Approach and Life Cycle Performance

This chapter reviews the activities and functions associated with the development approach, cadence, and life cycle phases of the project. This review highlights the key fundamentals, concepts, and terms that are emphasized by PMI, including how to select the appropriate development approach for your project deliverables and why this determination impacts your project life cycle and other key activities for the project.

This chapter addresses the following objectives from the PMP Exam Content Outline:

Domain	Task #	Exam Objective
People	Task 10	Build shared understanding
Process	Task 1	Execute project with the urgency required to deliver business value
Process	Task 9	Integrate project planning activities
Process	Task 13	Determine appropriate project methodology/methods and practices

"Do I Know This Already?" Quiz

The "Do I Know This Already?" quiz allows you to assess whether you should read this entire chapter thoroughly or jump to the "Exam Preparation Tasks" section. If you are in doubt about your answers to these questions or your own assessment of your knowledge of the topics, read the entire chapter. Table 3-1 lists the major headings in this chapter and their corresponding "Do I Know This Already?" quiz questions. You can find the answers in Appendix A, "Answers to the 'Do I Know This Already?' Quizzes and Review Questions."

Table 3-1   "Do I Know This Already?" Section-to-Question Mapping

Foundation Topics Section	Questions
Development Approach and Project Life Cycle Fundamentals	1–6
Development Approach Selection	7–8
Relationship Between Project Deliverables, Delivery Cadence, Development Approach, and Project Life Cycle	9
Impact on Other Project Factors	10

CAUTION   The goal of self-assessment is to gauge your mastery of the topics in this chapter. If you do not know the answer to a question or are only partially sure of the answer, you should mark that question as wrong for purposes of the self-assessment. Giving yourself credit for an answer you correctly guess skews your self-assessment results and might provide you with a false sense of security.

1. Why are the development approach and project life cycle important to a project?

   a. They are important aspects of planning and organizing a project.

   b. They determine what type of development team you need and how long the project will last.

   c. The project life cycle determines what type of development approach can be used.

   d. The development approach and subsequent project life cycle must support the effective delivery of business and stakeholder value from the beginning to the end of the project.

2. What is the difference between project life cycles and development life cycles?

   a. There is no difference. Both involve predictive, hybrid, and adaptive options.

   b. Development life cycles are standard life cycles independent of a given project.

   c. The project life cycle is influenced by the development approach life cycle but includes all the work of the project.

   d. The development life cycle is one of the phases of a project life cycle.

3. What is the best definition of a project life cycle?

    a. The process by which the project deliverables are produced by the project team

    b. The series of phases that a project passes through from start to completion

    c. The flow of a product from inception to retirement

    d. The process by which the project is managed from start to completion

4. What is meant by delivery cadence?

    a. It applies only to projects for the music industry.

    b. The timing and frequency of project deliverables.

    c. The natural flow and rhythm in which the project work occurs.

    d. The quality of the verbal communications by the project manager.

    e. The timing and frequency of the iterations in an adaptive/agile project.

5. What is the difference between an incremental and iterative development approach?

    a. An iterative approach is used for digital products, and an incremental approach is used for physical products.

    b. Incremental development is focused on product improvement. Iterative development is focused on development process improvement.

    c. There is no difference between them. They mean the same thing.

    d. Iterative development is used when progressive elaboration is needed to clarify and refine an initial idea, concept, or vision. Incremental development is focused on delivering components of the deliverable over a period time.

6. Which option best describes traits of adaptive/agile development approaches?

    a. Planning, requirements, design, development, testing, deployment

    b. Iterative and incremental development approaches, top-down management, changes are expected

    c. Sprints, use of backlogs, focus on perfect product, multiple product deliveries

    d. Iterative and incremental development approaches, constant feedback loops, changes are expected

7. Which option best describes the factors that need to be considered when determining the development approach for a project?

   a. The skills of the development team, the project budget, and the project schedule

   b. The development methodology of the sponsoring organization, non-negotiable milestone dates, and stakeholder expectation management

   c. The desires of the project team, the nature of the deliverables involved, and delivery cadence required

   d. All pertinent deliverable, project, and organizational variables

   e. The development approach that can be used to produce all the deliverables needed for the project

8. Which development approach should be used if the project is determined to be a high-risk project?

   a. It depends on the nature of the risks involved.

   b. Adaptive/agile approaches are always the best option for high-risk projects due to their focus on generating a working product as soon as possible to help manage uncertainty.

   c. Predictive development approaches are the best option for high-risk projects due to the importance placed on detailed planning up front.

   d. Hybrid development approaches are the best option for high-risk projects due to their use of the best aspects of predictive, incremental, and iterative approaches.

9. Which option best describes the typical relationship between project deliverables, delivery cadence, development approach, and project life cycle?

   a. Development approach => delivery cadence => project life cycle => deliverable

   b. Project life cycle => development approach => delivery cadence => deliverable

   c. Deliverable type => development approach => delivery cadence => project life cycle

   d. Delivery cadence => development approach => project life cycle => deliverable

10. Which of the following options best describe how determining the development approach and the project life cycle impacts project planning? (Choose two.)

    a. After the initial planning is done, the development approach can be determined.

    b. The development approach selection and the project life cycle determination are key aspects of project planning.

    c. The development approach selection and the project life cycle determination are done before any project planning.

    d. The development approach(es) selected will determine when and how frequently additional detail planning will occur.

Foundation Topics

Development Approach and Project Life Cycle Fundamentals

Let's review why the development approach and project life cycle performance domain is important. The development approach and subsequent project life cycle must support the effective delivery of business and stakeholder value from the beginning to the end of the project. On this surface, this seems rather common sense in nature, but as we all know, this is not always what happens in the real world.

> **NOTE** The development approach and subsequent project life cycle must support the effective delivery of business and stakeholder value from the beginning to the end of the project.

We will discuss how to determine which development approach to use for a project, but before we proceed, let's cover some key terms and concepts.

Project Life Cycle and Phases

One area of common confusion for PMP test takers is thinking the development life cycles and project life cycles are the same thing. They are not. It is understandable why there can be confusion on this topic because of how people use terms interchangeably, and, in fact, PMI contributes to this misunderstanding by referring to the three types of project approaches of predictive, hybrid, and adaptive, which also are the three base development approaches that PMI refers to as well.

Per PMI, a **_project life cycle_** is defined as the series of phases that a project passes through from start to completion. In other words, it encompasses all the work for all the **_deliverables_** produced by the project. This can include activities such as start-up, business case development, feasibility studies, product selection, visioning, training, deployment, pilot rollouts, and closure—all activities that are not necessarily covered by the development approach. Plus, a project might have multiple deliverables that each use a different development approach. They are all part of the overall project life cycle.

NOTE   The project life cycle encompasses all the work for all the deliverables produced by the project, not just the development approach.

As mentioned, in the PMI definition of project life cycle and implied in the preceding paragraph, a project life cycle is composed of phases. To clarify, the PMI definition of a **_project phase_** is a collection of logically related project activities that culminate in the completion of one or more deliverables. The specific phases (and the names used for the phases) of any project are dependent on many variables, but the industry/organizational methodology, nature of the project deliverables, the development approach, and the **_delivery cadence_** required are primary factors. Common project phase examples for a predictive project life cycle are Define, Design, Construct, Test, Deploy, and Close. Refer to Figure 3-1 for sample project life cycles for a predictive, hybrid, and adaptive project.

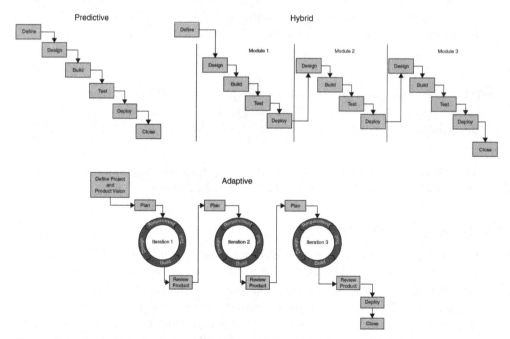

Figure 3-1   Project Life Cycle Examples for Predictive, Hybrid, and Adaptive Projects

In structured environments following a predictive or hybrid project life cycle, it is common to have exit criteria that must be met and accepted before the project can continue to the next project phase. Also, PMI does not prescribe a predefined set of project phases for a given project life cycle because it acknowledges the highly dependent nature of this process for any project scenario.

Product Life Cycle and Project Management Process Groups

Although we discussed this topic in Chapter 2, "Project Management 101," make sure you are clear on the differences between a project life cycle, a product life cycle, and the project management process groups, which are often referred to as the project management life cycle. Refer to Table 2-3 for a breakdown of the differences between projects and products. In summary, if you remember that a project produces a product, it makes sense that their life cycles cannot be the same. For further review, refer to Figure 3-2 for an illustration of the common product life cycle model.

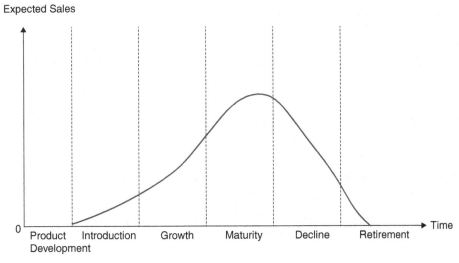

Figure 3-2 Product Life Cycle

The initial product life cycle phase of product development is composed of one or more projects to generate the product. After that, the product would be in the traditional operations and maintenance stage. However, there will be follow-up projects initiated on the product during its life cycle to add enhancements, to implement improvements or upgrades, and to respond to market feedback.

We also discussed the project management process groups in Chapter 2. Refer to Table 2-5 and Figure 2-3 for quick reminders. At times, these groups are confused with the project life cycle because they both are focused on projects, and three of the project management process groups (initiating, planning, and closing) can be names of project life cycle phases as well. The key to remember here is that the project life cycle deals with all the work involved in the project, not just the project management aspect, which is the focus of the project management process groups. In addition, the project management process groups are often repeated within a given project because they can be applied to each project life cycle phase within the project.

Delivery Cadence

We mentioned earlier that delivery cadence is a key factor in determining the project life cycle. Let's clarify this term and review the potential options.

 Per PMI, *cadence* refers to the rhythm of activities conducted throughout the project, and *delivery cadence* refers to the timing and frequency of project deliverables. Table 3-2 summarizes the options for delivery cadence.

Table 3-2   Summary of Delivery Cadence Options

Delivery Cadence	Description	Associated with Development Approach
Single	Single delivery at the end of the project	Predictive
Multiple	Multiple deliveries of the same deliverable throughout a project	Hybrid
		Iterative, Incremental
	Multiple deliverables with independent delivery schedules	Adaptive
	Deliverable can be delivered incrementally	
Periodic	Same as multiple delivery cadence but on a fixed schedule (i.e., every two weeks, monthly, etc.)	Hybrid
		Iterative, Incremental
		Adaptive
Continuous	Ability to deliver deliverable/product updates anytime and as frequently as needed	Adaptive
		Hybrid
	This is an option for digital products and requires DevOps practices	

Development Approach Options

Before we get into how to select an appropriate approach for a project, let's review the different development approach options that PMI covers in the *PMBOK® Guide*, Seventh Edition. PMI defines a development approach as a method to create and evolve the product, service, or result during the project life cycle. As mentioned before, PMI focuses on the three general development approaches of predictive, hybrid, and adaptive, but it also references the incremental and iterative approaches at times. This is a source of common confusion. In addition, people often use the terms *iterative* and *incremental* interchangeably, which leads to further confusion.

> **NOTE** A *development approach* is a method to create and evolve the product, service, or result during the project life cycle.

Development Approach Spectrum

The best way to think about the development approach is as a spectrum, as illustrated in Figure 3-3. On one end is the ***predictive development approach*** model. This is the waterfall, plan-driven, traditional approach where the deliverable is built following a sequential process, starting with requirements definition through deployment. On the other end of the spectrum is the adaptive model. This is commonly referred to as an agile approach and entails building the deliverable incrementally via a series of iterations where the scope of each iteration is determined by stakeholder priorities and feedback. In between these two ends of the spectrum, we have the ***hybrid development approach*** model. In general, the hybrid model involves certain aspects of the predictive approach combined with certain aspects of the adaptive model. Specifically, hybrid models leverage varying degrees of incremental and/or iterative development approaches. As one moves closer to a pure adaptive model, the use of incremental and iterative approaches increases.

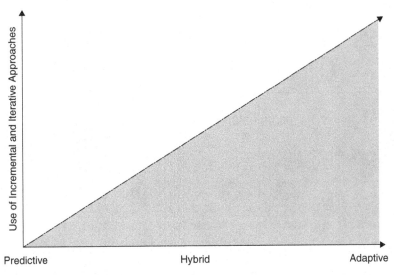

Figure 3-3 Development Approach Spectrum

Incremental and Iterative: What's the Difference?

Because we mentioned *incremental* and *iterative development approaches*, let's clarify what these two terms mean. At a high level, an incremental approach entails building and/or deploying the deliverable in chunks (pieces, modules, components). This approach is consistent with the PMI definition of an incremental approach, which states it is a development approach in which the deliverable is produced successively, adding functionality until the deliverable contains the necessary and sufficient capability to be considered complete. By contrast, an iterative approach entails building the deliverable starting from an initial simplified (low fidelity) implementation and then progressively elaborating on the solution until it contains all the features, details, and/or correctness to be considered complete (high fidelity). The classic example used to illustrate the differences between these two approaches is to think of a painting (as in a piece of art). In an incremental approach, the complete detail of each section is created a section at a time. The artist starts with creating the top section and then moves down to the next section, continuing this process until the final section is painted. With an iterative approach, the artist starts with a rough pencil sketch of the complete picture. From here, the artist creates another rendition that has finer granularity and perhaps some initial color shades. After each rendition (or iteration), the painting (product) can be reviewed for feedback. This process continues until the painting is considered completed and the stakeholders are satisfied. See Figure 3-4 for an illustration of this concept.

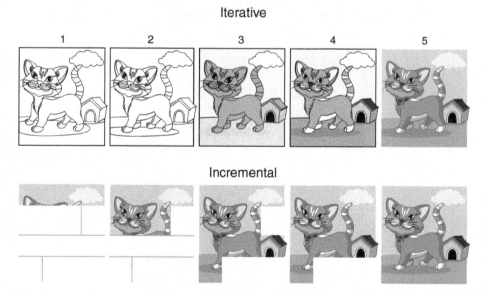

Figure 3-4   Painting Example to Illustrate the Difference Between Incremental and Iterative Approaches

Other examples of incremental approaches that can illustrate the difference include constructing a building, building a car, and deploying a human resources information software (HRIS) system. When you are constructing a building, the desired solution is planned out in great detail up front until you have a final blueprint. From the blueprint, the building is constructed in stages, starting with the foundation. The development of a new car involves outsourcing the parts/components development and then assembling the car in a step-by-step process until the final vehicle is complete. With an HRIS implementation, it is common to configure, test, and deploy modules over a period of time; for example, the payroll system first, then the retirement system module, then health insurance module, and so on. Each time a working module is deployed to production while work on the next module deliverable gets underway. This is done routinely to provide value to certain business functions as soon as possible, to manage the business process change management aspect, and/or to address development resource bandwidth limitations. At a high level, any deliverable that can be decomposed into lower-level work items that can be developed and/or tested in parallel are prime candidates for incremental approaches.

Iterative approaches are excellent for any situation where the complete solution is unknown, and the idea or concept needs to be flushed out. By using/building initial low-fidelity models or prototypes, the team captures initial ideas, visions, and requirements to have something tangible the stakeholders can review, test, and further clarify their requirements against. This process repeats itself until the correct and/or marketable solution is generated. An example of this would be the development of a new vaccine. At the beginning of the project, the final solution is unknown; however, through a series of repeated steps, potential solutions are developed and tested until one is determined to be effective and acceptable. Again, the development process is repeated many times, but there is just one final deliverable.

Adaptive Approach

Key Topic

As mentioned previously, on one end of the development approach spectrum is the *adaptive development approach*, more commonly referred to as an agile approach. In many ways, this approach is more than a development style; it is a mindset shift that originates from the Agile Manifesto created in 2001 for software development. The manifesto and the focus on a more adaptive approach were created in response to the issues many practitioners experienced with the traditional, waterfall, documentation-heavy process that was primarily used to build software. To be clear, the following is a summary of the common issues experienced from applying the traditional waterfall predictive approach to software (digital product) development:

1. Due to the length of many of these projects (often 18–24 months) and requirements defined at the beginning, the delivered system would often be outdated on the first day of deployment.

2. Stakeholders often had difficulty in being certain about defining requirements for a system that would not be implemented for another 18–24 months.

3. Software requirements are often vague and open to misinterpretation, so the delivered system often did not meet stakeholder expectations.

4. In addition to not meeting stakeholder functional expectations, there were often multiple changes, uncontrolled scope creep, and frequent rework, which led to the project being over budget and not meeting schedule milestones, which led to even more frustrations and unsuccessful projects.

Since then, the ideas and principles espoused by the manifesto have influenced the development approaches used across many industries, not just software development. As the terms *adaptive* and *agile* imply, the focus was on a more flexible, resilient approach that was focused on the people and on the deliverable. For clarification, let's review the 4 values and the 12 principles communicated in the Agile Manifesto at agilemanifesto.org:

Agile Manifesto Values

1. **Individuals and interactions** over processes and tools

2. **Working software** over comprehensive documentation

3. **Customer collaboration** over contract negotiation

4. **Responding to change** over following a plan

The authors of the manifesto acknowledge there is value in the items on the right, but they value the items on the left (in bold font) more.

Agile Manifesto Principles

1. Our highest priority is to satisfy the customer through early and continuous delivery of valuable software.

2. Welcome changing requirements, even late in development. Agile processes harness change for the customer's competitive advantage.

3. Deliver working software frequently, from a couple of weeks to a couple of months, with a preference to the shorter timescale.

4. Business people and developers must work together daily throughout the project.

5. Build projects around motivated individuals. Give them the environment and support they need and trust them to get the job done.

6. The most efficient and effective method of conveying information to and within a development team is face-to-face conversation.

7. Working software is the primary measure of progress.

8. Agile processes maintain a constant pace indefinitely.

9. Continuous attention to technical excellence and good design enhances agility.

10. Simplicity—the art of maximizing the amount of work not done—is essential.

11. The best architectures, requirements, and designs emerge from self-organizing teams.

12. At regular intervals, the team reflects on how to become more effective, then tunes and adjusts its behavior accordingly.

As you can see from the values and principles noted in the Agile Manifesto, an adaptive/agile approach is a mindset and cultural shift, not just a different way of developing something. This is the primary reason why it takes time to implement this approach in many organizations and why you will find many hybrid development approaches out there. In addition, you can also see why this approach would be difficult, if not challenging, to implement for situations where documentation is a key requirement, contracts are a key aspect, hard milestone dates exist, the business team is not readily available, the project team is large (multiple development teams), a development team is not collocated, or the development team cannot self-manage, just to name a few. To be clear, these are not showstoppers for an adaptive/agile approach, but this is why many environments end up with hybrid development approaches.

NOTE   An adaptive/agile approach is a mindset and cultural shift, not just a different way of developing something.

So, do you need to memorize the Agile Manifesto for the PMP exam? No. However, you should be familiar with the key traits and characteristics that most adaptive/agile development approaches share, such as the following:

- Iterative and incremental development

- Process that welcomes and anticipates change

- Focus on the deliverable; getting the work product in front of the customers quickly and often

- Constant feedback loops—on both the deliverable and the work process

- Business representative(s) working closely with the development team

- Development team that is self-organized, self-managed, and plans the work for each iteration

- Development team that works from a prioritized, groomed list of requirements (backlog)

To help illustrate this point, let's look at a typical development life cycle model for an agile methodology called Scrum (see Figure 3-5). This is the most popular agile methodology in practice and the one that any PMP exam questions tend to reference. However, other agile methodologies are in use, such as Lean, Kanban, Extreme Programming, Dynamic System Development Method, Feature-Driven Development, and Crystal.

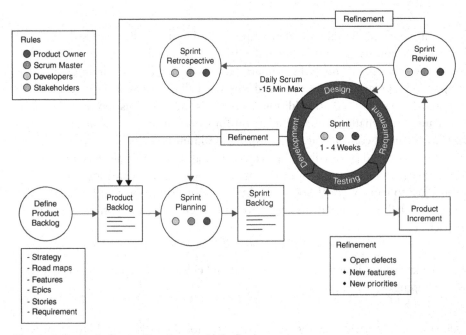

Figure 3-5   Agile Scrum Development Life Cycle

The primary characteristics of the Scrum agile life cycle are

1. All potential work is captured in the product backlog.

2. Each iteration (sprint) is scheduled for two to four weeks in duration.

3. The business/customer is represented by a full-time team member (product owner).

4. Each sprint has a planning session where the development team works with the product owner to agree on what can be delivered in the next sprint. The result is the sprint backlog.

5. On a daily basis, the development team has a short stand-up meeting to review what they accomplished the day before, what they plan to do today, and if they have any impediments to their work.

6. Each sprint results in a working increment of the deliverable that is reviewed by the stakeholders for feedback.

7. The feedback is captured in the product backlog for consideration in the next or future sprints.

8. Each sprint ends with a retrospective meeting with the core team to assess the work process and what, if any, adjustments need to be made to improve going forward.

Of course, there are more details we could go into regarding the Scrum process and the Scrum roles, but this is not a book (nor an exam) on the Scrum agile methodology. What's important for the PMP exam is to understand these common characteristics of the Scrum agile life cycle.

 # Development Approach Selection

Now that we've covered the key concepts and terms involved with development approaches and project life cycles, let's review how to determine which development approach is best for a given project. To do this, you must consider the three primary groups of variables: the targeted deliverable (product, service, or result), the project environment, and the organizational environment.

Deliverable Variables

The first area to focus on when determining a development approach is with the targeted deliverable (product, service, or result). In many cases, the nature of this deliverable dictates which development approach needs to be leveraged. The primary factors here are how clear and complete the deliverable requirements are, how easily the deliverable can be changed after development has started, and whether the deliverable can be decomposed into smaller components. We will expand on these topics, but let's first look at all the variables in this group:

■ **Degree of Innovation:** If the level of innovation involved is low, a more predictive approach can be used because this would imply the scope and requirements are well understood, and this is something the development team has done before. If the level of innovation is high due to the nature of the deliverable solution or due to the experience level of the development team in building the solution, an approach that leverages adaptive methods (incremental, iterative) is likely needed.

- **Requirements Certainty and Scope Stability:** As mentioned before, a predictive approach works well when the requirements are well understood, agreed upon, and unlikely to change. If the requirements do not meet these criteria or are complex in nature, a more adaptive approach is likely a better fit. In fact, PMI defines an adaptive approach as a development approach in which the requirements are subject to a high level of uncertainty and volatility and are likely to change during the project. Personally, I am not fan of this definition because it just states when to use the approach and does not actually define what the approach is, but we covered this issue earlier, and you can see the emphasis that PMI puts on the requirements certainty and scope stability variables when it comes to determining the development approach to use.

- **Ease of Change:** One of the more obvious variables in the group is the ease of change factor. If the nature of the product, service, or result to be generated by the project cannot incorporate changes easily or without a lot of cost, a more predictive approach is needed. This is why most digital-based products lend themselves to more adaptive approaches because they can be modified easily and quickly. Conversely, projects that are delivering physical products (i.e., buildings, cars, appliances) are not as well suited for adaptive approaches. This being said, the project can still use iterative approaches (like prototyping, modeling) during the planning, requirements, and/or design phases to improve their project outcomes.

- **Delivery Options:** Products, services, or results that can be developed and/or delivered in components lend themselves to iterative, incremental, and adaptive development approaches.

- **Risk:** The risk factor is interesting because it is not a simple one. The level of risk does not necessarily dictate the development approach that should be used. It is a matter of applying the proper approach to the situation. Products that are high risk in nature may require intensive analysis and detailed planning to reduce the threats involved. This would mean a more predictive approach. On the other hand, other high-risk products might need to be built incrementally and/or iteratively so that the team can adapt to what they learn to better manage the risk threats involved. And, of course, a project might need to employ both approaches to manage the risks involved.

- **Safety Requirements:** Products that have rigorous safety requirements tend to use more predictive or hybrid development approaches due to the importance of identifying, planning, defining, integrating, and testing all the necessary safety elements involved.

- **Regulatory Requirements:** Similar to the safety requirements variable, if the project exists within an environment that must adhere to strict regulatory oversight that requires specific processes to be followed and/or documentation to be generated, a more predictive or hybrid approach might likely be more appropriate.

Project Variables

The next area to focus on when determining a development approach is the project environment variables described next. In many cases, the nature of the project environment itself can dictate which development approach needs to be leveraged.

- **Stakeholder Availability:** To leverage a pure adaptive approach, there must be significant stakeholder involvement throughout the project, and an effective product owner role is paramount to any successful agile approach. If the stakeholder community cannot support this process or commitment of time, a more predictive or hybrid approach might be needed.

- **Schedule Constraints:** If there is a need to deliver something quickly, an adaptive or incremental approach may likely be needed. Conversely, if hard milestone dates must be met with specific deliverable requirements, a more hybrid or incremental approach may be needed.

- **Budget/Funding Availability:** Projects that have limited or uncertain budget funding might benefit from an iterative or adaptive approach where the focus is on delivering a minimum viable product as soon as possible. This provides the opportunity to get quicker stakeholder and/or market feedback that can then be used to justify the investment of additional funds into the product. On the other end of the spectrum, if the project has a larger than normal budget with high visibility, there might be the need to thoroughly plan the project and get necessary approvals before proceeding. This scenario would lend itself to more predictive or hybrid approaches.

- **Expectation Management:** This factor is not mentioned in the *PMBOK® Guide*, Seventh Edition, but it should be. As is often the case, even when the scope and requirements are well defined up front, there can still be value in using a more adaptive, iterative, or incremental approach in generating the deliverable to show a working product as soon as possible. This approach not only helps build confidence in the stakeholders, which can help potential concerns with the schedule or budget if they arise, but it can also serve to validate the requirements as early as possible in the project. It is not uncommon for a disconnect to occur between documented requirements and what the development team understood. In addition, a more adaptive approach provides the opportunity for the stakeholders to refine and/or add to the requirements for the deliverable.

- **Project Team Size and Location:** PMI has this listed under organizational variables in the *PMBOK® Guide*, Seventh Edition, but I think it fits better as a project variable. Adaptive approaches, especially agile, are structured for smaller teams (five to nine people) that are collocated together. In today's world, remote and virtual teams are becoming the norm. This situation can be challenging for these approaches, especially if the team lacks experience with agile approaches. Also, when teams are spread out globally and work times are not in sync within the team, an agile approach can be difficult for a team. In addition, many project situations have and require larger teams. There are adaptive-based methodologies and frameworks to manage larger and multiple agile teams, such as the Scaled Agile Framework (SAFe). Neither one of these factors is a showstopper for an adaptive approach, but this can be a reason why a more hybrid approach is needed in these situations.

Organizational Variables

The final area to focus on when determining a development approach is the organizational environment variables described here. In many situations, the structure, culture, or capability of the organization can dictate which development approach needs to be leveraged.

- **Organizational structure:** As we discussed in Chapter 2, the organizational structure impacts the nature of projects and the role of the project manager for projects operating in its environment. The more functional and hierarchical the organizational structure, the more challenging it can be to leverage an adaptive approach due to the emphasis placed on top-down management and more formal reporting structures. These environments tend to favor a more predictive approach. Conversely, organizations that are more project-oriented and have flatter structures will more naturally favor the self-organizing, self-managing project teams that are associated with adaptive approaches.

- **Culture:** If the organization is geared toward a top-down managing and directing way of working, a more predictive approach will be a better fit because the work is planned out in as much detail as possible up front and performance is measured against baselines. To leverage a more adaptive approach, the culture of the organization needs to support and be comfortable with the approach of self-managed project teams and the overall agile mindset. This is the reason a transition to a more adaptive, agile approach takes time for most organizations. It is not easy or quick to completely shift the working culture of an organization.

- **Organizational Capability:** Each one of these factors is closely related, and they tend to overlap each other. Also, organizational capability further gets into the transition aspect of moving from a traditional predictive approach to a more adaptive, agile approach. To successfully employ adaptive methods, there needs to be support from the executive level on down. In addition, organizational policies, reporting structures, the ways teams work with each other, and individual team members' attitudes and responsibilities must be aligned.

For each of these variables, if an organization lacks experience and competency with adaptive/agile methods, they must be accounted for when selecting the development approach, and it is often the reason why hybrid approaches are leveraged while an organization makes this transition.

Relationship Between Project Deliverables, Delivery Cadence, Development Approach, and Project Life Cycle

Now that we've reviewed the key fundamentals related to development approaches and project life cycle and discussed the factors that must be considered when selecting a development approach for a given project deliverable, let's tie this altogether and clarify the relationships involved and the important principles to know for the PMP exam.

The process starts with the type of deliverable the project needs to deliver. The nature of the deliverable will determine the options for how the project can be developed and thus which development approaches can be considered. From here, the delivery cadence options can be considered. This is a factor of the development approach, the urgency for delivering value to the stakeholders, and the deployment strategy needed to either manage risks or expectations. After the development approach and delivery cadence are determined, the project life cycle and its subsequent phases can be finalized.

Important Notes for the PMP Exam

> **NOTE** The selected development approach should be consistent with the deliverable variables and appropriate given the project and organizational variables involved.

A few important notes to understand and remember regarding the relationships between project deliverables, delivery cadence, development approach, and project life cycle:

- This process is applied to each targeted deliverable to be generated by the project.

- The selected development approach should be consistent with the deliverable variables and appropriate given the project and organizational variables involved.

- A project can have a different development approach and delivery cadence for each deliverable.

- These factors can change during the project as feedback is received and new understandings are gained, primarily with delivery cadence and deployment strategies.

- The project life cycle phases should facilitate the development approach and delivery cadence required.

  - This means the cadence for developing, testing, and deploying is represented in the project life cycle phases.

  - If the project contains multiple deliverables, the cadence for developing, testing, and deploying each deliverable is clearly represented in the project life cycle phases.

- The project life cycle and phases should connect delivery of business and stakeholder value from the beginning to the end of the project.

- The final project life cycle accounts for all the work of the project—from beginning to end, including all the work for each deliverable.

- There is no standard project life cycle or phases. Project life cycles are dependent on industry, organization, and number of deliverables, in addition to the factors already mentioned (development approach, delivery cadence).

Project Life Cycle: Development Approach Illustrations

As illustrated earlier in Figure 3-1, when the project has a single deliverable, the project life cycle will closely mirror the flow of the development approach selected. In most cases, the additional up-front start-up work and the project close phases need to be added to complete the life cycle. If the project has multiple deliverables, however, the final project life cycle can have a range of options. Like the single deliverable project, the project start-up and project close phases need to be accounted for. In addition, the development approach and delivery/deployment schedule for each deliverable need to be captured. In general, there are two approaches for this:

- The single deliverable project phases are maintained, but they may overlap to account for the different schedules or approaches for each deliverable.

- The deliverables are shown at the highest level, and the specific phases for each deliverable are shown at the second level. This approach can often be much easier for most stakeholders to see and understand when depicting the project life cycle for reporting purposes. See Figures 3-6 and 3-7 for examples.

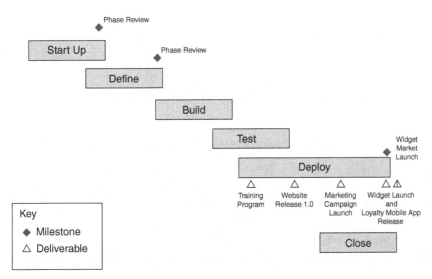

Figure 3-6 Project Life Cycle with Multiple Deliverables—Overlapping Phases

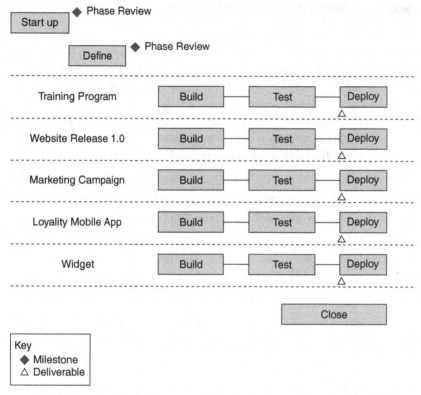

Figure 3-7   Project Life Cycle with Multiple Deliverables—Deliverable Bases

Community Center Project Example from *PMBOK® Guide*, Seventh Edition

Now let's look at the community center project example that PMI uses in the *PMBOK® Guide*, Seventh Edition, Section 2.3.6, when discussing this topic. The project life cycle illustration shown there would be an example of the first approach mentioned in the previous section. Personally, I think this is an awkward illustration, and it could be made clearer by placing each deliverable on its own flow thread. This would be an example of the second approach mentioned in the previous section. Figure 3-8 illustrates how the community center project life cycle would look if this approach was used.

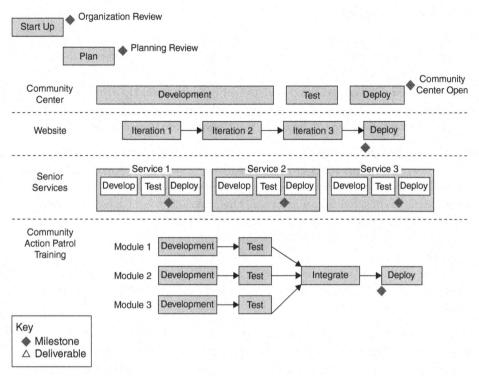

Figure 3-8 *PMBOK® Guide*, Seventh Edition, Community Center Project Example Project Life Cycle with Deliverable Focus

While we are looking at this community center project example from the *PMBOK® Guide*, Seventh Edition, I believe the description of the "senior services" deliverable using an iterative approach is not correct. Remember how we mentioned the common confusion between incremental and iterative development approaches before? This is a great illustration. In Section 2.3.3 of the *PMBOK® Guide*, Seventh Edition, the example indicates the senior services will include a Meals on Wheels program, transportation services, group outings/events, caregiver relief, and adult day care, with each to be delivered sequentially. This approach is incremental, and not iterative as indicated. Now, if this example planned to pilot the services, evaluate performance and feedback, adjust/improve the service as needed, and then roll out a final version of the service, that would be an iterative approach. Given how common these concepts are confused, and because the *PMBOK Guide* is a primary source for the PMP exam, I felt it was important to point out this discrepancy to assist in your exam preparations.

Hybrid Project Life Cycles

Before we leave this section, let's revisit the relationship between project types and development approach types. As noted previously, because PMI refers to the three general project approaches and three general development approaches with the same terms—*predictive*, *hybrid*, and *adaptive*—it is understandable if you assumed they were the same thing. And, for the most part, this is correct for predictive and adaptive. In the case of hybrid, however, it is important to note this distinction.

In a hybrid development approach, a project is using some elements of either incremental or iterative approaches or both, along with some elements of the predictive development approach. So any project using a hybrid development approach would be considered to be a hybrid project type. This makes sense and is rather straightforward. But it is possible to have a hybrid project type that does not use a hybrid development approach. How is this possible? Well, if a project is to generate two deliverables, one to be built using a predictive development approach and the other to be built using an adaptive development approach, the project is a hybrid project type because it uses multiple development approaches, but neither deliverable uses a hybrid development approach.

Perhaps not a common occurrence, but this scenario helps illustrate the differences between project life cycle types and development approaches and clarifies the subtle difference between the hybrid project approach and hybrid development approach.

Impact on Other Project Factors

As we have reviewed, you have a lot of factors and variables to consider when selecting the development approach(es) and project life cycle needed for a given project, especially with risk management, stakeholder expectation management, and capabilities of the organization and project team. These considerations overlap with the other performance domains and project management responsibilities. To help clarify all of this, let's quickly review how the development approach(es) and project life cycle interrelate to the other performance domains:

- **Planning:** There is obvious overlap with the planning performance domain because the selection of the development approach(es) and the project life cycle is a key element of initial project planning. In addition, the development approach(es) selected will determine when and how frequently the additional detail planning will occur.

- **Uncertainty:** The development approach is a key instrument in managing the uncertainty (risk) associated with a targeted deliverable. If there is risk around meeting regulatory requirements, then more planning might be needed up front, along with additional testing, required documentation, and rigorous processes and procedures. This would indicate a more predictive approach is needed. On the other hand, if there is significant risk around stakeholder acceptance or requirement stability, then a more iterative approach might be needed to get a minimum viable product in front of the stakeholders as soon as possible in order to better manage these aspects.

- **Stakeholder:** This was covered in the preceding paragraph for Uncertainty. Managing stakeholder expectations can be a key driver for selecting the delivery approach and delivery cadence for a given deliverable.

- **Team:** There is a push-pull relationship with the Team performance domain. The capabilities of the team must be considered when selecting the development approach, and then after the development approach is selected, the way the team works and the project leadership approach leveraged will be affected.

- **Project Work:** The selected development approach is a key determinant in the way the project work will be performed.

- **Delivery:** There is a tremendous amount of overlap with the Delivery performance domain because the delivery cadence can be a valuable tool for ensuring the project value is delivered in alignment with the business case and the benefits realization expectations. In addition, the product and quality requirements influence the development approach that needs to be used for a given deliverable.

Exam Preparation Tasks

As mentioned in the section "How to Use This Book" in the Introduction, you have a couple of choices for exam preparation: the exercises here, Chapter 18, "Final Preparation," and the exam simulation questions on the Pearson Test Prep practice test software.

Review All Key Topics

Review the most important topics in this chapter, noted with the Key Topic icon in the outer margin of the page. Table 3-3 lists a reference of these key topics and the page numbers on which each is found.

Table 3-3 Key Topics for Chapter 3

Key Topic Element	Description	Page Number
Paragraph	Importance of development approach and project life cycle	91
Paragraph	Difference between development life cycles and project life cycles	91
Paragraph	Definition of project life cycle	92
Paragraph	Definition of project phases	92
Paragraph	Key notes on project phases	93
Section	Product Life Cycle and Project Management Process Groups	93
Paragraph	Definition of cadence and delivery cadence	94
Table 3-2	Summary of Delivery Cadence Options	94
Section	Development Approach Spectrum	95
Section	Incremental and Iterative: What's the Difference?	96
Section	Adaptive Approach	97
Paragraph	Definition of Agile Manifesto	98
List	Summary characteristics of adaptive/agile development approaches	99
List	Summary of Scrum agile life cycle	100
Section	Development Approach Selection	101
Paragraph	Process flow from deliverable to project life cycle	105
List	Important notes for PMP exam regarding relationships between deliverable, development approach, delivery cadence, and project life cycle	106
Section	Hybrid Project Life Cycles	110
Section	Impact on Other Project Factors	110

Define Key Terms

Define the following key terms from this chapter and check your answers in the glossary:

project life cycle, deliverable, project phase, delivery cadence, cadence, development approach, predictive development approach, hybrid development approach, incremental development approach, iterative development approach, adaptive development approach

Review Questions

1. Which of the following would not be considered when determining the development approach to be used?

    a. Organizational culture

    b. Organizational performance management process

    c. Requirements certainty

    d. Nature and type of the deliverable

    e. Stakeholder availability

2. Which of the following descriptions would be considered examples of a hybrid development approach? (Choose two.)

    a. Define Product Vision, Sprint 1, Sprint 2, Sprint 3, Sprint N

    b. Requirements, Design, Development, Testing, Deploy

    c. Requirements, Sprint 1, Sprint 2, Sprint N, User Acceptance Testing, Deploy

    d. Requirements, Design 1, Develop 1, Test 1, Deploy 1, Design 2, Develop 2, Test 2, Deploy 2

3. Which of the following options describe a project life cycle? (Choose two.)

    a. Planning, requirements, development, testing, deployment, close

    b. Initiating, planning, executing, monitoring, closing

    c. Introduction, growth, maturity, decline, retirement

    d. Define, iteration 1, iteration 2, iteration 3, iteration N, deployment, close

4. A project is charged with deploying a new customer relationship management software package, a supporting mobile application, updating a legacy application, revising business processes, and supporting training modules for an organization that is new to adaptive approaches. Based on the nature and type of deliverables listed, what development approach(es) will likely be used for this project?

    a. Adaptive/agile for all deliverables (this is the current best practice)

    b. Predictive/waterfall for all deliverables (this is what the organization is most comfortable with)

    c. Hybrid for all deliverables

    d. Predictive for the mobile application, adaptive for the legacy application update, hybrid approaches for the rest

5. Which list best describes an agile development approach?

   a. Incremental and iterative development, strong project manager, minimal business involvement needed

   b. Sprints, Scrum master, product owner, focus on maximum product value

   c. Collaboration, expects change, deliver working product frequently, self-organizing teams

   d. Iterations of two to four weeks, tight partnership between business and development, schedule is highest priority

6. All of the following are common characteristics of Scrum agile development approaches except which one?

   a. Potential work is maintained in a product backlog.

   b. The business/customer is represented by a full-time team member (product owner).

   c. On a daily basis, the team meets for a brief stand-up meeting.

   d. Each sprint results in a working product that can be delivered to production.

7. Which of the following statements is not true regarding incremental and iterative development approaches?

   a. The incremental approach is closer to a predictive approach than an iterative approach is.

   b. Iterative approaches involve developing and deploying the final solution in pieces.

   c. Iterative approaches are better used for clarifying potential solutions.

   d. Both incremental and iterative approaches can use iterations in their development life cycle.

   e. Both incremental and iterative approaches are used in adaptive projects.

8. Which delivery cadence option indicates there will be multiple deliveries of the product on a fixed schedule?

   a. Continuous

   b. Monthly

   c. Periodic

   d. Iterative

9. Which option contains valid deliverable variables that should be considered when selecting a development approach?

   a. Risk, delivery options, organizational structure

   b. Degree of innovation involved, scope stability, expected ROI

   c. Expected duration of the product life cycle, requirements certainty, ease of change

   d. Requirements certainty, ease of change, safety and regulatory requirements

10. Which of the following statements is not true regarding the relationship between project deliverables, delivery cadence, development approach, and project life cycle?

    a. A project life cycle cannot include multiple development approaches and delivery cadences.

    b. The project life cycle and phases should connect delivery of business and stakeholder value from the beginning to the end of the project.

    c. There are no standard project life cycle phases. Project life cycles and phases are dependent on industry, organization, number of deliverables, development approach, and delivery cadence.

    d. These relationships can change during the project as feedback is received and new understandings are gained.

    e. The project life cycle phases should facilitate the development approach and delivery cadence required.

This chapter discusses the key processes, tools, and artifacts for starting a project and integration management. The following topics are covered:

- **What Is Integration Management?:** Review the project management plan and learn how each component is integrated to create the plan.

- **Initiating a Project:** Review the common processes, tools, and artifacts needed to start the project.

- **Planning a Project:** Examine the common processes, tools, and artifacts needed to plan the project.

- **Executing the Project:** Learn the common processes, tools, and artifacts needed to execute the project to deliver value.

- **Monitoring and Controlling the Project:** Review the common processes, tools, and artifacts needed to determine the performance of the project. Although change control is discussed in detail here, other important concepts of monitoring and controlling are discussed in Chapter 14, "Project Measurement."

## CHAPTER 4

Starting a Project and Integration

In this chapter, we discuss in detail the initiating, planning, and executing aspects of integration management as needed for the PMP exam. The monitoring and controlling aspects of change control are discussed here, but other important concepts of monitoring and controlling are discussed in Chapter 14, "Project Measurement." Chapter 15, "Closing a Project," discusses the closing processes in detail.

We discuss the principles related to the *PMBOK® Guide*, Sixth Edition; the *PMBOK® Guide*, Seventh Edition; and the Exam Content Outline (ECO).

This chapter addresses the following objectives from the PMP Exam Content Outline:

Domain	Task #	Exam Objective
People	Task 2	Lead a team
People	Task 3	Support team performance
People	Task 6	Build a team
People	Task 7	Address and remove impediments, obstacles, and blockers for the team
People	Task 9	Collaborate with stakeholders
People	Task 10	Build shared understanding
People	Task 11	Engage and support virtual teams
Process	Task 1	Execute project with the urgency required to deliver business value
Process	Task 2	Manage communications
Process	Task 3	Assess and manage risks
Process	Task 4	Engage stakeholders
Process	Task 7	Plan and manage quality of products/deliverables
Process	Task 9	Integrate project planning activities
Process	Task 12	Manage project artifacts
Process	Task 15	Manage project issues
Process	Task 16	Ensure knowledge transfer for project continuity
Business	Task 2	Evaluate and deliver project benefits and value

"Do I Know This Already?" Quiz

The "Do I Know This Already?" quiz allows you to assess whether you should read this entire chapter thoroughly or jump to the "Exam Preparation Tasks" section. If you are in doubt about your answers to these questions or your own assessment of your knowledge of the topics, read the entire chapter. Table 4-1 lists the major headings in this chapter and their corresponding "Do I Know This Already?" quiz questions. You can find the answers in Appendix A, "Answers to the 'Do I Know This Already?' Quizzes and Review Questions."

Table 4-1   "Do I Know This Already?" Section-to-Question Mapping

Topics Section	Questions
What Is Integration Management?	1
Initiating a Project	2–3
Planning a Project	4–6
Executing the Project	7–8
Monitoring and Controlling the Project	9–10

CAUTION   The goal of self-assessment is to gauge your mastery of the topics in this chapter. If you do not know the answer to a question or are only partially sure of the answer, you should mark that question as wrong for purposes of the self-assessment. Giving yourself credit for an answer you correctly guess skews your self-assessment results and might provide you with a false sense of security.

1. Who should the project manager interact with when performing integration processes?

   a. The sponsor

   b. Team members

   c. Key decision makers on the project

   d. Any stakeholder

2. Which of the following is not documented in the project charter?

   a. Requirements

   b. Business justification

   c. Team ground rules

   d. Identified resources

3. Of the following, which represent the purpose of creating the project charter? (Choose two.)

    a. Officially authorizes the project to begin

    b. Documents the baseline budget for the project

    c. Creates the detailed scope of the project

    d. Ensures stakeholders have a clear and common understanding of the project

    e. Details the deliverables and timelines of the project

4. When is the project management plan baselined?

    a. When all stakeholders have approved and signed off

    b. When the sponsor and senior management have approved and signed off

    c. When all the required stakeholders have approved and signed off

    d. When the project team has approved and signed off

5. You are near the end of a sprint when a stakeholder identifies some additional requirements they would like to include. What should you do?

    a. Decline the request because you are near the end of the sprint.

    b. Add the requirement to the product backlog.

    c. Perform an impact analysis and send a change request to the change control board.

    d. Implement the additional requirement.

6. The project manager has completed the project management plan and sent it to the sponsor, other key stakeholders, and team leads for their approval. Upon review, one of the team leads notices an important activity is missing and requests that it be added to the project management plan. What should the project manager do?

    a. Perform an impact analysis of the missing activity.

    b. Submit a change request because the team lead has already performed the impact analysis and stated that the activity needs to be added.

    c. Advise the team lead that adding the activity at this stage is gold plating.

    d. Add the missing activity to the project management plan.

7. You are requesting a status from your team. One team member states that they are 60 percent complete and the activity has cost $48,000 so far. How would you classify these results?

    a. Work performance information

    b. Work performance data

    c. Work performance figures

    d. Work performance reports

8. Which of the following are examples of business value? (Choose three.)

    a. 25 percent increase in sales

    b. Finish by September 30

    c. 3 percent increase in market share

    d. Our product will be well-known nationwide

    e. Project budget of $150,000

9. Your team lead has approached you with an issue that you think might be a quick and easy fix. However, this was not in the original scope of the project. What should you, as project manager, do next?

    a. Tell the team lead to go ahead and fix the issue because it's a quick and easy fix.

    b. Perform an impact analysis.

    c. Document and submit the change request to the change control board.

    d. Inform the sponsor.

10. You are managing a project for a client to move a data center and call center offshore. Many changes have been made throughout the project, but you notice that during meetings team members frequently refer to different versions of the same document, which is causing confusion. What would have prevented this?

    a. Assigning one team member to ensure all documents are up to date

    b. Implementing an adequate change control system

    c. Ensuring the file management system procedures are being followed

    d. Implementing an adequate configuration management system

Foundation Topics

Understanding the vision and purpose of a project is the key to successful planning, and communicating the vision and purpose of a project regularly is the key to successful implementation.

Every project needs to have a purpose and needs to align with the strategic direction of the organization. If it does not, you need to ask, "Why are we doing this project?"

In this chapter, we discuss the initiation and integration elements of projects and how the project manager must balance the constraints, processes, and needs of stakeholders so that project success can be achieved.

We first discuss the initiation of the project and describe the major artifacts for starting a project. We then move on to the planning of a project and discuss the many artifacts that constitute the ***project management plan***. We also discuss the aspects of executing a project to achieve project success before finally moving on to the monitoring and controlling aspects of integration management.

All of these processes appear in the *PMBOK® Guide*, Sixth Edition, knowledge area of integration management, so let's begin with integration management.

What Is Integration Management?

Project management processes and procedures are performed throughout the project multiple times, simultaneously. Although technical project work may be performed once on certain projects (especially on predictive projects), the project management processes themselves are performed throughout. The constraints of budget, schedule, resources, risks, scope, quality, regulations, and standards all impact one another, so the project manager must balance all of these factors simultaneously when managing a project. The project manager must guide the team and ensure they are collaborating and working together to achieve project success. The project manager must also understand the strategic objectives of the project and ensure they align with the goals and expectations of the program and the portfolio.

Integration management is the key to performing these processes and a critical success factor on projects. It is an essential skill set for project managers. This is also the first knowledge area of the *PMBOK® Guide*, Sixth Edition, which describes integration management as "the processes and activities to identify, define, combine, unify and coordinate the various activities within the project management process groups."

As with any definition, it may sound a little confusing, so let's examine what it means. Knowledge areas represent the areas of project management that need to be properly planned, managed, and controlled, and integration management is the area in which the project manager must have expertise. A failure in any one knowledge area may lead to a failure of the project. However, all knowledge areas impact one another, so the processes and activities of all knowledge areas must be performed simultaneously. For example, the scope of the project directly impacts the cost and schedule, and vice versa. When you are determining any changes to the scope of a project, you simultaneously think about the impact to the budget, timeline, resources, risks, quality, and other factors. If material prices suddenly increase, your project may end up going over budget, and this may result in a reduction of the scope of the project. A sudden increase in processing of raw materials is usually accompanied by delays in delivery of said raw materials, which in turn has an impact on the project schedule.

As a project manager, you must balance all these constraints and processes to ensure project success.

> **NOTE**   Remember, the six major constraints on a project are
>
> - Scope
> - Schedule
> - Budget
> - Resources
> - Quality
> - Risk
>
> These six constraints are also six of the knowledge areas of the *PMBOK® Guide*, Sixth Edition, process map.

Integration management is not a standalone knowledge area by itself, but moreover it is a combination of all the other knowledge areas. The fact that you are performing the tasks of all the knowledge areas simultaneously means that you are integrating the processes of your project. Integration management is sometimes known as the "master" knowledge area because it includes all other knowledge areas and essentially means that processes are performed concurrently.

Whereas the tasks of other knowledge areas may be delegated to team members and specialists (such as development of the schedule, budget, and risk management process), the processes of integration can be performed only by the project manager because the PM brings all of these processes together as a unified whole. The project manager brings teams and team members together to perform all the tasks of the project in unison. Thus, on predictive projects the project manager is ultimately accountable for the project by ensuring that all these processes work in unison.

Table 4-2 shows the *PMBOK® Guide*, Sixth Edition, integration management processes and the process groups each process relates to. This is an extract from page 25 of the process map in the *PMBOK® Guide*, Sixth Edition.

Table 4-2   Integration Management Processes and Process Groups

Process Group Knowledge Area	Initiating	Planning	Executing	Monitoring and Controlling	Closing
4.0 Project Integration Management	4.1 Develop Project Charter	4.2 Develop Project Management Plan	4.3 Direct and Manage Project Work	4.5 Monitor and Control Project Work	4.7 Close Project or Phase
			4.4 Manage Project Knowledge	4.6 Perform Integrated Change Control	

Notice that this is the only row of the process map that is fully populated, further signifying the importance of this knowledge area. In performing each of these processes of integration management, the project manager performs all the respective processes in the knowledge areas that fall below integration management on the process map.

Initiating a Project

The initiating process group refers to the processes required to start a new project or start a phase of an existing project. The purpose is to

- Ensure stakeholders have a clear and common understanding of the project or phase

- Align stakeholders' expectations with the project purpose at the beginning of the project or phase

- Ensure that the project aligns with the organization's strategic objectives

- Ensure each phase aligns with the project's objectives

- Officially authorize the project to begin

However, we all know what happens in reality! Stakeholders might agree and understand the goals at the kickoff of the project, but they can rapidly forget them as the project progresses, leading to scope creep and unnecessary additional work throughout the project. So, it is the project manager's responsibility to ensure that stakeholders have the same clear and common understanding of the goals throughout the project.

During the initiating stage of the project, the ***project charter*** is authorized by the sponsor, which allows the project manager to start detailed planning and to obtain resources for the project. Key stakeholders are also identified, and the project manager holds several meetings to ensure stakeholders understand and agree to their roles and responsibilities on the project. Involving the sponsor, customers, and other key stakeholders early in the project aims to create a shared understanding of the goals and success criteria and increases the likelihood of project acceptance and stakeholder engagement.

There are two processes in the initiating process group of the *PMBOK® Guide*, Sixth Edition, process map:

- Develop Project Charter
- Identify Stakeholders

Chapter 5, "Stakeholder Engagement," describes the Identify Stakeholders process in detail. The Develop Project Charter process is discussed here.

Develop Project Charter

Develop Project Charter is the first of the *PMBOK® Guide*, Sixth Edition, processes; it establishes the authorization for the project to begin. This process documents how the project is aligned to the strategic objectives of the project, creates a formal record of the project, and describes the organization's commitment to the project.

During this process, the project manager may be identified and assigned if they haven't been already, and the project manager either assists the sponsor in writing the project charter, or the project manager may write the entire charter with the sponsor signing the charter after it is written. In all cases, the sponsoring entity must sign the project charter.

After the project charter has been authorized by the project sponsor, the project manager can start planning activities and assigning resources.

Key Artifacts of Developing the Project Charter

Several artifacts are related to developing the project charter. Some of these artifacts are starting points (inputs) for developing the project charter, and some artifacts are created as a result of this process (an output). The sections that follow describe these artifacts (business documents, project charter, project overview statement, and assumptions log) in more detail.

Business Documents

For PMI's purposes, *business documents* are artifacts that are generally originated outside the project and used as a starting point (or an input) to developing the project charter. PMI refers to two such documents, as described in the sections that follow.

The Business Case

PMI defines the ***business case*** as "a documented economic feasibility study to establish the validity of the benefits." It documents the reasons and objective for project initiation and provides the basis to measure success and progress throughout the project life cycle.

A business case may be developed for a variety of reasons, such as

- Market demand

- Organizational need

- Customer request

- Technological advancement

- Legal requirements

- Ecological impacts

- Social need

The business case can include many items but typically contains the following:

- Business Need

    - Identifies the gap, the problem, or the opportunity

    - Documents the reasons for doing the project and what would happen if you don't do this project

    - Documents the value that should be achieved by performing the project and how the project aligns to the strategic goals of the organization

- Analysis of the Situation

    - Identifies the organization's goals, strategies, and objectives

    - Identifies the root cause of the gap, problem, or opportunity

    - Identifies any known risks and critical success factors

    - Decision criteria for actions to take to address the gap, problem, or opportunity, such as

        – Required actions

        – Desired actions

        – Optional actions

    - Alternative courses of action

The business case also describes the recommended course of action and the plan for evaluating and measuring the benefits that will be delivered should the project be approved.

Benefits Management Plan

The *benefits management plan* documents how the benefits of the project will be realized. It describes how and when the benefits of the project will be delivered and describes the mechanisms that should be in place to measure those benefits. The exact benefit naturally varies from project to project as does the timeframe of when the benefit will be achieved. This is also dependent on the life cycle.

For example, a process improvement project may realize expected benefits immediately after the project is closed. However, the benefits of a project to create a new product expected to increase sales by $200 million a year might not be realized for a few years. Predictive projects typically realize benefits after the project is closed, whereas an agile project generally realizes benefits at the end of each sprint during the project.

The benefits management plan is developed early in the project, sometimes while the business case is being developed, and it typically contains the following:

- **Target Benefits:** Describes the value the organization will achieve by performing this project.

- **Strategic Alignment:** Describes how the value aligns with the strategic direction of the organization. Sometimes this may be obvious; sometimes it may not. For example, with a project to create a new product expected to increase sales by $200 million a year, it might be obvious to most people how that project fits in with the goals of the organization (increase sales and profits). However, a process improvement project that impacts only one department might not be as well understood as to how this project benefits the whole organization.

- **Timeframe:** Describes when the benefits will be realized.

- **Benefits Owner:** Describes who will record and monitor the benefits.

- **Metrics:** Provides measurements that will be used to determine benefits realization.

- **Assumptions:** Describes any assumptions you are making when planning the expected benefits.

- **Risks:** Describes any risks involved in achieving the benefits (for example, competitors may build a similar product).

In addition, a benefits management plan should identify other stakeholders who might need to be involved in achieving the benefits (such as the sales and marketing team to promote a new product).

Per PMI, this document needs to be progressively elaborated on over time.

The Project Charter

The project charter is the formal authorization for the project to begin and, after it is signed by the sponsor, allows the project manager to apply organizational resources to project activities. It documents the business justification for the project and the reasons for the project to exist. The project charter is a high-level document that describes the measurable objectives and related success criteria; and it ensures a common understanding by the stakeholders of the key deliverables, milestones, and the roles and responsibilities of all involved.

The components of the project charter might include the following:

- Identities of the project manager and the sponsor and their authority levels

- High-level budget and schedule (as constraints, not baselines)

- High-level scope and requirements

- High-level assumptions and constraints

- High-level risks

- Any preassigned physical resources or team resources, such as specialized machines or key team members on the project

- Any key stakeholders who have been identified

- Summary of milestones and exit criteria in case of project failure

- The stakeholder who will approve the deliverable

Although a summary document, the project charter is not a document that should be written quickly or without much thought. Because it constitutes the formal authorization for the project, care should be taken to involve appropriate decision makers and other key stakeholders to ensure everyone has a clear and common understanding of the project. Although a high-level document, it must also be a SMART document (Specific, Measurable, Achievable, Realistic, Time-bound). There are other small variations of this acronym, too.

Project Overview Statement

Another document that conveys the intent and vision of a project is the project overview statement. It communicates the intent and vision of the project and contains the following:

- Problem or opportunity

- Project goal

- Project objectives

- Success criteria

- Assumptions, risks, and obstacles

Authorization of the project starts when the project charter is signed, or a project overview statement is approved. Then the project manager can start spending money on the project and obtaining resources.

Assumption Log

The assumption log documents all the detailed assumptions and constraints identified throughout the project. For example, if you need to use a machine that is shared among other teams, and that machine is available for only two hours a day, that constraint is documented in the assumption log. The team now knows that any activities that use said machine need to be scheduled during those available hours only.

Planning a Project

The *PMBOK® Guide*, Sixth Edition, discusses planning in the planning process group. The *PMBOK® Guide*, Seventh Edition, discusses planning in the Planning Performance domain.

Planning is the foundation for all project success. Many projects fail due to inadequate planning. Planning is considered one of the critical steps toward project success because it provides the structure and foresight for the execution and monitoring steps of a project. It is an essential guide for the project manager, project teams, stakeholders, and sponsors to achieve successful completion of each stage of the project.

However, there are different levels of planning based on the size and nature of the project and the development approach. In predictive projects, detail planning is done at the beginning of the project, and any changes to the plan need to be constrained and go through a change control process. In agile, only a high-level "relative estimate" is made at the beginning of the project, with the detailed estimates performed per sprint.

Per the *PMBOK® Guide*, Seventh Edition, "the Planning Performance domain addresses the activities and functions associated with the initial, ongoing, and evolving organization and coordination necessary for delivering project deliverables and outcomes."

Throughout the planning process, the project manager must consider internal and external factors that could impact the project. The PM needs to identify assumptions and constraints that could lead to uncertainty and risks on the project. The project manager also needs to progressively elaborate on projects to ensure correct ranges are calculated and management plans are updated. However, planning also needs to be an efficient process. If there are many unknowns and many uncertainties on a project (risks), it is challenging to perform detailed planning of the scope. In this case, more time should be spent on planning for risk, and the scope should be progressively elaborated over time. The project manager and the project team determine the exact parameters of planning.

Some of the key points regarding planning are that

- Time spent on planning should be appropriate for the project. It is very easy to "overplan" when there are many uncertain parameters that impact the project. Likewise, not enough planning may lead to issues and problems during delivery.

- Planning is sufficient to deliver value and manage stakeholders' expectations. The purpose of a project is to deliver value for the customer, so the project manager and/or team must plan sufficiently to deliver the value. The exact meaning of value differs based on many parameters, such as the nature of the project, the stakeholders, and the industry. This issue is discussed in more detail later in the "Executing the Project" section of this chapter.

- Project plans are progressively elaborated on throughout the project life cycle to adapt to changes as needed. This is true for both predictive and adaptive projects. A change to one project constraint may lead to a change in another constraint, so plans need to be able to adapt (even on predictive projects).

Variables that impact project planning can include

- **Development Approach**
  - Based on whether this is a predictive, adaptive, incremental, iterative, or hybrid project, this approach can influence how much planning and the type of planning that needs to be done.
  - You might need to plan phases, iterations, increments, or sprints.

- **Project Deliverables:** The product or service that is being delivered determines the type and extent of planning. For example, a construction project requires extensive planning to minimize scope changes, whereas the scope of research and development projects can be dynamic.

- **Organizational Requirements:** The company's governance, policies, procedures, and culture determine project planning procedures.

- **Market Conditions:** External factors such as scarcity of resources and competition determine the level of planning that needs to be performed. If, for example, a competitor is releasing a superior product to yours, the schedule for your upgrade project may need to be moved forward, thus impacting planning.

- **Legal or Regulatory Requirements:** Your project might need regular approvals from regulatory authorities before proceeding to the next stage. This step needs to be planned, but any delays need adjustment to the schedule and plans. For example, construction projects require inspections at various stages. If the inspector doesn't approve the deliverable, it needs to be fixed before the building team can continue to the next stage.

The *PMBOK® Guide*, Sixth Edition, defines the planning process group as consisting of the processes required to establish the scope of the project, refine the objectives, and define the course of action required to attain the objectives that the project was undertaken to achieve.

Twenty-four processes in the *PMBOK® Guide*, Sixth Edition, process map are associated with the planning process group, as shown in Table 4-3. There are 49 processes altogether in the entire process map, and almost half of them are in planning, showing that PMI has placed a huge emphasis on planning a project.

Table 4-3 *PMBOK Guide*, Sixth Edition, Knowledge Areas and Processes Associated with the Planning Process Group

Knowledge Area	Planning Processes
Project Integration Management	Develop Project Management Plan
Project Scope Management	Plan Scope Management
	Collect Requirements
	Define Scope
	Create WBS (Work Breakdown Structure)
Project Schedule Management	Plan Schedule Management
	Define Activities
	Sequence Activities
	Estimate Activity Durations
	Develop Schedule

Knowledge Area	Planning Processes
Project Cost Management	Plan Cost Management
	Estimate Cost
	Determine Budget
Project Quality Management	Plan Quality Management
Project Resources Management	Plan Resource Management
	Estimate Activity Resources
Project Communications Management	Plan Communications Management
Project Risk Management	Plan Risk Management
	Identify Risks
	Perform Qualitative Risk Analysis
	Perform Quantitative Risk Analysis
	Plan Risk Responses
Project Procurement Management	Plan Procurement Management
Project Stakeholder Management	Plan Stakeholder Management

In this chapter, we concentrate on the integration management aspects of planning. The other planning processes are discussed in the appropriate chapters related to those knowledge area topics.

The *PMBOK® Guide*, Sixth Edition, planning process for integration management is called Develop Project Management Plan, which includes the plans for all the other knowledge areas.

Table 4-4 highlights the *PMBOK® Guide*, Sixth Edition, process that we describe in this section.

Table 4-4 *PMBOK® Guide*, Sixth Edition, Develop Project Management Plan

Process Group / Knowledge Area	Initiating	Planning	Executing	Monitoring and Controlling	Closing
4.0 Project Integration Management	4.1 Develop Project Charter	4.2 Develop Project Management Plan	4.3 Direct and Manage Project Work 4.4 Manage Project Knowledge	4.5 Monitor and Control Project Work 4.6 Perform Integrated Change Control	4.7 Close Project or Phase

The Project Management Plan is made up of many planning documents (artifacts), as follows:

- Subsidiary Management Plans, which include
    - Scope Management Plan
    - Requirements Management Plan
    - Schedule Management Plan
    - Cost Management Plan
    - Quality Management Plan
    - Resource Management Plan
    - Communications Management Plan
    - Risk Management Plan
    - Procurement Management Plan
    - Stakeholder Engagement Plan
- Baselines, which include
    - Scope Baseline
    - Schedule Baseline
    - Cost Baseline
- Additional Components, which include
    - Change Management Plan
    - Configuration Management Plan
    - Performance Measurement Baseline
    - Project Life Cycle
    - Development Approach
    - Management Review

Understanding the purpose of each of the components of the project management plan is important, so let's discuss each of these components.

Subsidiary Management Plans

Each of the *subsidiary management plans* documents how you are to plan, execute, manage, and control the respective knowledge area. They do not contain the actual results of that knowledge area.

For example, the requirements management plan does not contain any requirements. It documents the procedures for collecting requirements. It documents how you are going to collect requirements, what tools you are going to use to collect requirements, and the level of details you need to collect requirements. It also documents procedures for missed requirements and procedures for adding new requirements.

Likewise, the cost management plan does not tell you what the project is going to cost. It documents how you are going to estimate cost, the formulae used, the assumptions made, and the procedures for trying to get back on track if you start to go over budget.

All subsidiary management plans document procedures on how to plan, execute, manage, and control each particular knowledge area.

EXAM TIP!   Whenever you see a document that has the name *management plan* in its title, immediately you know it is a how-to document or a procedures document.

The only subsidiary management plan that does not have the words *management plan* in the title is the stakeholder engagement plan. However, it, too, documents procedures on how to engage and motivate stakeholders.

It's also important to understand that a project manager does not know all these procedures at the beginning of the project. The project manager must work with the project team to figure out all these procedures throughout the project and progressively elaborate on the plan documents as necessary.

Baselines

A *baseline* is simply the approved version of a plan. Plans need to be approved by appropriate stakeholders, such as the project manager, sponsor, project leadership team, and key members of the project team. During planning, the project manager, senior management, and other key stakeholders determine who will have such approval responsibilities.

The three basic baselines—the scope baseline, schedule baseline, and cost baseline—represent the approved versions of the scope, schedule, and budget, respectively. In addition, a fourth baseline, the performance measurement baseline, represents these three basic baselines combined.

These baselines represent the plan for the project, and actual results are compared against the baselines. However, the main significance of the baselines is that any changes to the baselines must go through a change control process.

On predictive projects, changes must be properly controlled, so changes always need to go through a change control process.

- The work of the project is executed according to the baseline.

- Actual results are compared to the baseline.

- Subsequent changes must go through the change control process.

- Project may be re-baselined after sign-off from appropriate stakeholders.

On pure agile projects, there are no baselines. The scope of the work is determined by the product backlog, which will change as user stories are added, removed, and reprioritized.

 Additional Components

Two additional management plans and an additional baseline are listed under this subsection, as follows:

- **Change Management Plan:** Documents the procedures for change control.

- **Configuration Management Plan:** Documents procedures regarding version control.

- **Performance Measurement Baseline:** This artifact is a combination of the scope, schedule, and cost baselines.

Three other documents listed in this section are

- **Project Life Cycle:** Discussed in Chapter 3, "Development Approach and Life Cycle Performance," these are the series of stages a project goes through from start to finish.

- **Development Approach:** This document identifies the approaches used, such as predictive, agile/adaptive, iterative, incremental, or hybrid.

- **Management Review:** This document provides the points on the project where appropriate stakeholders will review project progress and make appropriate decisions.

EXAM TIP!   Make sure you know each component of the project management plan and the purpose of each artifact that makes up the project management plan.

EXAM TIP!   If you look at the Planning column on the process map, you will notice that the first process for each of the knowledge areas always starts with "Plan *x* Management," where *x* refers to the knowledge area. So, in Scope Management, the first process is Plan Scope Management; in Schedule Management, the first process is Plan Schedule, and so on. Table 4-5 shows an extract of the process map that specifically relates to the planning process group and the processes we are referring to here. To learn the artifacts that are created in each of these processes, simply move the word *Plan* to the end, so artifacts are the "*x* Management Plan." In Plan Scope Management, the artifact created is the Scope Management Plan; in Plan Schedule Management, the artifact created will be the Schedule Management Plan; in Cost Management, the artifact created is the Cost Management Plan, and so on. The only exceptions are Integration Management, which is the "master" knowledge area encompassing all the plans, and Scope Management, where there is an additional Requirements Management Plan.

Remember that each management plan documents *how* you are to plan, execute, monitor, and control the particular knowledge area. They are documenting procedures.

Before you can perform any of the project management processes of any knowledge area, you first need to figure out how you are going to perform those processes, and those procedures are documented in the "*x* Management Plans," and hence the reason the "Plan *x* Management" process always comes first.

Table 4-5 is an extract of the *PMBOK® Guide*, Sixth Edition, process map highlighting the planning group and the processes referred to in the preceding exam tip.

Table 4-5   *PMBOK® Guide*, Sixth Edition, Processes in Planning

Process Group Knowledge Area	Initiating	Planning
4.0 Project Integration Management	4.1 Develop Project Charter	4.2 Develop Project Management Plan
5.0 Project Scope Management		5.1 Plan Scope Management
		5.2 Collect Requirements
		5.3 Define Scope
		5.4 Create WBS

Process Group Knowledge Area	Initiating	Planning
6.0 Project Schedule Management		6.1 Plan Schedule Management
		6.2 Define Activities
		6.3 Sequence Activities
		6.4 Estimate Activity Durations
		6.5 Develop Schedule
7.0 Project Cost Management		7.1 Plan Cost Management
		7.2 Estimate Costs
		7.3 Determine Budget
8.0 Project Quality Management		8.1 Plan Quality Management
9.0 Project Resource Management		9.1 Plan Resource Management
		9.2 Estimate Activity Resources
10.0 Project Communications Management		10.1 Plan Communications Management
11.0 Project Risk Management		11.1 Plan Risk Management
		11.2 Identify Risks
		11.3 Perform Qualitative Risk Analysis
		11.4 Perform Quantitative Risk Analysis
		11.5 Plan Risk Responses
12.0 Project Procurement Management		12.1 Plan Procurement Management
13.0 Project Stakeholder Management	13.1 Identify Stakeholders	13.2 Plan Stakeholder Engagement

Executing the Project

Executing the project refers to implementing the plan and performing the work of the plan to create the deliverables.

The *PMBOK® Guide*, Sixth Edition, processes of executing in integration management are

- Direct and Manage Project Work
- Manage Project Knowledge

The *PMBOK® Guide*, Seventh Edition, discusses execution and delivery of the project in the following Performance domains:

- Project Work Performance Domain
- Delivery Performance Domain

We discuss the main contents of these Processes and Performance domains as they relate to the PMP exam.

First, let's examine the purpose of executing the project. The main purpose of execution is to deliver the business value of the project.

The exam content outline (ECO) mentions two tasks related to business value as follows:

- **Process Domain Task 1:** Execute the project with the urgency required to deliver business value.
- **Business Environment Domain Task 2:** Evaluate and deliver project benefits and value.

With two ECO tasks mentioning value, you can see the significance that PMI places on this term for the PMP exam.

It is important to understand what is meant by *business value*.

 What Is Business Value?

Business value is the net quantifiable benefit derived from the business endeavor that may be tangible, intangible, or both. The reason for doing a project in the first place is to realize the business value, and this value varies depending on the project. For example, the benefit of one project may be to increase market share, whereas the benefit of another may be to improve processes. Benefits can also be intangible; for example, the benefits of a homeowner building a house are that the owner moves into their dream home.

Some examples of tangible benefits include

- Financial
- Market share
- First to market
- New customer
- Technological
- Improvements

- Social

- Equity

Some examples of intangible benefits include

- Goodwill

- Brand recognition

- Reputation

- Strategic alignment

When does the business value get realized? It depends!

The time frame determining when business value will be realized is dependent on many factors. On a predictive project, the business value generally is realized after the close of the project, whereas on an agile project, the business value is realized at the end of each sprint. The benefits of a process improvement project may be realized at various increments throughout the project, whereas a new product development project aimed at increasing sales, profits, and market share may not be realized for several months or even years after the start of production.

At a project level, business value needs to be defined and understood during the early stages of the project. The project charter documents what success and failure mean on the project.

What Does Project Success Mean?

Is project success achieved by being within schedule and budget? Is that the true measure of project success?

For the most part, many people will say yes to this question. For many project managers, the classic success criteria for a project are being within schedule and within budget.

However, is that really a true and accurate measure of success? There is no right or wrong answer to this; it depends on many factors and situations.

For example, let's say a new product development project was expected to increase sales by $5 million a year, and this project finished 10 percent ahead of schedule and 5 percent under budget. At this point, you would be congratulating yourself on a job well done; however, if the sales ended up so low that the company went out of business, would this be considered a success now?

On the other hand, if this same project ended up 10 percent behind schedule and 20 percent over budget, you would initially be concerned by these metrics and might need to explain to senior management what went wrong. But if the sales doubled expectation, then would you consider this a failed project? Absolutely not.

So, measuring project success and failure based on budget and schedule alone may not always be the best metrics to use. You need to look at the overall picture and consider the business value. Success on a project should be determined by whether the business value was attained.

There are various different ways of measuring business value, such as

- Benefit-Cost Ratio

- Return on Investment (ROI)

- Internal Rate of Return (IRR)

- Present Value (PV)

- Net Present Value (NPV)

On adaptive projects, business value is realized at the end of each sprint when the product owner approves the deliverables, which in turn creates the potentially shippable product increment. Two important terms related to this are

- **_Minimum Viable Product (MVP)_:** This is the smallest collection of features that can be included for a product to be considered functional. These are the bare-bones, no-frills type of functionality required for the product or system to work. As an analogy, these could be considered the must-haves of the MoS-CoW analysis. The aim is to do the minimum amount of work to deliver value to the customer.

- **_Minimum Business Increment (MBI)_:** This is the smallest amount of value that can be added to a product or service that benefits the business. The aim is to deliver the highest value first.

Now that you understand business value, plus the success and failure of a project, let's further discuss the execution of the project within this context.

The Project Work Performance domain of the *PMBOK® Guide*, Seventh Edition, results in the efficient and effective project performance where the team uses appropriate processes and tools to complete the work and produce the deliverables. The project work keeps the team focused and the project activities running smoothly by managing the workflow; effectively and efficiently communicating with stakeholders; and managing materials, equipment, supplies, logistics, and vendors.

The project manager and the project team should regularly review the processes and procedures to identify any inefficiencies and bottlenecks and resolve issues and impediments. The team might use lean systems such as the value stream map to identify such bottlenecks and use continuous improvement tools such as retrospectives and lessons learned to make small, incremental, and continuous improvement steps. The project manager has the responsibility to maintain the team's focus on the work and ensure the sense of urgency is instilled to deliver the work in a timely manner.

Now let's discuss the two *PMBOK® Guide*, Sixth Edition, processes of executing in integration management.

Direct and Manage Project Work

The project manager is the visionary leader of the project and as such must constantly communicate the goals and value to stakeholders throughout the project. The project manager must also ensure that deliverables and goals are met throughout the project by ensuring that the team is consistently performing the appropriate tasks to meet those goals and expectations. The project manager must therefore instill a culture of urgency throughout the project to ensure deliverables are being met and stakeholders agree with the timeline of these deliverables.

Direct and Manage Project Work is the process of implementing the plan and leading the execution of the plan. The project manager leads the team through the execution of tasks and activities. The result of executing the work is to create the deliverables of the project, which then are tested as part of the quality management process (discussed in Chapter 11, "Project Quality").

Another major result of this process is to create the work performance data that will be analyzed and compared to the plan to create the work performance information and summarized in the work performance report.

Let's look at these terms in detail:

- *Work Performance Data (WPD):* This refers to raw observations or actual results. This data provides no context and must be analyzed to understand what it means. For example, a page of numbers collected by market research may be meaningless without any analysis. For a project, an example might be, "We have spent $50,000 so far on this project."

- *Work Performance Information (WPI):* This is the interpretation of the data, and it provides some meaning to what the data means. For example, after the pages of numbers from the previous example have been analyzed, the interpretation of those numbers is the work performance information. A project example is, "We are $5,000 over budget."

  Based on the previous example, if you have spent $50,000 so far but should have spent $45,000, you are $5,000 over budget. In this example, the $50,000 is the work performance data (actual results), the $45,000 is the plan, and the $5,000 over budget is the work performance information. To get the work performance information, you should always compare the actual results with the plan.

- *Work Performance Report (WPR):* This is a representation or a summary of the work performance information in a physical or electronic report format that is used for decision-making and shows the status of the project. Because the information contains the data and the plan, it could be regarded as containing all three.

> **EXAM TIP!**   Work performance data is created as part of the Direct and Manage Project Work process. Work performance information and work performance reports are both created as part of the Monitoring and Controlling process and the Measurement Performance domain.

Manage Project Knowledge

Learning new knowledge, reusing existing knowledge, and transferring knowledge are important skill sets for team members and critical success factors for collaboration and project success.

Team members must not hoard knowledge but should share their knowledge with other team members and stakeholders as needed. This aids in collaboration and engagement. When we all learn from one another, we all develop new skills and understanding, and we all win.

Knowledge transfer also includes passing on information and knowledge to other stakeholders, such as the ongoing operations team. At the end of the project, the project team will pass on pertinent information to the production team or operations team so that they understand the capabilities and weaknesses of the deliverable. This information will be in the form of documentation, meetings, work shadowing, and training the production staff.

There are two classifications of knowledge:

- *Explicit Knowledge:* This knowledge is tangible and easily codified into words, pictures, numbers, chart, graphs, reports, and so on. For example, this book is considered explicit knowledge.

- *Tacit Knowledge:* This knowledge is more intangible and personal, based on beliefs, thought processes, insights, and experiences. This type of knowledge is more difficult to express and codify. For example, your experience as a project manager and your approach to resolve an issue based on your past experience are tacit knowledge.

Knowledge management refers to both explicit knowledge and tacit knowledge. You should always learn new knowledge and reuse existing knowledge (lessons learned).

Knowledge transfer refers to both explicit and tacit knowledge. Knowledge within an organization exists on three levels:

- **Individual Knowledge:** This is mostly tacit knowledge but can include some explicit knowledge.

- **Project Knowledge:** This is mostly explicit knowledge because it refers to project documentation.

- **Organization Knowledge:** This is mostly explicit knowledge because it refers to the organization's documentation (OPA). This term also refers to such knowledge as the skills and experiences of employees that can be reused across the organization.

Tacit knowledge generally resides within the minds of individuals, and it is not possible to force people to share their knowledge and experiences. Consequently, creating an atmosphere of trust among team members is important so that they are motivated to share their experiences and knowledge. Even the best tools and processes will not work if people are not motivated to share what they know or pay attention to what others know. Effective transfer of knowledge includes both knowledge management tools and documentation as well as interactions and networking between people.

A key artifact of Manage Project Knowledge is the lessons learned register, which documents what went well, what went badly, and what improvements can be made. However, that is not the only artifact for knowledge management. All project documentation is a form of knowledge transfer, so all project documents are used for managing project knowledge.

> **EXAM TIP!**   The lessons learned register is a current project document (an artifact). A lessons learned repository refers to historical documentation (an OPA).

Monitoring and Controlling the Project

Monitoring and controlling refers to comparing the actual results with the plan, which is a task that a project manager performs throughout the project. This is the process of tracking, reviewing and regulating the performance of the project to determine whether *corrective actions*, *preventive actions*, or *defect repair* (rework) is needed. You are essentially determining the health of the project by comparing metrics. For example, you need to determine whether the project is ahead of schedule or behind schedule by comparing the actual schedule with the planned schedule. You also need to determine whether the project is over or under budget by comparing the actual amount spent with the planned amount that should have been spent.

- The actual results are known as work performance data.

- This is compared against the plan to determine the variance.

- The interpretation of the variance is considered work performance information.

For example,

- "We have spent $30,000 so far on this activity" is our work performance data.

- "We should have spent $25,000 so far on this activity" is our plan.

- "The difference of –$5,000 is our variance."

- "Therefore, we are $5,000 over budget so far" is our work performance information.

Any changes to the baseline must go through a change control process.

On adaptive projects, monitoring and controlling may compare the actual number of user stories approved so far versus what was planned at this stage (or the actual story points delivered versus the story points planned).

For more details on monitoring and controlling, see Chapter 14. Here we concentrate on one aspect, integrated change control.

Integrated Change Control

On predictive projects, having a robust and efficient change control process is vital to ensure changes are properly controlled and approved. Otherwise, the project may end up with runaway costs, it may fall way behind schedule, and tasks may be performed inefficiently and haphazardly.

The perform integrated change control process of the *PMBOK® Guide*, Sixth Edition, is the process of reviewing, approving, and managing all changes on a project.

The project manager must properly control all changes on a project. The PM does not need to eliminate all changes, but those changes do need to be properly controlled. The project manager needs to prevent unnecessary changes to a project.

Why is that?

On predictive projects, most changes are going to cost money! You need to determine who is going to pay for it. So, changes need to go through a proper change control process to avoid scope creep, gold-plating, and uncontrolled costs. Of course, there may be other impacts to the project as well, such as schedule and resources, but regardless, they still need to be properly controlled.

There are many reasons why you would need to go through a change control process, such as

- Team members realize they missed a requirement.

- The customer wants to include some additional requirements.

- Senior management decides to increase the scope.

- A machine breaks down and needs to be fixed or replaced (corrective action).

- One of the components of the machine is wearing down and may cause the machine to fail. You need to replace that part before the machine fails (preventive action).

- There are regulatory changes.

These are just a few reasons why you may need a change on a project. This is not an exhaustive list by any means.

Key Artifact of Integrated Change Control: Change Management Plan

The change management plan documents procedures regarding change control, and each organization has its own procedures regarding change control, which are documented here. Following are some of the items that the change management plan can include:

- **Identifies who has the authority to approve or reject changes**—Generally, the change control board (CCB) is the authority to approve or reject requested changes. The change management plan documents who will be part of the change control board and what level of authority each member has. Even if there is no official change control board, there still must be some authority who can approve or reject changes, even if this authority is one person. If no one has been identified initially, the authority may be the project sponsor. The project manager, too, may have a certain authority to approve or reject changes, which are initially documented in the project charter but also are documented here. For example, if the project manager has the authority to approve changes up to the value of $5,000, this is documented in the project charter and also documented in the change management plan.

- **Identifies who can submit a change request:** The entire change control process needs to be properly controlled, and that includes who can submit a change request to the change control board. Although any stakeholder on a project can propose a change, there should be only a limited number of people who can actually submit the change request document to the CCB. Generally, the project managers have this authority, but the change management plan identifies who these people are. They determine whether the change is valid, is relevant for the project, and adds value to the project.

- **Identifies what constitutes a change:** Generally, any changes that impact the baseline must go through the change control process. As the team is planning the project, any work identified is added to the plan. When the scope, schedule, and costs have been baselined, any identified changes must go through the change control process. However, each organization may have its own definition of what constitutes a change, which also is documented here. For example, "Any task that is less than two hours of work will not be considered a change." If that is the case, it is documented here.

- **Describes the change control process:** Each organization has its own procedures regarding change control, but a basic understanding of PMI's general process is needed for the PMP exam. This process is discussed next.

- **Describes documentation and templates that must be used and updated during the change control process:** Each organization has its own templates and documents that must be used for requesting changes, analyzing changes, and submitting change requests.

 Key Artifact of Integrated Change Control: Configuration Management Plan

Configuration management refers to version control of artifacts, ensuring that team members and stakeholders are accessing the latest version of documents. The configuration management plan documents the configuration management system and procedures.

Distinguish this with the version control system:

- Configuration management retrieves the latest version of the document.

- Version control allows access to the previous versions of the documents.

Steps Involved in the Change Control Process

Each organization has its own procedures for change control, but the following are the basic steps that you need to know for the PMP exam:

Step 1.   A stakeholder identifies the need for a change.

- This is documented in the change log.

- This request may be initiated verbally, but it must still be documented.

Step 2.   Perform an impact analysis.

- The team analyzes the change to determine the impact to the budget, schedule, resources, and other constraints.

- You also need to determine the impact to other areas of the project, such as other project processes or impacts to other project teams.

- You also identify any possible alternative actions.

Step 3.   Submit the change request to the change control board.

Step 4.   Follow the steps outlined in the change management plan to obtain approval (or rejection) from the appropriate authority (CCB, sponsor, or other authority).

Step 5.   Update the change log with the status and any other project documents to reflect the change. Communicate the status to any other interested stakeholders.

Step 6.   Implement the change.

Step 7.   Verify/test the change (control quality).

EXAM TIP!   An impact analysis always involves quantified values—for example,

- "This defect will take two weeks to fix, and we need one additional resource" is an impact analysis because there are quantified values involved.

- "This defect is a quick and easy fix" or "This is a major change" is *not* an impact because there are no quantified values. The terms *quick and easy* and *major* are subjective.

The project manager might not perform the actual analysis but will utilize subject matter experts and team members.

The change authority may come from outside of the organization (such as a government agency). For example,

- Making changes to a building may require approval (permits) from the local village or town council.

Change Control in an Adaptive Environment

For the most part, the day-to-day work of an agile project does not always require a change control process in the same way as a predictive project. Any new user stories are added to the product backlog, which is regularly reprioritized. Only the high-priority user stories are implemented in a sprint. So, in an adaptive environment, change control is built into the agile process.

In addition, the many levels of feedback cycles that are performed frequently on an agile project ensure that potential changes are communicated and understood to ensure an adequate change management process is in place.

However, any major changes to the vision of the agile project or any additional sprints needed will require an approval process. The approval process in agile is beyond the scope of the PMP exam.

Exam Preparation Tasks

As mentioned in the section "How to Use This Book" in the Introduction, you have a couple of choices for exam preparation: the exercises here, Chapter 18, "Final Preparation," and the exam simulation questions on the Pearson Test Prep practice test software.

Review All Key Topics

Review the most important topics in this chapter, noted with the Key Topic icon in the outer margin of the page. Table 4-6 lists a reference of these key topics and the page numbers on which each is found.

Table 4-6 Key Topics for Chapter 4

Key Topic Element	Description	Page Number
Table 4-2	Integration Management Processes and Process Groups	123
Section	Key Artifacts of Developing the Project Charter	124
Section	Benefits Management Plan	126
Section	The Project Charter	127
List	The project management plan is made up of many planning documents	132
Section	Subsidiary Management Plans	133
Section	Baselines	133

Key Topic Element	Description	Page Number
Section	Additional Components	134
Exam Tip!	Components of the project management plan	135
Section	What Is Business Value?	137
List	MVP and MBI	139
List	WPD, WPI, and WPR	140
List	Two classifications of knowledge	141
Section	Key Artifact of Integrated Change Control: Change Management Plan	144
Section	Key Artifact of Integrated Change Control: Configuration Management Plan	145
Section	Steps Involved in the Change Control Process	146

Define Key Terms

Define the following key terms from this chapter and check your answers in the glossary:

project management plan, project charter, business documents, business case, benefits management plan, subsidiary management plans, baselines, business value, minimum viable product (MVP), minimum business increment (MBI), work performance data (WPD), work performance information (WPI), work performance report (WPR), explicit knowledge, tacit knowledge, corrective action, preventive action, defect repair, configuration management

Review Questions

1. Who is responsible for integrating the activities of a project?

   a. The project manager

   b. The project manager and the project team

   c. The project manager and subject matter experts

   d. The sponsor and the project manager

2. Your project has a tight deadline, and planning needs to start immediately; otherwise, there may be risks of delays. The sponsor has not signed the project charter and will not be available for another two weeks. What should you do?

   a. Explain the urgency of the situation to the sponsor but start planning the project. You can have the sponsor sign the project charter when they are available.

   b. Explain the urgency of the situation to the sponsor but do not start work until you have a signed project charter.

   c. Explain the urgency of the situation to the sponsor and escalate to senior management for resolution.

   d. Explain the urgency of the situation to the sponsor and request senior management assign another sponsor.

3. Which of the following are not components of the project management plan? (Choose two.)

   a. Risk management plan

   b. Schedule baseline

   c. Requirements documentation

   d. Resource management plan

   e. Risk register

4. You are an experienced team facilitator recently hired by your company to lead its first agile project. Your team members are asking which artifacts they will need to update as the project progresses. Which of the following is not an artifact used in Agile?

   a. Sprint backlog

   b. Product backlog

   c. Schedule baseline

   d. Burndown chart

5. Which of the following is work performance information?

   a. "We have spent $80,000 so far on this deliverable."

   b. "We are four weeks into the project and have completed 50 tasks."

   c. "We are 10 percent complete."

   d. "We are 10 percent over budget."

6. You are managing a project using a new approach for your organization. There are three distinct phases that are divided into several short iterations, and each iteration will deliver a valuable product to the organization. What are these products best described as?

    a. Minimum business increment

    b. Deliverables

    c. Minimum viable product

    d. Requirements

7. You are in a meeting with your team. You present some reports, show a PowerPoint presentation, and discuss your own past experiences to offer insight on how to improve certain procedures on the project. Which of the following is true?

    a. You are discussing lessons learned, which is tacit knowledge, but your experience is explicit knowledge.

    b. Your reports and PowerPoint presentation would be classified as explicit knowledge, whereas your experience would be tacit knowledge.

    c. Your reports and PowerPoint presentation would be classified as tacit knowledge, whereas your experience would be lessons learned knowledge.

    d. Your reports and PowerPoint presentation would be classified as tacit knowledge, whereas your experience would be explicit knowledge.

8. You are managing a small construction project, and one of the team leads informs you that there is a problem with the plumbing, but it will be a quick and easy fix. What should you do next?

    a. Tell the team member to go ahead and make the fix.

    b. Perform an impact assessment.

    c. Create the change request.

    d. Notify the change control board.

9. The agile team and product owner are in a meeting discussing a feature, but there is much confusion between team members about the coding. After some discussion, it transpires that one developer was looking at a piece of code from the day before and another from an hour ago. What did the team probably fail to do?

    a. Implement an adequate file management system.

    b. Update the communication management plan.

    c. Communicate with one another.

    d. Implement an adequate configuration management system.

10. Regarding change, the project manager's attention is best spent doing which of the following?

    a. Informing the sponsor and stakeholders of changes

    b. Tracking and recording changes

    c. Building relationships with the change control board members

    d. Preventing unnecessary changes

This chapter covers the key PMI processes, artifacts, and tools for successfully managing stakeholders throughout a project. Stakeholder engagement and collaboration are key themes throughout the PMP exam.

- **Stakeholder Management:** Learn how this section fits in to the process model and performance domain model of the *Guide to the Project Management Body of Knowledge* (*PMBOK® Guide*) and identify the materials you need to know for the topics on stakeholder management for the PMP exam.

- **Identify Stakeholders:** Review common tools to identify and prioritize stakeholders, such as the stakeholder grid and the salience model.

- **Plan Stakeholder Engagement:** Learn the importance of stakeholder engagement and review the stakeholder engagement assessment matrix and the stakeholder register.

- **Manage Stakeholder Engagement:** Review the execution of the plan to engage stakeholders.

- **Monitor Stakeholder Engagement:** Learn the importance of constantly appraising stakeholder engagement level throughout a project.

Stakeholder Engagement

The Stakeholder Performance domain discusses the procedures and activities a project manager and team must perform to work with and engage stakeholders. The project manager must identify all stakeholders on a project, determine their potential impact and influence on the project, and develop appropriate management strategies to engage stakeholders. The PM needs to perform these activities throughout the project to ensure everyone has a clear and common understanding of the expectations and goals of the project. Stakeholder engagement is considered a critical success factor on a project.

This chapter addresses the following objectives from the PMP Exam Content Outline:

Domain	Task #	Exam Objective
People	Task 9	Collaborate with stakeholders
People	Task 10	Build shared understanding
People	Task 13	Mentor relevant stakeholders
Process	Task 4	Engage stakeholders

"Do I Know This Already?" Quiz

The "Do I Know This Already?" quiz allows you to assess whether you should read this entire chapter thoroughly or jump to the "Exam Preparation Tasks" section. If you are in doubt about your answers to these questions or your own assessment of your knowledge of the topics, read the entire chapter. Table 5-1 lists the major headings in this chapter and their corresponding "Do I Know This Already?" quiz questions. You can find the answers in Appendix A, "Answers to the 'Do I Know This Already?' Quizzes and Review Questions."

Table 5-1   "Do I Know This Already?" Section-to-Question Mapping

Foundation Topics Section	Questions
Identify Stakeholders	1–6
Plan Stakeholder Engagement	7–8
Manage Stakeholder Engagement	9
Monitor Stakeholder Engagement	10

CAUTION   The goal of self-assessment is to gauge your mastery of the topics in this chapter. If you do not know the answer to a question or are only partially sure of the answer, you should mark that question as wrong for purposes of the self-assessment. Giving yourself credit for an answer you correctly guess skews your self-assessment results and might provide you with a false sense of security.

1. Of the following, who would be considered a stakeholder on a project? (Choose all that apply.)

   a. Your customers

   b. Senior management of your organization

   c. End users of your product

   d. The project manager

   e. The project team

   f. PMO

   g. Steering committee

   h. Government agencies that need to approve the final deliverable

   i. Vendors and suppliers

2. Which of the following stakeholders is the highest priority for the project manager?

   a. High power and low interest

   b. Definitive stakeholders

   c. High power and low influence

   d. Demanding stakeholders

3. A new director joins your organization, and you know that this director's division will be highly impacted by your project. What should you do next?

    a. Email the new director introducing yourself and explaining the project.

    b. Update the stakeholder register.

    c. Set up a meeting with the new director and discuss the project and any requirements the director may have.

    d. Update the communication management plan with the communication needs of the new director.

4. A stakeholder is requesting project status daily but has no decision-making responsibilities on the project. How would you classify this stakeholder on the power and interest grid?

    a. Keep informed

    b. Manage closely

    c. Monitor

    d. Keep satisfied

5. When should you identify stakeholders on a project?

    a. At the beginning of the project

    b. At the beginning of each phase of the project

    c. Throughout the project

    d. While developing the project charter

6. When should you stop identifying stakeholders on a project?

    a. When the project is closed

    b. After you start the closing process of the project

    c. After all stakeholders have been identified

    d. When the senior stakeholders on the project direct you to do so

7. You are determining your stakeholders' current engagement levels compared to where you want them to be. Which of the following would help you determine these levels?

    a. Stakeholder engagement assessment matrix

    b. Stakeholder management plan

    c. Stakeholder register

    d. Resource calendar

8. A new stakeholder has been identified on your project, and you are trying to determine the best approach and strategy to involve and collaborate with this stakeholder. Which artifact should you refer to?

   a. Stakeholder engagement assessment matrix

   b. Stakeholder engagement plan

   c. Salience model

   d. Power and interest grid

9. Which is the best way to meet stakeholders' expectations?

   a. Keep stakeholders regularly informed throughout the project.

   b. Hold weekly status meetings.

   c. Hold daily status meetings.

   d. Host team building sessions with stakeholders.

10. As you are performing data analysis of your stakeholders, it becomes apparent that some stakeholders are resistant to this project. You find this resistance surprising because this project would benefit those stakeholders. What would be the best approach to handle this situation?

   a. Determine a strategy for dealing with these resistant stakeholders and avoid giving them too much information about the project in case they start giving pushback.

   b. Engage them as early as possible to clearly outline their roles and responsibilities on the project.

   c. Add them to the stakeholder register and identify them as resistant in the stakeholder engagement assessment matrix.

   d. Schedule a meeting with them and clearly outline the goals of the project as per the project charter and discuss the items in the benefits management plan.

Foundation Topics

Stakeholder Management

The stakeholder performance domain can be summarized using the six steps shown in Figure 5-1.

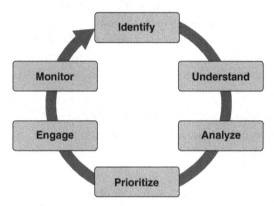

Figure 5-1 Stakeholder Engagement Steps

The first step is to identify the stakeholders and then understand their power, interest, and influence on the project.

Next, you must plan how to engage your stakeholders by understanding, analyzing, and prioritizing the stakeholders based on factors such as power, legitimacy, and influence.

After you have a plan, you must now execute the plan by physically engaging your stakeholders.

Throughout the project, stakeholders' engagement levels may change. You must constantly monitor their engagement levels and ensure they are at the appropriate desired engagement level that would lead to project success.

For the exam, it is important to understand that whether you are a project manager, team lead, or team facilitator (Scrum master), you are responsible for collaborating with, engaging, and motivating all stakeholders on your project.

Now, let's define who a stakeholder is because different people might have different perceptions of the term stakeholder.

PMI defines a *stakeholder* as "an individual, group or organization that may affect, be affected, or perceive itself to be affected by a decision, activity, or outcome of a project, program or portfolio." A stakeholder may be impacted positively or negatively or may influence a project positively or negatively. Normally, you might immediately think of the customer and senior management as being stakeholders of a project. They are definitely stakeholders on a project—major stakeholders at that. However, they are not the only stakeholders.

You, as the project manager, are a stakeholder on your project because the project is impacting you (*you* are managing the project), and how you manage the project can determine the success or failure of the project. Your team members are stakeholders on the project for the same reason. Vendors working on your project or supplying you with raw materials or equipment are stakeholders on the project because a delay in delivering those materials may delay your project.

A senior director in another division of your organization who has nothing to do with your project—although initially you might not consider this person a stakeholder—may actually end up being a stakeholder if this person can influence a decision maker on your project.

However, not all stakeholders are equal. Some stakeholders have higher influence, or higher power or interest, than other stakeholders. You need to manage some stakeholders more closely than other stakeholders. There are other stakeholders you don't need to worry about as much on a day-to-day basis during the project.

Because you are a project manager, it is vital for you to recognize and identify all stakeholders on your project and prioritize your stakeholders to determine who needs more attention, who needs immediate attention, and which stakeholders are higher and lower priority.

Remember, the number one job skill for a project manager is communication. But who is the project manager communicating with? Stakeholders!

To follow on with this theme, the number one success factor on a project is considered to be stakeholder engagement. If all stakeholders are engaged and motivated on your project, then the results are generally positive on your project. Obviously, in reality, that is easier said than done, but it's something you need to consider as a success factor on a project.

NOTE   There are many success factors on a project, and the project manager needs many skills to manage a project. Communication is one among many skills the project manager must possess, but communication is considered the main skill. Likewise, there are many success factors on a project, but stakeholder engagement is considered the main one.

PMI introduces four processes for stakeholder management in the *PMBOK® Guide*, Sixth Edition, which begins with identifying and prioritizing stakeholders and then further goes on to discussing stakeholder engagement. Table 5-2 shows the *PMBOK® Guide*, Sixth Edition, processes associated with the Stakeholder Management knowledge area.

Table 5-2 An Extract of the *PMBOK® Guide*, Sixth Edition, Process Matrix Showing the Stakeholder Management Processes

13.0 Project Stakeholder Management	13.1 Identify Stakeholders	13.2 Plan Stakeholder Engagement	13.3 Manage Stakeholder Engagement	13.4 Monitor Stakeholder Engagement

Four processes span the initiating, planning, executing, and monitoring and controlling process groups, respectively. We discuss each of these processes in detail later in this chapter, but here's a summary:

- **Identify Stakeholders:** This refers to the process of finding who is impacted by the project, or who could influence a project, including decision makers and team members.

- **Plan Stakeholder Engagement:** This is the process of determining how to engage and motivate stakeholders and how to keep them engaged and motivated throughout the project.

- **Manage Stakeholder Engagement:** This refers to managing stakeholders' expectations and building trust among stakeholders (an important role for a project manager).

- **Monitor Stakeholder Engagement:** This refers to monitoring the overall relationships with stakeholders and adjusting strategies to keep stakeholders engaged.

Identify Stakeholders

As mentioned previously, a project manager's key skill set is communication. However, before you can communicate with stakeholders, you need to know who those stakeholders are; otherwise, how are you going to communicate with them? And how will you know what information to communicate to them if you don't know who they are? One of the important tasks of a project manager is to identify stakeholders throughout the project.

You can only stop identifying stakeholders after the project is closed. Even at the deployment or go-live stage, or when moving the product to ongoing operations, you will be identifying new stakeholders (end users, for example, are often identified toward the end of the project).

However, as mentioned earlier, not all stakeholders are equal, so you have to prioritize your stakeholders based on their power, interest, and influence on the project.

Common Tools and Techniques for Identifying Stakeholders

There are many ways of identifying stakeholders throughout the project. The following methods are identified in the *PMBOK® Guide*, Sixth and Seventh Editions and are commonly asked about in the exam.

- **Expert Judgment:** Your own knowledge and experience will identify some stakeholders in your project, along with knowledge and experience of other team members, subject matter experts, and in fact, other stakeholders themselves.

- **Meeting**—As a project manager, you might feel you spend half your time in meetings. That is just the nature of the role, but any meeting you are in may identify stakeholders on your project.

- **Data Gathering**

  - **Questionnaires and Surveys:** You may send out questionnaires or surveys with some standard questions to determine stakeholders' involvement, interest, and influence on the project.

  - **Brainstorming:** This technique is used to gather as many ideas as possible.

- **Data Analysis**

  - **Stakeholder Analysis:** This refers to analysis of project roles, position in the organization, interest, expectations, and contribution (among others). This analysis can be used to prioritize stakeholders.

  - **Document Analysis:** Reviewing documents such as prior project files, regulatory requirements, and industry standards can help identify stakeholders on your project.

- **Data Representation**

  - **Stakeholder Grid (Power and Interest, Power and Influence, Impact and Influence):** These points are discussed in more detail in the "Stakeholder Grid" section, which follows.

- **Salience Model:** This model is discussed in more detail in the later "Salience Model" section.

- **Stakeholder Cube:** This 3D version of the stakeholder grid shows three variables instead of two.

- **Direction of Influence:** This issue is discussed in more detail in the later "Direction of Influence" section.

Stakeholder Grid

A *stakeholder grid* is a type of classification model that a project manager may use to prioritize stakeholders and determine a management approach to stakeholders based on their power or level of interest, influence, or impact on the project. There are three types of stakeholder grids:

- Power and interest grid

- Power and influence grid

- Impact and influence grid

The most common of these is the power and interest grid, shown in Figure 5-2.

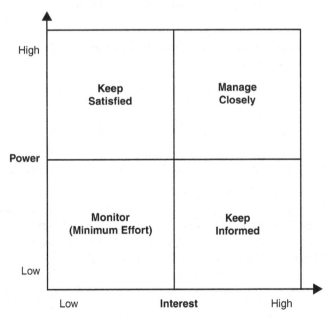

Figure 5-2 Power and Interest Grid

Power (on the y-axis) refers to the level of authority a stakeholder has on the project. If a stakeholder has high power, it means that this person can either cancel the project or change direction of the project. Here are some examples of stakeholders with high power:

- Sponsors
- Customers
- Key decision makers
- PMOs
- Project leadership team
- Key stakeholders who have sign-off responsibilities
- Senior (C-level) executives of an organization

Interest (on the x-axis) refers to the level and frequency of information the stakeholder needs about your project. If a stakeholder has high interest, then that person needs regular information about the project. If the stakeholder has low interest, then just the occasional snippet of information would suffice. Following are some examples of stakeholders with high interest:

- The project team (they need constant information about the details of the project)
- Vendors working on the project (they may need regular but appropriate information about their aspect of the project)
- Customers
- PMOs
- Key decision makers
- Project leadership team
- Key stakeholders who have sign-off responsibilities

Stakeholders who have both high power and high interest would be placed in the top-right quadrant of the grid, where the project manager's management strategy would be "manage closely." These are the key stakeholders on your project—key decision makers such as the customer, project leadership team, and stakeholders who have sign-off responsibility.

Think about this in reality: If key stakeholders at several pay scale levels above you ask you a question about your project, what do you do? You probably drop everything to answer their question. You might even anticipate the questions these stakeholders may ask and prepare an answer in case they ask it, or even address the question yourself before they ask it! These stakeholders are your highest priority stakeholders, the ones you absolutely do not want to disappoint on your project.

Stakeholders who have high power but low interest would fall into the top-left quadrant, where the strategy would be "keep satisfied." You may wonder how that situation arises. You might think that if someone has high power, then surely that person automatically has high interest.

Not necessarily. Senior executives in your organization can cancel your project at any time, so they would be high power. But do they care on a day-to-day basis what is going on in your project? Usually, they do not. Normally, they just need to know that the project is progressing and their investment in this project is money well spent (they are kept satisfied).

Stakeholders who have low power but high interest would fall into the bottom-right quadrant, where the strategy is "keep informed," which just means constant information flow. These stakeholders need regular information about the project, such as team members and vendors. They cannot cancel a project nor make a major decision on a project, but they certainly need data and information to do the work on the project.

Stakeholders who have low power and low interest would fall into the bottom-left quadrant, where the strategy is "monitor." These would be the lowest-priority stakeholders who have no decision-making authority on the project but sporadically might need pieces of information about it. For example, an end user of a process improvement project may be wondering how a particular process will work after the project goes live.

NOTE *Power* refers to power on the project (not necessarily power within the organization). For example, a senior director of another division in your organization may be high power, but if this person is not involved on your project or if no project activities or outcomes impact this person or their division, then this director would not be considered high power for the purpose of the project. However, this senior director may be able to influence a key decision maker on your project, in which case you might now consider the person to have influence on your project.

Instead of a power and interest grid, you may create a power and influence grid (power on the y-axis, influence on the x-axis). A third type of grid is influence and impact, where influence is on the y-axis and impact is on the x-axis. Regardless of the type of grid, the exact same diagram as Figure 5-2 would be relevant.

Salience Model

Another stakeholder classification model is the *salience model*, which has three variables: power, legitimacy, and urgency, shown as a Venn diagram in Figure 5-3.

1. Dormant stakeholder
2. Discretionary stakeholder
3. Demanding stakeholder
4. Dominant stakeholder
5. Dangerous stakeholder
6. Dependent stakeholder
7. Definitive stakeholder
8. Non-stakeholder

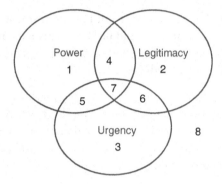

Figure 5-3   Salience Model

Power has the same meaning here as it does for the stakeholder grid—namely, that these stakeholders can either cancel a project or change the direction of a project.

Legitimacy means that these stakeholders are appropriately involved or impacted by a project. A senior executive of your company may have the power to cancel your project but have no legitimate day-to-day involvement on your project.

Urgency refers to how quickly stakeholders need immediate attention or regular information about the project.

A stakeholder who falls into area 1 (possessing only power, no legitimacy or urgency) is known as a dormant stakeholder. This person has no day-to-day decision-making capabilities on the project, is not involved in the project, nor does this person need regular day-to-day information about the project. For example, the CEO of a company can cancel a project; however, this executive might have no legitimate involvement on the project, nor would they need regular day-to-day urgent information about the project.

A stakeholder who falls into area number 2 is known as a discretionary stakeholder. This person doesn't have high power on the project or need information urgently but nonetheless is legitimately involved or impacted by the project in some way. For example, a local charity that receives food donations from a restaurant chain may be impacted by a new corporate directive. The charity is a legitimate stakeholder but has no power or urgency on this new corporate directive project.

A stakeholder who falls into area number 3 is known as a demanding stakeholder. Although this person doesn't have high power or legitimate involvement in the project, they might be very vocal about their thoughts and requirements and might try to influence other stakeholders. For example, if the project is to build a busy road through a quiet neighborhood, the local residents impacted may be very vocal about their discontent.

A stakeholder who falls into area number 4 and has both power and legitimacy but no urgency is known as a dominant stakeholder. For example, if you are building a house, you need a permit from your local authority. This authority has power (can reject your permit) and legitimacy (needs information about your project to determine whether to approve or reject the permit and will inspect the building at various points on the project) but doesn't urgently need any of this information. This stakeholder will make the decision when you provide the information needed.

A stakeholder who falls into area number 5 and has power and urgency but no legitimacy is known as a dangerous stakeholder. For example, a senior director whose preferred project was voted down by senior management in favor of another project may try to sabotage the other project.

A stakeholder who falls into area number 6 and has legitimacy and urgency but no power is known as a dependent stakeholder. For example, these stakeholders might be local residents of an area where you are doing public construction.

A stakeholder who falls into area number 7 has power, urgency, and legitimacy; this person is known as a definitive stakeholder. These would be your highest priority stakeholders and the ones whom you would be managing very closely—for example, customer contacts, senior decision makers on your project, PMO, the project leadership team, to name a few.

Anyone who is outside of this model (possesses no power, urgency, or legitimacy) would be classed as a non-stakeholder and fall into area number 8.

"But wait!" I hear you say. Technically, wouldn't the rest of the world be non-stakeholders in this case? True. But that is not what this term refers to. As an example, think of a member of the project leadership team who has now left the organization. That person was previously a stakeholder, but this project has nothing to do with them anymore, so you would now classify that person as a non-stakeholder.

Direction of Influence

As a project manager, you have influencing skills. You will use this skill to influence the decisions of appropriate stakeholders so that they are doing what is best for the project. For example, you will influence decision makers to make the right decisions for the project, and you will influence team members to perform tasks that will be beneficial for project success.

Influencing does not mean forcing someone to do something. It is about winning people over and getting them on your side to do what is best for the project.

Per PMI, influencing is hierarchical and occurs in four directions:

- **Upward (Senior Management):** Means you are influencing stakeholders hierarchically above you in the organization (stakeholders who are pay scales above you).

- **Downward (Team):** Means you are influencing stakeholders hierarchically below you in the organization (such as team members and junior analysts).

- **Sideward (Peers Within the Organization):** Means you are influencing peer stakeholders within your organization (employees who are neither above you nor below you in the organization's hierarchy but still impacted by or could influence the project).

- **Outward (External Stakeholders):** Means you are influencing stakeholders outside of your organization (such as vendors and suppliers).

In each case, you will adjust your communication style accordingly.

Common Artifact: The Stakeholder Register

Stakeholders are documented in the *stakeholder register*, which contains such information as

- Name
- Position/title in the organization
- Role on the project
- Manager
- Contact information
- Influence
- Power
- Supportive or resistant?

Figure 5-4 shows a stakeholder register. Note that this is not a template that you should be using on your project. It is just a simple example of a stakeholder register.

| Project ID | | | | Project Manager | | | | | |
| Project Name | | | | Sponsor | | | | | |

Name	Title	Role	Location	Contact Info	Supportive, Neutral or Resistant?	Power (H, M, L)	Interest (H, M, L)	Internal or External?	Comments

Figure 5-4 A Stakeholder Register

EXAM TIP! Whenever you identify a new stakeholder on the project, the first thing you do is update the stakeholder register. An exam question will rarely state directly that you have identified a new stakeholder. Instead, it will give you a scenario where you will need to determine whether a new stakeholder has been identified.

Plan Stakeholder Engagement

After a stakeholder has been identified, you need to determine the appropriate strategies to engage and motivate that stakeholder throughout the project depending on power, interest, influence, legitimacy, urgency, or any other factors you may have determined.

Stakeholder Engagement Assessment Matrix

One of the key artifacts for documenting stakeholders' engagement is the *stakeholder engagement assessment matrix*, an example of which is shown in Figure 5-5.

Stakeholder	Unaware	Resistant	Neutral	Supportive	Leading
A	C			D	
B		C		D	
C			C		D
D				C, D	

C = Current Engagement Level
D = Desired Engagement Level

Figure 5-5 A Stakeholder Engagement Assessment Matrix

PMI has identified five engagement levels of a stakeholder:

- **Unaware:** These are stakeholders who are unaware that the project exists.

- **Resistant:** These stakeholders do not want the project to be a success and may take active steps to ensure its failure.

- **Neutral:** These stakeholders are indifferent to the success or failure of the project. It makes no difference to them whether the project is a success or failure.

- **Supportive:** This group of stakeholders is satisfied that the project will be a benefit and want the project to be a success.

- **Leading:** These stakeholders want the project to be a success and are actively engaged to ensure project success.

Based on this matrix, you can determine your management strategy on how to communicate with your stakeholders. You can make determinations such as which stakeholders need the most attention, which ones you don't have to worry about as much, or which stakeholders need immediate attention.

As a project manager, you should try to have all the *C*s and *D*s in the same box.

For example, in Figure 5-5, stakeholder D is currently supportive of the project, and you want this person to be supportive of the project. So you don't need to spend a lot of time trying to engage and motivate this stakeholder because this person is already engaged and motivated. Stakeholder D is already where you want them to be, so you just need to ensure they remain engaged and motivated.

Stakeholder A, however, is unaware of the project, but you need this person to be supportive. So, what do you think would be the first thing to do here? Find out why they are unaware of the project. Maybe they're on vacation, or maybe they were not invited to the information session discussing the project. Whatever the reason, you may determine that this stakeholder is your highest priority stakeholder right now and that you immediately need to reach out to them and discuss the project.

Stakeholder B is currently resistant to the project, but you want them to be supportive. Again, the first step is to determine why they are resistant. Perhaps it was due to misinformation about the project that they received that is making them resistant to the project. So perhaps they may now be your highest priority stakeholders that you now need to reach out to, to give them correct information. This situation may be challenging if they have already decided against the project, but at least, even if you don't convince them enough to become supportive, they may become neutral. Neutral is still better than resistant because a resistant stakeholder may take active steps to try to ensure the project is not a success, whereas a neutral stakeholder does not care.

However, if a resistant stakeholder is negatively impacted, you know they will be much more challenging to deal with, so you need to adjust management approach and communication style accordingly.

NOTE The priority of each stakeholder depends on many factors, such as power, interest, and urgency, as discussed before. You need to consider all these factors together when trying to determine your management strategy.

Stakeholder Engagement Plan

Another key artifact is the stakeholder engagement plan.

NOTE The stakeholder engagement plan is one of the subsidiary management plans that make up the project management plan. It is the only subsidiary plan that does not have the phrase *management plan* in its title. However, it is still a how-to document—a document that contains procedures.

The ***stakeholder engagement plan*** therefore documents how you are to engage and motivate stakeholders. It contains the procedures to prioritize stakeholders based on power, influence, legitimacy, and so on, and documents the various management strategies based on their engagement levels. It identifies the actions required to promote productive involvement of stakeholders in making decisions and executing tasks throughout the project. It contains the stakeholder engagement assessment matrix and outlines steps involved in moving stakeholders to the appropriate engagement level.

NOTE As with all components of the project management plan, the stakeholder engagement plan is progressively elaborated over time as more is known about the project. You may not know all these strategies at the beginning of the project, but as you learn, you update!

Manage Stakeholder Engagement

One of the major responsibilities of a project manager is to manage stakeholders' engagement throughout the project. If communication is the number one job skill for a project manager, then surely managing stakeholders' engagement and expectation should be considered the number one job description. How does a project manager manage stakeholders' expectations? By communication.

The project manager communicates and collaborates with all stakeholders, including team members, vendors, key decision makers, as well as customers and senior management. You always want to try to have a productive working relationship and build trust among all your stakeholders throughout the project.

A key principle for engaging and motivating stakeholders is to involve them as early in the project as possible. Remember, depending on the project, different stakeholders will be involved at different times on the project, so you must define and share a clear vision for the project at the beginning of their involvement on the project and continue sharing the vision throughout the project. Involving decision makers early in the project will give them a vested interest in the project and thereby increase their engagement. Likewise, holding team members accountable for their work and decisions will also increase their engagement and collaboration. Addressing risks and resolving issues in a timely fashion will build trust among key stakeholders.

Some of the key skills you utilize to engage stakeholders include

- **Communication skills:** The way to collaborate with any stakeholders is to communicate with them.

- **Conflict management:** You need to utilize this skill because there will be disagreement between stakeholders.

- **Cultural awareness:** You need to adjust your management and communication style based on organization culture and external culture.

- **Political awareness:** You might need to navigate through office politics to get work done.

- **Negotiation:** You need to negotiate tasks and resources to perform those tasks.

- **Observation and conversation:** You will naturally observe stakeholders' attitudes and mindsets throughout the project.

Monitor Stakeholder Engagement

As with all monitoring and controlling processes, you compare actual results with the plan. In this case, the project manager compares the stakeholders' current engagement level with the desired engagement level and adjusts management strategies accordingly. Through ongoing observation and monitoring, if you detect a discrepancy between the two, you will utilize your skills and strategies to correct those discrepancies and work to continually improve stakeholder perceptions.

If stakeholders show concern about the project, you will address those concerns. If you see supportive stakeholders beginning to wane in their support, you will act accordingly and try to win their level of support. If resistant stakeholders begin to negatively impact the project, again you will act accordingly, this time to ensure the negative impact is either eliminated or at least kept to a minimum.

EXAM TIP! When stuck on a question, always look at option choices that refer to engaging, motivating, and collaborating with stakeholders (including team members). You always want to take the proactive approach, so always look for options that are proactive rather than reactive. For example, if you've identified an issue, always address the issue immediately rather than waiting for a stakeholder to point out the issue before you address it.

Exam Preparation Tasks

As mentioned in the section "How to Use This Book" in the Introduction, you have a couple of choices for exam preparation: the exercises here, Chapter 18, "Final Preparation," and the exam simulation questions on the Pearson Test Prep practice test software.

Review All Key Topics

Review the most important topics in this chapter, noted with the Key Topic icon in the outer margin of the page. Table 5-3 lists a reference of these key topics and the page numbers on which each is found.

Table 5-3 Key Topics for Chapter 5

Key Topic Element	Description	Page Number
Paragraph	Definition of a stakeholder	158
Section	Stakeholder Grid	161
Section	Salience Model	164
Exam Tip	Updating the stakeholder register	167
Figure 5-5	A Stakeholder Engagement Assessment Matrix	167
Section	Stakeholder Engagement Plan	169

Define Key Terms

Define the following key terms from this chapter and check your answers in the glossary:

stakeholder, stakeholder grid, interest, salience model, power, legitimacy, urgency, stakeholder register, stakeholder engagement assessment matrix, stakeholder engagement plan

Review Questions

1. You are the project manager of a new project, and you know from past experience that one of the key stakeholders on the project constantly requests changes throughout a project. You want to avoid this situation. What should you do?

   a. Avoid communicating too many results with this stakeholder. The less they know, the fewer changes they will request.

   b. Involve the stakeholder as early as possible and request their input regularly throughout the project.

   c. Consider this situation as a risk to the project and update the risk register.

   d. Observe this stakeholder's involvement, and if this becomes an issue, then escalate to the sponsor.

2. Who would least likely be considered a stakeholder in the following situations?

   a. A building inspector who has to approve the work before the owners are allowed to move in

   b. The vendor that you have decided to order raw materials from this one time and that you have never done business with before

   c. A technical expert whom you sometimes refer to for advice

   d. End users of a system's implementation project

3. You are part of the way through a project, but before you can move to the next stage, you need to get approval from a local government agency. What direction of influence does this government agency fall into in relation to your organization?

   a. Upward

   b. Downward

   c. Outward

   d. Sideward

4. A senior decision maker on your project has recently left your organization and is no longer impacted by the project, nor will this person have any influence on the project. What should you do next?

   a. Update the risk register because this person was a key decision maker.

   b. Notify the team.

   c. Reach out to the replacement.

   d. Update the stakeholder register identifying this person as a non-stakeholder.

5. Which of the following tools might you use to identify stakeholders throughout your project? (Choose three.)

   a. Questionnaires and surveys

   b. Check sheet

   c. Meetings

   d. Statistical sampling

   e. Expert judgment

6. You are analyzing a document and notice that one of your stakeholders is unaware of the project, but you want them to be supportive. What document are you most likely analyzing?

   a. Stakeholder engagement plan

   b. Stakeholder engagement assessment matrix

   c. Salience model

   d. Power and interest grid

7. A stakeholder has power, legitimacy, and urgency. How would you classify this stakeholder?

   a. Definitive stakeholder

   b. Manage closely

   c. Demanding stakeholder

   d. Dangerous stakeholder

8. Your project is currently over budget and behind schedule, and you are looking at the stakeholder engagement assessment matrix. From this document, what indicates to you that you need to take some action to engage and communicate with the stakeholder?

   a. There is a C in the Resistant column.

   b. There are a C and D in the same column.

   c. The C and D are in different columns.

   d. There is a D in the Supportive column.

9. If senior management doesn't want you to spend time writing a project charter because they don't see the value, what should you do?

   a. Continue writing the project charter and show senior management afterward how the charter benefitted the project.

   b. Stop writing the project charter to comply with their request.

   c. Review the benefits of the project charter with them.

   d. Escalate the issue to the sponsor.

10. From the following table, which stakeholder will be the project manager's highest priority stakeholder to reach out to?

Stakeholder	Unaware	Resistant	Neutral	Supportive	Leading
A	C			D	
B			C	D	
C					C, D
D				C, D	

This chapter covers the following topics on scope management:

- **What Is Scope Management?:** Review the concepts of scope and learn why managing scope is a critical success factor for a project.

- **Planning Scope Management:** Review the process for planning the scope of the project.

- **Collecting Requirements:** Learn the common tools and artifacts needed to successfully collect requirements from appropriate stakeholders.

- **Scope Definition:** Examine the development of the scope statement.

- **The Work Breakdown Structure (WBS):** Review the purpose of the work breakdown structure and the scope baseline.

- **Validate Scope:** Review the process of customer acceptance of the deliverables.

- **Control Scope:** Identify the project manager's responsibility for properly controlling the scope of a project.

- **Agile Considerations for Scope Management:** Examine the agile approach to managing scope.

## CHAPTER 6

Project Scope

Project managers always dream of projects going successfully and smoothly without a hitch. Unfortunately, for the most part, that usually remains a dream!

Many factors impact the project throughout the project life cycle, and these factors can have an impact on the scope. Factors such as risks, budget, availability of resources, changes to the external and internal business environment, supply chain issues, needs and wants of stakeholders, and many more factors all directly impact the scope of the project.

This chapter discusses the processes, tools, and artifacts for Scope Management from both the traditional style of project management and agile. We discuss the traditional style first and then examine the adaptive approach toward the end of the chapter.

This chapter addresses the following objectives from the PMP Exam Content Outline:

Domain	Task #	Exam Objective
People	Task 2	Lead a team
People	Task 4	Empower team members and stakeholders
People	Task 9	Collaborate with stakeholders
People	Task 10	Build a shared understanding
Process	Task 1	Execute project with the urgency required to deliver business value
Process	Task 4	Engage stakeholders
Process	Task 7	Plan and manage quality of products/deliverables
Process	Task 8	Plan and manage scope
Process	Task 10	Manage project changes
Process	Task 17	Plan and manage project/phase closure or transitions
Business	Task 1	Plan and manage project compliance
Business	Task 1	Evaluate and deliver project benefits and value

"Do I Know This Already?" Quiz

The "Do I Know This Already?" quiz allows you to assess whether you should read this entire chapter thoroughly or jump to the "Exam Preparation Tasks" section. If you are in doubt about your answers to these questions or your own assessment of your knowledge of the topics, read the entire chapter. Table 6-1 lists the major headings in this chapter and their corresponding "Do I Know This Already?" quiz questions. You can find the answers in Appendix A, "Answers to the 'Do I Know This Already?' Quizzes and Review Questions."

Table 6-1   "Do I Know This Already?" Section-to-Question Mapping

Foundation Topics Section	Questions
What Is Scope Management?	1
Planning Scope Management	2
Collecting Requirements	3
Scope Definition	4
The Work Breakdown Structure	5–6
Validate Scope	7
Control Scope	8
Agile Considerations for Scope Management	9–10

CAUTION   The goal of self-assessment is to gauge your mastery of the topics in this chapter. If you do not know the answer to a question or are only partially sure of the answer, you should mark that question as wrong for purposes of the self-assessment. Giving yourself credit for an answer you correctly guess skews your self-assessment results and might provide you with a false sense of security.

1. Common scope failures on projects are a result of which of the following? (Choose all that apply.)

    a. Miscommunication

    b. Scope creep

    c. Misunderstanding

    d. Misinterpretation

    e. Gold-plating

2. Senior management has decided to increase the scope of your project. Which of the following would you need to consult to determine the next steps?

   a. Requirements documentation

   b. Scope management plan

   c. Scope statement

   d. WBS

3. Which of the following tools can be used for requirements elicitation? (Choose two.)

   a. Interviewing

   b. Ishikawa diagram

   c. Backlog grooming

   d. Observation

   e. Pareto chart

4. Your team is on track to finish your project by the end of the year, but your customer informs you that due to a new discovery, the project has to finish a month earlier. Which artifact would you update to reflect this change?

   a. Scope management plan

   b. Scope statement

   c. Product backlog

   d. Traceability matrix

5. Which of the following are components of the scope baseline?

   a. Scope statement, WBS, activities

   b. WBS, control accounts, activities, WBS dictionary

   c. Scope statement, WBS, code of accounts, tasks

   d. WBS dictionary, WBS, scope statement

6. Senior management is asking about the purpose of a work breakdown structure. Of the following, what do you not tell them?

   a. The WBS allows team members to see how their work impacts other areas of the project.

   b. The WBS shows dependencies between work packages.

    c. The WBS is a communication tool for stakeholders.

    d. The WBS allows for team buy-in.

7. A team member hears the term *Validate Scope* and is confused as to its purpose. Which of the following is not a response you would give to this team member?

    a. The purpose of Validate Scope is to allow the customer to test the deliverable against the requirements.

    b. The purpose of Validate Scope is to allow the customer to sign off on the deliverables.

    c. The purpose of Validate Scope is to allow the team to test the deliverable to ensure it meets all requirements.

    d. The purpose of Validate Scope is to allow the customer to point out features that do not meet their requirements.

8. Because your stakeholders are requesting additional features that they would like to add that were not part of the original scope of the project, you are analyzing the scope of these additions and ensuring these requests go through the proper change control channels. Which of the following would best describe what you are doing?

    a. You are ensuring stakeholders are engaged throughout the project by recognizing their requests.

    b. You are allowing scope creep because these additional features were not part of the original scope of the project.

    c. You are validating the scope of the project.

    d. You are controlling the scope of the project.

9. You notice that two team members are having a really hard time implementing their user stories. As you investigate further, you realize that both user stories are large and complex, so the challenge is not surprising. What should you do to address this problem?

    a. Assign additional team members to work on those larger user stories.

    b. Break down the large user stories into smaller user stories.

    c. Send the two team members for additional training.

    d. Reassign these user stories to more experienced team members and assign smaller user stories to these two team members.

10. Which of these is an example of a user story?

    a. As a travel agent, I want to find vacation deals for my customers.

    b. I want a four-bedroom house and a two-car garage built within six months.

    c. This wall should be painted blue.

    d. As a call center analyst, I want to input customers' first and last names and postal codes so that I can pull up their accounts quickly.

Foundation Topics

What Is Scope Management?

The Scope Management knowledge area addresses the understanding of the requirements and needs of the project. Scope Management is all about defining the boundaries for the project—what is included and what is excluded. Understanding the scope ensures you are completing all the work necessary for project success... and *only* the work necessary for project success. You are not performing any additional work. It is vital for all stakeholders to share this understanding throughout the project so that all stakeholders are focused on the goals and accomplishments of the project. In short, if your project is to build a bike, you ensure that you are building a bike and don't end up building a tank!

Some of the common failures on projects related to Scope Management are

- Misunderstanding of requirements

- Miscommunication of requirements

- Misinterpretation of requirement by the various teams involved on the project

- Scope creep

- Gold-plating

- Customers not entirely understanding what requirements they need

Many of you have likely seen something similar to this comic related to misunderstood requirements in Figure 6-1.

Unfortunately, these misunderstandings happen all too frequently on projects, so the Scope Management knowledge area attempts to address them.

As a project manager, you are trying to prevent the following:

- ***Scope Creep:*** The uncontrolled expansion of work while still being held accountable to your original time and budget. It is not simply adding features to the product at the request of the customer, which is what many people assume scope creep to be. Adding such features is perfectly acceptable if the changes are properly controlled. If the customer agrees to pay for the additional work and allows adjustment to the schedule and other plans, that is not considered scope creep. It is an addition to scope, which is perfectly acceptable if controlled properly.

| How the Customer Explained It | How the Project Leader Understood It | How the Engineer Designed It | How the Programmer Wrote It | How the Sales Executive Described It |
| How the Project Was Documented | What Operations Installed | How the Customer Was Billed | How the Help Desk Supported It | What the Customer Really Needed |

Figure 6-1 Misunderstood Requirements

If a customer requests additional features to a product and you agree and add those features, that is considered scope creep. If, on the other hand, you follow the change control process by performing an impact analysis, submitting a change request to the change control authority, and having the change approved before adding those features, that is not considered scope creep.

- *Gold-plating*: A type of scope creep in which the team members themselves initiate a change or additional work without any request from the customer. For example, a web developer adds an extra page to a website, but the customer didn't actually request that additional page.

In both cases, the changes could result in additional costs and other impacts to the project, so you must go through the proper change control channels to have any additions to scope properly approved before making any updates. We cover the details of the change control process in Chapter 4, "Getting a Project Started and Integration."

The approach to managing the scope differs depending on the life cycle approach. We first discuss the predictive (traditional) approach to scope management, and then we discuss the adaptive approach.

Understand the following:

- **Product Scope:** The feature and functions of the product. This term describes what you are creating and therefore relates to the product requirements.

- **Project Scope:** The work that needs to be performed to produce the deliverable. This term relates to the steps and procedures involved in developing the product, and because it relates to how you are to deliver the product, it relates to the project management plan.

  It is usually understood that the product scope is included in the project scope (per PMI).

The *PMBOK® Guide*, Sixth Edition, processes related to scope management are as follows:

- Plan Scope Management

- Collect Requirements

- Define Scope

- Create WBS

- Validate Scope

- Control Scope

We discuss each process as it relates to the PMP exam.

Planning Scope Management

The first process of Scope Management is Plan Scope Management. This process refers to how you are going to plan, execute, monitor, and control the scope and requirements of the project. The purpose is to provide guidance and direction to manage the scope and requirements throughout the project. These procedures are documented in the scope management plan and the requirements management plan.

Key Artifacts of Plan Scope Management

Two key documents are created when planning the scope of the project, and both are progressively elaborated on over the life of the project. The sections that follow describe these two documents.

Scope Management Plan

The scope management plan documents *how* the scope will be defined, developed, and controlled. It describes the *procedures* for preparing the scope statement; explains how to create the work breakdown structure; and documents the process, guidance, and procedures for managing scope changes. For example, it documents what to do if senior management decides to increase the scope of the project during the project after the plan has been baselined.

The scope management plan does *not* document the scope of the project itself (that is documented in the scope statement, covered later).

Requirements Management Plan

The requirements management plan documents *how* the requirements collection process will be planned, executed, and changes managed and controlled. It describes the *procedures* for collecting requirements and documents when requirements will be collected and where will they be documented. It describes the procedures for adding new requirements and the process for missed requirements.

You might need to collect many types of requirements (discussed in the next section), and each type of requirement may have different procedures for collection and documentation. All these various procedures are documented here.

The requirements management plan does *not* document the requirements itself (those are documented in the requirements documentation, discussed later).

Key Tools and Techniques of Plan Scope Management

The common tools (or methods) described in the list that follows are used across many of the 49 *PMBOK® Guide*, Sixth Edition, processes and refer to actions taken or knowledge utilized to perform the work of the process.

- **Expert Judgment:** You use your own knowledge and experience and the knowledge and experience of other team members and subject matter experts to plan the scope of the project.

- **Alternatives Analysis:** There are different ways of determining, validating, and evaluating the scope of the project. You determine all these different approaches when planning your project.

- **Meetings:** You will attend many meetings with team members, customers, and other stakeholders before you can all agree to the scope of the project and procedures.

Collecting Requirements

PMI defines the process of Collect Requirements as "the process of determining, documenting and managing stakeholders' needs and requirements to meet objectives." This means you need to understand what the customer wants, what the customer needs, what you are going to deliver, and how you are going to deliver it. Many causes of failure on a project are a direct result of either misunderstanding or miscommunicating requirements (note Figure 6-1 earlier).

Even the customers might not always know exactly what requirements they need, so the project manager and the project team must work with customers to help them identify and ensure they have a common understanding of the requirements. As an example, if you hire an architect to design an eco-friendly house and don't know anything about house construction and house design, you would expect the architect and team to work with you to help you agree to a design that fits your needs. Simply picking out pictures in a magazine or online would not constitute your understanding what you want or what you need. Steve Jobs once said, "People don't know what they want until you show it to them." People did not realize they needed the iPod until it was shown to them.

At the corporate level, whether it's an IT project, a facilities project, a process improvement project, or any type of project, all stakeholders need to understand what is to be delivered, how it is to be delivered, and when it is to be delivered.

There are many types of requirements, including the following:

- **Product Requirements:** These are the agreed-upon conditions or capabilities of a product, service, or outcome that the project is designed to satisfy.

- **Project Requirements:** These are the actions, processes, or other conditions the project needs to meet, such as milestone dates, contractual obligations, budget, and constraints.

- **Business Requirements:** These conditions define the business need of the project, including the critical success criteria. They describe why a project is needed and how it will benefit the organization.

- **Stakeholder Requirements:** Also known as *user requirements*, these conditions relate to how users might use the product and what requirements or features they might need.

- **Quality Requirements:** These are the quality standards the product needs to abide by.

- **Compliance Requirements:** These are the standards and regulations that the product and the project must abide by. The standards could be internal to the organization or external. Regulations always come from a government body.

- **Transition Requirements:** Once the product or service has been built, you need to understand how to move this to production/ongoing operations/go-live (every industry has its own terminology related to this).

- **Functional Requirements:** These are conditions describing the behavior of the product.

- **Nonfunctional Requirements:** These additional requirements are needed to correctly use the product or service. Common examples of nonfunctional requirements include

  - **Safety and Security:** What are the safety protocols when using the product or service?

  - **Availability:** If the service suddenly becomes unavailable, how long will it take to restore?

  - **Continuity of Service:** If there is a disaster, how quickly can the service be restored?

  - **Capacity:** What are the speed and performance of the product or service?

The product is still functional without these nonfunctional requirements; however, it might not operate at its full capacity. For example, a machine can still be fully functional if safety measures are not implemented; however, the people around that machine might be in danger. These safety requirements would be considered nonfunctional requirements.

The preceding list provides just some examples of the types of requirements. This is not an exhaustive list by any means, because every industry or organization might need to collect its own unique types of requirements.

Key Tools and Techniques of Collect Requirements

Depending on the industry, size, and nature of the project, there are many different ways of collecting requirements. The different types of requirements also determine which method to use to collect those requirements. The following are some of the more common requirements elicitation techniques that are asked about in the PMP exam.

■ **Expert Judgment:** You use your own knowledge and experience and the knowledge and experience of other team members and subject matter experts to plan your scope planning process.

■ **Brainstorming:** This technique is used to generate as many ideas as possible.

■ **Interviews:** In this technique, stakeholders are asked what they want or what they need out of this project. This may be a formal or informal process.

■ **Focus Groups:** This technique brings together predetermined stakeholders or subject matter experts to get their opinions and ideas.

■ **Questionnaires and Surveys:** Usually, this approach is used if there are a large number of stakeholders to get requirements from or if you need some initial high-level requirements before digging deeper into those requirements.

■ **Benchmarking:** The technique involves comparing against a standard (personal, organization, industry, or government).

■ **Document Analysis:** Using this technique, you might refer to historical project files to see what requirements were involved on a prior, similar project. Or you might need to refer to government regulations to determine compliance requirements for the product or project. For example, if you are building a house, you need to know the building codes and regulations for the municipality.

■ **Voting:** If there are multiple alternatives (such as two possible designs of a website), you may vote on it. There are three types of voting methods:

  ■ **Unanimity:** Everyone agrees to one option over the other (unanimous decision).

  ■ **Majority:** The option with at least 51 percent of the vote is chosen.

  ■ **Plurality:** The option with the largest percent of vote or largest voting block is chosen (you might not get a 51 percent majority, especially if there are more than two options).

These are also known as group decision-making techniques.

■ **Autocratic Decision-Making:** In this technique, one person makes a decision for the whole group. Note, however, that in some cases this could also be considered a type of group decision-making; for example, if the team has previously decided that if they cannot reach a consensus, the person appointed will decide for them.

- **Multicriteria Decision Analysis:** There could be many factors and criteria that could impact a decision, so all of them need to be considered and evaluated.

- **Affinity Diagram:** This technique provides a way to group similar ideas together.

- **Mind Mapping:** This technique involves a type of flow chart used to generate ideas from diverse groups of stakeholders.

- **Nominal Group Technique:** This technique is a continuation of brainstorming, where the ideas generated are discussed, voted, and ranked.

- **Observation/Conversation:** Sometimes you need to observe the process to start collecting requirements (for example, on a process improvement project, you need to observe the current process before you can identify gaps and inefficiencies to improve upon).

- **Facilitation:** As a project manager, you will facilitate workshops, meetings, interviews, focus groups, and so on, to elicit requirements.

- **Context Diagram:** This is a type of flow chart showing how the system and processes interact with people.

- **Prototypes:** This technique employs a standard working model or a mockup and a way of beginning to collect requirements or getting early feedback from customers. For example, a small company wishing to develop a company website might need to see some templates or generic websites to determine which design it prefers, and this can be a starting point for collecting requirements of the website.

Key Artifacts of Collect Requirements

The sections that follow describe the two key artifacts that document requirements.

Requirements Documentation

The *requirements documentation* includes all the various requirements for the project and defines what is needed from the project and the product. Per PMI, "the requirements documentation describes how the individual requirements meet the business need for the project."

By documenting requirements, stakeholders are agreeing to a product or service that is to be delivered. A well-documented requirement must meet the following criteria:

- **Clear:** It must be free from misinterpretation.

- **Concise:** It must be written in its simplest form for stakeholders to understand.

- **Verifiable:** You must be able to easily verify that the requirement is being met.

- **Consistent:** There are no contradictory statements between requirements.

- **Complete:** It must represent the full set of needs for the project or iteration.

- **Traceable:** You can trace the requirements across the project life cycle.

As mentioned previously, there are many types of requirements, and each has its own requirements documentation.

Requirements Traceability Matrix

The requirements traceability matrix is a grid that traces activities back to the product requirements, and the product requirements back to the business need. It is used to track requirements throughout the project life cycle. It might expose scope creep and gold-plating and ensures that requirements are not missed and that the business value is being delivered.

Scope Definition

Define Scope is the process of setting the boundaries of the project. It describes the functions and features that will be included in the deliverable and what will not. After the project team has collected the appropriate requirements, they can proceed to creating the scope statement, which describes the work that will be performed and the work that will not and develops a detailed description of the project and product.

Key Tools and Techniques of Define Scope: Product Analysis

The team will analyze the product to determine what is to be delivered and how. This product analysis generally refers to asking questions about a product or service and forming answers to describe the use, characteristics, and other aspects of the deliverable. Common examples of product analysis are as follows:

- Product Breakdown
- Systems Analysis

- Systems Engineering
- Value Analysis
- Value Engineering

Key Artifact of Define Scope: Scope Statement

The *scope statement* is a detailed description of the product scope and project scope; it includes major deliverables, assumptions, constraints, and requirements. It also describes the deliverables in detail and provides a common understanding of the scope among stakeholders. The detailed plans and work breakdown structure are developed from the scope statement.

The details of the scope statement differ depending on the project, industry, and organization but generally include the following:

- Project Objective
- Scope Description
- Deliverables
- Requirements
- Assumptions
- Constraints
- Acceptance Criteria
- Exclusions

The Work Breakdown Structure (WBS)

The *work breakdown structure*, or WBS, is a graphical hierarchy that shows all the work that needs to be accomplished on the project. It is a hierarchical decomposition of the total scope to be carried out by the project team to accomplish the objectives. It does not contain the actual activities but does include the work package that groups activities together.

The advantages of using a work breakdown structure are as follow:

- Is easy to understand
- Serves as a communication tool among stakeholders
- Allows team members to understand how their work fits in to the overall project

- Promotes team buy-in

- Becomes the foundation for planning

Figure 6-2 shows a simple work breakdown structure.

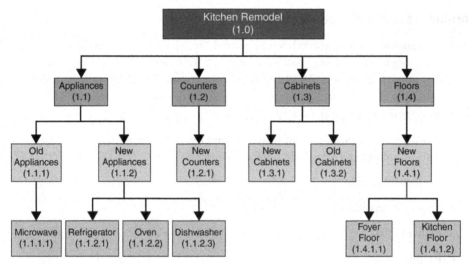

Figure 6-2 A Work Breakdown Structure

In this example, the project is a simple kitchen remodeling project, and the WBS here captures all the work that needs to be performed. In this case, you need appliances, countertops, cabinets, and flooring. You can keep one old appliance (the microwave), but you need to purchase other new appliances (refrigerator, oven, and dishwasher).

This WBS captures all the work that needs to be performed on the project so that no work is missed. Notice that there are no activities in the WBS. Activities are shown in the activity list, which is discussed in Chapter 7, "Project Schedule."

The WBS is the foundation for planning and extensively used in predictive projects. Using the WBS, you can create the activities, schedule, and budget and use it for earned value calculations.

You need to understand a few important components of the WBS:

- ***Work Package:*** This is the lowest level of the WBS, often referred to as deliverables, and which will eventually be broken down into activities. Costs and duration can be managed at this level.

- *Control Account:* This is a level above the work package and represents a management point where scope, budget, and schedule are compared to earned value for project performance evaluation. This is the level where you perform calculations and comparisons to determine the health of the project.

- **Code of Accounts:** This is the unique numbering system used to identify each component of the WBS and shows how each WBS item flows up and down the WBS. Any combination of alphanumeric characters can be used, and this is especially important when the WBS spans multiple pages.

- **Planning Package:** The best way to think of the planning package is as a "placeholder." It has been determined that there is some work to do, but you do not have any details yet. It is generally below the control account, with known work content but without any known detailed activities.

Figure 6-3 summarizes how the preceding components relate to the WBS.

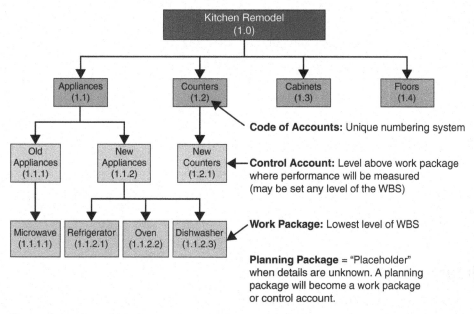

Figure 6-3 Components of the Work Breakdown Structure

Key Tool and Technique for Creating WBS: Decomposition

Decomposition is the method used to divide the project scope and the deliverables into smaller manageable parts to create the WBS. The level of decomposition is determined by the project manager and is based in the size and nature of the project, the industry, exact parameters, or any other factor.

Key Artifact of Creating the WBS: The Scope Baseline

Remember from the previous section that any baseline is the approved version of the plan. So, it is fitting that the *scope baseline* is the approved version of the scope. The scope baseline is made up of three components:

- **Scope Statement:** The detailed description of the product scope and project scope

- **WBS:** The hierarchical decomposition of the total scope

- **WBS Dictionary:** A document that supports the WBS and contains all the details regarding the WBS, such as

    - Description of the work

    - Assumptions and constraints

    - Schedule estimates and milestones

    - Cost estimates

    - Responsible team or organization

    - Acceptance criteria

    - Resources required (both physical and team resources)

EXAM TIP! Make sure you know the three components of the scope baseline for the exam. You can get direct questions asking about it.

Validate Scope

Validate Scope is the process of formalizing the acceptance of the deliverable.

Question: Who accepts the deliverable?

Answer: The customer!

The Validate Scope process is the responsibility of the project manager to gain the acceptance of the deliverable from the customer before the phase, deliverable, or project is closed. The customer (not the team or project manager) determines whether the product, service, or deliverable meets the acceptance criteria.

For the customer to accept the deliverable, they first need to inspect or test the deliverable. Some industries may refer to this as "acceptance testing" or "user acceptance testing," where the customer performs multiple tests to determine the feasibility of the deliverable. As a much simpler example, if you have hired contractors to remodel your home, you, as a customer, are constantly reviewing their work to determine progress and whether they are performing the work they were hired to do. You are validating scope.

Before the customer can perform acceptance testing, your project team should have tested the product first to ensure it meets the customer's requirements before handing it over to the customer for their inspection. The team's testing is quality control (which refers to the Control Quality section covered in Chapter 11, "Project Quality"). However, the ultimate acceptance comes from the customer.

The Validate Scope process is performed throughout the project whenever the customer needs to sign off on a deliverable before the project moves to the next stage or phase. During planning, the project manager and the project management team determine the frequency and timings of such acceptance and sign-off.

If there are disputes relating to the deliverable, they must be resolved, and disputes may need to go through the Change Control process.

In agile, the equivalent of the Validate Scope process occurs during the sprint review meeting where the agile team demos the deliverable to the product owner (customer), and the product owner approves or rejects the user stories.

Control Scope

Control Scope is purely the responsibility of the project manager, who monitors the status of the project scope and product scope and ensures changes are properly controlled. In short, the way to control the scope of the project is to perform Integrated Change Control throughout the project. If any changes impact the product scope or project scope (or any of the baselines), you must go through the Change Control process to prevent unnecessary changes to the project.

If changes are not properly controlled, the end result can lead to scope creep and gold-plating, so the benefit of the Control Scope process is to maintain the scope baseline throughout the project life cycle.

The project manager needs to ensure that the team is delivering what the customer wants, what the customer needs, and that the deliverables are meeting the requirements.

A large percentage of misunderstanding and project failures have their origins in the requirements gathering and requirements management processes. The frustrating thing about these situations is that most of these issues can or could be avoided. You, as a project manager, need to consider and contemplate the following common problems regarding requirements as you are monitoring the progress of your project:

- **Requirements Are Not Well Written:** The requirements are ambiguous, inconsistent, and too high level.

- **Requirements Are Incomplete:** If they are incomplete, you cannot properly define the solution.

- **Unstated Expectations:** The list of requirements does not accurately reflect all the expectations held by the stakeholders for the targeted solution.

- **Inflexible Process:** Although specifications do need to be agreed on and finalized at certain points, defining requirements is an evolutionary process, and things do change. The system for managing requirements must anticipate this reality, which is one of the strong aspects of using an agile approach.

- **Inadequate Definition Process:** This is the age-old problem with language. Using statements to describe a targeted solution creates many opportunities for misunderstandings and misperceptions. In most cases, you need to employ other techniques and methods to verify that you are defining the right solution. Techniques that help stakeholders visualize the final work product or solution are especially helpful.

- **Lack of Education:** Often, the stakeholders who are defining the solution requirements don't fully understand the entire requirements process and the significance or impact of their decisions.

- **Ineffective Review Process:** Some examples of an ineffective review process include using a process that is not a good match for the reviewers' natural working method or schedule, using a process that does not ensure reviewers are engaged, or using a process that does not make it easy to see what changed from the previous version.

- **Using the Wrong Tool for the Job:** In addition to the challenges with leveraging the right techniques and methods to elicit requirements, the wrong tool is used to capture, store, and manage the documented requirements.

Agile Considerations for Scope Management

Scope management in an agile/adaptive environment is handled very differently to traditional/predictive projects. For PMP purposes, an agile project is known as a release that is typically six to nine months long (however, predictive and hybrid projects may have releases too). Each agile release contains several sprints that are typically one to four weeks in length. During planning for the release (Release Planning), the agile team, the product owner, and the team facilitator work with the customer to collect requirements for the release. These requirements are collected and broken down from epics, to features, and eventually into *user stories*, which are then prioritized by the product owner to create the product backlog. During each sprint, the agile team selects some higher-priority user stories that are then implemented during the sprint. The team decides how many user stories and which stories to implement in a given sprint. Toward the end of the sprint, the agile team delivers or demonstrates the functionality to the product owner. This demonstration is performed at the sprint review ceremony, where the product owner will approve or reject the deliverable. The approved deliverables are then considered a "potentially shippable product," which can move into production. The team hosts a sprint retrospective ceremony after the sprint review to discuss lessons learned, and this meeting also serves as a sprint closeout meeting. The sprint review ceremony is the equivalent of the Validate Scope process because the customer (in this case, the product owner who represents the customer) will approve or reject the deliverable.

During the sprint, if a new requirement (or user story) is identified, it is placed into the product backlog, and all backlog items are reprioritized. If any user stories get rejected from the product owner, they too get placed back into the product backlog and are reprioritized for a future sprint. Any planned user stories that do not get implemented during the sprint are also moved back into the product backlog and reprioritized for a future sprint. Note that these user stories are not automatically moved into the next sprint; they are first placed into the product backlog, along with any new user stories that have been identified and then reprioritized. If those user stories are still high priority, they are moved into the next sprint; otherwise, they are moved into another future sprint.

Reprioritization of the product backlog is often referred to as backlog grooming.

Table 6-2 highlights a few major differences between traditional predictive projects and agile/adaptive projects.

Table 6-2 Traditional Predictive Projects vs. Agile/Adaptive Projects

	Traditional Project	**Agile/Adaptive Project**
Requirements	All requirements must be collected and approved at the beginning of the project, and all requirements need to be delivered at the end of the project.	Requirements are prioritized, and only high-priority requirements (user stories) are delivered during any sprint.
Customer Value	The team delivers the product once, at the end of the project after all the work is complete and all requirements have been met. The customer does not receive value until the end of the project.	Because the user stories are prioritized, the customer receives value regularly and constantly throughout the project, based on the length of the sprint.
Project Changes	Any changes must be constrained as much as possible and must go through a proper change control process for approval before any changes are made.	Through constant feedback loops, as the business environment changes (whether internal or external), agile projects allow for changes to the project requirements. If a new user story is high priority, another user story must be lower priority. Only high-priority items are delivered in a sprint.
Work Completion	Any work that is incomplete or not functioning correctly by the end of a deliverable must be fixed before it is delivered, which often means the project ends up falling behind schedule.	You do not extend a sprint. Any work that has been rejected by the product owner or any work that was incomplete by the team is simply placed into the product backlog and reprioritized for a future sprint, even if the work is 95 percent complete. However, the work is not "backed out" in any way. The team takes this into consideration when planning subsequent sprints.

A hybrid project might use a mix of predictive and agile approaches, so the principles of both agile and predictive would apply.

Product Backlog

The *product backlog* is a prioritized list of user stories used to deliver the product and is derived from the roadmap. The product backlog represents the entire scope of the agile project (or release), but this can change as the project progresses. As new user stories are identified and as the business environment changes, priorities can change, and consequently, the product backlog is modified.

User stories are prioritized by the product owner, so it is the product owner's responsibility to create the product backlog. The product owner works with the agile team to determine these priorities.

For example, if Story B is dependent on Story A, then Story A must be completed first before you can start implementing Story B. Therefore, Story A is a higher priority than Story B. The product owner may not always know these dependencies and relationships, but the agile team is able to determine them. So, the product owner works with the team to determine these priorities and dependencies of user stories. The product backlog is ultimately the product owner's responsibility and accountability.

User stories are constantly reprioritized and the backlog updated throughout the project based on factors such as

- New requests
- New discoveries
- Rejected user stories
- Incomplete user stories
- Defects from prior sprints
- Changes in internal and external environment

These are just a few factors among many that may require reprioritization of the backlog. This is also known as *backlog grooming*.

User Story

A user story represents a requirement and is generally written in an informal way to explain functionality from a user's perspective. User stories will be written using the following template:

"As a *<Role>*, I want *<Functionality>*, so that *<Business benefit>*."

- **Role:** Describes who will perform this functionality (the end user)
- **Functionality:** Describes what the user is trying to accomplish
- **Business Benefit:** Describes why the user is trying to perform this function

For example, the following is a simple user story:

As a call center analyst, I want to search clients by first and last name so I can look up their records quicker.

In this case:

The *Role* is the "call center analyst."

The *Functionality* is "search clients by first and last name."

The *Business benefit* is "look up their records quicker."

User stories must always be written in this way. You should be able to write a user story on a simple flash card, so you can think of the product backlog as being a series of prioritized electronic flash cards, each containing a requirement.

The purpose of going down to this granular level is simple: It is to alleviate any misunderstanding. Remember Figure 6-1 showing the misinterpretation of requirements? When requirements are large and vague, they are naturally open to misinterpretation. When a requirement can be progressively elaborated down to one sentence that contains the role, function, and benefit, there is no question of what is to be implemented, and there is much less chance of being open to misinterpretation.

So now let's discuss how the team breaks down a user story to this kind of granular level.

Of course, even on an adaptive project, you will collect high-level user stories that need to be progressively elaborated and broken down into smaller user stories. The hierarchical decomposition in agile is as follows:

Epics > Features > User Stories > Tasks

In its simplest form, a very high-level agile requirement is known as an epic. This is broken down into features, which eventually will be broken down into individual tasks or activities.

An epic is essentially a large body of work that can be delivered across multiple sprints, whereas a feature contains functional components that group functionality together.

A large user story must always be broken down into smaller user stories. How does a team know whether a user story is a "good" user story? It must meet certain criteria that is summarized by the INVEST acronym:

- **I**ndependent: The user story is not dependent on other user stories and can be worked on independently by the team, and therefore can be prioritized.

- **N**egotiable: It is not a contract, but more of a conversation, that captures the essence of what is needed.

- **V**aluable: It must provide business value to the customer.

- **E**stimable: You are able to estimate the user story in terms of approximate size and level of effort, which can be used for prioritization.

- **S**ize (small): It is small enough to break into tasks to meet the definition of done.

- **T**estable: It is small enough to test to ensure it meets the definition of done.

When the user story meets the preceding criteria, the team members know they have a good user story. If just one of the criteria is not met, it is not considered a good user story, so the team will work to meet that criterion by generally splitting the user story into smaller user stories until all criteria are met.

For the exam, you should know a couple of other important terms:

- **Definition of Done:** These are the criteria used to determine if the work is complete. Early on in an agile project, the agile team, product owner, and team facilitator will work together to determine the definition of done. These are the acceptance criteria that the product owner uses during the sprint review ceremony to accept or reject a deliverable. If the user story meets the definition of done, the product owner accepts it. If it does not, the product owner rejects that user story. Thus, for PMP exam purposes, even if the user story is 99 percent complete, if it does not meet the definition of done, it is rejected. In agile, the work is either complete, or it is not complete (unlike a traditional predictive project where it is perfectly acceptable to state a deliverable is 90 percent complete and then give an estimate of when it will be complete).

- **Definition of Ready:** This is the team's checklist for a user-centric requirement that has all the information the team needs to be able to begin working on it. The user stories must be immediately actionable, and the team must be ready to perform the work. The definition of ready must be met before the work can start on a user story in a sprint.

Agile Prioritization Techniques

As mentioned several times throughout this book, user stories are prioritized in agile. Many methods can be used to prioritize user stories, but the four commonly asked about on the PMP exam are as follows:

- **MoSCoW Analysis:** MoSCoW stands for

  - **Must Have:** These are the showstopper features that, if absent, would render the product unusable. These features are non-negotiable and must be delivered; otherwise, the product is not considered functional.

  - **Should Have:** These features are needed and add value, but the product could still be functional without them. You can go into production without these features if needed, but they would still need to be delivered later.

  - **Could Have:** These are the "nice to have" features but not necessarily needed by the customer. The customer might do a cost-benefit analysis on these items to determine whether they are worth adding.

  - **Won't Have:** These features are not needed and provide no value.

- **Kano Model:** This prioritization model is based on four categories of customer preferences:

  - **Dissatisfiers:** These features, if not present, would dissatisfy the customer. Similar to the "must have" in MoSCoW, these are non-negotiable features.

  - **Satisfiers:** These features bring value to the customer and are features that the customer expects.

  - **Exciters:** These features bring high value to the customer, and the customer is very happy with them.

  - **Indifferent:** These features have no impact to the customer, and the customer does not care whether the feature is there. They are less likely to use the feature even if present.

- **100-Point Method:** Each team member is given 100 points to spread across a certain number of user stories. The team member assigns more points to the higher-priority user stories. The user stories then can be prioritized based on the total number of points assigned by the team.

- **Paired Comparison Analysis:** This technique is used to compare multiple factors at a time. It compares successive pairs and prioritizes one over another. The following is a simple example of a Paired Comparison analysis.

Let's say you are trying to determine the main motivators for your employees and have identified nine factors that could be considered motivators. Figure 6-4 shows these nine factors down the side and across the top. Each successive pair is compared against one another, and then a "count and rank" is performed, shown at the bottom.

In this example, the team has determined that appreciation is their biggest motivator, followed by financial benefits, followed by work conditions.

	A	B	C	D	E	F	G	H	I
A: Appreciation		A	A	A	A	A	A	A	A
B: Achievement			C	B	B	B	G	B	B
C: Work condition				C	C	C	G	C	C
D: Power					D	D	G	D	I
E: Creativity						F	G	E	I
F: Interest							G	F	I
G: Financial benefits								G	G
H: Relationship									I
I: Self development									
Count	8	5	6	3	1	2	7	0	4
Rank	1	4	3	6	8	7	2	9	5

Figure 6-4 A Paired Comparison

Agile Consensus-Gathering Techniques

Because the agile team determines the work for each sprint, members must agree to the work and need to come to a consensus throughout the project. If they cannot reach a consensus regarding the priority of work, the relative estimates of size of the work, the assignment of the work, or the level of effort of the work, these would be major impediments for the team.

Agile teams use many consensus-gathering techniques, but the following four are most commonly asked about on the PMP exam:

- **Fist of Five**
  - Each team member raises their hand.
  - Team members who raise all five fingers are in complete agreement.
  - Team members who raise no fingers (raise their fist) are in complete disagreement.
  - There are various levels of agreement and disagreement based on how many fingers a team member has raised.

- **Roman Voting**

  - This is a simple thumbs up or thumbs down.

  - Thumbs up means they agree.

  - Thumbs down mean they disagree.

- **Polling**

  - Team members discuss and share their point of view.

  - A vote is made, and if unanimous, the team moves on to the next topic of discussion.

  - If objections are raised, further discussions are made on this topic, and subsequent votes are made until a consensus is reached.

- **Dot Voting**

  - Each team member is given a certain number of sticky dots, which they use to prioritize user stories.

  - The greater number of dots a user story has means higher priority.

  - These dots could be prioritized based on a color-coding classification instead of based on the number of dots.

Agile Estimation Techniques

Agile teams do not estimate the work based on timeline and budget like on predictive projects. Instead, they use the concept of relative estimating to determine the level of effort to implement a user story compared to one another. A base point is determined, and subsequent user stories are compared against this base point.

The three agile estimation techniques commonly asked about on the PMP exam are as follows:

- T-shirt Sizing

- Story Pointing

- Planning Poker

The sections that follow describe each technique in more detail.

T-shirt Sizing

Team members use the common knowledge of sizes of T-shirts, such as Extra Small, Small, Medium, Large, Extra Large (XS, S, M, L, XL). A base point is established, and user stories are compared to this base point to determine the relative size of user stories based on this classification.

Story Pointing

The story pointing technique relies on the Fibonacci numbering sequence to assign work estimates for a user story.

In a Fibonacci sequence, the next number in the sequence is the sum of the previous two numbers. Thus:

1, 2, 3, 5, 8, 13, 21 …

The team uses this set of numbers to determine the relative estimate of user stories and show the true magnitude of the relative size of user stories compared to another.

You do not always have to use a strict Fibonacci sequence; a modified sequence of numbers would suffice also. The team decides.

Consider the following example of story pointing:

Using the following Fibonacci sequence of numbers, provide your relative estimate for the size of each of these animals:

Use the Fibonacci sequence: 1, 2, 3, 5, 8, 13, 21, 34, 55

Table 6-3 provides the story pointing example.

Table 6-3   Story Pointing Example

Animal	Story Points
Golden Retriever	
Camel	
Elephant	
Zebra	
Rat	

Table 6-4 provides the answer to the story pointing example.

Table 6-4 Story Pointing Example: Answer

Animal	Story Points
Golden Retriever	5
Camel	21
Elephant	55
Zebra	13
Rat	2

In this example, we are not physically taking a tape measure and measuring the sizes of these animals. Based on our knowledge of these animals, these are the relative estimates we have come up with. The elephant is by far the biggest animal here, so we assign it the highest value in our sequence (55). The Golden Retriever is a much smaller animal than an elephant, so we have assigned it a 5 to show how much smaller this dog is compared to an elephant.

There is no right or wrong answer to the preceding question. This is based on one team member's opinion. Another team member might have a slightly different opinion, in which case team members will discuss and eventually reach a consensus.

Likewise, this approach would be performed for user stories in a release and sprint.

Planning Poker

The Planning Poker method also uses a Fibonacci sequence, or modified Fibonacci sequence, and uses the same principles as story pointing. This time, though, each team member is given a deck of cards representing a Fibonacci sequence (or modified Fibonacci sequence).

1. The team members discuss the user story with the product owner and team facilitator.

2. Each team member does a relative estimate of the size of the story.

3. Each team member lays down a card to indicate their relative estimate of the size of the story.

4. Team members with the highest and lowest values explain their evaluations.

5. Successive rounds are played until the relative ratings converge to the same value.

Because user stories vary by size and relative level of effort, the team determines how many story points they will implement in a sprint rather than the number of user stories.

Exam Preparation Tasks

As mentioned in the section "How to Use This Book" in the Introduction, you have a couple of choices for exam preparation: the exercises here, Chapter 18, "Final Preparation," and the exam simulation questions on the Pearson Test Prep practice test software.

Review All Key Topics

Review the most important topics in this chapter, noted with the Key Topic icon in the outer margin of the page. Table 6-5 lists a reference of these key topics and the page numbers on which each is found.

Table 6-5   Key Topics for Chapter 6

Key Topic Element	Description	Page Number
List	Scope Creep and Gold Plating	182
Exam Tip	The terms *uncontrolled*, *unapproved*, or *undocumented*	184
Section	Scope Management Plan	185
Section	Requirements Management Plan	185
List	Components of the WBS	192
Section	Key Artifact of Creating the WBS: The Scope Baseline	194
Exam Tip	Scope baseline	194
Section	Validate Scope	194
Section	Agile Considerations for Scope Management	197
Section	User Story	199
Section	Agile Prioritization Techniques	201
Section	Agile Consensus-Gathering Techniques	203
Section	Agile Estimations Techniques	204

Define Key Terms

Define the following key terms from this chapter and check your answers in the glossary:

scope creep, gold-plating, requirements documentation, scope statement, work breakdown structure, work package, control account, decomposition, scope baseline, Validate Scope, user story, product backlog

Review Questions

1. You are managing a project to create a new online shopping portal for your client, who has an international reach. Your team lead, Michael, realizes that the checkout page could be improved by the addition of a currency conversion function. Adding this function requires minimum effort, so he decides to add this in. What mistake did Michael make?

   a. This is considered scope creep and should have gone through the change control process before implementing.

   b. There is no mistake. Because this is minimum effort, it is okay to add in this functionality.

   c. This is gold-plating and should have gone through the change control process.

   d. Michael should have discussed this with the team first.

2. You have been notified that a new senior director has joined your organization, and this director's division will be impacted by your project. You update the stakeholder register and then reach out to the new senior director, who tells you that there are new processes for collecting requirements from the managers of this division. What should you do next?

   a. Reach out to the managers to introduce yourself.

   b. Invite the managers to a requirements gathering meeting.

   c. Update the stakeholder register and add in the new managers.

   d. Update the requirements management plan.

3. You have been reassigned to manage a project after the original PM suddenly quit. As you begin to familiarize yourself with the project, you notice that some of the functionality implemented was not part of the original project scope, and you don't understand which requirements these activities relate to. How could the original project manager have avoided this situation?

   a. The original PM should have done a better job of documenting requirements in more detail.

   b. The original PM should have created a requirements traceability matrix.

   c. The original PM should have created a more detailed WBS.

   d. The original PM should have developed a change control process.

4. To bring a new senior stakeholder up to speed on your project, which of the following would be the most informative document for them to review?

    a. Business case

    b. Work breakdown structure

    c. Scope management plan

    d. Scope statement

5. Which of the following are not part of the scope baseline? (Choose two.)

    a. Tasks

    b. WBS

    c. Requirements

    d. WBS dictionary

    e. Scope statement

    f. Work package

6. You are the PM on a project developing a new model of smart doorbells. The doorbell will record short video clips of activity and send alerts to the user's phone app. It will also have a function to recognize faces and automatically unlock the door for "approved" people. The project has been progressing well, and you are now in the testing phase but have already encountered some issues with the facial recognition feature of the doorbell. Your customer contact is observing some of those tests and performing some light testing themselves but is not providing any feedback or comments to the team because they know that testing is not complete. The team lead has informed you that the root cause of the problem been discovered and will take an additional 15 hours to fix. Which of the following is true?

    a. The customer is validating scope.

    b. The next step you should take is to perform an impact analysis.

    c. The team is validating scope.

    d. The customer is performing quality control.

7. You are the project manager of a systems implementation project. Your team has started testing a deliverable with the customer observing the process. The testing has uncovered many defects that are all being duly noted and submitted back to the appropriate technical team members to fix. Some of these

fixes have an impact on the project, so you are performing an impact analysis and submitting the request to the CCB. Which of the following statements is correct?

   a. The PM is performing quality control, the team is performing validate scope, and the customer is observing.

   b. The PM is performing validate scope, the team is performing quality control, and the customer is performing quality assurance.

   c. The PM is performing change control, the team is performing quality assurance, and the customer is performing quality control.

   d. The PM is controlling the scope, the team is performing quality control, and the customer is performing validate scope.

8. You are an agile coach attending a meeting at the beginning of a release, and you observe that the meeting has been quite productive. The team and the product owner collaborated to determine the priority of user stories to develop the product backlog, and now the team facilitator is determining the definition of done that should be used for rest of the project. What comment would you give to the attendees of this meeting?

   a. Commend the team, team facilitator, and the product owner for such a productive meeting.

   b. Advise the team and the team facilitator that they should work with the product owner to determine the definition of done.

   c. Advise the attendees that the definition of done should be determined by the product owner.

   d. Advise the team it is too early to determine the definition of done. This should be performed at the beginning of each sprint

9. Which of the following agile ceremonies and predictive processes are closely related?

   a. Iteration Retrospective and Control Scope

   b. Release Planning and Define Scope

   c. Iteration Review and Validate Scope

   d. Sprint Review and Close Project or Phase

10. You are the team facilitator of an inexperienced but motivated agile team. The team is asking about the methods they should use to prioritize their user stories and tasks. What should you tell them? (Choose two.)

    a. They should use T-shirt sizing to prioritize larger to smaller user stories.

    b. They should use Paired Comparison to prioritize various factors at a time.

    c. They should use Planning Poker, which uses a Fibonacci sequence to prioritize user stories.

    d. They should use the 100-Point Method, which distributes 100 points across the user stories.

    e. They should use the Roman Voting method to prioritize the user stories.

This chapter covers the following topics in schedule management:

- **Plan Schedule Management:** Review the process for planning the schedule and developing the project management plan.

- **Define Activities:** Continue the discussion of the work breakdown structure by decomposing work packages into activities.

- **Sequence Activities:** Learn the precedence diagramming method of determining the proper order of project activities.

- **Estimate Durations:** Review the tools for determining duration activities and work packages.

- **Develop and Control the Schedule:** Learn the common processes, tools, and artifacts for developing, maintaining, and controlling the schedule.

- **Schedule Management Considerations for Agile:** Review the adaptive approach to schedule management.

## CHAPTER 7

Project Schedule

Schedule management is often referred to as time management and includes the processes, tools, and artifacts needed for timely and successful completion of the project. A project schedule documents what work should be performed, when it should be performed, and when it should be completed. It is vital for the project manager to first plan the schedule correctly and develop a sound project schedule that meets the SMART (Specific, Measurable, Achievable, Realistic, Time-bound) determination. Just as important is to manage the schedule and ensure deadlines are being met and the project does not go behind schedule. Many internal and external factors can impact the management of the schedule, and the project manager must manage and control them.

This chapter discusses the processes, tools, and artifacts for schedule management from both the traditional style of project management and agile. We discuss the traditional style first and then talk about the adaptive approach toward the end of the chapter.

This chapter addresses the following objectives from the PMP Exam Content Outline:

Domain	Task #	Exam Objective
People	Task 2	Lead a team
People	Task 3	Support team performance
People	Task 10	Build a shared understanding
Process	Task 1	Execute project with the urgency required to deliver business value
Process	Task 3	Assess and manage risks
Process	Task 6	Plan and manage schedule
Process	Task 9	Integrate project planning activities
Process	Task 13	Determine appropriate project methodology/methods and practices
Business	Task 2	Evaluate and deliver project benefits and value

"Do I Know This Already?" Quiz

The "Do I Know This Already?" quiz allows you to assess whether you should read this entire chapter thoroughly or jump to the "Exam Preparation Tasks" section. If you are in doubt about your answers to these questions or your own assessment of your knowledge of the topics, read the entire chapter. Table 7-1 lists the major headings in this chapter and their corresponding "Do I Know This Already?" quiz questions. You can find the answers in Appendix A, "Answers to the 'Do I Know This Already?' Quizzes and Review Questions."

Table 7-1   "Do I Know This Already?" Section-to-Question Mapping

Foundation Topics Section	Questions
Plan Schedule Management	1
Defining Activities	2
Sequencing Activities	3–4
Estimate Durations	5–6
Developing and Controlling the Schedule	7–8
Schedule Management Considerations for Agile	9–10

CAUTION   The goal of self-assessment is to gauge your mastery of the topics in this chapter. If you do not know the answer to a question or are only partially sure of the answer, you should mark that question as wrong for purposes of the self-assessment. Giving yourself credit for an answer you correctly guess skews your self-assessment results and might provide you with a false sense of security.

1. You have been told to use the critical path method using the zero-method rule with a tolerance limit of +/– 10 percent. Where would you document this?

    a. Schedule baseline

    b. Project schedule

    c. Work performance information

    d. Schedule management plan

2. Which of the following would be considered activities as opposed to a work package? (Choose two.)

    a. Order windows

    b. Master bedroom

    c. Electrical rewiring

    d. Check vendor references

    e. Plumbing work

3. You are managing a project to install a large machine in a manufacturing plant. You cannot start testing the machine until the machine is fully installed and configured correctly. What dependency does this describe?

    a. Discretionary

    b. Start to finish

    c. Mandatory

    d. External

4. You need to clear a parking lot covered in snow and decide one person should start clearing the snow before the other person starts putting down rock salt. What relationship does this best describe?

    a. Start to start

    b. Finish to start

    c. Start to finish

    d. Finish to finish

5. You need to develop a new website for a large customer that is in the business of selling many types of household products. You know that your organization did a similar project for a similar organization and that website took six months to develop. You therefore estimate that this project will take about six months as well. Which estimating tool do you use?

    a. T-shirt sizing

    b. Parametric estimating

    c. Analogous estimating

    d. Relative estimating

6. You have an expected activity duration of 26 days, optimistic value of 18 days, and pessimistic value of 67 days. Calculate the PERT.

    a. 26 days

    b. 31.5 days

    c. 8.2 days

    d. 37 days

7. Your project is running behind schedule, but you have plenty of float on some activities. You decide to move resources from noncritical path activities to critical path activities. What are you performing?

   a. Crashing

   b. Resource leveling

   c. Fast-tracking

   d. Resource smoothing

8. Your customer has approached you and told you that you now need to finish the project two weeks earlier than anticipated. What does this mean in terms of the critical path?

   a. You have a negative float of two weeks.

   b. You have a project float of two weeks.

   c. Your project will be delayed by two weeks.

   d. You have a positive float of two weeks.

9. Which of the following scheduling tools would you use on an agile project? (Choose two.)

   a. Three-point estimating

   b. On-demand scheduling

   c. Iterative schedule with a backlog

   d. Critical path method

   e. Bottom-up estimating

10. Your team is using an adaptive methodology and planning the current release. Which of the following would be the most relevant here?

    a. Gantt chart

    b. Product roadmap

    c. Critical path method

    d. Three-point estimating

Foundation Topics

The Schedule Management knowledge area addresses the planning and managing of processes, tools, and artifacts to complete the project deliverables on time. It provides a detailed plan to show when the product will be delivered throughout the project life cycle.

The *PMBOK® Guide*, Sixth Edition, processes related to schedule management are as follows:

- Plan Schedule Management
- Define Activities
- Sequence Activities
- Estimate Activity Duration
- Develop Schedule
- Control Schedule

The *PMBOK® Guide*, Seventh Edition, discusses the schedule as part of the Development Approach and Life Cycle Performance domain and the Planning domains.

We discuss each process in detail as it relates to the PMP exam. Because these processes mostly relate to predictive projects, we discuss the predictive approach first and then discuss the agile approach.

Plan Schedule Management

The first Schedule Management process is Plan Schedule Management, and this process refers to how you are going to plan, execute, monitor, and control the schedule. The purpose is to provide guidance and direction regarding the planning of the schedule and execution of the project activities. These procedures are documented in the schedule management plan.

Many factors will impact the schedule, which you, as a project manager, need to consider when planning the project and adjust for when executing the project. Following are some common factors:

- **Availability of Resources:** For example, you schedule plumbing work based on the availability of the plumber and machine work based on the availability of the machine and its operator.

- **Decisions on Whether to Perform the Work In-House or Use Vendors:** This is also known as make-or-buy analysis, discussed in more detail in Chapter 12, "Project Procurement." Your scheduled performance of the work may be different from a vendor's scheduled performance of the work.

- **Budget:** The budget of the project may impact the scope of the work (and hence the schedule to deliver the scope), the raw materials used, and resources utilized, which in turn may lead to changes in the schedule.

- **Risks:** Identification of risks may impact accuracy and ranges of the schedule estimate.

- **Life Cycle Utilized:** Is it a single delivery or multiple deliveries? Is there a tight deadline or a rolling deadline? Is it a predictive project or an adaptive project?

- **Employee Capabilities:** A more-experienced team may need less time than a less-experienced team.

- **Employee Availability:** As with capability, if well-experienced team members are unavailable and you have to hire less-experienced team members for the project, this decision impacts the timeline for the project.

- **External Business Environment Changes:** These can include changes to regulations and standards, supply chain issues, and geographical location.

- **Internal Environment Changes:** These can include reorganizations, organizational change management, management changes, and changes to processes and procedures.

- **Stakeholder's Request for Changes During the Project:** Requests for scope changes impact the schedule. Whether a stakeholder requests additional requirements, or a team member finds issues and design flaws during the project, these factors can all directly impact the schedule.

- **Any Constraint Identified During the Project That Might Have an Impact on the Schedule:** An impact on the schedule is itself a major constraint on the project. Constraints can include the scope, budget, resources, quality, risk, and any other factors identified during the project.

This is not an exhaustive list; these are just a few common examples of factors that impact the schedule. There are many more that depend on the industry, size, and nature of the project and the particular situation.

Key Artifact: Schedule Management Plan

The schedule management plan documents how the schedule is going to be planned, developed, and controlled. It establishes the procedures for planning, developing, and managing the schedule and documents what the team must do if you end up behind schedule or if there are changes to the schedule. It does not document the schedule itself but documents the procedures related to developing and managing the schedule.

The schedule management plan documents items such as

- The methodology and approach to developing the schedule. Many methodologies and models can be used to develop a schedule. One of the methods is the critical path method, which we discuss later in this chapter.

- Levels of accuracy, which specify the acceptable ranges for the schedule.

- Units of measure such as days, weeks, and staff hours.

- Performance measurements to determine whether you are ahead of schedule or behind schedule.

- How activities will be defined and progressively elaborated.

- The format of the schedule, as well as reporting formats.

- Criteria for developing, executing, and controlling the project schedule.

- Rules of performance measurements to be used (such as earned value).

- Control thresholds to be used for monitoring schedule performance.

- Process descriptions to explain how schedule management processes are to be documented throughout the project.

EXAM TIP!   This list represents just some examples of the type of information contained in the schedule management plan; it is not an exhaustive list. For the exam, understand that any procedures regarding the schedule are documented in the schedule management plan. Do not try to memorize a list of such items.

Define Activities

Per PMI, Define Activities is the process of identifying and documenting the specific actions to be performed to produce the project deliverables.

In scope management, you break down the project to the work package. In schedule management, you further break down work packages into individual activities. These activities provide a basis for estimating, scheduling, executing, monitoring, and controlling the work of the project. Remember, for PMP exam purposes, activities are not included in the WBS. The lowest level of the WBS is the work package.

Activities are documented in the activities list, which is a separate document to the WBS. This list normally includes verbs (actions words), whereas work packages contain nouns.

In the WBS example in Figure 7-1, the work package labeled *refrigerator* could be broken down into the activities outlined.

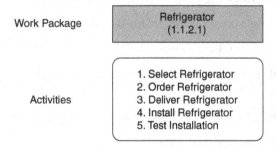

Figure 7-1   Activities versus Work Packages

Notice, the words *Select*, *Order*, *Deliver*, *Install*, and *Test* are verbs in this context (action words), indicating that they are activities, whereas *Refrigerator* is a noun, indicating it is a work package. On the exam, you may be asked to distinguish between a work package and an activity, so make sure you understand this concept.

Sequence Activities

The process of sequencing activities refers to placing **project activities** in their proper order and defining the logical sequence of the work. Activities can be dependent on other activities. Some activities can be run in parallel. Some activities must start before another can start. These dependencies and logical relationships need to be analyzed and determined by the team before a schedule can be developed.

Precedence Diagramming Method (PDM)

One method for constructing a schedule model and sequencing activities is called the **precedence diagramming method** (PDM), also known as activity on node

(AON). You need to understand the concepts of precedence relationships, activity dependencies, and leads and lags as they relate to the precedence diagramming method.

Precedence Relationships

You must be aware of four types of logical relationships for the PMP exam:

- **Finish to Start:** You must finish one activity before you can start the next activity. In Figure 7-2, Task A needs to finish before you can start Task B. You usually try to perform most tasks using this relationship; you like to finish one task before you start another.

- **Start to Start:** One activity must start before another activity can start, but both run in parallel. In Figure 7-2, Task A needs to start before you start Task B.

- **Finish to Finish:** One activity must finish before another activity can finish, but both run in parallel. In Figure 7-2, Task A needs to finish before Task B can finish.

- **Start to Finish:** One activity must start before another can finish. In Figure 7-2, Task A needs to start before you finish Task B.

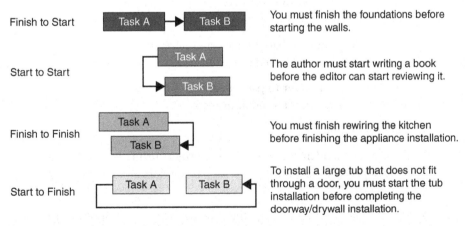

Figure 7-2 Activity Relationships

Activity Dependencies

You must be aware of four types of activity dependencies for the PMP exam:

- **Mandatory Dependency** (also known as *hard logic* or *hard dependency*)

  - Tasks must be performed in a certain way or in a certain sequence due to physical conditions, laws of science, or logic.

  - For example, when building a traditional house, you must dig the foundation before beginning the framing. You cannot decide to build the roof first and then frame the house and dig the foundation last. The work must be done in the correct order.

  - Likewise, you cannot test a system until you have built the system. If the system is not there, what are you going to test?

  - Contracts also fall under this section. If you are contractually obligated to perform a certain task or perform it in a certain sequence, that, too, would be a mandatory dependency

- **Discretionary Dependency** (also known as *soft logic* or *preferred logic*)

  - You can determine when to run tasks and when to sequence them. You can move activities around and resequence as you see fit.

  - For example, you will paint bedroom 1 first, then bedroom 2, then bedroom 3. But you can easily decide to paint bedroom 3 first if you wanted to.

  - Preferred logic means that you have a preference for the order of activities, but they can be changed if needed.

  - For example, you prefer to paint bedroom 1 first, but if you need to paint bedroom 3 first, you can do that instead.

- **External Dependency**

  - These are dependencies outside of the project team's control and generally dependent on a third party, such as vendors and government compliance.

  - For example, you cannot start the construction project until you have a signed permit.

- **Internal Dependency**

  - These are dependencies within the project team itself and within the team's control.

- For example, you need a developer to write code to customize a payroll system, but that developer is busy writing code for an employee onboarding system. You are dependent on that team member completing their current work before they can start the payroll customization. However, you might be able to move priorities around so that the developer can work on the payroll coding before finishing the employee onboarding system if you determine the payroll is higher priority.

EXAM TIP!   Be careful with internal and external dependencies. Internal dependencies refer to dependencies within the project team itself, not necessarily within the organization. So waiting on data from another department within the organization that is not part of your project team is considered an external dependency.

Dependencies may also be a mix, such as

- Mandatory Internal

- Mandatory External

- Discretionary Internal

- Discretionary External

Leads and Lags

A *lead* refers to adjusting the timelines of successor activities so they can start earlier. In Figure 7-3, if Activity B starts, say, two days before Activity A completes, you have a two-day lead.

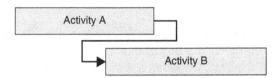

Figure 7-3   A Lead

A *lag* is an imposed delay due to the nature of the work and is always built into the schedule during planning. For example, on a construction project, when you have poured concrete into the foundation, you need to leave the concrete to cure (harden) before you can start framing. If it takes one week for the concrete to cure, during this week you cannot perform any activities, so you have a one-week lag. This lag has already been identified and built into the schedule (shown in Figure 7-4).

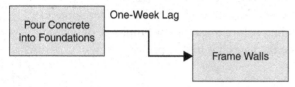

Figure 7-4   A Lag

Estimate Durations

The Estimate Durations process refers to estimating the length of activities and work packages and determining timelines, such as start and end dates of activities and work packages. The duration can be calculated using any unit of measure that makes sense for the project, industry, or organization, such as days, weeks, months, staff hours, or full-time equivalents. The project manager and the team determine the unit of measure to use early in the project and document the units of measure in the schedule management plan. Of course, these activity estimates will be progressively elaborated throughout the project.

Many factors can impact the duration estimate, including

- **Scope of the Work:** Naturally, the bigger the scope of a project, the more time is needed to complete the work.

- **Life Cycle Approach:** The level of details depends on the exact life cycle approach for the project. For example, a predictive project has a detailed plan documented on a Gantt chart, whereas an adaptive project is higher level and is documented on a product roadmap.

- **Availability of Resources:** The schedule is directly affected by the availability of both physical resources and team resources. For example, if many teams share a machine, the availability of that machine determines when you can run the activities that use that machine.

- **Skillsets of Team Members:** A new or inexperienced team may need more time to perform the work than a well-experienced team.

- **External Factors (EFs):** For example, supply-chain issues impact your schedule and affect your duration estimates for each activity.

- **Risks:** Internal and external uncertainties always affect your duration estimates, which is the reason that you usually estimate a range for the duration.

- **Intrinsic Factors:** These factors are inherent on the project, such as constraints. All constraints identified on a project can impact the duration of the project.

- **Law of Diminishing Returns:** An increase in one unit of input does not necessarily lead to an increase in one unit of output. As you are increasing your input (say, increasing the number of resources), you will reach a point that additions will yield progressively smaller increases in output. For example, doubling the number of team members does not halve the time to perform the work.

- **Advances in Technology:** New and advanced machines may require less time to perform the work than older machines.

- **Parkinson's Law:** This is also known as procrastination. This is the point at which work expands to fill the time available. So, if a team is given three weeks to perform a five-hour task, they will take three weeks to perform it! We have all had such experiences!

Some important terms that you need to understand regarding estimate durations are as follows:

- **Activity Duration Estimate:** The quantitative assessment of how long it will take to complete an activity (a plan).

  - Does not consider lags or stoppage time, but the estimated work period.

  - For example, you plan to spend two hours on day 1, three hours on day 2, and two hours on day 3 working on this activity. That means your duration estimate is seven hours.

- **Elapsed Time:** The actual calendar time required for an activity from start to finish.

  - Includes lags, weekends, holidays, and stoppage times.

  - For example, a duration estimate of three weeks + one week lag = four weeks of elapsed time.

  - From the previous example, you plan to spend two hours on day 1, three hours on day 2, and two hours on day 3 working on this activity. That means your duration estimate is seven hours, but your elapsed time is three days.

- **Effort:** The number of labor units required to complete a scheduled activity; for example, 100 hours' worth of work, or 100 person-hours.

- **Duration:** The number of work periods required to complete an activity. This includes business days.

Estimating Methods

The PMP exam commonly asks about the following four estimating methods for predictive projects (the agile estimating methods are discussed in Chapter 6, "Project Scope"). All four of these estimating techniques are relevant for both schedule management and cost management:

- **Analogous Estimating (also known as Top-Down Estimating)**

  - This technique uses a prior similar activity to make a high-level estimate for this activity and includes adjustments for any known differences.

  - For example, the last time you installed a similar server, it was 15 hours' worth of work, so the analogous estimate would be 15 hours. If you know that previously you had well-experienced analysts installing the server but this time have only new and inexperienced team members, you can make adjustments accordingly.

  - Advantage: This type of estimate is quick and easy because it relies on historical information.

  - Disadvantage: The estimate might not be very accurate.

- **Parametric Estimating**

  - This technique uses first principles, a rule of thumb, or a statistical relationship to extrapolate results.

  - For example, if it takes 1 hour to lay down 25 meters of cable, how long will it take to lay down 1000 meters of cable?

  - After doing the math, you find the answer is 40 hours.

  - Advantage: This type of estimating may be more accurate than analogous, and it is still quick and easy because you are using simple math.

  - Disadvantage: The parameters may not always scale.

    - In this example, just because the first 25 meters of cable took 1 hour, that doesn't necessarily mean that laying down 1000 meters will take a full 40 hours. Parametric estimating does not take into consideration learning curves and economies of scale.

    — Parametric estimating also includes situations such as "If it takes a team of 5 team members two weeks to complete an activity, then 10 team members will be able to perform the same work in one week." That is not the case! As we have all experienced, doubling the number of team members does not halve the time to do the work!

- **Bottom-Up Estimating**

  - In this detailed estimating technique, further analysis of each activity is performed in granular detail, and the results are aggregated through the work breakdown structure.

  - Advantage: The estimates are very accurate because this is the most accurate approach of the four estimating methods.

  - Disadvantage: Because you go to a granular level of detail, this approach is time consuming and therefore an expensive approach to estimating. This is also not possible for many types of projects. In fact, on many projects, due to uncertainties (risks), it is not possible to even get to this granular level of detail. Bottom-up is used best on well-understood projects where parameters are certain, or the uncertainties are easily identified and well understood.

- **Three-Point Estimating**

  - A three-point estimate is simply an average of three points commonly known as optimistic, pessimistic, and most likely (sometimes referred to as realistic).

  - This technique is used to estimate cost or duration by applying the three points when there is uncertainty.

  - Two types of three-point estimating incorporate a simple average and a weighted average.

  - In the next section we expand on the two types of three-point estimating.

Three-Point Estimating

Three-point estimating involves calculating an average of three points and using those points to estimate a confidence range. The three points are as follows:

- **Most Likely (M):** Based on the resources and current factors, this is how long you think the activity should take.

- **Optimistic (O):** This would be the best-case scenario of how long the activity could take.

- **Pessimistic (P):** This would be the worst-case scenario of how long the activity could take.

NOTE   Sometimes most likely (M) can be referred to as realistic (R).

The sections that follow describe the two types of three-point estimates.

Triangular Distribution

Triangular distribution is also known as simple average or a straight average, and the formulae needed for the confidence range calculation are as follows:

$$\text{Mean} = \frac{\text{Optimistic} + \text{Most Likely} + \text{Pessimistic}}{3}$$

$$\text{Standard Deviation } (\sigma) = \frac{\text{Pessimistic - Optimistic}}{3}$$

Triangular distribution is less likely to appear on the exam, so we concentrate on the other type of three-point estimating known as the PERT (or beta distribution), which uses a weighted average and is more likely to appear on the exam.

Beta Distribution (or PERT)

The program evaluation and review technique (PERT) is a weighted average of the three points (optimistic, most likely, pessimistic). It is also referred to as the *expected activity duration*.

The mean and standard deviation formulae now become:

$$\text{Mean (PERT)} = \frac{\text{Optimistic} + (4* \text{Most Likely}) + \text{Pessimistic}}{6}$$

$$\text{Standard Deviation } (\sigma) = \frac{\text{Pessimistic - Optimistic}}{6}$$

In this case, you weight the most likely number by 4, and because there are now six data points (four Ms, an O, and a P), you divide by 6.

So, let's put this into context. Let's say a senior manager asks for a time estimate of an activity. You say, "This activity should take 16 days, but if things go well, it might take only 10 days, but if things go badly, it might end up taking 34 days."

In this case:

Most Likely = 16

Optimistic = 10

Pessimistic = 34

By plugging the numbers into the PERT formula, you see the following:

$$PERT = \frac{10 + (4*16) + 34}{6} = 18 \text{ days}$$

The 18 days in this case are the PERT, or weighted average, or the expected average duration.

To determine the range, you need to make another calculation, the Standard Deviation (referred to as sigma or σ). In this example, by plugging the numbers into the standard deviation (SD) formula, you see the following:

$$SD (\sigma) = \frac{34 - 10}{6} = 4 \text{ days}$$

To calculate the range, you take the PERT and do the following:

1. Add the standard deviation to get an upper range.

2. Subtract the standard deviation to get a lower range.

In the example, the range is as follows:

$$\text{Range: } = PERT + \sigma = 18 + 4 = 22$$
$$PERT - \sigma = 18 - 4 = 14$$

Let's expand on standard deviation a little further, based on what you need to know for the PMP exam.

The following are the standard deviation (sigma) percentages that you need to know for the exam:

1σ = 68.26 percent

2σ = 95.46 percent

3σ = 99.73 percent

6σ = 99.9997 percent

You can see there are six standard deviation levels (for the exam, you do not need to know the percentages for 4σ and 5σ), but you have just one formula for standard deviation.

So which σ percentage does the standard deviation formula refer to?

It refers to 1σ (1 standard deviation). And because 1σ is 68.26 percent, you say that the range that you calculated is to a confidence level of 68.26 percent (or 68 percent):

$$\text{Range: } \begin{array}{l} = 18 + 4 = 22 \\ 18 - 4 = 14 \end{array} \Big\} \; 68\%$$

If you wanted to calculate to a 95 percent confidence level (or 95.46 percent), you would simply multiply the standard deviation level by 2 and then add and subtract from the PERT.

Thus, in the example, if

  1σ = 4, then

  2σ = 2*4 = 8, and

  3σ = 3*4 = 12

So, the range based on a 95 percent confidence is

$$\text{Range: } \begin{array}{l} = 18 + 8 = 26 \\ 18 - 8 = 10 \end{array} \Big\} \; 95\%$$

The range based on a 99.73 percent confidence is

$$\text{Range: } \begin{array}{l} = 18 + 12 = 30 \\ 18 - 12 = 6 \end{array} \Big\} \; 99.73\%$$

One additional term that you may come across on the exam is *activity variance*. The only fact you need to know for activity variance is

  Variance = σ^2

So, in the example,

  Standard Deviation (σ) = 4

Therefore,

  Activity Variance = σ2 = 42 = 16

EXAM TIP!   The default method to use is always the PERT method. If the question does not state whether to use the triangular distribution or the PERT method, use the PERT method. Use triangular distribution only if the question specifically tells you to use triangular.

EXAM TIP! Make sure you read the last sentence first to ensure you know what you need to calculate. The scenario could give you optimistic, most likely, and pessimistic values and the question could ask you to calculate standard deviation. Because the scenario gives you all three values, you may inadvertently calculate the PERT instead of the standard deviation (and, of course, PERT would be one of the option choices given!).

The Advantages and Disadvantages of the Predictive Estimating Techniques

Table 7-2 compares the advantages and disadvantages of the four predictive estimating techniques.

Table 7-2   The Predictive Estimating Techniques

Technique	Advantages	Disadvantages
Analogous	Quick and easy	Not very accurate
Parametric	Can be more detailed than analogous	Might not scale
Bottom-Up	Very detailed analysis, very accurate	Time consuming
Three-Point (PERT)	For well-understood activities, can be very accurate	If any one of the 3 estimates (optimistic, most likely or pessimistic) are inaccurate, the whole PERT estimate can be inaccurate

The Predictive and Adaptive Estimating Methods

In this chapter, we covered the four estimating methods for predictive projects. In Chapter 6, we discuss three estimating methods for adaptive (agile) projects. Remember that on adaptive projects, agile teams do not initially estimate timelines or budget but perform a relative estimate of user stories. The estimating methods for predictive and adaptive projects are as follows:

- **Predictive Methods**

    - Analogous Estimating

    - Parametric Estimating

    - Bottom-Up Estimating

    - Three-Point Estimating

- **Adaptive Methods**
  - T-Shirt Sizing
  - Story-Pointing
  - Planning Poker (Scrum Poker)

Develop and Control the Schedule

After the team members have defined the activities, sequenced them, and estimated the duration for each activity, they can develop the overall schedule for the project by estimating start and end dates for each activity. Project teams can use various approaches and methodologies for this task, but the one that is more commonly asked about on the exam is the critical path method, discussed later in this chapter.

Key Artifacts in Developing the Schedule

The key artifacts in developing the schedule are as follows:

- **Project Schedule:** This key artifact shows the start and end dates of the overall project and start and end dates of each activity or work package. This includes the early start, late start, early finish, late finish, and durations for each activity. It also includes the sequences of the activities, their logical relationships, and dependencies. It is often shown as a Gantt chart, and most teams use a software tool to develop and track the schedule performance.

- **Schedule Baseline:** This key artifact is simply the approved version of the project schedule. After the schedule has been developed, it needs to be approved by appropriate stakeholders (typically the project manager(s), the sponsor(s), the project leadership team (senior stakeholders), and key members of the project team). These stakeholders would be determined during planning and documented in the schedule management plan. After they have approved and signed off on the schedule, this means that it has been baselined. Actual results are compared against this baseline, and any changes to the baseline must go through the change control process.

- **Gantt Chart:** This bar chart shows scheduled activities and progress of the schedule, developed from the software tool that the team uses to develop the schedule.

Figure 7-5 shows a sample Gantt chart.

Detail	Month 1		Month 2		Month 3		Month 4		Month 5		Month 6	
Ethnography												
Fieldwork Observation		■	■	■								
Depth Interview												
Fieldwork				■	■	■						
Topline Report							■					
Holiday						■						
Progress Report			■			■			■			
Quality Control							■	■	■			
Analysis								■		■		
Outline Report & Presentation											■	

Figure 7-5   A Gantt Chart

> ■ **Milestone Chart:** A milestone is a significant point on a project, or a key deliverable. The milestone chart is similar to a Gantt chart, but it is a summary overview of these significant points.

Key Tools for Developing the Schedule

The sections that follow describe the key tools for developing the schedule.

Resource Optimization Techniques

The term *resource optimization techniques* refers to adjusting levels of resources to ensure no resources are overallocated or underallocated. You want to ensure that all resources are utilized at the optimal level. In its simplest form, let's say you are managing four teams on a project. One team is consistently putting in 60+ hours a week, but the other three teams each rarely have more than 35 hours of work a week. In this scenario, resources are not optimally utilized (one team is overutilized, and the other three are underutilized).

What is the logical solution in this situation?

You can either move some activities from the overworked team to the other three underutilized teams or move team members from the underutilized team to the overutilized team. In each case, you are trying to optimize the workload. This is known as *resource optimization*.

There are two types of resource optimization:

- *Resource Leveling*

    - This term refers to readjusting the start and end dates based on the availability of resources.

    - This type of resource optimization might end up changing the critical path, and you may end up falling behind schedule.

    - Figure 7-6 shows a simple example of resource leveling.

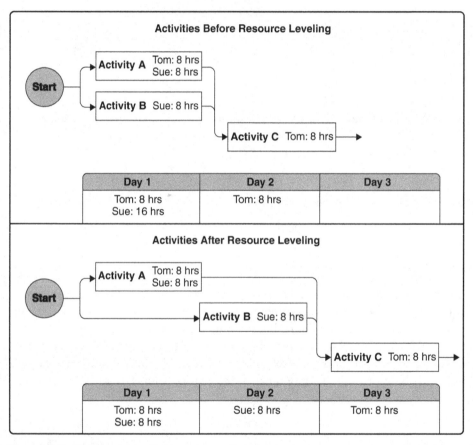

Figure 7-6   Resource Leveling

- *Resource Smoothing*

    - Here, resources are moved from noncritical path activities to critical path activities.

■ In this situation, you cannot fall behind schedule, so adjustments can be made only within the amount of total float and free float.

See the section "Network Diagraming and the Critical Path Method (CPM)" later in this chapter for a detailed discussion on floats and critical path terminology.

Schedule Compression Techniques

Schedule compression is used to either shorten or accelerate the schedule without reducing the scope or quality of the work. There are two types of schedule compression techniques:

■ *Crashing*

■ This technique involves adding additional resources to critical path activities.

■ Approving overtime, hiring additional workers, or paying for expedited services are examples of crashing.

■ This results in increased cost and risk to the project.

■ *Fast-Tracking*

■ Activities that had originally been planned to run sequentially are now going to be run in parallel.

■ This technique increases risk but can also increase cost because crashing and fast-tracking are often performed simultaneously.

■ You can do this only if you have a discretionary dependency. If a mandatory dependency exists between two activities, you are not able to fast-track.

Monte Carlo

A Monte Carlo is a random iterative computer model that shows probability distributions based on risks that could impact the project (in this case, impact the schedule) and is used for simulation modeling. In its simplest, the team first calculates three-point estimates for each activity. Then you will build a probability distribution based on the many risks and uncertainties identified on the project.

Figure 7-7 shows a very simple example of the results of a Monte Carlo.

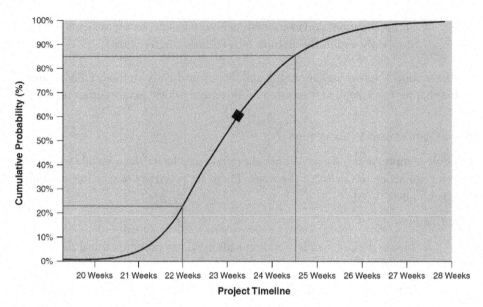

Figure 7-7   A Monte Carlo Analysis

Based on this, what would be the likelihood of the project finishing by week 22?

Answer: About 23 percent. So it is not a good idea to set the schedule for a planned finish date of week 22. The 85 percent probability is between 24 and 25 weeks, so that would seem like a more reasonable estimate. Plus, as new risks are identified or as risk responses are planned, you can perform what-if analyses—for example, what would happen to the schedule if risk A materialized, or risk B was to be avoided?

Network Diagraming and the Critical Path Method (CPM)

The *critical path* method is one way of developing a schedule and the one that PMI has chosen as part of its principles and standards.

Before we examine the basic steps, let's define some important terms:

- **Critical Path:** The longest path through a network that represents the earliest completion for the project.

- **Float:** The amount of time an activity can be delayed, which is built into the schedule. Three types of floats are discussed toward the end of this section. *Float* is essentially the same as *slack* or *cushion*, but for CPM, the term *float* is used.

While you're calculating the critical path, any activities that fall on the critical path have a zero float (no slack or cushion); however, critical path is always considered to be the path with the least amount of float.

So, let's look at a simple example to understand this concept: Imagine you have only two independent activities to perform, and each activity starts at the same time and is performed by two separate teams. Activity 1 will take 5 days, and activity 2 will take 20 days.

Question 1: How long will the project take?

Answer: 20 days.

Both activities are performed in parallel, so the earliest you can finish is 20 days. So, the critical path is the longest path, and it represents the earliest completion for the project.

Question 2: If activity 1 takes 5 days and activity 2 takes 20 days, activity 1 can be delayed. How long can it be delayed by?

Answer: 15 days.

In other words, activity 1 has a float of 15 days. It can be delayed by up to 15 days, and there will be no impact on the 20-day deadline.

Question 3: What happens of activity 2 gets delayed?

Answer: That will delay the entire project.

The whole principle behind critical path is that if any activity on the critical path is delayed, it delays the entire project.

The critical path method utilizes five basic steps as follows:

Step 1.   Calculate the critical path.

Step 2.   Float on the critical path is initially set to zero.

Step 3.   Calculate the early start and early finish (this step is known as the *forward pass*).

Step 4.   Calculate the late finish and late start (this step is known as the *backward pass*).

Step 5.   Calculate float on noncritical path activities.

Let's examine the five basic steps using the network diagram in Figure 7-8.

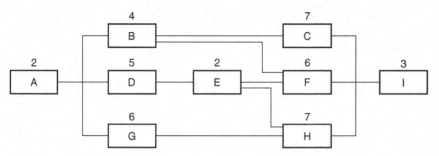

Figure 7-8 Network Diagram

On any network diagram, such as the one shown in Figure 7-8, each box represents an activity, and the lines between the activities (sometimes shown as arrows) represent the dependencies and relationships between each activity.

Thus, in Figure 7-8 activities B, D, and G are dependent on A. C is dependent on B, and so on. The activities in this diagram have a finish-to-start relationship.

As you develop a schedule using the critical path method, you can use the convention depicted in Figure 7-9, which shows the most common convention used for placing identifiers of each activity:

- The number on the top left of each box represents the early start (ES) of the activity.

- The number on the top right of each box represents the early finish (EF) of the activity.

- The number on the bottom left of each box represents the late start (LS) of the activity.

- The number on the bottom right of each box represents the late finish (LF) of the activity.

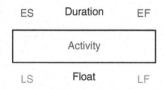

Figure 7-9 Common Convention Used in the Critical Path Method

In the middle of the boxes, going from top to bottom, the numbers or characters represent the following:

- Duration of the activity

- Name of the activity

- Total float of the activity

There are two methods of performing a forward pass and a backward pass, and both methods are dependent on the early start (ES) of the first activity:

- **Zero Method:** The first activity has a start date of 0. Assuming the durations are in days, this means that subsequent activities start the same day as the current activity finishes (or the same time period that you are using—weeks, months, and so on). In this example, as soon as you finish Activity A, you can start work on activities B, D, and G the same day. As soon as B finishes, you can start work on C and F immediately, and so on. You can also think of this as a 24-hour workday (such as machines in a manufacturing plant). As soon as work is completed on one machine, you can immediately start work on the next machine.

- **One Method:** The first activity has a start date of 1. Assuming the durations are in days, this means that subsequent activities start the following day (the day after the current activity finishes—or the following time period that you are using—weeks, months, and so on). In this example, after Activity A finishes, you start work on activities B, D, and G the following day. After B finishes, you start work on C and F the day after B finishes, and so on. You can also think of this as an 8-hour workday (such as for each team member). This assumes a team member works 8 hours per day, completes work by the end of the work-day, and the next work will start the following day.

Let's look further at both methods and then discuss when to use the methods based on exam questions.

Zero Method

First, let's look at the zero method because it is the easier of the two methods. Following the five steps outlined earlier, based on the network diagram shown earlier, you can do the following:

Step 1.   Calculate the critical path.

First, figure out all the paths.

Next, compute the total duration of each path (sum up each path duration).

Critical path is the *longest* path through the network (in this case, ADEHI):

ABCI = 2+4+7+3 = 16

ABFI = 2+4+6+3 = 15

ADEFI = 2+5+2+6+3 = 18

ADEHI = 2+5+2+7+3 = 19

AGHI = 2+6+7+3 = 18

Step 2.   Float on the critical path is initially set to zero.

The network diagram now looks as shown in Figure 7-10.

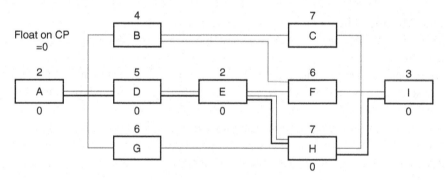

Figure 7-10   Step 1

Step 3.   Calculate the early start and early finish (this step is known as the forward pass):

a. ES of first activity is time 0.

b. EF = ES + Duration.

c. ES of successor = EF of prior task.

d. If a task is dependent on two or more predecessors, the *highest* number wins.

The network diagram now looks as shown in Figure 7-11.

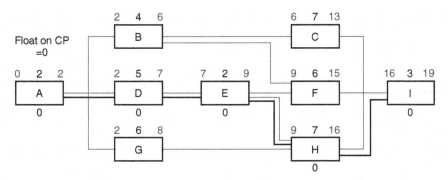

Figure 7-11   Forward Pass Using the Zero Method

Step 4.   Calculate the late finish and late start (this step is known as the backward pass):

Start at the last activity on the critical path and work backward.

a. On all critical path activities (LF = EF) and (LS = ES).

b. LF of predecessor = LS of successor.

c. LS = LF – Duration.

d. If a successor task has more than one predecessor, the *lowest* number wins.

The network diagram now looks as shown in Figure 7-12.

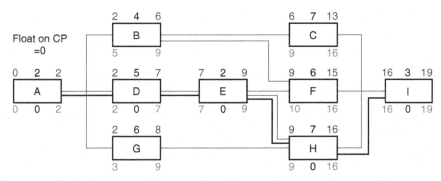

Figure 7-12   Backward Pass Using the Zero Method

Step 5.   Calculate float on non-critical path activities.

Total Float = LF – EF (also LS – ES)

The network diagram now looks as shown in Figure 7-13.

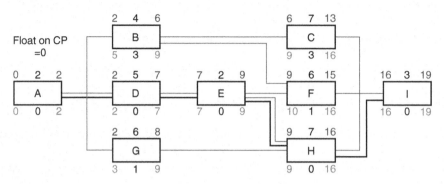

Figure 7-13   Float on All Activities

One Method

Now let's examine the one method of developing the critical path. Remember, in the one method, the start of the first activity is labeled 1, and subsequent activities start the following day (or following time period).

The previously listed steps 1 and 2 are the same, so we start with step 3.

Step 3.   Calculate early start and early finish (this step is known as the forward pass):

    a. ES of first activity is time 1.

    b. EF = ES + Duration –1.

    c. ES of successor = EF of current +1.

    d. If task is dependent on two or more predecessors, the *highest* number wins.

The network diagram now looks like Figure 7-14.

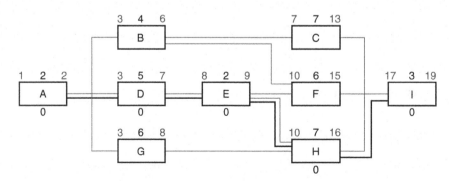

Figure 7-14   Forward Pass Using the One Method

Step 4. Calculate late finish and late start (this step is known as the backward pass):

Start at the last activity on critical path and work backward.

a. On all critical path activities, (LF = EF) and (LS = ES).

b. LF of predecessor = LS of current –1.

c. LS = LF – Duration +1.

d. If a successor task has more than one predecessor, the *lowest* number wins.

The network diagram now looks like Figure 7-15.

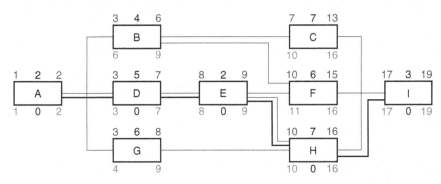

Figure 7-15   Backward Pass Using the One Method

Step 5. Calculate float on noncritical path activities.

Total Float = LF – EF (also LS – ES)

The network diagram now looks like Figure 7-16.

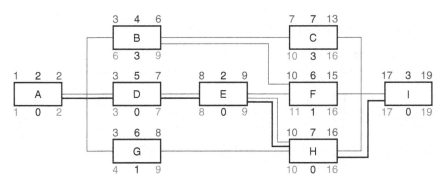

Figure 7-16   Float on All Activities

Comparing the Zero Method and the One Method

As you compare the two methods, you will notice the only difference: the ES and LS for each activity have increased by one using the one method. Everything else remains the same: the critical path, floats, EF, and LF of each activity all remain the same.

If you wanted, you could calculate the zero method first and then add a 1 to the left side of the boxes for each activity (ES and LS) to convert it to the one method.

Which method should you do on the exam? For the most part, it shouldn't matter, depending on the question. If the question simply asks you to calculate the float for an activity, or the EF or LF of an activity, you will get the same answer using either method. So, use whichever method you find easier. The only time it makes a difference is if the question specifically asks for the ES or LS.

EXAM TIP!   The exam question rarely tells you which method to use and never uses the term *zero method* or *one method*. If it is relevant to the question, you need to read the scenario carefully to determine which of the two methods to use.

Three Types of Floats

There are three types of floats:

- *Total Float*

    - This is the time an activity can be delayed without delaying the *end date* of the project.

    - The floats that you calculated for the preceding activities are the total floats of those activities (for example, B and C have total floats of 3).

    - If the question asks for the total float of a path, you choose the largest float of any activity on a path (not cumulative).

    - For example, if the question asks for the total float of ABEFI, the total float is 3 (not 4).

    - You never add float values together; you always take the highest float.

- *Free Float*

    - This is the time an activity can be delayed without delaying an *early start* of any successor activity.

    - For example, activity B using the zero method has an EF of 6, but activity C has an ES of 6. Therefore, B has a free float of zero, even though it has a total float of 3.

- The calculation of the free float differs slightly based on the zero and one methods, as follows:

  — Zero Method: ES of successor – EF of current (predecessor)
  — One Method: ES of successor – (EF of current + 1)

- **Project Float**

  - This is the time a project can be delayed without impacting an externally imposed project deadline or another project.

  - The question provides the externally imposed deadline.

  - In the example, let's say the customer stated that as long as you finish by day 21, they will be fine. You have calculated the CP to be 19 days, so you have 2 days of additional cushion before you impact the customer's deadline. This cushion is the project float.

  - Project Float = Deadline – Critical path

In addition, floats can be negative or positive:

- **Negative Float:** This can mean one of two things. Either

  - The project is behind schedule (the critical path has been delayed). For example, if activity D finishes on day 8 instead of day 7, you are 1 day behind schedule, and you have a negative float of 1 day.

    Or it can mean

  - Time has been taken away. For example, if it is determined that the project must finish on day 17 instead of day 19, you have 2 days of negative float.

- **Positive Float:** The project is ahead of schedule (a critical path activity has finished early). For example, if activity D finishes on day 6 instead of day 7, you are 1 day ahead of schedule, so you have a positive float of 1 day.

Monitoring and Controlling the Schedule

As with all monitoring and controlling processes, controlling the schedule means comparing actual results with the plan. In this case, you determine metrics by asking yourself these questions:

- Are we ahead of schedule?

- Are we behind schedule?

- How much work has been completed versus how much is outstanding?

- What work is left to complete, and when will it be completed?

- How have changes impacted the schedule?

- Do we need to re-baseline the schedule?

- Do we need to reprioritize work?

- Are the vendors performing the work during the timeframe agreed?

- How many user stories have been accepted versus how many should have been accepted by now (for agile projects)?

- What is the velocity? This is the rate at which deliverables are produced, validated, and accepted per sprint (for agile projects only).

As always, the preceding is not an exhaustive list, but just some considerations to make when controlling the schedule.

Schedule Management Considerations for Agile

Adaptive projects do not use Gantt charts like predictive projects. Instead, adaptive projects make the use of a **_product roadmap_**, like the one shown in Figure 7-17.

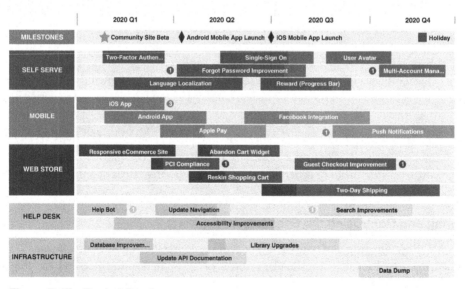

Figure 7-17   Product Roadmap

At first glance, it might look like a Gantt chart; however, it is very different. The "swim lanes" show actual products (not activities), and the timelines (Q1, Q2, and so on) are approximate timelines, not actual start and end dates of activities. Several sprints are planned to create each product.

Agile Release Planning

An agile project is known as a *release*, and typically a release is three to nine months long, containing several iterations (or sprints). Agile release planning provides a high-level summary of the release schedule based on the product roadmap and the vision (usually documented in the project charter).

During agile release planning, the team determines the number of sprints in the release, decides the length of each sprint, and allows the product owner and the team to determine deliverables for each sprint.

Figure 7-18 shows the relationship between the product vision, roadmap, release planning, and sprint planning.

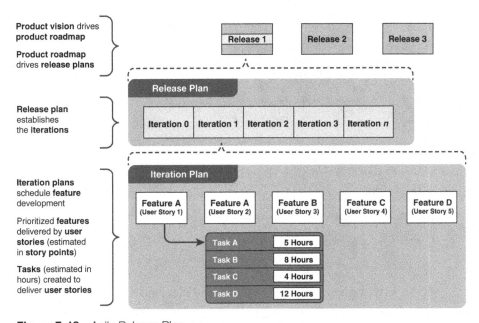

Figure 7-18   Agile Release Plan

Spikes

Spikes are time-boxed research or experiments, often in the form of an additional sprint or user story, and are used when additional information or research is needed. There are two common types:

- **Architectural Spikes:** Used when teams need a better understanding of requirements or a better understanding of the technology.

- **Risk Spikes:** Used when significant risks have been identified and further analysis needs to be done to determine how they will impact the project and deliverable.

Agile Schedule Approach

There are two basic approaches to the schedule when it comes to agile development:

- **Iterative Scheduling with a Backlog**
  - Uses rolling wave planning
  - Allows changes/adaptations throughout the release
  - Delivers business value early and incrementally
  - Provides a specific time window, usually two to four weeks
  - Prioritizes user stories based on priority and time
  - Adds new stories to backlog
  - Reprioritizes user stories as needed (backlog grooming)
  - Does not always work well if there are complex dependency relationships

- **On-Demand Scheduling**
  - Work "pulled" from queue by team members when they have available bandwidth
  - Based on Kanban and Lean methodologies
  - Provides incremental business value
  - Levels out work of team members
  - Works best when activities can be divided into equal amounts
  - Does not work well when there are complex dependency relationships

As a reminder, large user stories must be broken down into smaller user stories. A good user story meets the INVEST criteria discussed in Chapter 6, "Project Scope." For iterative scheduling with a backlog and on-demand scheduling to work, user stories must meet the INVEST criteria (Independent, Negotiable, Valuable, Estimable, Small, Testable).

Adaptive projects use a time-boxed approach where work is prioritized so that it can be planned and performed during a specific timeframe. For example, team members determine which user stories they will be able to implement during their two-week sprint. They determine how best to plan and utilize their four-hour sprint review meeting to efficiently demonstrate the product increment to the product owner during this timeframe. Likewise, each agile ceremony is time-boxed. This allows for team members to work more efficiently and reduce the amount of non-value-added work during a sprint.

Exam Preparation Tasks

As mentioned in the section "How to Use This Book" in the Introduction, you have a couple of choices for exam preparation: the exercises here, Chapter 18, "Final Preparation," and the exam simulation questions on the Pearson Test Prep practice test software.

Review All Key Topics

Review the most important topics in this chapter, noted with the Key Topic icon in the outer margin of the page. Table 7-3 lists a reference of these key topics and the page numbers on which each is found.

Table 7-3   Key Topics for Chapter 7

Key Topic Element	Description	Page Number
Section	Define Activities	219
Section	Precedence Relationships	221
Section	Activity Dependencies	222
Section	Leads and Lags	223
Section	Estimating Methods	226
Section	Resource Optimization Techniques	233
Section	Schedule Compression Techniques	235
Section	Schedule Management Considerations for Agile	246

Define Key Terms

Define the following key terms from this chapter and check your answers in the glossary:

project activities, precedence diagramming method, lead, lag, resource leveling, resource smoothing, crashing, fast-tracking, critical path, total float, free float, product roadmap

Review Questions

1. As you roll on to manage an existing project with a tight deadline, you make a new discovery that will add additional tasks and may affect the schedule. What should you do next to determine how to move forward?

   a. Consult with the team.

   b. Review the schedule management plan.

   c. Update the risk register.

   d. Perform an impact analysis.

2. A junior project manager and a key stakeholder are in disagreement. The junior PM delivered the WBS to the stakeholder, who is very upset that it is incomplete. It is missing the activities, and the stakeholder wants to know how this basic mistake could have happened. How should you, as the senior PM, handle this situation?

   a. Coach the junior PM on the fundamentals of the WBS and ask that the WBS be developed again, showing activities.

   b. Because time might be limited, you should create the WBS yourself and include the activities.

   c. Explain to the key stakeholder that the junior PM is correct not to include activities.

   d. Explain to the key stakeholder that there are many ways of creating a WBS and this is one way. You can create another WBS showing the activities if they so want.

3. What type of dependency is being described in the following situation? You are managing the modernization of a local high school building. You are about to begin the process of completely removing and remodeling the home economics classroom. The update involves removing all the current gas cooktops and replacing them with safer electric induction cooktops. To safely remove all the cooktops, you must first disconnect all the gas lines.

      a. Discretionary

      b. Hard logic

      c. Internal

      d. Preferred

4. Your initial plan was to finish all configuration work before testing would start. However, due to some delays, you have decided to start testing even though configuration is not yet complete. Which of the following would best describe this situation?

      a. You have changed a mandatory dependency to a discretionary dependency.

      b. You have changed soft logic to hard logic.

      c. You have changed a start to finish relationship to a finish to start.

      d. You have changed a finish to start to a start to start relationship.

5. You are coaching your junior project managers and are trying to determine the duration of activities. You need to deliver the final product on the deadline date, but some uncertainties can affect the estimated duration of activities. Which of the following is the best tool to use?

      a. Bottom-up estimating

      b. T-shirt sizing

      c. Parametric estimating

      d. Three-point estimating

6. You are managing a project where the product has to be delivered by a deadline that cannot be extended. You notice that one team is consistently working a lot of overtime while other teams are sometimes working less than 40 hours per week. What should you do to ensure team members' work is spread across teams evenly?

      a. You should use resource leveling to ensure team members are utilized optimally.

      b. You should remove low-performing team members and replace them with high-performing team members.

      c. You should use resource smoothing to ensure team members are optimally utilized.

      d. You should use fast tracking to ensure items are running in parallel.

7. The customer has set a strict project deadline of 85 days for completion. As you review the project schedule, you notice that one of your paths has a total float of 11 days, and another has a total float of 14 days. Your critical path has a total duration of 55 days, and one of your activities has a free float of 5 days. What is the project float?

   a. 30 days

   b. 14 days

   c. 0 days

   d. 25 days

8. You are the manager on a project to build a new wing for the local hospital. The ribbon-cutting ceremony is set, and many high-profile local dignitaries will be present, so the deadline is set firm and approaching fast. Unfortunately, the project is behind schedule. You work with your customer to discuss the best way to bring the project back on track, and the customer decides to crash the schedule. Of the following, which is the greatest concern to you?

   a. Increased cost

   b. Stakeholder's buy-in

   c. Finding the additional resources to perform the work

   d. Getting approval from the change control board

9. In which of the following methods do team members pull the work from a queue?

   a. Iterative scheduling with a backlog

   b. Critical path method

   c. Resource leveling

   d. On-demand scheduling

10. As team members work with the product owner to prioritize user stories, it has become obvious that they need a better understanding of the requirements because this is a new technology that they are not familiar with. What is the best approach to handle this situation?

    a. Extend the schedule of the sprints to allow for additional time to analyze the requirements and the new system.

    b. Create a spike experiment for further investigation.

    c. Adjust the sprints so that the first sprint focuses on learning the new system and requirements.

    d. Ensure the team has the tools and information to perform further analysis.

This chapter covers the following topics in the Cost Management knowledge area:

- **Plan Cost Management:** Examine the common processes, tools, and artifacts needed to estimate costs on a project and determine the budget for the project.

- **Estimate Costs:** Review the process and tools for estimating costs of activities, work packages, and other components of the project.

- **Determine Budget:** Review the process of aggregating costs to ascertain the time-phased budget for the project.

- **Control Costs:** Briefly examine the process of tracking cost across the project. This topic is discussed in more detail in Chapter 14, "Project Measurement."

## CHAPTER 8

Project Cost

In this chapter, we discuss in detail the cost management approach of projects as needed for the PMP exam and discuss the common process tools and artifacts needed for successful cost management. We specifically discuss the principles related to the *PMBOK® Guide*, Sixth Edition; the *PMBOK® Guide*, Seventh Edition; and the Exam Content Outline (ECO).

This chapter addresses the following objectives from the PMP Exam Content Outline:

Domain	Task #	Exam Objective
People	Task 2	Lead a team
People	Task 8	Negotiate project agreements
People	Task 9	Collaborate with stakeholders
People	Task 10	Build a shared understanding
Process	Task 1	Execute project with the urgency required to deliver business value
Process	Task 5	Plan and manage budget and resources
Process	Task 6	Plan and manage schedule
Process	Task 7	Plan and manage quality of products/deliverables
Process	Task 8	Plan and manage scope
Process	Task 9	Integrate project planning activities
Process	Task 10	Manage project changes
Process	Task 11	Plan and manage procurement
Business Environment	Task 2	Evaluate and deliver project benefits and value

"Do I Know This Already?" Quiz

The "Do I Know This Already?" quiz allows you to assess whether you should read this entire chapter thoroughly or jump to the "Exam Preparation Tasks" section. If you are in doubt about your answers to these questions or your own assessment of your knowledge of the topics, read the entire chapter. Table 8-1 lists the major headings in this chapter and their corresponding "Do I Know This Already?" quiz questions. You can find the answers in Appendix A, "Answers to the 'Do I Know This Already?' Quizzes and Review Questions."

Table 8-1   "Do I Know This Already?" Section-to-Question Mapping

Foundation Topics Section	Questions
Plan Cost Management	1–3
Estimate Costs	4–8
Determine Budget	9
Control Costs	10

CAUTION   The goal of self-assessment is to gauge your mastery of the topics in this chapter. If you do not know the answer to a question or are only partially sure of the answer, you should mark that question as wrong for purposes of the self-assessment. Giving yourself credit for an answer you correctly guess skews your self-assessment results and might provide you with a false sense of security.

1. You are halfway through the project and have been given a new set of formulae to determine the financial health of your project. Where would these formulae be documented?

   a. The formula register

   b. Cost baseline

   c. Cost estimate

   d. Cost management plan

2. How would you best classify the cost of raw materials on a project?

   a. Direct

   b. Variable

   c. Fixed

   d. Indirect

3. Which of the following would be an indirect cost on your project?

   a. Benefits for employees in your organization

   b. Renting specialized equipment for your team members

   c. Travel expenses for team members to clients' offices

   d. Raw materials

4. Your customer is requesting a detailed and accurate cost estimate for an upcoming deliverable. Which of the following would you most likely use?

   a. Parametric estimating

   b. Planning poker using a Fibonacci sequence

   c. Analogous estimating

   d. Bottom-up estimating

5. What is a rough order of magnitude (ROM) range on an estimate of $200,000?

   a. $100,000–$300,000

   b. $190,000–$220,000

   c. $150,000–$350,000

   d. $100,000–$400,000

6. You are delivering a cost estimate to your customers, and it has taken some time to estimate. However, the customers are pleased with the estimate because there is an accurate breakdown of each detailed cost category, and they feel they are in a much more informed position to make the right decision. What estimating tool was most likely used here?

   a. Bottom-up estimating

   b. Analogous estimating

   c. Parametric estimating

   d. Planning poker

7. Earlier on this project, your team lead expressed concerns that a vendor may delay shipment of some vital raw materials for the project due to factors beyond their control. If these raw materials are not delivered on time, the entire project would come to a halt until they could be delivered. You have come to a critical point on the project, and the vendor informs you that they indeed need to delay this shipment due to these exceptional circumstances. You decide to order these raw materials from a different vendor who is going to charge a lot more. Where would you get the additional funding for the more expensive raw materials?

   a. Management reserves because this is due to factors beyond the vendor's control

   b. Management reserves because this is a known risk

    c. Contingency reserves because this is due to factors beyond the vendor's control

    d. Contingency reserves because this is a known risk

8. You are in a meeting with some team members and discussing material costs for certain activities. Your team is tasked with painting 100 rooms for a large hotel. One of your team members thinks that each room should take about four hours to complete, including the closets, bathrooms, and all the edges and corners and should use about two gallons of paint. You know the cost each gallon of paint and the charge-out rate for each team member. What is the best estimating tool to use in this case?

    a. T-shirt sizing

    b. Analogous estimating

    c. Parametric estimating

    d. PERT estimating

9. You are finalizing the costs for work packages, activities, and contingency reserves. Because this is such a large project, there are many phases and deliverables for this project, and each stage of the project requires a separate approval and sign-off. For this deliverable, you have estimated a total cost of $930,000. The senior management staff has informed you that they will be able to release only $310,000 per quarter, so you should plan activities accordingly. Which tool do you employ to do this?

    a. Project budget

    b. Cost aggregation

    c. Funding limit reconciliation

    d. Cost baseline

10. You are comparing actual results to the plan and making calculations to determine the project's rate of performance. What are you doing?

    a. Cost aggregation

    b. Estimating costs

    c. Controlling costs

    d. Reserve analysis

Foundation Topics

Cost is arguably regarded as the most significant constraint on a project. Most organizations and individuals do not have an unlimited budget, so managing costs to the budget is a major responsibility for the project manager. In most cases, senior management regards success or failure of a project based on cost management and whether the project is over or under budget. Rightly or wrongly, they are often only concerned with the bottom line. If costs are not managed properly, then runaway costs can lead to project failures, which can lead to negative impacts on the organization.

The Cost Management knowledge area addresses the planning, estimating, budgeting, financing, funding, managing, and controlling of all the costs on a project. As a project manager, you need to account for all the expenses on your project.

The *PMBOK® Guide*, Sixth Edition, processes related to cost management are as follows:

- Plan Cost Management

- Estimate Cost

- Determine Budget

- Control Cost

The *PMBOK® Guide*, Seventh Edition, discusses the budget in the Planning Performance domain and mostly summarizes the main points of the *PMBOK® Guide*, Sixth Edition.

We discuss each process in detail as it relates to the PMP exam.

EXAM TIP!   Many students tend to confuse the Estimate Cost and Determine Budget processes because they sound similar. The difference between them is that Estimate Cost refers to estimating individual costs for each component of the project (such as activities and work packages). When you know these individual costs, you can aggregate them to calculate the overall budget for the project (which is the Determine Budget process).

Plan Cost Management

The first process of Cost Management is Plan Cost Management; this process refers to how you are going to plan, execute, monitor, and control the cost and budget of the project. The purpose is to provide guidance and direction regarding the planning of the budget and varies based on many factors, such as industry, reporting standards, methodology, life cycle, and whether the organization has a formal approach to cost management. These procedures are documented in the cost management plan.

Following are the four basic categories of cost:

- *Direct Costs*: These costs are directly attributable to your project because of your project. You must have these expenses; otherwise, you cannot do your project. Generally, equipment, supplies, raw materials, labor, and machines are considered direct costs.

- *Indirect Costs*: Generally, these costs are shared among different teams, business units, or departments. Costs such as overheads and utilities are examples of indirect costs.

- *Variable Costs*: These costs vary with the amount of usage, such as travel expenses, hourly contractors, or credit card fees.

- *Fixed Costs*: These costs are fixed over time, so you pay the same amount over a time period, such as rent, equipment leases, and insurance premiums. In each case, you pay the same monthly amount.

Many costs straddle more than one of the categories, so you can have

- Direct Variable Costs

- Direct Fixed Costs

- Indirect Variable Costs

- Indirect Fixed Costs

However, the most significant costs on your project are always Direct Costs. They are the maximum expenses on your project because you cannot perform your project without these expenses.

Other Cost Considerations

In addition to the four basic categories of cost, other cost-related factors that you must consider for a project include the following:

- **Financing**: The cost of financing your project could be a direct or indirect cost to your project. For example, if your organization takes a bank loan specifically to finance your project, the interest on the loan is a direct cost to the project. If, however, the organization took the loan to finance various activities in the organization and your project is one of them, the interest is an indirect cost.

- **Life Cycle Costing:** This factor refers to the full life of the product, not just the cost of implementation or development and installation. It also includes such costs as maintenance over the life of the product, upgrades, fixes, salvage costs, and depreciation.

- **Sunk Costs:** These costs have already been spent and are not considered for any future decision-making.

Many factors impact the cost and budget for a project and vary depending on the industry, size, and nature of the project and the particular situation. Some examples are

- Geographical location
- Cost of raw materials
- Cost of quality
- Labor expenses
- Risks
- Scope of the project
- Scope changes
- Schedule
- Availability of resources (both physical and team resources)
- Employee capabilities
- Employee availability
- Make or buy decisions
- External business environment changes (such as changes to regulations and standards, supply chain issues, exchange rates, and so on)
- Internal environment changes (such as reorganizations, organizational change management, and so on)

These are just a few examples. Almost every activity that is performed on a project or any decision that is made on a project most likely has some kind of cost implication.

Key Artifact of Plan Cost Management: Cost Management Plan

The *cost management plan* documents how the cost of individual activities, work packages, and the budget will be planned, developed, and controlled. It establishes the procedures for planning, developing, and managing the cost and budget, and it documents what the team must do if they end up going over budget or if there are changes to the budget. It does not document the budget itself.

The cost management plan documents items such as the following:

- The methodology and approach to determining the budget. You can use many methodologies and models to develop the cost and budget for a project. One of the methods is earned value management (EVM), which is discussed in Chapter 14.

- Tolerance limits for going overbudget (the acceptable range).

- Units of measure and levels of accuracy.

- Levels of precision. Are you estimating costs to the nearest penny or the nearest thousands of dollars?

- Performance measurements to determine whether you are over budget or under budget, and what to do if you are over budget.

- Control thresholds to be used for monitoring cost performance.

- Process descriptions to explain how the cost management processes are to be documented throughout the project.

The preceding are just some examples of the type of information contained in the cost management plan; it is not an exhaustive list.

Agile Considerations

Because the scope of adaptive projects is not fully defined at the beginning, performing detailed cost calculations is not possible due to the frequency of updates and changes. Instead, simple estimates may be used to generate high-level forecasts and progressively elaborated over time. Using rolling wave planning, you can often determine a more detailed cost estimate for each upcoming sprint.

Any high-level estimates are based on known labor costs and any known nonlabor fixed costs. Because pure agile works best on knowledge-based projects, the maximum expense is the labor expense of team members. And because the charge-out rate for each team member is known, estimating the high-level cost of each iteration and, therefore, the release, is possible.

For example, based on each team member's labor rate and fixed system usage expenses, you can estimate a one-month sprint to cost $20,000. If there are 10 sprints, you can estimate the cost of the release to be $200,000. It makes no difference to the cost whether a developer writes one piece of code versus another piece of code or whether the tester tests one piece of code versus another piece of code. These team members are paid to write and test a piece of code, respectively, so moving user stories around makes no difference to the cost of a sprint.

Estimate Costs

The Estimate Costs process refers to estimating costs of individual activities, work packages, and other components of a project. Costs are usually calculated as a range and take into consideration any assumptions made in the assumption log and risks identified in the risk register. The estimates are progressively elaborated over the life cycle of the project. Any additional assumptions and risks identified as a result of estimating costs and developing the budget are updated in the assumption log and risk register, respectively.

Two estimating ranges that you need to know for the PMP exam are as follows:

- *Rough Order of Magnitude (ROM)*

  - This is of the range –25% to +75%. This is a wide range that is used during the initiating phases or if starting the project when not much information is known.

  - For example, the ROM range on an estimate of $100,000 is $75,000 to $175,000. Every industry and organization may have its own ranges for the ROM, but this range is according to PMI's standards.

- *Definitive Estimate*

  - This is of the range –5% to +10%. When you are well into planning, you should be at the definitive range of the estimate.

  - For example, the definitive range on an estimate of $100,000 is $95,000 to $110,000. Different types of cost estimates and levels of accuracy are needed at different points along the project.

Key Tools for Estimating Cost

The following sections discuss a few methods for estimating costs on a project that are commonly asked about on the exam. We have discussed some of them in detail in other chapters because many tools and techniques are common across many processes. We list the predictive and adaptive methods separately.

Estimating Methods: Predictive

Commons tools for estimating costs on predictive projects are as follows.

- Analogous Estimating (discussed in Chapter 7, "Project Schedule")

- Parametric Estimating (discussed in Chapter 7)

- Bottom-Up Estimating (discussed in Chapter 7)

- Three-Point Estimating (discussed in Chapter 7)

- Expert Judgment

- Cost of Quality (discussed in Chapter 11, "Project Quality ")

- Reserve Analysis (discussed later in this chapter)

Although the first four estimating methods were discussed in Chapter 7, the same principles also apply here. The only difference is that in this section, the units of measure are in terms of a monetary value, whereas in Chapter 7 the measure was based on time.

Estimating Methods: Adaptive

The following estimating methods for agile projects were discussed in detail in Chapter 6, "Project Scope." Remember, in agile, the teams initially perform relative estimates of user stories rather than detail estimates of time and cost.

- T-Shirt Sizing

- Story Pointing

- Planning Poker (Scrum poker)

Reserve Analysis

Risks are a major constraint to a project, and any funds you have to set aside to respond to risks are a consideration for the budget. Risks are discussed in detail in Chapter 13, "Uncertainty," but for this section, there two types of risk reserves:

- **Contingency Reserves**: This is money that you (as the project manager) have set aside for known risks (also referred to as *known unknowns*). You are responsible for contingency reserves and they are included in the cost baseline.

- **Management Reserves**: This is money that senior management sets aside for unknown risks on a project (also referred to as *unknown unknowns*). As the project manager, you are not responsible for management reserves, and this money is not included in the cost baseline. Only after the budget and contingency reserves have been depleted do you reach into the management reserves. As an analogy, you could think of management reserves as a rainy day fund.

Contingency reserves are considered a direct cost to your project because they are included in the cost baseline.

Contingency reserves and management reserves are discussed in more detail in Chapter 13.

Determine Budget

The Determine Budget process refers to aggregating the costs of individual activities, work packages, and other components of the project to establish the cost baseline. This includes all the funds authorized to execute the project (except management reserves).

Key Tool: Cost Aggregation

Figure 8-1 provides a simple example of *cost aggregation*.

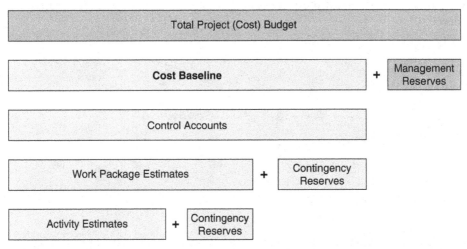

Figure 8-1 Cost Aggregation

You should read this diagram from the bottom up.

The first row (bottom row) shows the activity estimate, which refers to the cost of individual activities of a project. Based on any risks identified for this activity, you may set aside funds in contingency reserves.

When you add up all the activity cost estimates and contingency reserves, this gives the work package estimate. Based on additional risks identified at the work package level, you may set aside some additional funds in contingency reserves.

Thus, you roll up each layer of the work breakdown structure. The cost of the overall project (the top box of the WBS) is known as the cost baseline. This is the approved version of the budget that you, as project manager, are responsible for.

Upon the addition of management reserves by senior management, you now have the total project budget (or total cost budget). Remember that you, as the project manager, are not responsible for the management reserves and therefore not responsible for the total project budget. You (the project manager) are responsible up to and including the cost baseline.

The cost baseline is the time-phased budget, not just the final budget at the end of the project. It is often shown as an S-curve, such as Figure 8-2.

The expenditure rate at the start of the project is not going to be very high as you are mainly planning the work and not utilizing too many resources. As you start executing and purchasing raw materials and using resources, the rate of expenditure is going to increase. Toward the end of the project, when the product is made, and you don't need to utilize or purchase as many resources, the rate of expenditure is reduced.

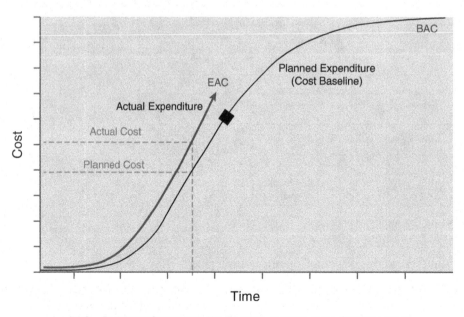

BAC = Budget at Completion (the Baseline Budget, or the Cost Baseline)
EAC = Estimate at Completion (the Forecasted Budget)

Figure 8-2 Time-Phased Budget

The *Budget at Completion (BAC)* line shows the cost baseline through the project (or the planned expenditure rate throughout the project). This expenditure needs to be approved and signed off by the appropriate stakeholders, so the cost baseline is not just one final budget at the end of the project but the time-phased budget throughout the project.

Estimate at Completion (EAC) refers to the forecasted budget and is calculated at various points along the project. The EAC line shows the actual expenditure to date, and the difference between the actual cost and planned cost tells how much over budget or under budget you are at a point on the project.

These terms, along with the other earned value management terms, are discussed in more detail in Chapter 14.

EXAM TIP!   Understand that there is no cost baseline in agile. Baselines are set only for predictive projects.

Key Tool: Funding Limit Reconciliation

Funding limit reconciliation refers to reconciling the amount of work that needs to be done with any funding limits imposed by senior management or the customer, or the customer's ability to pay for the work.

For example, for a $1 million project, your senior management may impose a funding limit of $100,000 per month. You therefore need to adjust your plan accordingly so that the work is performed based on a funding of $100,000 per month. You plan your project based on an expenditure rate of $100,000 per month. Senior management may impose such funding to control the cash outflow of the organization.

Control Costs

The Control Costs process refers to monitoring the status of the project to determine whether the project is on budget, under budget, or over budget. As the project manager, you update the project costs and manage changes to the cost baseline.

You also compare the actual costs (work performance data) to the cost baseline to determine the work performance information. Any changes to the baseline due to additional work, internal business changes, or external business changes need to go through a change control process.

Many methods and approaches to cost management are industry specific. The approach that the PMI uses as its standard is earned value management (EVM), also known as earned value analysis (EVA). This approach is discussed in more detail in Chapter 14.

Exam Preparation Tasks

As mentioned in the section "How to Use This Book" in the Introduction, you have a couple of choices for exam preparation: the exercises here, Chapter 18, "Final Preparation," and the exam simulation questions on the Pearson Test Prep practice test software.

Review All Key Topics

Review the most important topics in this chapter, noted with the Key Topic icon in the outer margin of the page. Table 8-2 lists a reference of these key topics and the page numbers on which each is found.

Table 8-2   Key Topics for Chapter 8

Key Topic Element	Description	Page Number
List	Four basic categories of cost	260
Section	Key Artifact of Plan Cost Management: Cost Management Plan	262
Paragraph	Rough order of magnitude	263
Section	Estimating Methods: Predictive	264
Section	Estimating Methods: Adaptive	264
Section	Reserve Analysis	264
Section	Key Tool: Cost Aggregation	265
Section	Key Tool: Funding Limit Reconciliation	267

Define Key Terms

Define the following key terms from this chapter and check your answers in the glossary:

direct costs, indirect costs, variable costs, fixed costs, cost management plan, rough order of magnitude (ROM), definitive estimate, contingency reserve, management reserve, cost aggregation, Budget at Completion (BAC), Estimate at Completion (EAC), funding limit reconciliation

Review Questions

1. Penny is compiling a list of costs incurred so far on a project. She must categorize these costs so that she can present the amount of direct cost incurred. Which of the following should Penny include in this list?

   a. Benefits for employees in the organization

   b. Expense incurred in meeting the regulatory standards for the company

   c. Costs incurred for maintaining coffee stations around the office

   d. Travel expenses to the customer's office

2. You have rolled onto a project where the customer has not been very happy with the progress. The scope of the project has not been defined very clearly, there are many versions of the same documentation, and stakeholders do not feel engaged on the project. Which document do you review to determine how to manage negative cost variances?

   a. Configuration management plan

   b. Scope management plan

   c. Stakeholder management plan

   d. Cost management plan

3. You are reviewing an artifact that documents the formulae to use to calculate the budget, the acceptable budget tolerance range, and units of cost measurement. Which artifact are you reviewing?

   a. Code of accounts

   b. Funding limit reconciliation

   c. Cost management plan

   d. Budget forecasts

4. You are in a meeting with team members to the discuss costs of activities. Your team will be painting 250 rooms for a large hotel chain. An experienced team member states that, based on historical experience, each room should take about three hours to complete, and from this number, you can figure out how long the whole project should take and how much it should cost. What is the best estimating tool to use in this case?

   a. Analogous estimating

   b. Bottom-up estimating

   c. Planning poker

   d. Parametric estimating

5. You are hosting a project kickoff meeting for a high-visibility project that has a fixed deadline. Discussions include high-level scope, budget, schedule, and stakeholder involvement. A senior manager insists on a detailed budget so that they can estimate cash flows for the organization. How should you respond?

   a. You should comply with senior management's request and try your best to estimate the budget in as much detail as possible.

   b. Advise senior management that the best you can do at this stage is a rough order of magnitude (ROM) range of –25% to +75%.

   c. Advise senior management that the best you can do at this stage is a rough order of magnitude (ROM) range of –50% to +50%.

   d. Advise senior management that the best you can do is a relative estimate.

6. You are estimating the cost of an activity on your project, and you come across some documentation from a prior project that would be very helpful. This activity is almost identical to the activity performed on that prior project, so you can use those figures as a direct comparison, especially in terms of scope, risks, and project team requirements. Which of the following tools provides the most accurate cost estimates?

   a. Analogous estimating

   b. T-shirt sizing

   c. Parametric estimating

   d. Bottom-up estimating

7. Which of the following are included in the cost baseline? (Choose three.)

   a. Work package cost estimate

   b. Contingency reserves

   c. Management reserves

   d. Activity cost estimate

   e. Project budget

   f. Resource management plan

8. You are on your third sprint, and senior management is concerned that you have not created a cost baseline yet for your project. They want you to immediately start work on creating the cost baseline. What should you do?

   a. Comply with senior management and immediately start working on the cost baseline.

   b. Explain to senior management that a cost baseline is not needed for this project.

c. Reach out to the team to create the baseline.

d. Consult the cost management plan to determine what to do next.

9. As project manager, you are working on finalizing the costs for all the work packages, activities, control accounts, and contingency reserves. Which document do you produce as a result of this effort?

a. WBS

b. Cost baseline

c. Cost aggregation

d. Project budget

10. You are on a project to develop an aircraft engine and are working on finalizing the costs for work packages, activities, and contingency reserves. Which tool are you utilizing?

a. Project budget

b. Cost aggregation

c. Funding limit reconciliation

d. Cost baseline

This chapter covers the following topics regarding managing resources and the team.

- **Planning For and Acquiring Project Resources:** Review the key processes, tools, and techniques for defining how physical and team resources will be managed and securing the targeted resources.

- **High-Performing Teams:** Review the characteristics of high-performing teams, management principles that support them, techniques for better team performance, and key team development models.

- **Project Leadership:** Review the key components and skill sets of project leadership, techniques for better project leadership, the value of the servant leadership approach, the aspects of a project that need leadership, and how leading a project is different from managing a project.

- **Special Project Situations:** Review the principles and techniques in managing special project situations like challenging project teams, cross-cultural projects, and virtual project teams.

Managing Resources and the Team

This chapter reviews the activities and functions associated with planning and acquiring project resources and with the development and performance of the *project team*. This review highlights the key fundamentals, concepts, and terms that are emphasized by PMI, including how to develop and manage a high-performing project team, characteristics of a high-performing team, and the importance of leadership and interpersonal skills in establishing a high-performing team culture.

In the *PMBOK® Guide*, Sixth Edition, planning and acquiring resources and managing the project team are covered by these project resource management knowledge area processes:

- Plan Resource Management

- Estimate Activity Resources

- Acquire Resources

- Develop Team

- Manage Team

- Control Resources

NOTE Some aspects of control resources will be covered in Chapter 14, "Project Measurement."

In the *PMBOK® Guide*, Seventh Edition, one of eight project performance domains is the Team Performance domain. This demonstrates that PMI recognizes the importance that this project management area has on project success.

Per the *PMBOK® Guide*, Seventh Edition, if this performance domain is effectively executed, the project team can demonstrate these outcomes:

1. **Shared ownership:** All project team members are clear on the project vision and objectives, and the project team takes ownership of the deliverables and project outcomes.

2. **High-performing team:** The project team collaborates, trusts each other, is empowered, adapts to change, and is resilient when faced with challenges.

3. **Applicable leadership and other interpersonal skills are demonstrated by all project team members:** Project team member leadership styles are appropriate for the context and environment of the project. Project team members apply critical thinking and demonstrate effective interpersonal skills.

In this chapter, we discuss the principles from the respective *PMBOK® Guide*, Sixth Edition, and *PMBOK® Guide*, Seventh Edition, sections mentioned and address the following objectives from the PMP Exam Content Outline:

Domain	Task #	Exam Objective
People	Task 1	Manage conflict
People	Task 2	Lead a team
People	Task 3	Support team performance
People	Task 4	Empower team members and stakeholders
People	Task 5	Ensure team members/stakeholders are adequately trained
People	Task 6	Build a team
People	Task 7	Address and remove impediments, obstacles, and blockers for the team
People	Task 8	Negotiate project agreements
People	Task 9	Collaborate with stakeholders
People	Task 11	Engage and support virtual teams
People	Task 12	Define team ground rules
People	Task 13	Mentor relevant stakeholders
People	Task 14	Promote team performance through the application of emotional intelligence
Process	Task 4	Engage stakeholders
Process	Task 5	Plan and manage budget and resources
Process	Task 9	Integrate project planning activities
Process	Task 16	Ensure knowledge transfer for project continuity
Business Environment	Task 4	Support organizational change

"Do I Know This Already?" Quiz

The "Do I Know This Already?" quiz allows you to assess whether you should read this entire chapter thoroughly or jump to the "Exam Preparation Tasks" section. If you are in doubt about your answers to these questions or your own assessment of your knowledge of the topics, read the entire chapter. Table 9-1 lists the major headings in this chapter and their corresponding "Do I Know This Already?" quiz questions. You can find the answers in Appendix A, "Answers to the 'Do I Know This Already?' Quizzes."

Table 9-1 "Do I Know This Already?" Section-to-Question Mapping

Foundation Topics Section	Questions
Planning For and Acquiring Project Resources	1–2
High-Performing Teams	3–6
Project Leadership	7–11
Special Project Situations	12

CAUTION   The goal of self-assessment is to gauge your mastery of the topics in this chapter. If you do not know the answer to a question or are only partially sure of the answer, you should mark that question as wrong for purposes of the self-assessment. Giving yourself credit for an answer you correctly guess skews your self-assessment results and might provide you with a false sense of security.

1. Per PMI, what are the three processes that comprise planning for and acquiring project resources?

    a. Plan resource management, estimate activity resources, procure resources

    b. Estimate activity resources, budget resources, acquire resources

    c. Plan resource management, estimate activity resources, interview resources

    d. Plan resource management, estimate activity resources, acquire resources

2. Which element is not normally part of a project's resource management plan?

    a. A visual description of how the project roles will be organized and the reporting relationships

    b. A listing of the resource requirements for the project

    c. A description of the project roles and their subsequent authority, responsibility, and competence

    d. Descriptions of how the team and physical resources will be identified and acquired for the project

3. What are some characteristics of high-performing teams?

    a. They have highly skilled technicians who do whatever it takes to accomplish project goals.

    b. They are self-managed and use agile practices.

    c. They have clarity on their responsibilities and take ownership of their assignments.

    d. They trust each other, collaborate well together, and accomplish more as a combined group than they could collectively as individuals.

4. What term is used to describe the Tuckman Ladder team development model?

    a. Orientation, Trust-Building, Commitment, High-Performance

    b. Introductions, Team Building, Team Conflicts, Team Synergy

    c. Forming, Storming, Norming, Performing

    d. Storming, Forming, Performing, Norming

5. What are some management principles that can maximize team performance?

    a. Adapt the management approach to match what is needed for the team and project situation, plan as a team, involve the team in every decision

    b. Set clear expectations, recognize and reward, facilitate team synergy

    c. Understand the motivators for each team member, keep the team focused, hold any celebrations for the project completion

    d. Facilitate team collaboration, leverage mentoring, assign tasks to force team members to work on their weaknesses

6. What are three management techniques that can improve team performance?

    a. Leverage pairing and mentoring opportunities, set up a project repository, apply a Theory X management mindset

    b. Develop a team charter, set up a team collaboration environment, share leadership responsibilities

    c. Leverage expertise, resolve conflicts right away, use agile approaches

    d. Develop team rituals, confirm task assignments are understood, meet with the team daily no matter what

7. What are the four primary components of leadership skills per PMI?

   a. Conflict management, decision-making, emotional intelligence, servant leadership

   b. Servant leadership, critical thinking, public speaking, motivation

   c. Salesmanship, charisma, emotional intelligence, decision-making

   d. Establishing and maintaining vision, critical thinking, motivation, and interpersonal skills

8. What are the four aspects of emotional intelligence?

   a. Showing self-control, reading body language and other nonverbal cues, thinking before acting, having empathy

   b. Remaining calm under pressure, possessing social media skills, reading people's minds, understanding your own emotions

   c. Recognizing other people's feelings, possessing social awareness, building rapport, having empathy

   d. Self-awareness, self-management, social awareness, and social skill

9. What is a benefit of making project decisions with the team?

   a. It allows the senior members of the team to influence the less experienced team members.

   b. It makes the team accountable for the decision, not the project manager.

   c. It leverages the knowledge, expertise, and experience of diverse individuals.

   d. It allows decisions to be made faster.

10. What approaches are key to effectively address and resolve conflicts?

   a. Keep communications open and respectful, focus on the issues (not the people), focus on the present and the future (not the past), and search for alternatives together

   b. Address them quickly, deal with the participants face-to-face, always look for compromise, and approach conflict as a problem to be solved

   c. Avoid addressing until conflict escalates, keep communications open and respectful, and understand the root cause of the conflict

   d. Focus on the issues and the people involved, approach conflict as a problem to be solved, and keep communications open and respectful

11. What variables can impact the leadership style needed on a given project?

   a. Use of agile approaches, organization experience level with type of project, PMO requirements, and location of project team members

   b. Emotional intelligence of the project team, organizational governance structures, risk level of the project, and budget amount of the project

   c. Team experience level with type of project, maturity level of the project team, organizational governance structures, and location of project team members

   d. Maturity level of the project team, organizational governance structures, use of adaptive approaches, and location of project team members

12. What is a recommended first action step when dealing with poor performers on the project team?

   a. Take swift action because the rest of the team is watching.

   b. Verify the expectations the individual had for their current assignment.

   c. Reassign their assignment to someone else on the team.

   d. Contact their supervisor and past project managers.

Foundation Topics

Planning For and Acquiring Project Resources

Resource management, and in particular planning for and acquiring project resources, is a vital component of overall project planning, cost management, schedule management, risk management, and procurement management. These project management activities overlap and occur in concert with each other. In addition, project resources are key constraints on projects and a common source for project risks.

When we speak of project resources, we are including all project resources—both the human project team members and any/all physical resources that are needed by the project team to complete the work of the project. To clarify, the physical resources include any facilities, infrastructure, tools, supplies, and raw materials needed by the project.

As with most things with projects and project management, what is needed for resource planning and acquiring resources varies depending on the sponsoring organization, the industry, the project type and complexity, and the project life cycle approach to be used. For example, planning for physical and team resources is much less predictable in high-variability projects. In these projects, the need for quick supply agreements and lean methods is vital to controlling costs and meeting schedule milestones.

In all cases, the project manager is responsible for planning, managing, and controlling all resources on the project. With that in mind, let's review the key processes, tools, and artifacts related to planning for and acquiring project resources that you need to know for the PMP exam.

Key Processes

First, we examine the key processes involved with planning for and acquiring project resources.

Plan Resource Management

The first key process is Plan Resource Management. As the process name suggests, it is the process for defining how to estimate, acquire, manage, and utilize physical and team resources. The key artifact resulting from this process is the resource management plan (reviewed later in this chapter). The primary value of this process is establishing the approach and the management effort level needed for managing project resources based on type and complexity of project. The approach is of particular importance when it comes to ensuring that sufficient resources are available when the project needs them to successfully complete the project. This is especially true when there is competition for targeted resources or when the supply of those targeted resources is low or scarce.

Although the resource management plan often includes the project roles and skill sets that will be needed and even the grade and quality of the required physical resources, this artifact and this process are not focused on identifying exactly who will be on the team or the exact physical resources that will be needed. They are both focused on capturing how the project resources will be identified, acquired, and managed throughout the project.

If your project has needs for physical resources, it is important to determine if the performing organization uses specific resource management method(s) to manage critical resources such as Kaizen, total productive maintenance (TPM), lean management, just-in-time (JIT) manufacturing, and theory of constraints (TOC). You need to understand these methods and incorporate them into your resource planning efforts.

Estimate Activity Resources

The next process is Estimate Activity Resources. This process involves estimating how many team members are needed and what skill sets are required to complete the work. It involves estimating the raw materials, supplies, equipment, and facilities that are needed, including the type, grade, and quality of those physical resources.

As with all planning activities, this one is tightly integrated with other planning activities, especially work activity planning and cost estimating, and is often flushed out in an iterative manner during the planning process and as needed throughout the project.

The resource estimates should be consistent with other estimating performed and should occur at the same level of granularity. These estimates should be for the work activity and/or work package level and then aggregated up to determine overall needs at the project level.

The primary artifacts resulting from this process are the resource requirements, the basis of estimates (which documents how those resource estimates were derived), an updated assumptions log (updated with any assumptions made or constraints identified), and a resource breakdown structure (RBS).

Acquire Resources

The Acquire Resources process is the next step in the effort to plan for and acquire project resources. This process involves the effort to secure the team members and physical resources needed for the project. When this step is complete, names are assigned to each role on the project team; the work facilities, equipment, and supplies are obtained; and any raw materials needed are ordered.

When you are the project manager, the key items to note in this process are the following:

1. Acquiring internal resources involves using your negotiation and interpersonal skills with various resource managers to obtain the best-suited individuals when you need them.

2. Acquiring external resources involves working with procurement and may involve selection processes if there are not predefined supplier arrangements in place.

3. Any discrepancy between the desired skill set or cost for the project team role and in the skill set or cost in the team member actually assigned needs to be accounted for in the other project planning aspects (budget, schedule, risks, quality) and in the team training plan.

4. In addition, if any of the targeted resources will not be available when needed or there is a risk of them not being available when needed, this also needs to be accounted for in the other project planning aspects.

Key Artifacts and Tools

Now that we have reviewed the highlights of the key processes involved with planning for and acquiring project resources, let's look at the key artifacts and tools involved with planning for and acquiring resources that you want to know for the exam.

Pre-Assignment Tools

Pre-assignment tools include any mechanism used to evaluate and assess potential candidates for your project team. Most anyone who has gone through an interview and hiring process for a new job is instinctively familiar with these methods. These methods would be used in the process of acquiring resources to fill the defined project team roles. The common pre-assignment tools include the following:

- Attitudinal survey
- Specific assessments
- Structured interviews
- Focus groups
- Ability test

As mentioned previously, the project manager does not always have as much control on who gets assigned to their project as they would like. This normally depends on the size, nature of the project, and the industry. Whenever possible, the project manager and the project are best served in selecting candidates that best fit the technical and interpersonal skills needed for the project.

SWOT Analysis

A SWOT (strengths, weaknesses, opportunities, and threats) analysis is a common tool used in various capacities in a project, and applying this analysis to your project team would be one of them. Although this analysis would not be completed until the project team is fully formed and assigned, it can help to start the analysis as you are evaluating candidates. The key reasons to use a SWOT analysis on your project team include the following:

- Understand skills and competencies of the team
- Identify areas of weakness to recognize training needs
- Organize teams around their strengths
- Perform team skill appraisal

This analysis is even more important if you had to compromise on resources due to lack of availability of the targeted resources or if selected team members did not have all the skills or experiences desired.

For an example of a resource planning SWOT analysis template, refer to Figure 9-1.

#	STRENGTHS (+)
1	Several team members have deep knowledge of the business domain
2	Core development team has successfully worked together before
3	Several team members have worked on complex high-risk projects before
4	Experienced Scrum master
5	

#	WEAKNESSES (–)
1	Team has limited experience with agile methodology and practices
2	Team has limited experience with DevOps approach and practices
3	Several members have limited experience with the projected dev toolset
4	
5	

#	OPPORTUNITIES (+)
1	Senior team members can mentor the newer members
2	Business domain knowledge within the team to propose solution ideas
3	
4	
5	

#	THREATS (–)
1	Several team members have more than 2 weeks of PTO to use before end of the year
2	Team members will be working across multiple time zones
3	Technical leader has received several lucrative offers from other firms
4	
5	

ANALYSIS SUMMARY & EVALUATION NOTES
This is a talented, professional team with a history of successful projects
Recommend team training on agile, DevOps for entire team
Recommend training on targeted development tools for select team members
Provide incentive to technical leader to remain with the project until completion, and pair him closely with Steve for all project efforts

Figure 9-1 SWOT Analysis Template

Training

Training is important to PMI, and it should be a high priority for you as well. Training is the process by which individual team members acquire new skills or enhance existing skills. In most cases, training is needed when dealing with new technologies or processes, or when individual team members do not have the prerequisite experience in a given skill set that is needed to successfully complete project assignments.

The first step is to identify the requisite competencies and skill sets needed for each role on the project. Then you need to identify areas of weakness to recognize training needs. This is where your SWOT analysis can be helpful.

It is recommended that the team or project manager create a training plan to capture the required training. From here, a training calendar can be developed and should also be incorporated into the project schedule. In addition, the cost of the training is a direct cost to your project and should also be factored into the project budget.

Three important notes about training:

- Training is not limited to formal classroom or virtual training courses. It can also include coaching, on-the-job training, mentoring, simulations, and documentation reviews.

- To be the most effective, training should be provided as close as possible to the point needed in the project so the new skills and knowledge are not lost over time.

- Training is a great motivator for project team members.

 Resource Management Plan

As referenced earlier in the discussion of the Plan Resource Management process, the *resource management plan* is the artifact that captures how the project resources will be managed throughout the project, and it is a subsidiary plan to the overall project management plan. As with all project management plans, the exact composition and the detail within the plan vary depending on the industry, organization policy and procedures, and the nature of the project itself. In addition, it is common for the resource management plan to be organized in two sections: one for the team resources and another for the physical resources.

The common elements of a resource management plan include the following:

- **Identification of Resources:** Describes how the team and physical resources will be identified for the project.

- **Acquiring Resources:** Describes how resources will be acquired; in particular, which ones will be internally sourced versus ones that will be external and need to involve procurement.

- **Roles and Responsibilities:** Describes the project roles and their subsequent authority, responsibility, and competence.

- **Project Organizational Chart:** Provides a visual illustrating how the project roles will be organized and the reporting relationships.

- **Project Team Resource Management:** Describes how team members should be defined, staffed, managed, and released.

- **Training:** Captures the training strategies that will be utilized for team members.

- **Team Development:** Captures methods for developing the team.

- **Resource Control:** Describes physical resources and how the acquisition of physical resources will be optimized for project needs and will be available when needed on the project.

- **Recognition Plan:** Describes what recognition and rewards will be given to team members and when they will be given.

Team Charter

For the PMP exam, the ***team charter*** is a key artifact for the project team. The team charter documents the values, agreements, and operating guidelines for the project team. And like most project management artifacts, it can be updated during the project as new discoveries are encountered and as circumstances change during the project. There are no set elements of a team charter, but common elements include the following:

- Team values

- Team agreements

- Communication tools and guidelines

- Decision-making criteria and process

- Conflict resolution process

- Meeting guidelines

- Other team agreements and team protocols

- Ground rules that clarify acceptable and unacceptable behavior

To clarify, this artifact should be developed with the team after it is formed. As we discuss later, it is an activity to help establish team ownership of the project, but it should be accounted for during the planning process. Many of these resource management artifacts are started during planning and then completed after the team forms. The team charter is a prime example of this.

Resource Requirements

The resource requirements document lists all the team and physical resources needed by the project at the work package or activity within a work package level by the type and quantity. From this level, the resource needs for any higher level, including the project as a whole, can be determined.

This document often includes the assumptions and constraints that led to the decision to use the targeted resources. In addition, this information is used hand in hand with work and cost estimating.

Resource Breakdown Structure (RBS)

The resource breakdown structure (RBS) is a hierarchical representation by category and type of all the team and physical resources needed by the project. It is a helpful tool to use with stakeholders to summarize the resource needs of the project and to ensure all resource needs are accounted for. Like the resource requirements document, the RBS is used along with the work breakdown structure (WBS) and cost estimating methods to improve the quality of the project planning process.

Figure 9-2 shows an RBS template.

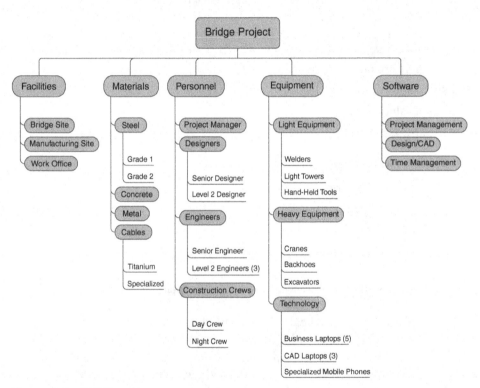

Figure 9-2 RBS Template

Responsibility Assignment Matrix (RAM)

The responsibility assignment matrix (RAM) illustrates the connections between the project work packages (or activities) with the project team members. In particular, it documents which team members are assigned and responsible for each work item. This illustration is normally captured in a matrix/table form with the project team members along one axis and the work items along the other axis. Then each intersectional cell is used to capture what level of involvement the team member has with that given work item.

A RAM can be captured for any and all work levels with the WBS, so there is flexibility depending on your intended audience.

The most common form of a RAM is an RACI chart. RACI is an acronym for Responsible, Accountable, Consulted, and Informed. Figure 9-3 shows an RACI matrix template.

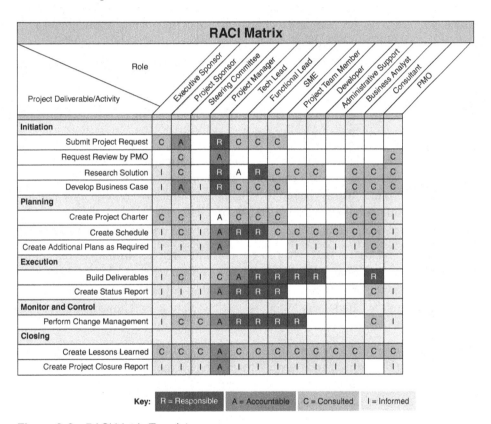

RACI Matrix													
Project Deliverable/Activity	Executive Sponsor	Project Sponsor	Steering Committee	Project Manager	Tech Lead	Functional Lead	SME	Project Team Member	Developer	Administrative Support	Business Analyst	Consultant	PMO
Initiation													
Submit Project Request	C	A		R	C	C	C						
Request Review by PMO		C		A									C
Research Solution	I	C		R	A	R	C	C	C		C	C	C
Develop Business Case	I	A	I	R	C	C	C				C	C	C
Planning													
Create Project Charter	C	C	I	A	C	C	C				C	C	I
Create Schedule	I	C	I	A	R	R	C	C	C	C	C	C	I
Create Additional Plans as Required	I	I	I	A			I	I	I	I		C	I
Execution													
Build Deliverables	I	C	I	C	A	R	R	R	R		R		
Create Status Report	I	I	I	A	R	R	R				C		I
Monitor and Control													
Perform Change Management	I	C	C	A	R	R	R	R			C		I
Closing													
Create Lessons Learned	C	C	C	A	C	C	C	C	C	C	C	C	C
Create Project Closure Report	I	I	I	A	I	I	I	I	I	I	I		I

Key: R = Responsible   A = Accountable   C = Consulted   I = Informed

Figure 9-3   RACI Matrix Template

Resource Calendars

The resource calendar maps the project resources to the project calendar and documents the actual availability of resources (physical and team) to the project work efforts. The resource calendar identifies working days, shifts, holidays, vacation time, training days, and when physical resources are expected to be available. This information should be incorporated into the scheduling tool used by the project.

High-Performing Teams

Next, let's get into managing the project team and why the Team Performance domain is important. On any project, after taking everything into account, the project team is expected to deliver. And the key to doing this is having a high-performing project team. You can have the greatest plan in the world, but if your core project team can't get the work done as expected, it really doesn't matter. Conversely, a high-performing project team can go a long way in compensating for inadequate planning and other less-than-ideal project environments. As the ***project manager***, you are responsible for developing and fostering an environment and a team culture that maximizes the performance of your project team. Even when the team members have the requisite skill sets, they need to work together and collaborate effectively for project success, and the project manager can greatly influence this experience.

Characteristics of High-Performing Teams

Before we delve into the management principles and techniques that lead to better project team performance, let's be clear on the goal. In other words, what do high-performing teams look like? What do they have in common? Do they all look and act the same? Although no two teams ever perform in precisely the same manner, and every team has its unique strengths, high-performing teams share a core set of traits:

- **Clarity:** This trait is likely the most important. High-performing teams know where they are going, what they are doing, and why they are doing it. They understand the project goals and priorities, they have clear roles and responsibilities, and they understand their assigned work tasks and how their piece fits in with the rest.

- **Commitment:** Members of high-performing teams are committed to the success of the project, and they take ownership of the project outcomes. They demonstrate a persistence and determination to get the job done. The source of the commitment is not always the same. It might be personal, to the team, to the customer, or to the organization.

- **Professional:** High-performing teams are professional about their work. Members take individual responsibility for the quality of assigned work, personal communications, and interactions with all stakeholders, especially with each other. This involves the effective use of leadership and ***interpersonal skills***.

- **Synergy:** High-performing teams develop a synergistic force about them that allows them to accomplish more as a combined team than they could do collectively as individuals. This synergy is developed over time, but generally results when the team has the right mix of skills and experiences, has a healthy team orientation, and has clearly defined roles and responsibilities.

■ **Trust:** High-performing teams display a great deal of trust in each other and in their project leader. Trust is earned over time, and keys to building this trust include demonstrating effective leadership and interpersonal skills and creating a collaborative team environment with an open exchange of ideas.

Team Development Models

Now that you have a better sense for what a high-performing team looks like, let's review two team development models that help the project manager support the project team and its development to a high-performing unit. In addition, you should know these models for the exam.

Tuckman Ladder

The first model, the Tuckman model, is the one that is routinely referenced by people when they use the expression "forming, storming, norming, performing" to describe the process of how teams come together and develop over the life of the project. Officially, the model is known as the Tuckman Ladder, and it describes the five stages of team development.

1. **Forming:** This is the initial stage when the project team first comes together. Team members go through the process of meeting each other and learning each other's position on the team, along with their skill sets and backgrounds.

2. **Storming:** This is the stage when team members' personalities, strengths, and weaknesses emerge, and initial conflicts can occur as the team discovers how to work together and explore which ideas and approaches will be used. This process can complete quickly or linger for a long time. Poor performing teams often never get past this stage. This is also the stage where leadership and interpersonal skills are key, so the team can advance to the stage of growth.

3. **Norming:** This is the stage when the team is working together and starting to function as a cohesive group. Everyone knows their roles and understands how to work with everyone else. There may still be some challenges during this stage, but they are handled and resolved quickly.

4. **Performing:** This is the stage that high-performing teams get to. The team operates efficiently, works together well, focuses on what is best for the team, has developed a synergy about them, and is producing quality work.

5. **Adjourning:** This is not part of the original Tuckman Ladder model but was added by him in a second edition. This is simply the stage when the project work is completed, and the team disbands to move on to their next assignments.

The key takeaways from this model are that high-performing teams get to the performing stage of team development, not all teams make it to each stage, and some times teams have to return to a prior stage to reset before they can return to a prior stage and/or advance beyond that. An area to be particularly mindful about is the addition and departure of team members and what that does to the team dynamic. When these changes occur to the team composition, the team returns to the forming stage and works its way back through the process. This can be very quick, but it does occur. The key to determining the impact of the change and the team dynamics is the role the team member is performing and the interpersonal skills of either the team member who left or who is joining the team. The more of a leadership role it is, the more impact there could be. And if the departing team member provided a lot of the social bonding glue to the team fabric, there is likely to be more impact with their absence. This is an area where the project manager needs to both monitor closely and help facilitate a new team dynamic.

> **TIP** The project team can go through these team development stages constantly throughout the project life cycle as team members are rolling on and rolling off the project.

Drexler/Sibbet Team Performance Model

The second model is the Drexler/Sibbet Team Performance Model, developed by Allan Drexler and David Sibbet. Their model describes team performance in seven steps. Steps 1–4 address creating a project team, and Steps 5–7 address project team sustainability and performance. Step 6 (High Performance) is obviously the indication the team has become a high-performing team. Table 9-2 summarizes the key aspects of this model.

Table 9-2 Drexler/Sibbet Team Performance Model Summary

Step	Step Name	Description
1	Orientation	This step answers the Why question. The project team learns the purpose and mission of the project.
2	Trust Building	This step answers the Who question. The project team learns about each other, including the skills and abilities that each brings to the project. In addition, any key stakeholders that can influence the project are reviewed.
3	Goal Clarification	This step answers the What question. The project team elaborates on the high-level project information to get a better understanding of requirements, assumptions, acceptance criteria, and stakeholder expectations.

Step	Step Name	Description
4	Commitment	This step answers the How question. The project team starts to develop plans to achieve the project goals. This often includes milestone schedules, high-level budgets, resource needs, and initial release plans.
5	Implementation	In this step, the high-level plans are decomposed into greater detail, and the team starts working together.
6	High Performance	In this step, the team has worked together for a while, is working well together, experiences synergies, and does not require much oversight.
7	Renewal	This step can occur anytime there is a change on the project or project team. This could be a change in the deliverables, project team membership, project leadership, project environment, or stakeholders.

When a change occurs, the team may need to evaluate whether past behavior and actions are still sufficient or if the team needs to return to a prior step to reset expectations and/or ways of working together. |

Management Principles to Maximize Team Performance

Key management principles that are paramount to maximizing team performance include the following:

- **Adapt management style:** Although as a rule, a collaborative, servant-leadership management approach to leading project teams is the most effective in most situations, you might need to adjust your style depending on the project phase, the needs of your particular team, and the project environment. We discuss tailoring the project leadership style and *servant leadership* in more detail later.

- **Get the right people:** Whenever possible, personally select the members of your core team. You should have the best understanding of the skills, abilities, and behaviors that are needed for project success. In particular, get people who have a track record of success. As any successful project manager will attest, having the right people is 80 percent of the battle. Of course, in the real world, you don't always have this luxury, and we talk about that in the "Techniques for Challenging Project Team Situations" section later in this chapter.

    One aspect to note here for the PMP exam is the difference between I-shaped skills and T-shaped skills. The "I" and "T" references pertain to the depth and breadth of the skill sets a particular team member possesses. I-shaped refers to someone who is deep in a particular skill set needed by the project but has minimal skills in any other skill needed by the project. The T-shaped reference indicates someone who has deep skills in at least one skill needed by the project and some talent/knowledge in the other skills areas needed by the project (that is, breadth).

For adaptive/agile projects, more value is placed on individuals with T-shaped skills given the smaller team sizes and their self-organizing nature.

TIP   Agile teams value individuals with T-shaped skill sets.

- **Plan as a team:** A major component of modern project management is the idea that planning is a team activity. This was a heavy emphasis in the planning chapters. Why is this key? If the team develops the project plan, it becomes "their" plan and "their" schedule. With this come a much higher level of commitment, buy-in, and accountability and much less time spent battling the issues you get when this is not present.

- **Develop a team charter:** To align individual expectations with desired team behaviors, develop a team charter that defines the guidelines, procedures, and principles by which the team will operate. The important thing here is develop this with the team. This way, much like the overall project plan and schedule, it becomes theirs.

EXAM TIP   For the exam, understand the purpose and content of the Team Charter and that it should be developed as collaborative process with the project team.

- **Keep the team focused:** One of the most important things a project manager can do is to make sure each team member is simultaneously crystal clear on the big picture of the project (mission, objectives, and priorities) on one hand and focused on the immediate task on the other. To focus, not only must each team member have clear work assignments and roles, but the project manager needs to be an umbrella for them. As an umbrella, the project manager protects the team members from the politics, noise, and other factors that distract them and slow their progress.

- **Set clear expectations:** To encourage maximum team productivity, nothing is more important than making sure team members understand what is expected from them in advance. This applies to both work assignments and team protocols. A key aspect of this expectation-setting activity is to review the completion criteria for any work assignment up front. This step alone goes a long way in preventing rework and increasing productivity.

- **Facilitate productivity:** Continuing our productivity theme, the focus of the project manager should be on doing everything to enable each team member to be as productive as possible. What does this mean? It means the following:

  - Ensure that work assignments are clear and understood.

  - Provide the tools, resources, and procedures to facilitate team collaboration.

  - Provide all resources that are needed to accomplish the work in a timely fashion.

  - Facilitate resolution to any issue impeding work assignment completion.

  - Anticipate issues that might affect work productivity and take action to mitigate or prevent them (risk management at the work task level).

- **Improve marketability:** A key goal a project manager can have for every person on their team is to improve their marketability through their experiences on the project. In the end, the only real job security one has is to always be "marketable"...and to continuously improve. A project manager should look for ways to improve skills, build competencies, enhance résumés, and help each person make progress on their career goals. This mindset is key to both how work tasks are assigned and sold to the respective individuals. This also involves the use of training to help accomplish these goals and is priority for PMI. In particular, a project manager should find out who desires to become project managers or to gain project management skills, and then assign roles and responsibilities throughout the project to facilitate the growth of these leadership skills.

- **Leverage individual strengths:** An extension of the previous principle, this one has three primary components:

  - Look for the strengths that each person brings to the table but understand their weaknesses. This approach keeps the project manager positive and is especially important when the project manager has not personally selected the team or when they have been given a team member with a reputation. This aspect may also involve identifying opportunities for training.

  - Understand what drives people, their motivators, and what they care about. Not only will this help position people to do better, but it will also enable the project manager to reward and recognize them more effectively.

  - Align project roles and responsibilities with each team member's "sweet spot" as much as possible. The sweet spot is the combination of natural strengths and personal motivators.

- **Recognize and reward:** This principle has three primary aspects:

> **NOTE**   Look for opportunities to recognize and reward the behaviors and accomplishments that will lead to project success, and prioritize team-level rewards over individual rewards.

- **PR agent:** A project manager should pretend they are the public relations agent for each one of their team members. In addition to providing timely feedback and appreciation directly to each person, they can make sure the right people (especially the people who influence their career advancements and compensation) know about the excellent work the person is doing throughout the project. This should not wait until the end of the project or at annual review time; it is much more effective and meaningful if it is communicated as it happens.

- **Celebrate:** A project manager should take the time and make plans to celebrate interim milestones along the way. This supports the idea of acknowledging efforts throughout the project and helps to build team momentum.

- **Rewards:** There are two key items here: First, look for ways during initial project planning and throughout the project to allow the team members to share in the rewards (profits) if the project accomplishes certain goals. Second, if the project team or specific team members are asked to perform heroic efforts, set up an incentive that will both reward and acknowledge the special efforts. As a rule, the rewards should be team based. This helps build team synergy, collaboration, and accountability. This aspect is important to PMI too.

- **Facilitate team synergy:** Especially early in the project, a project manager should use methods to help build the cohesiveness of the team. Most teams naturally go through the traditional "forming, storming, norming, and performing" stages, but a project manager can do some things to be a positive influence on this process. Depending on how much the given project team has worked together before and where they are physically located, the specifics differ, but as a guide, a project manager should focus on the following:

  - **Build relationships:** Set up team-building outings, team lunches, team meetings, and so on to enable relationships to begin and grow.

  - **Foster team collaboration:** Set up the tools that make it easy for the team to work together regardless of work locations; look for opportunities to have multiple team members work together on a single assignment to encourage knowledge sharing and reduce risk around isolated pockets of expertise in addition to improving overall team performance.

■ **Set up team procedures:** Determine what rules, guidelines, and protocols are needed to help establish team productivity (such as modes of communication, core hours, standard meeting times, work standards, work processes, and administrative procedures).

■ **Focus on visible progress:** Structure the project approach so that the team can get some early, visible progress. Not only does this create enthusiasm for the stakeholders, but it does the same for the core team too. In addition, track the team's progress and accomplishments in a very visible fashion. This helps build enthusiasm, and it encourages pride and accountability in project efforts.

Techniques for Better Team Performance

With an understanding of what a high-performing team looks like and the related management principles as the foundation, let's review a few techniques that generally lead to better project team performance:

■ **Conduct team kickoffs:** Conduct separate kickoff meetings with your core team at the beginning of each phase. This is an excellent way to reset expectations on project context, project goals and priorities, team member roles and responsibilities, team member assignments, project schedule, and team procedures.

On adaptive/agile projects, the sprint ceremonies of sprint planning and sprint retrospective accomplish this.

TIP Utilize mini-kickoff meetings at the beginning of each project phase, not just the start of the entire project, to reset expectations.

■ **Co-locate:** This is not always possible, and it is becoming more uncommon as project work becomes increasingly distributed. However, the results speak for themselves. When project team members are physically located in the same area, it is much easier to build relationships, share ideas and experiences, collaborate on assignments, develop answers to problems, and increase team synergy.

EXAM TIP For the exam, PMI always assumes co-location to be the best way for teams to work together, and the project manager should always strive to co-locate team members as much as possible.

- **Use meeting time wisely:** To communicate both respect and value for individuals' time and to help team productivity, have a definite purpose or need for any team meeting and confirm that this purpose is understood by all team members. At a minimum, conduct a general team status meeting each week to share knowledge and lessons learned, and to provide gentle peer pressure accountability. The need for formal meetings varies depending on the project approach utilized, how the team is naturally collaborating, the composition of the team, team productivity, and the list of outstanding issues.

- **Set standards:** Especially on projects where multiple individuals might be doing the same type of work or when work is outsourced, develop and communicate the standards the work must meet to be accepted. Setting standards helps clarify expectations, reduces rework activity, improves quality, and leverages expert knowledge. This can also be captured in the team charter.

- **Leverage expertise:** This is an invaluable method to improve team performance and improve the skills of multiple individuals, especially in cases where the project involves newer technologies, the primary resource pools do not have adequate skill levels, or the organization needs to avoid allocating their most senior, sought-after talent on a single project.

- **Resolve conflicts right away:** High-performing teams do not let intrateam conflicts or project issues linger because they can adversely affect team productivity if they do. As the project manager, you need to facilitate resolutions quickly. This does not mean that you do not listen and make rash judgments. It means that you deal with it—don't avoid it. In all cases, it is very important that you stay objective, treat all sides with respect, place your focus on potential solutions, and seek out win-win scenarios.

- **Prepare for client interactions:** To better manage client expectations and avoid unproductive issues, prepare the team for direct client interactions. Make sure they understand the project from the client's perspective, the expectation the client has of the team's abilities, specific actions to take if they need assistance when they are with the client, and any talking points to either avoid or emphasize.

- **Set up a project repository:** To help facilitate team productivity, share knowledge, and protect project assets, set up a common repository that is accessible by all core team members to store project work products and project management deliverables.

- **Set up a team collaboration environment:** To encourage and make it easy for the team to work together on project work items—especially when the team is distributed or virtual in nature—set up the appropriate collaboration tools and environments. This normally means setting up one or more online tools to enable team members to do one or more of the following: discuss topics (group chat), facilitate team meetings (web conferencing), view and edit a common work product, and track changes to a work product.

- **Develop team rituals:** To help build team unity, develop specific rituals that engage the entire team. Examples include going out to lunch together on a certain day each week, sharing breakfast together on a certain day each week, celebrating individual birthdays or anniversaries, and so forth.

- **Share leadership responsibilities:** To help team members develop leadership skills and to help build commitment to the project, look for opportunities to share leadership responsibilities. This is natural on larger and cross-functional projects.

- **Leverage pairing and mentoring opportunities:** An effective technique to foster team building, collaboration, and trust and to provide growth opportunities is to leverage pairing and/or mentoring work arrangements. In a pairing arrangement, two team members are assigned to the same high-level task with the intent of learning together and from each other along the way. In a mentoring arrangement, a more experienced team member coaches a less experienced team member.

- **Effective task assignments:** We've talked about this one in various ways many times already, but the point we want to emphasize here is that you can't just assume a task assignment is understood and will be done because it appears on the schedule and there is a person's name beside it. The keys here are the following:

    - Instill a sense of ownership on assigned tasks. Look for modules or domains that specific people can have lead responsibility over.

    - Verify that the person assigned the work is clear on task completion criteria. This way, you avoid the need to micromanage your team.

    - Ensure that one person is primarily responsible for a task and that you have buy-in on that responsibility.

    - Ensure that the level of schedule detail is appropriate to effectively assign and monitor work.

- **Plan for orientation:** For any new team member joining your project, there is an introductory orientation period. Your goal is to streamline this period and have each team member at maximum productivity as soon as possible. Some recommended action items include the following:

    - **Protect your schedule:** Do not assume the new team member will be 100 percent productive on day one. The length of the ramp-up period will be specific to the project, work assignments, and previous work experiences.

- **Prepare an orientation packet:** Put yourself in the new team member's shoes and think about what you need to know to get a solid understanding of the project environment.

- **Set up the work environment in advance:** In any project environment where team members need specific equipment, tools, or access privileges to do their work, do whatever you can to get them set up before the team member starts. If you can't, you should account for this ramp-up time in your schedule.

- **Invest the time up front:** Plan on spending time with any new team member up front. By investing focused attention with any new team member, you can better communicate your energy for the project and the expectations for the project, their role, and their contributions. This is a clear case where spending a little extra time up front prevents the need to spend a lot more time down the road on team productivity issues.

- **Plug in:** To help facilitate the performance team, you must stay connected with the team. The keys here are to stay visible, use the same communication channels the team is using, take time to meet with each team member one on one, and make sure the team knows you are there to help them be productive.

- **Personality Indicators and Psychometrics:** These can be used to gain a better understanding of team members' personalities and can even be used as a type of team building exercise. They can be used to encourage team members to improve interaction, build trust, and align their personalities with career progression. Some personality type categories include introverts, extroverts, pragmatists, innovators, and process-followers; however, they should not be used to judge anyone or make assumptions of anyone but should be an exercise to understand one better. Common types of personality assessment tools include

  - Myers-Briggs Type Indicator (MBTI)

  - Big Five Personality Model (OCEAN: Openness, Conscientiousness, Extroversion, Agreeableness, and Neuroticism)

  - DISC (Dominance, Influence, Steadiness, Conscientiousness)

  - True Colors

  - TRACOM

Project Leadership

As you can see from the previous sections, a project environment must have effective project leadership and a positive team culture to achieve its maximum potential. In the Project Team performance domain, the Power Skills from the PMI Talent Triangle we discussed in Chapter 2, "Project Management 101," really come into play.

> **NOTE**   Power Skills are the knowledge, skills, and behaviors needed to guide, motivate, and direct a team to help an organization achieve its business goals. This category used to be referred to as Leadership.

Here, we review the aspects of a project that need leadership and how leading a project is different from managing a project. In addition, we explore the key components and skill sets of project leadership, techniques for better project leadership, and the value of the servant leadership approach.

More Than Managing

The process of leading a project is more than managing the project. To be clear, an effective project manager employs both management and leadership to accomplish the project objectives. The key is finding the proper balance between the two and using the approach that is the best fit for their personality and the needs of the project organization, environment, and team. Table 9-3 (taken mostly from the *PMBOK® Guide*, Sixth Edition, Section 3.4.5) summarizes the differences between management and leadership.

Table 9-3 Comparing Leadership and Management

Leadership	Management
Uses relational power	Uses positional power
Best for developing	Best for maintaining
Focus on vision, alignment, motivation, and inspiration	Focus on operational issues and problem solving
Do the right things	Do things right
Innovation focus	Administrative focus
Focus on relationships with people	Focus on systems and structure
Inspires trust	Relies on control
Focus on long-range vision	Focus on near-term goals
Focus on the horizon	Focus on the bottom line

Leadership	Management
Challenge status quo	Accept status quo
Ask what and why	Ask how and when

The process of leading a project entails employing the right balance of management and leadership to guide the people involved (team, stakeholders, organization) toward the accomplishment of the project's objectives. This process involves understanding your own personality and the leadership style needed for the project organization, environment, and project team. If we look back at Chapter 2, many of the roles a project manager performs involve leadership, including the following:

- **Planner:** Ensures the project is defined properly and completely for success, all stakeholders are engaged, a work effort approach is determined, and processes are in place to properly execute and control the project.

- **Point Person:** Serves as the central point of contact for all oral and written project communications to key stakeholders.

- **Facilitator:** Ensures that stakeholders and team members from different perspectives understand each other and work together to accomplish the project goals.

- **Aligner:** Gains agreement from the stakeholders on project definition, success criteria, and approach; manages stakeholder expectations throughout the project while managing the competing demands of time, cost, and quality; gains agreement on resource decisions and issue resolution action steps.

- **Problem Solver:** Utilizes root-cause analysis process experience, prior project experiences, and technical knowledge to resolve unforeseen technical issues and take any necessary corrective actions.

- **Umbrella:** Works to shield the project team from the politics and noise surrounding the project so they can stay focused and productive.

- **Coach:** Determines and communicates the role each team member plays and the importance of that role to the project success, finds ways to motivate each team member, looks for ways to improve the skills of each team member, and provides constructive and timely feedback on individual performances.

- **Salesperson:** Focuses on selling the benefits of the project to the organization, serving as a change agent, and inspiring team members to meet project goals and overcome project challenges.

In addition, many qualities of successful project managers described in Chapter 2 have strong leadership elements, including the following:

- **Takes ownership:** Takes responsibility and accountability for the project; leads by example; brings energy and drive to the project; without this attitude, all the skills and techniques in the world will only get you so far.

- **Showcases savviness:** Understands people and the dynamics of the organization; navigates tricky politics; is able to quickly read emotionally charged situations; thinks fast on their feet; builds relationships; and leverages personal power for benefit of the project.

- **Exudes intensity with a smile:** Balances an assertive, resilient, tenacious, results-oriented focus with a style that makes people want to help; consistently follows up on everything and their resolutions without annoying everyone.

- **Remains the eye of the storm:** Demonstrates an ability to be the calm eye of the project hurricane; has a high tolerance for ambiguity; takes the heat from key stakeholders (senior executives); exhibits a calm, confident aura when others are showing signs of issue or project stress.

- **Maintains a strong customer-service orientation:** Demonstrates an ability to see each stakeholder's perspective; has the ability to provide a voice of all key stakeholders (especially the sponsor) to the project team; possesses strong facilitation and collaboration skills and excellent active listening skills.

- **Stays people-focused:** Understands that methodology, process, and tools are important, but without quality people, it's very difficult to complete a project successfully; acts ethically; protects his team; and takes a teaching approach.

- **Always keeps an eye on the ball:** Stays focused on the project goals and objectives. There are many ways to accomplish a given objective, which is especially important to remember when things don't go as planned.

- **Demonstrates controlled passion:** Balances passion for completing the project objectives with a healthy detached perspective. This allows the project manager to make better decisions, to continue to see all points of view, and to better anticipate risks.

- **Provides context understanding:** Understands the context of the project— the priority that the project has among the organization's portfolio of projects and how it aligns with the overall goals of the organization.

- **Looks for trouble:** Constantly looks and listens for potential risks, issues, or obstacles; confronts doubt head-on; deals with disgruntled users right away; understands that most of these situations are opportunities and can be resolved up front before they become full-scale crisis points.

Where Leadership Is Needed on a Project

There are three key points to know about leading a project:

1. There are many aspects and different styles of project leadership.

2. The project manager is not the sole provider of project leadership.

3. Specific leadership providers vary depending on the project environment.

To clarify these ideas, Table 9-4 reviews the different leadership styles and Table 9-5 describes project areas where leadership is needed and who could provide it. Note that for adaptive/agile projects, the reference to Team Leader(s) in Table 9-5 includes the Scrum master and product owner roles.

Table 9-4   Project Leadership Styles

Leadership Style	Description
Direct	Hierarchical, with project manager making all decisions
Consultative	Factors in opinions from other key advisors, but the leader makes the decisions
Servant Leadership	Facilitates rather than manages; provides coaching, training, and removes work impediments
Consensus/Collaborative	Seeks input from all team members equally and welcomes all ideas and suggestions; the team comes to an agreement
Situational	Style changes to fit context, maturity, and experience of the team
Laissez-faire	"Hands off" leader—allows the team to make their own decisions and establish their own goals
Transactional	Focuses on goals, feedback, and accomplishment to determine rewards
Transformational	Empowers followers through idealized attributes and behaviors, inspirational motivation, encouragement for innovation and creativity, and individual consideration
Charismatic	Inspires others, possesses high influencing skills, has high energy, and is enthusiastic
Interactional	Combination of transactional, transformational, and charasmatic

Table 9-5 Project Leadership Areas

Project Area	Leadership Provided By
Direction and plan	Project sponsor
	Senior management
	Project manager
	Technical leader(s)
	Product management
Organizational influence	Project sponsor
	Senior management
	Project manager
	Technical leader(s)
	Product management
Commitment	Project sponsor
	Senior management
	Project manager
	Project team
	Product management
Stakeholder expectations	Project manager
	Project sponsor
	Senior management
	Product management
	Project team
Facilitation	Project manager
	Team leader(s)
Communications point	Project manager
	Team leader(s)
Project team	Project manager
	Team leader(s)
	Technical leader(s)
Conflict resolution	Project manager
	Team leader(s)
	Project team

Project Area	Leadership Provided By
Managing business change	Project sponsor
	Senior management
	Project manager
Technical issues	Project manager
	Technical leader(s)
	Project team
Business issues	Project sponsor
	Senior management
	Product management
	Project manager
	Team leader(s)
Managing risks	Project sponsor
	Senior management
	Product management
	Project manager
	Team leader(s)
	Technical leader(s)
	Project team

Leadership Skills

We have discussed the importance of project leadership and reviewed how it is implemented on projects with high-performing teams. In addition, we noted that PMI indicates that a key measure of effective team performance is the application of leadership and interpersonal skills by all team members. Let's take a moment to explicitly review what comprises leadership, team, and interpersonal skills per PMI.

When you think of leadership skills, what comes to mind?

- The ability to create and sell a vision?

- The ability to motivate and inspire a group of people?

- The ability to be aware and sensitive to various culture norms, practices, and beliefs?

- The ability to think logically, analyze objectively, and identify root causes of challenging situations?

- The ability to make decisions and/or the ability to leverage the team when making key decisions?

- The ability to effectively resolve conflicts?

- The ability to be self-aware and control one's own emotions, actions, and words?

- The ability to empathize with others and understand their perspective?

- The ability to understand the politics of the organization and to get things done?

- The ability to effectively implement management practices and systems?

- The ability to negotiate for resources?

If you answered yes to these questions, you are on the right track. As you can see, leadership skills are rather straightforward, and PMI takes a similar straightforward approach in breaking down leadership, team, and interpersonal skills too. The key leadership, team, and interpersonal skills per PMI are as follows:

- Establishing and maintaining vision

- Critical thinking

- Motivation

- Emotional intelligence

- Decision-making

- Conflict management

- Influencing

- Negotiation

- Recognizing the value of diversity, equity, and inclusion

For each of these skill areas, we clarify what is covered and review any applicable models that you should be aware of for the exam.

Establishing and Maintaining Vision

The ability to create a clear, concise project purpose and a clear picture of the desired future state the project will deliver is an essential leadership skill. The shared vision of the project target contributes to better team collaboration, serves as a strong day-to-day motivational tool, helps to guide project decisions along the way, and keeps project efforts from getting off track.

Critical Thinking

Critical thinking is the ability to apply open-minded, rational, disciplined, logical, evidence-based thinking to project efforts. It also involves a high level of self-awareness to recognize one's own bias and faulty assumptions. This leadership skill is important for all project team members, but as the project manager, you set the example that others on the team can model. Some key areas on projects where critical thinking comes into play include the following:

- Identifying root causes of problems

- Dealing with ambiguity and complexity

- Identifying bias, unstated assumptions, false premises, faulty logic, and emotional appeals

- Analyzing data and evidence to evaluate arguments and perspectives

- Observing events to recognize patterns and relationships

- Applying inductive, deductive, and abductive reasoning appropriately

- Researching and gathering unbiased, well-balanced information

- Discerning the use of language and the influence it has on oneself and others

Motivation

The ability to motivate a project team throughout the project life cycle is an essential leadership skill. This skill entails understanding the primary motivators for each member of the team and then applying this understanding to get the best performance from each individual and ultimately the entire team as a whole.

We review the four most common motivational models that are used in this endeavor, but the key ones to understand for the exam are extrinsic and intrinsic motivators. Extrinsic motivators include salary, rewards, bonuses, and promotions. Intrinsic motivators include achievement, challenge, autonomy, personal growth, responsibility, opportunity to make a difference, relationships, and opportunity to be part of a team. As a rule, extrinsic motivators have a ceiling regarding their effectiveness. When people feel they are fairly compensated and rewarded, the motivational effect is minimized; however, if these extrinsic motivators are not being met, they can act as a demotivating force. For project work especially, the intrinsic motivators drive optimal individual and team performance.

As mentioned previously, PMI includes four *motivation* models in the *PMBOK® Guide*, Seventh Edition, as references. Table 9-6 summarizes these models and provides a quick study guide to help your preparation efforts.

Table 9-6 Motivation Models

Model	Developed By	Description
Hygiene and Motivational Factors	Frederick Herzberg	Insufficient hygiene factors (compensation, company policies, work environment) lead to worker dissatisfaction.
		Sufficient hygiene factors do not necessarily lead to worker satisfaction.
		Motivational factors (achievement, advancement, growth) determine worker satisfaction level.
Intrinsic versus Extrinsic Motivators	Daniel Pink	Extrinsic motivators (compensation) have limited impact.
		Intrinsic motivators are more effective for complicated and challenging work, like projects.
		Three types of intrinsic motivators are autonomy, mastery, and purpose.
Theory of Needs	David McClellan	All people are motivated by relative need levels of achievement, affiliation, and power.
		The strength of each need varies depending on an individual's experiences and culture.
		Achievement people are motivated by challenging work.
		Affiliation people are motivated by being part of a team.
		Power people are motivated by increased responsibility.
Theory X, Y, and Z	Douglas McGregor (Theory X and Y) Abraham Maslow and William Ouchi (Theory Z)	**Theory X** assumes people work solely for income and have no goals or ambitions.
		Management style is top-down and hands-on. It is commonly used in hierarchical organizations and in production, labor-intensive environments.
		Theory Y assumes people are intrinsically motivated to do good work.
		Management style is more coaching based and encourages creativity and discussion. This style is common in creative and knowledge worker–based environments.
		Theory Z (Maslow) assumes people are motivated by self-realization, values, and a higher calling.
		Management style focuses on learning insights and meaning/value of the work.
		Theory Z (Ouchi) assumes people are motivated by providing a job for life with a focus on well-being of the employee and their family.
		Management style focuses on high productivity, morale, satisfaction.

Emotional Intelligence

If interpersonal skills are the foundation for effective leadership, then emotional intelligence is the material used to build that foundation. For many people, when they think about others with interpersonal skills, they are seeing emotional intelligence in action. Per PMI, *emotional intelligence* is defined as the ability to identify, assess, and manage the personal emotions of oneself and other people, as well as the collective emotions of groups of people. In other words, emotional intelligence is the ability to be aware of and control one's own emotions while simultaneously being able to recognize and understand the emotions and feelings of others.

> **NOTE** Per PMI, emotional intelligence is defined as the ability to identify, assess, and manage the personal emotions of oneself and other people, as well as the collective emotions of groups of people.

As stated previously, projects are performed by people and for people, and no other skill is more important for building and sustaining positive work relationships and high-performing project teams than emotional intelligence. You can also see the strong connection between emotional intelligence and servant leadership. Without emotional intelligence, servant leadership would be very difficult. The ability to remain under control, listen actively, and dial into how others are feeling and responding is essential for all project communications, team collaboration, and leadership endeavors.

Although there are many models to explain emotional intelligence, most of them agree on these four aspects:

- **Self-Awareness:** This is the ability to see ourselves for how we really are, including understanding our own emotions, goals, motivations, strengths, and weaknesses.

- **Self-Management:** This is the ability to think before acting, to remain under control, and not to respond impulsively.

- **Social Awareness:** This is the ability to recognize, consider, understand, and empathize with other people's feelings. This includes the ability to read body language and other nonverbal communications.

- **Social Skill:** This is the ability to put the other three aspects into action and is focused on building rapport, finding common ground, managing groups of people, and building social networks.

Together, these four aspects of emotional intelligence form a quadrant. Table 9-7 captures the relationships among these aspects. The aspects for oneself are on top, and the aspects for others on bottom. The awareness aspects are on the left, and the managing aspects are on the right.

Table 9-7 Emotional Intelligence Quadrant

	Awareness Focus	**Management Focus**
Oneself	Self-Awareness	Self-Management
Others	Social Awareness	Social Skill

Decision-Making

When we think of an effective leader, we often think of someone who can make decisions and leverage the team in the decision-making process in an effective manner.

The key points to understand about decision-making for the exam are as follows:

- Unilateral decisions offer the benefit of time but run the risk of demotivating team members who are impacted by the decision and did not have the opportunity to provide input.

- Group decisions offer the benefit of leveraging the knowledge, expertise, and experience of a diverse team but take time and take team members away from their primary tasks at hand.

- The art and skill of decision-making are comprised of knowing what decisions can be made unilaterally and which ones are better done with the group.

- When group decisions are needed, the key is to use techniques that minimize time required, reduce the impact of groupthink, and reduce the influence of dominant personalities on the team.

- The best group decision techniques are ones that leverage a diverge/converge pattern.

  - This means team members are approached individually first for their ideas and potential solutions.

  - Then the group converges to review the potential solutions and reach consensus on the final decision.

  - Common techniques for reaching a final decision include Roman voting, fist to five voting, and Wideband Delphi estimating.

- For decisions outside the authority of the project team, the team can evaluate alternatives, including the impact of each, and present the options to the authorized individual or team. This approach is aligned with the concept of "don't bring me problems, bring me solutions" that most senior management team members appreciate and value.

Conflict Management

Conflict management is an inherent nature of the project manager role. Projects, by their very nature, are an ongoing endeavor in managing and balancing the natural conflicts between scope, schedule, budget, and quality. And, of course, anytime people are involved, there are going to be conflicts. It is just a natural part of people working together. The way conflicts are approached and handled can make all the difference in the success of the project and the performance of the project team. If conflicts are not handled well, it can lead to team frustration, lack of trust, and overall reduced team morale and motivation.

The key is to look at conflicts as natural, as an opportunity to improve, and as something to proactively manage. To clarify, a conflict does not necessarily mean team members are arguing or fighting; it just means there is a disagreement. And natural disagreements are going to occur as teams determine how they are going to work together, how they are going to accomplish the project work, and how they are going to resolve the various technical issues that arise during the project.

If they are addressed well when they are small, a project can avoid situations that can derail the intended outcomes of the project. In most cases, the project manager should let the team members try to resolve the conflict themselves using their own interpersonal skills. Conflicts can escalate if team members feel their idea/solution/opinion is the only way to proceed and/or if they are not genuinely considering the input of the other team member. Per PMI, if the team members cannot resolve the conflict, then on a more predictive project, the project manager would step in to facilitate, and on a more adaptive project, the whole team would get involved due to the self-organizing nature of adaptive teams, which includes managing conflicts. This reinforces the importance of the entire team demonstrating leadership and interpersonal skills and not just the project manager.

We have discussed many qualities and techniques of effective project management and project leadership that come into play here. The following approaches are key to effectively addressing and resolving conflicts:

- Keep communications open and respectful.

- Focus on the issues, not the people.

- Focus on the present and the future (not the past).

- Search for alternatives together.

EXAM TIP   For the PMP Exam, here are some key conflict management themes per PMI:

- Conflict is simply a disagreement between team members (which is natural), not necessarily that they are fighting and arguing.

- If team members are disagreeing, let them try to resolve the situation first. If they cannot, then on a

    - **Predictive project:** The project manager steps into facilitate.

    - **Agile project:** The whole team steps in because they are self-organizing, which includes managing conflicts.

- Conflict management is the key (not necessarily conflict resolution) because you cannot always resolve a conflict, but it certainly needs to be managed so that it doesn't have negative consequences on the project.

Although many models out there describe how to address and resolve conflicts, for the exam, we advise being familiar with the one from Ken Thomas and Ralph Kilmann that describes six ways of addressing conflict. The model focuses on the relative power between the parties involved and the desire to maintain a positive relationship between the parties. Table 9-8 summarizes the Thomas-Kilmann model for addressing conflicts.

Table 9-8   Ken Thomas and Ralph Kilmann Conflict Management Model Summary

Approach	Description	Used When
Confronting/ Problem Solving	Approaching the conflict as a problem to be solved.	The relationship between parties is important.
Collaborating	Approaching the conflict by incorporating and learning about multiple views and perspectives.	There is trust between participants and time to reach consensus. The PM often serves as facilitator for conflicts within the project team.
Compromising	Conflict is resolved by agreeing to get some aspects of what each party wants but not all.	The parties involved are not going to be fully satisfied with any resolution option. This approach is also best used when parties involved are of equal relative power status.

Approach	Description	Used When
Smoothing/ Accommodating	Used when reaching the higher priority goal is more important than the conflict itself. This approach maintains harmony in the relationship and creates goodwill between the parties.	The parties involved are not of equal relative power or authority; for example, a conflict between project sponsor and a project team member.
Forcing	One party with more relative power or authority forces its will/ decision on the other party.	There is not enough time to collaborate or problem solve.
Withdrawal/ Avoiding	The conflict is not addressed for the time being.	A problem may go away on its own. It is a no-win situation. A cooling-off period is needed until parties involved can reconvene with calmer states of mind.

Although the goal of the project manager and the project team is to avoid conflicts escalating, for the exam, you should know the different levels of conflict that can exist. These conflict levels are known as the Leas model of conflict resolution, and Table 9-9 provides a summary of them. These levels are not self-contained, and behaviors may overlap and change.

Table 9-9 Leas Model: Five Levels of Conflict

Conflict Level	Description
Problem Solving	Team members collaborate to resolve the issue. Differences are identified, then shared and discussed among members. This level is a problem- or task-oriented conflict, not a person- or relationship-oriented conflict.
Disagreement	Team members are opinionated and believe that only their solution will work; they disregard other opinions. Personalities and issues mix; therefore, problems cannot be identified. At this stage, people begin to distrust one another and make problems personal.
Contest	Team members start taking sides and forming cliques. A win/lose dynamic emerges, followed by taking sides, distorted communication, and personal attacks. Conflict objectives shift from focus on self-protection to winning the argument. People feel threatened or invigorated and ready to fight.
Crusade (sometimes called Flight/Flight)	Teams are polarized, and the goal is simply to win (without considering what the correct solution should be). Conflict participants may shift from winning to trying to hurt or get rid of their opponents. Intervention is required.

Conflict Level	Description
World War (sometimes called Intractable Situation)	Teams are not talking to one another. People are now incapable of having a clear understanding of issues. Efforts to destroy others' reputations, positions, or well-being are common. This eventually ruins relationships.

Influencing

Because project managers often have little to no direct authority over team members, especially in matrix organizations, the ability to influence stakeholders on a timely basis is vital to project success. The skills needed here overlap with several other areas, including emotional intelligence, conflict management, negotiation, and decision-making. Of particular importance is the ability to do the following:

- Persuade

- Employ active and effective listening skills

- Be aware of and consider the perspectives of others

- Clearly articulate points and positions

- Gather relevant information to address issues and reach agreements while maintaining mutual trust

Another key aspect of influencing to be aware of is that the project manager can influence in four directions, and all are generally needed for a successful project:

- Upward (toward senior management)

- Downward (toward team members)

- Sideways (stakeholder peers within the organization)

- Outward (stakeholders outside of the organization)

Negotiation

Negotiation is the ability to reach an agreement between two or more parties, and like the influencing skill, it does overlap with other skill sets mentioned in this section, especially influencing, decision-making, conflict management, and emotional intelligence.

The project manager often needs to negotiate with functional managers and procurement departments for project resources. In addition, the project manager often needs to use negotiation to gain support for the project within the organization and to resolve conflicts within the team.

The team members might need to negotiate roles and responsibilities, tasks, priorities, and conflicts. On agile teams, they negotiate the relative estimate of tasks and which user stories they will be working on too.

Although there are many negotiation models, the Stephen Covey "Think Win-Win" model is highlighted by PMI in the *PMBOK® Guide*, Seventh Edition. This model is effective for all interactions, not just negotiations. In this model, there are three possible outcomes:

- **Win-Win:** This is the optimal outcome. Each person is satisfied with the outcome.

- **Win-Lose/Lose-Win:** This is the competition mindset where, in order to win, the other person has to lose.

- **Lose-Lose:** This outcome results when the competitive mindset overwhelms collaboration and both parties end up worse off.

So the goal, of course, is win-win outcomes, and to achieve these results, the following elements need to be present:

- **Character:** The parties are mature; they demonstrate integrity and the perspective that there is enough value for each party.

- **Trust:** The parties trust each other, establish agreements on how to operate, and are accountable to each other.

- **Approach:** Each party is willing and able to see the situation from the other's perspective. They work together to identify key issues and concerns. They agree on what an acceptable solution looks like and then work together on options to achieve an acceptable solution.

Recognizing the Value of Diversity, Equity, and Inclusion

One leadership skill that has gained more importance in both life and on the PMP exam is the trait to recognize the value of diversity, equity, and inclusion in the project team composition.

By including individuals from different genders, cultures, age groups, physical traits, and industry and work backgrounds, you are more likely to have a team that can think "outside the box" and solve problems more effectively. With their diverse knowledge bases and experiences, combined with an environment of mutual trust and collaboration, they can identify solutions and resolve problems quicker as compared to a team where everyone has similar backgrounds and experiences.

Psychological safety goes hand in hand with diversity and refers to empowering the team by creating and maintaining a healthy work setting that embraces diversity and is built on trust and mutual respect. Team members should be comfortable being themselves in their work setting.

Keys to Better Project Leadership

Now that we've reviewed what project leadership is and the components of leadership skills, let's discuss a few keys to better project leadership. This discussion helps reinforce what we have covered and will better prepare you for the exam.

To guide a group of unfamiliar project stakeholders and project team members to accomplish something that has not been done before, the project manager must leverage leadership and interpersonal skills. In addition, the leadership style needs to be tailored to the specific needs of the given project, environment, and stakeholders. Let's review the keys to more effective project leadership:

1. **It's about the people:** There are those who maintain that project management is about managing a process (or a workplan) and not about managing people. Are they serious? Who does the work? People. An effective project leader takes a holistic view that puts people first. This approach results in a focus on establishing and building relationships and a focus on gaining an authentic understanding and buy-in from each stakeholder.

2. **Visualize the goal...and the way there:** This is the traditional leadership ability of providing direction to the team. Not only does a project leader need to clearly see the end and be able to create this picture for everyone else, but they must also understand how the team is going to get there. The ability to see this big picture is vital to keeping the project focused on its primary objectives.

3. **See with "their" eyes:** This skill is not natural for many but is an invaluable one if you can do it. Look at your project from the perspective of the other stakeholders. What do they see? What are they thinking? What do they need? This ability to take another's perspective is foundational to building better relationships, developing requirements, managing communications, managing expectations, and building a productive project team.

4. **Earn their trust:** Effective leaders are trusted by senior management to do the right thing and get the job done. They are trusted by other stakeholders because they manage with integrity and consistently seek win-win scenarios to any project challenge.

TIP Be the first to take responsibility and the last to take credit.

5. **Earn their respect:** How do you earn the respect of project stakeholders when you do not have position power? Four key behaviors affect the level of respect granted you by project stakeholders:

   ■ **Show respect:** First of all, show respect to each person you are dealing with. Listen to them: *Really* listen to them, respect their time, and respect their knowledge, experience, and perspectives.

   ■ **Be real:** Deal with reality, not what it should be or could be. Your willingness to acknowledge and confront the realities of the project will be key to your overall effectiveness.

   ■ **Be fair:** People might not always like final decisions, but they will respect the decision and you if they feel you handled the situation in a fair manner. An approach to team management, decision-making, and conflict resolution that emphasizes fairness is key to earning the respect of others.

   ■ **Be consistent:** Lead by example, stick with your decisions, maintain your principles, do what you say you are going to do, and be emotionally steady.

6. **Facilitate progress:** As a project leader, you are focused on accomplishing the project objectives, and you realize that one of the most important jobs you have is to make it as easy as possible for your team to complete its work. How do you do this? Think of yourself as a conduit for progress, an enabler, a productivity enhancer. Some key actions include the following:

   ■ Anticipate issues, work to prevent them, and confront and resolve the ones that do occur—quickly.

   ■ Create an open and honest team environment where members are encouraged and comfortable to exchange their thoughts and ideas.

   ■ Facilitate the decision-making process.

   ■ Get needed information quickly.

   ■ Ensure the team has the structure, process, and tools to be as productive as possible.

   ■ Work to reduce the doubt and uncertainty factor for others.

7. **Take ownership:** Let there be no doubt in anyone's mind about who is responsible for this project. An ownership mindset manifests itself in a persistent, results-focused, no-excuses attitude that is undeniable and contagious to the other team members.

8. **Be resilient:** Like the proverbial willow tree that shows its true strength when confronted with a ferocious wind, a project leader is able to quickly adapt their approach and style to best meet the needs of the project. Through a creative and flexible mindset, a project leader understands that there are many ways to achieve the targeted goals and works to make it happen.

9. **Be a teacher:** A great model for the modern project manager is that of a teacher. In many situations, you are literally educating all stakeholders regarding their roles and responsibilities in a project approach. But in all project situations, taking a teaching mentality—a mindset that sincerely wants others to learn, grow, and improve—rather than a judgmental view will be paramount to your leadership effectiveness.

10. **Strive for excellence:** An important trait of effective project leaders is their ability to create confidence that the project will be well managed and that it will accomplish its goals. How do you do this? Be very good at what you do, know what you are doing, and exude competence and professionalism (note: we did not say *arrogance*). The three simple keys here are be prepared, be organized, and never stop learning and improving.

11. **Compensate for weaknesses:** A leader is humble enough, has enough self-awareness, and is team focused enough to recognize personal weaknesses. From this recognition, the leader then builds a team and delegates responsibilities to properly compensate. Again, it is difficult to be proficient at everything, and it is much easier to leverage the strengths of yourself and of your team to get the job done.

12. **Showcase self-control:** As a rule, most effective project leaders are models of self-control. They are consistent and positive in their behaviors and are generally immune from egocentric approaches and significant shifts or swings in their emotional stability (especially negative ones). In addition, they are able to remain calm under pressure and serve as a model for others during stressful times.

13. **Balance team tone with sense of urgency:** It is important to provide a positive environment where team members feel a sense of value and are empowered to contribute to the overall success of the project. However, you also need to create a sense of urgency in order to keep the project moving along and ensure tasks are completed on a timely basis. You need to ensure the team understands the value of the project and how this project helps achieve the strategic goals of the organization. The project manager must therefore balance the tone with urgency:

    - **Tone:** Use fluid communication and engagement and promote positive interaction between team members.

    - **Urgency:** Emphasize the vision of the project and commit to delivering this value timely.

14. **Tailor to meet the needs of the project:** Because every project is unique, an effective project leader adapts their style to meet the needs of the project, the environment, and the stakeholders. Common variables that can impact the leadership style needed include

- **Experience with the type of project:** Organizations and project teams with experience with the type of project to be undertaken often tend to be more self-managing and require less hands-on leadership. Conversely, if the project type is new to the organization and key team members, then more oversight and direct leadership may be needed.

- **Maturity of the project team members:** The level of maturity, experience, and competency with the technical aspects among the project team may dictate different levels of oversight and guidance needed within the project team itself. A team with more mature/experienced/competent individuals should require less oversight and guidance. A team member new to the technical specialty, new to the team, or new to the organization will often require more attention and guidance. Of course, this is also an excellent opportunity to leverage those more mature individuals as the technical leaders and mentors for the others.

- **Organizational governance structures:** As we referenced before, all projects operate within an organizational structure and governance system. This structure or governance system may require projects to be managed in a certain way. This expectation or requirement may strongly influence how centralized or distributed the authority and accountability aspects of the project team management can be.

- **Distributed project teams:** We talk about this in the section "Techniques for Leading Virtual Projects."

TIP   When you're dealing with people, nothing beats a face-to-face meeting, active listening, and a humble spirit.

Servant Leadership Approach

Although we discussed numerous project leadership keys in the previous section, it really boils down to a simple, practical mindset that drives the thoughts, words, and actions of an effective project leader. It is a mindset of "service first" and not "me first." The approach is called *servant leadership*, and it was popularized by Robert Greenleaf in 1970 in his book *The Servant as Leader*. Since then, the philosophy of servant leadership has been steadily growing in popularity and now serves as the foundation for most modern leadership training programs.

In a project environment, where you are stakeholder-focused, where you must effectively relate to others to get work done, and where you must completely understand the needs and requirements of your customers to deliver the proper solution, it is a very practical management approach to take. It is a synergistic approach for any organization (or project) that values strong customer-service and team-focused approaches in their leaders.

To better illustrate what is meant by a servant leadership approach, and why it gives you the best chance of doing the right work, the right way, for the right people on your project, let's look at the prominent characteristics of this philosophy:

- Asserts a strong service orientation; leads by expanding service to others

- Emphasizes listening, patience, respect, and responsiveness

- Takes the perspective of others; maintains the best interests of others

- Accepts responsibility; takes initiative

- Encourages collaboration and trust; empowers individuals

- Seeks growth and improvement in all team members, organization, and community

- Solicits input and feedback from all stakeholders, especially in the decision-making process

- Insists on the use of skills to influence and persuade, not manipulate

- Spotlights a strong integrity principle—the ethical use of power

PMI defines servant leadership as the practice of leading the team by focusing on understanding and addressing the needs and development of team members to enable the highest possible team performance. This definition is fine and fits very well for the Team Performance domain, but the servant leadership mindset influences the interactions with all project stakeholders, not just the project team.

Like all project management and leadership skills, a servant-leadership mindset is not an all-or-nothing approach. It is a spectrum between a total egocentric, leader-first mindset on one end and a complete servant-first thought pattern on the other end. The goal is to do your best, continue to learn, and work to improve over time, just as you do with the other skill set areas.

NOTE The servant leadership approach to project management gives you the best chance of doing the right work, the right way, for the right people.

Special Project Situations

To better illustrate how effective project leadership is applied, let's review techniques for managing a few special project situations. Doing so helps reinforce these concepts and principles, as well as better prepares you for the exam.

Techniques for Challenging Project Team Situations

Project managers may find themselves in some situations with a project team that is not high performing. This can often happen if the team or certain team members are preassigned to the project effort. In these situations, the project manager still needs to get the work done, and the goal is to improve team performance. Although we could spend an entire chapter on all the problem situations a project manager might encounter, let's examine some common challenging situations related to project team performance and review action steps that can be taken to improve the situation. This examination also illustrates how the leadership and interpersonal skills reviewed earlier can come into play.

1. **Poor performers:** Poor performers generally fall into two categories: unacceptable work results or unacceptable behaviors. In many cases, the poor performance is a result of unclear expectations. If faced with this situation, keep these action items in mind:

> **TIP** Keep in mind that the rest of the team is watching how the project manager deals with poor performers. The challenge is to strike a balance between handling the person fairly and not letting the poor performance become a drag on the team.

   - **Seek to understand:** On first occurrences, don't overreact. Verify the expectations that they had, seek to understand what is going on and their particular situation, and take responsibility for any lack of clarity. This should always be the first step.

   - **Provide feedback:** After you have proper information, provide specific feedback to the team member as soon as possible in a private setting. Focus on the behavior or result, not the person.

> **EXAM TIP** For the PMP exam, there are two important themes for managing team member performance that is not meeting expectations:
>
> 1. Try to understand the team member's situation.
>
> 2. Any performance feedback should be timely, discreet, and specific.

- **Enable success:** Do everything that you can do to enable each team member's success. Provide resources. Knock down obstacles. Provide every opportunity for their performance to improve.

- **Initiate backup plans:** At the same time, you cannot assume their performance will get better. At the first signs of performance issues, start thinking about what you can do to mitigate the impact to the project if you do need to replace the team member or if the performance does not improve.

- **Cut your losses:** Assuming you've done everything mentioned so far, there comes a time when you must cut your losses. The main reason why a poor performer needs to be removed is the effect it can have on the performance and morale of the rest of the team.

2. **High-maintenance staff:** This group of team members includes those individuals who have a reputation of either being difficult to work with or possessing unusual personalities. In most cases, these are the people you need for your key critical path tasks...of course. Here are two key recommendations for these situations:

   - **Check for yourself:** Don't assume the reputation (the perception) is totally true. Verify for yourself. In many cases, these individuals are unfairly labeled. These labels often say more about the people who are uncomfortable working with individuals who are different from them than anything else.

   - **Treat them the same:** Use the same approach with them as you would any other team member. Work to understand their motivators, clarify expectations, avoid surprises, and help them be successful.

3. **Schedule developed without team:** PMI emphasizes the importance and the value in developing the detail project plan and schedule with the team. However, there are times this might not occur. If you find yourself in a situation where either you or your team members are asked to take responsibility for a schedule that they did not help develop, you must take the time to review the schedule. You need to get a buy-in from the team members before continuing. Two important items for consideration here:

   - **Understand the schedule assumptions:** In many of these situations, team members totally dismiss the merits of a schedule because they are not aware of the assumptions that serve as the foundation for the schedule. Key assumptions include those about resource ability and quality level of work product (completion criteria).

- **Identify risks:** If there are gaps between the schedule assumptions and project reality, or if you cannot get commitment from the team, you have some new project risks, if not outright issues. Follow your designated risk and issue management procedures to handle it.

Techniques for Leading Cross-Cultural Projects

With many project teams being global in nature and/or composed of team members from different cultures, let's review a few techniques specific to leading cross-cultural project teams:

- **Be respectful:** Take time to consider the effect that the different cultures, time zones, holiday schedules, and workday schedules will have on the project. Common impact areas are terminology, risk management, communications planning (including best times for status meetings), and the project schedule.

- **Understand potential culture impacts:** Understand potential cultural effects on project communications and team interactions. Specifically, be aware that due to cultural differences, others might not be as assertive or willing to speak up to the degree you would expect. In addition, review any conventions that you plan to use for status reporting. Make sure the conventions do not convey some unintended meaning and that everyone is comfortable using them.

- **Listen for understanding:** Even with a common language (in most cases, English), the use and the sound of the language can vary dramatically. The key here is to kick your active listening skills into high gear and focus on understanding. Don't let yourself get distracted or tune out because of accents or the irregular use of certain words. Stay engaged, be patient, ask questions, clarify terms, and don't stop until you are comfortable that you're on the same wavelength with your cross-cultural partners.

- **Plan on more formality:** To reduce the impact of cultural differences and ensure mutual understanding, cross-cultural projects are more mechanical, formal, and by the book. You just need to plan on this and realize that project management shortcuts should be avoided in these environments.

Techniques for Leading Virtual Projects

Any project that consists of team members not co-located in the same physical location is a virtual project to some degree. The more geographically dispersed the team members and the more interaction that is done with non–face-to-face communications, the more virtual the project is.

With the continued advances in communications and information technology, and the common everyday use of mobile phones, remote network access, email, web mail, pagers, and instant messaging, the ability of people to productively collaborate on common work is increased dramatically. And, of course, the reduced office costs and the increased ability to leverage outsourcing options are very attractive to most organizations.

However, these potential productivity gains and cost reductions do not happen automatically, especially in the demanding environment of most projects. A tremendous amount of energy is needed to plan, coordinate, and manage a virtual project team. And although all the team procedures, protocols, and ways of working details would be documented in the team charter, let's review a few techniques specific to leading virtual project teams:

1. **Get some face-to-face time, especially early:** If there is any way possible to get face time with your virtual team members, do it. Face-to-face interaction is instrumental in building trust, developing relationships, and jump-starting project momentum. A few recommendations on this topic include

   - Get everyone together for the project kickoff meeting.

   - Try to co-locate the team for the first stage (or as long as you can), and then let team members return to their remote locations.

   - If none of these are possible, try a mini-kickoff session that focuses on planning and identifying risks, and strongly encourage everyone to use video conferencing, especially for initial meetings.

   - Depending on the project phase and the nature of the work, look at split work environments (such as two days on-site, three days remote, or one week on-site every month).

   - If it's available, look to leverage video conferencing as much as possible, especially for initial team meetings. If not, consider creative use of digital pictures.

2. **Establish team norms:** Facilitate the rules and procedures that will guide team interactions and productivity with the team. Key items include the following:

   - Core hours everyone needs to be available (online)

   - Access to team members during noncore hours

   - Preferred team communication and collaboration mechanisms

   - Preferred meeting times, especially important when members are in different time zones

   - Reporting status

   - Project repository

- Contingency plans for network or phone outages
- Team directory

3. **Responsiveness is the difference-maker:** The key to successful virtual project teams is responsiveness. If people are easily accessible and respond quickly, most organizations couldn't care less where people are working. These environments do require team members to be professional and mature.

4. **Set up protocols for virtual meetings:** Virtual meetings are the lifeblood of a virtual project team. Here are some key reminders to make these meetings more productive:

   - Use technologies that are available to everyone.
   - Use technologies that are reliable for everyone.
   - Use technologies that meet the security requirements of the project and sponsoring organizations.
   - Ensure that everyone understands how to use the technologies.
   - Make sure to send agenda and reference materials in advance of the meeting (or just post to the project repository and send a link to it).
   - Review protocols for asking questions.
   - Keep discussions focused on items that pertain to all participants. For other items, take them offline. Stop the discussion and assign an action item to schedule a separate meeting with those involved.
   - Instant messaging conferences might be appropriate for core team meetings.

5. **Establish clear time zone references:** In this age of global teams, multiple time zones, and daylight savings time, take the time to review and clarify time zone designations and conventions. This goes a long way in avoiding meeting time conflicts. Two recommendations that can be helpful for this situation:

   - Use the newer time zone references, such as Eastern Time (ET) to refer to whatever time it is on the East Coast rather than Eastern Standard Time (EST) or Eastern Daylight Savings Time (EDST).
   - Reference city or state to clarify the intended time, such as Chicago time, London time, or Arizona time.

6. **Verify productivity early:** To ensure that the virtual work environment generates the expected level of productivity needed for project success, pay close

attention to initial work efforts. The fundamentals of work assignments apply the same here, but they're even more important:

- Invest time to clarify work expectations and completion criteria.

- Provide all necessary resources.

- Keep work packages small—less than the standard reporting period.

7. **Use preferred communication methods of customer and sponsor:** Either as part of your initial communications planning or as an observation you make during the project, make sure to communicate with your sponsor and your key customers in the manner they prefer and in the manner that best fits their learning style. If this is in person, meet them in person. If it is via phone at 7:30 a.m., call them at 7:30 a.m. If it is email at the end of the day, email them. The two important things to note here are the following:

   - The communication mechanisms you use for the core project team might likely be different than what you use for sponsor and customer communications.

   - Use the methods they prefer, not what you or the core project team prefers. This approach leads to fewer miscommunications and expectation management.

Forms of Power

Being a leader is ultimately about winning people over, influencing people to make the right decisions, and ensuring tasks are performed. A project manager must have negotiation skills to be able to navigate through the office politics to get things done. As a result, how other people perceive the person's power can be a leading factor in how the project manager or leader influences others.

A leader or manager can be seen to exert various forms of power. They are not mutually exclusive, and an individual may possess more than one form of power.

- **Positional power (also known as formal, legitimate, or authoritative power):** This power has been assigned to an individual due to their position, title, or job description. For example, a senior director has a certain authority in the organization only because they have been promoted to that role. A project manager has a certain authority on the project (documented in the project charter) purely because they have been assigned the project management role.

- **Expert power:** Others recognize the individual as the expert in the field and will follow their advice because they recognize them as the authority in the field. This authority can be based on the individual's subject matter expertise, knowledge, skills, education, or certification. This authority is always earned (never assigned).

- **Reward power:** The individual recognizes and appreciates the efforts of the team and team members and provides praise and encouragement. If they have the authority, they may offer financial incentives and perks to team members based on their efforts and performance. For example, a manager might hand out gift cards for strong performance, thanking team members for their contributions.

- **Penalty power (also known as punitive or coercive power):** The individual does not recognize the efforts of their team or team members and constantly threatens them to perform their work. Team members are in constant fear of repercussions, and that is what the manager believes is driving the team to do their work

- **Referent power:** People respect the individual because others admire or respect them due to some credibility they have earned. For example, a retired athlete who at one time was an expert in the sport is respected. People will remember and respect this person's achievement for many years and decades to come.

- **Personal or charismatic power:** The individual gains the respect of others simply due to their personality or charisma.

- **Relational power:** Others respect the individual based on who the person associates with. For example, if the child of the CEO of your company joins your team, you will probably treat them with more respect than other team members. The only reason why you will treat them with more respect is because they are the son or daughter of the CEO.

- **Representative power:** The team has appointed the individual to represent them.

- **Informational power:** The individual has the ability to control, gather, and distribute information.

- **Situational power:** The individual gains the respect or admiration of others for their performance during a unique situation or crisis.

- **Ingratiating power:** The individual can apply flattery or other common ground to win cooperation.

- **Pressure-based power:** The individual pressures others to make decisions by limiting freedom of choice.

- **Guilt-based power:** The individual imposes an obligation or sense of duty to others.

- **Persuasive power:** The individual has the ability to provide arguments that move others to the individual's desired course of action.

- **Avoiding power:** The individual feels they have the power to refuse participation.

Exam Preparation Tasks

As mentioned in the section "How to Use This Book" in the Introduction, you have a couple of choices for exam preparation: the exercises here, Chapter 17, "Final Preparation," and the exam simulation questions on the Pearson Test Prep practice test software.

Review All Key Topics

Review the most important topics in this chapter, noted with the Key Topic icon in the outer margin of the page. Table 9-10 lists a reference of these key topics and the page numbers on which each is found.

Table 9-10   Key Topics for Chapter 9

Key Topic Element	Description	Page Number
List	Key outcomes for effective team performance execution	273
Section	Planning For and Acquiring Project Resources	279
Section	Acquire Resources	281
Section	Training	283
Section	Resource Management Plan	284
Section	Characteristics of High-Performing Teams	288
Section	Tuckman Ladder	289
List	Management principles to maximize team performance	291
Section	Techniques for Better Team Performance	295
Section	More Than Managing	299
Section	Where Leadership Is Needed on a Project	302
Section	Leadership Skills	304
Paragraph	Extrinsic and Intrinsic Motivators	306
Table 9-6	Motivation Models	307
Section	Emotional Intelligence	308
List	Key decision-making points	309
List	Key conflict management approaches	310

Key Topic Element	Description	Page Number
Table 9-8	Ken Thomas and Ralph Kilmann Conflict Management Model Summary	311
Section	Keys to Better Project Leadership	315
Section	Servant Leadership Approach	318
Section	Special Project Situations	320

Define Key Terms

Define the following key terms from this chapter and check your answers in the glossary:

project team, resource management plan, team charter, project manager, interpersonal skills, critical thinking, motivation, emotional intelligence, conflict management, negotiation, servant leadership

Review Questions

1. A project manager who remains calm under pressure, thinks before they act, can put themselves in the other person's shoes, and naturally builds rapport with other people is exhibiting what skill?

    a. Self-awareness

    b. Motivation

    c. Emotional intelligence

    d. Trust-building

    e. Coaching

2. In which stage of the Tuckman Ladder team development model do initial conflicts emerge?

    a. Forming

    b. Performing

    c. Storming

    d. Norming

3. What are some actions that the project manager can take to maximize productivity of the team? (Choose two.)

    a. Let the team work out their issues on their own.

    b. Ensure work assignments are clear and understood.

    c. Provide the tools, resources, and procedures to facilitate team collaboration.

    d. Let the team take responsibility for obtaining the resources needed to accomplish their work.

    e. Ask the team members for status daily to keep them on track.

4. Which action item by the project manager may not help a new team member to be as productive as soon as possible?

    a. Assign a mentor to the new team member.

    b. Prepare an orientation packet that provides context for the project and the team operating environment.

    c. Set up their work environment in advance.

    d. Invest more time with the new team member.

    e. Assign them a challenging work assignment as their first task.

5. In what ways does an effective project manager demonstrate leadership? (Select all that apply.)

    a. Shields the project team from the politics and noise surrounding the project

    b. Looks for ways to motivate each team member and help them improve

    c. Takes responsibility and accountability for the project

    d. Exhibits a calm, confident aura when others are showing signs of issue or project stress

    e. Focuses more on the project management processes and not on the people involved in the project

6. What are examples of other team members, besides the project manager, providing leadership on a project? (Select all that apply.)

    a. A technical leader remaining quiet about potential risks because they do not want to concern the project manager

    b. The technical leaders providing input on the direction and plan for the project

    c. The project sponsor influencing organizational politics and providing commitment to the project plan

    d. The product owner influencing and guiding stakeholder expectations

    e. Senior management championing the business process changes that will result from the project to the impacted stakeholders

7. Why is critical thinking an important attribute for all project team members? (Select all that apply.)

    a. Improves ability to identify root causes of problems

    b. Prioritizes analyzing data and evidence to evaluate arguments and resolve issues

    c. Allows decisions to be made faster

    d. Decreases the impact of bias, unstated assumptions, and emotional appeals

    e. Improves ability to understand how the use of language impacts others

8. Which approaches for conflict management as described in the Thomas-Kilmann model are most common for conflicts within a high-performing team? (Choose three.)

    a. Smoothing/Accommodating

    b. Compromising

    c. Confronting/Problem-Solving

    d. Forcing

    e. Collaborating

9. What are some ways a project manager can earn the respect of the project team and other project stakeholders? (Choose all that apply.)

    a. Show respect to them.

    b. Be fair in how you make decisions and deal with conflicts.

    c. Openly confront the realities of the project situation.

    d. Focus on what should be happening, not on the current realities of the project.

    e. Demonstrate the behaviors you want others to emulate.

    f. Change your mind on decisions often and easily.

    g. Actively listen to each person you interact with.

10. Which statements reflect a servant leadership mindset? (Choose all that apply.)

    a. Encourages collaboration and trust

    b. Takes the perspective of others and maintains the best interest of others

    c. Seeks growth and improvement in all team members

    d. Assigns all responsibility to others to encourage their growth

    e. Exhibits a strong integrity principle

    f. Makes decisions unilaterally out of respect for other stakeholders' and team members' time

    g. Emphasizes a coaching approach to managing people

11. What is the primary value of planning resource management for a project?

    a. To define all the resources needed for the project so this information can be incorporated into the project budget and the project schedule

    b. To clarify when the procurement department will need to be involved in the project

    c. To ensure that sufficient resources are available when the project needs them

    d. To establish the approach and the management effort level needed for managing project resources based on type and complexity of the project

12. Which tools can be used by a project manager to assess the fit for any potential candidate for a project role? (Choose all that apply.)

    a. Resource requirements

    b. Attitudinal surveys

    c. Structured interviews

    d. Ability tests

    e. Training plan

    f. Team charter

This chapter covers the following topics regarding communications management on projects:

- **Plan Communications Management:** Review the common tools and artifacts needed to communicate effectively and efficiently to stakeholders.

- **Manage Communications:** Review the process of creating, collecting, distributing, storing, retrieving, and disposing of information.

- **Monitor Communications:** Review the process of ensuring the information needs of stakeholders are being met.

- **Agile Approach to Communications:** Review the agile approach for communicating between teams and stakeholders.

## CHAPTER 10

Project Communications

In this chapter we discuss in detail the communication management aspects for project managers (PMs) and team members to successfully meet the project needs of stakeholders. We discuss the principles related to the *PMBOK® Guide*, Sixth Edition, the *PMBOK® Guide*, Seventh Edition, and the Exam Content Outline (ECO).

This chapter addresses the following objectives from the PMP Exam Content Outline:

Domain	Task #	Exam Objective
People	Task 9	Collaborate with stakeholders
People	Task 10	Build shared understanding
People	Task 11	Engage and support virtual teams
Process	Task 2	Manage communications
Process	Task 4	Engage stakeholders
Process	Task 12	Manage project artifacts
Process	Task 16	Ensure knowledge transfer for project continuity

"Do I Know This Already?" Quiz

The "Do I Know This Already?" quiz allows you to assess whether you should read this entire chapter thoroughly or jump to the "Exam Preparation Tasks" section. If you are in doubt about your answers to these questions or your own assessment of your knowledge of the topics, read the entire chapter. Table 10-1 lists the major headings in this chapter and their corresponding "Do I Know This Already?" quiz questions. You can find the answers in Appendix A, "Answers to the 'Do I Know This Already?' Quizzes and Review Questions."

Table 10-1 "Do I Know This Already?" Section-to-Question Mapping

Foundation Topics Section	Questions
Plan Communications Management	1–4
Manage Communications	5–7
Monitor Communications	8–9
Agile Approach to Communications	10

CAUTION   The goal of self-assessment is to gauge your mastery of the topics in this chapter. If you do not know the answer to a question or are only partially sure of the answer, you should mark that question as wrong for purposes of the self-assessment. Giving yourself credit for an answer you correctly guess skews your self-assessment results and might provide you with a false sense of security.

1. Video conferencing is a type of which communication method?

    a. Interactive

    b. Formal verbal

    c. Pull

    d. Tight matrix

2. You are managing a military project with top secret designation. As a result, some teams are not allowed to communicate with other teams. Where would you document this constraint?

    a. Communication management plan

    b. Requirements documentation

    c. Team charter

    d. Project charter

3. Repeating the message is an example of?

    a. Noise

    b. Barrier

    c. Feedback

    d. Interactive communication

4. You are managing a large project with many global teams. Recently, you have noticed that some team members are not receiving the information they need, some are not being invited to meetings, some are not receiving the reports they need, and some team members are receiving the wrong reports. In this situation what should you do first?

    a. Follow up with team members to ensure you understand what reports and information the team members need and which meetings they need to be invited to.

    b. Review the information distribution detailed in the communication management plan.

    c. Set up a meeting with the team to ensure everyone is on the same page.

    d. Ensure all teams receive all reports and invite all team members to all your meetings.

5. In which of the following situations would formal written communication not be valid?

    a. Submitting a change request

    b. Creating the project charter

    c. Taking notes during a stakeholder's status meeting

    d. Requesting changes to the contract

6. You are having a problem with a team member's performance. What would be the most appropriate type of communication for addressing this issue with the team member initially?

    a. Formal verbal

    b. Formal written

    c. Informal verbal

    d. Informal written

7. You are managing 15 analysts and developers on your project, but 2 more are added. How many more communication channels are there?

    a. 31

    b. 153

    c. 136

    d. 33

8. During a meeting with stakeholders, two of the stakeholders tell you that they never received the report that you are presenting. The other stakeholders did receive them, and you confirm that the two stakeholders were on the distribution list. You didn't print any spare copies of the report because it is a very large document with more than 50 pages. The two stakeholders are visibly upset but later realize the report went into their junk mail. What could have prevented this situation?

    a. You should have followed up with all the meeting attendees to confirm they received the report.

    b. You should have consulted the stakeholder engagement plan to determine how you could have prevented this situation.

    c. You should have consulted the stakeholder engagement assessment matrix to ensure the two stakeholders are supportive of the project.

    d. You should have anticipated this issue before the start of the meeting and printed copies of the report.

9. Osmotic communication works best in which of the following situations?

    a. In a tight matrix

    b. Virtual teams using regular video-conferencing tools

    c. Face-to-face conversation

    d. In a strong matrix organization

10. You are a team facilitator mentoring a junior team member. You are showing this team member a chart that shows what user stories are yet to start, what has been started, and what has been finished. What chart are you showing the team member?

    a. Burn down chart

    b. Burn up chart

    c. Kanban board

    d. Work performance report

Foundation Topics

Communication is the exchange of information and is a vital job skill for project managers. We can argue that it is a PM's number one job skill. In fact, project managers generally spend 90 percent of their time communicating, engaging, and collaborating with stakeholders. Project managers therefore need to ensure communication is effective and efficient:

- **_Effective Communication_**: Provides the right information to the right stakeholders at the right time, via the correct medium, addressing the audience.

- **_Efficient Communication_**: Provides only the information needed in the shortest possible time. No more, no less.

The Communication Management knowledge area addresses the planning, managing, and monitoring of activities necessary to ensure that the information needs of the project and stakeholder are met. The project manager must first develop a strategy to communicate with stakeholders and then carry out these strategies effectively and efficiently.

The _PMBOK® Guide_, Sixth Edition, processes relating to Communication Management are as follows:

- Plan Communication Management

- Manage Communication

- Monitor Communication

In the sections that follow, we discuss each process in detail as it relates to the Exam Content Outline (ECO) and the PMP exam.

Plan Communications Management

The first process of communications management is Plan Communications Management, and this process refers to how you are going to plan, execute, monitor, and control the flow of information so that the correct information is delivered to the appropriate stakeholders in a timely manner. On many projects, information may be confidential or restricted, so it is vital for these projects to have a detailed and robust communication plan.

As a project manager, you need to ensure you are sending relevant information to appropriate stakeholders, not every single piece of information to every stakeholder. Many organizations manage communications quite inefficiently, which is why you often have a full inbox of emails that do not pertain to you, or you are invited to many unproductive meetings. The purpose of the Communications knowledge area is to address these issues.

The basic principle of planning is to determine the stakeholder's information needs and formulate the communication approach of all stakeholders. You need to determine

- Who needs the information?
- What information do they need?
- How often do they need it?
- Why is it important to them?
- How will it be delivered?
- When will it be delivered?

The Importance of Project Communications

Project communications are important not only for the obvious reason of keeping stakeholders properly and consistently informed on the status, progress, and impact of the project, but they are a key determining factor to the overall success of the project. Why is this? Here are a few key reasons:

- **Managing Expectations:** We discuss managing expectations in greater detail in Chapter 5, "Stakeholder Engagement," and Chapter 9, "Project Team," but for now, we'll just say that the quality and effectiveness of your communications will have a tremendous impact on stakeholder perceptions regarding the project and your role as a leader.

- **Managing the Project Team:** Your ability to communicate is the prominent factor affecting how well you manage and lead the project team.

- **Reducing Conflicts:** There are enough challenges executing your average project within the customary time, fiscal, and resource constraints without adding unnecessary conflicts that result from misperceptions, lack of information, or nonexistent issues—all of which can result from ineffective communications.

- **Saving Grace:** Solid project managers know there are two skills that will carry them in almost any project situation: organization and communication. Being excellent in these areas, especially project communications, will compensate for shortcomings in almost every other area.

It's also worth noting that there are many mediums for communication and many ways of communication. Communication is not just about talking and conversing with one another; it also refers to documentation. In fact, much of the project manager's time communicating is spent on documentation. Examples of communication on a project might include

- Status reports (discussed in Chapter 14, "Project Measurement")
- Progress review meetings
- Kickoff meetings
- Executive reports
- Presentations
- Financial reports
- Government (or external agency) reports
- Issue logs
- Risk register
- Change logs
- Responsibility assignment matrix (such as the RACI chart)
- Project organization chart
- Any project meeting (in any form/option)
- Any project documentation
- Project collaboration and engagement tools

It can also include organizational change management communications, such as

- Project name/identity
- Project website (portal)
- Enterprise social networking platforms
- Organizational change management plan
- Frequently asked questions (FAQs) references
- Awareness campaigns
- Newsletters
- Public relations notices

■ Roadshows

■ Individual meetings with key stakeholders

Key Tools and Techniques of Plan Communications Management

Developing an appropriate plan and approach for effective communication between stakeholders requires utilizing various strategies and tools to ensure effective and efficient communication. The sections that follow discuss some of the key tools and techniques in greater detail.

Communication Model

It is well known that passing information from one person to another will reduce the value of that information each time it is passed to the next person. If person 1 tells something to person 2, who then passes that message to person 3, who then passes it to person 4, each time the message will be diluted slightly until eventually the message will be completely changed.

The sender-receiver communication model attempts to address this issue and identify areas where the message may be diluted, misinterpreted, misconstrued, or interfered with. If you can identify these areas, you can potentially improve communication to reduce any misunderstanding.

Figure 10-1 shows an example of a sender-receiver model.

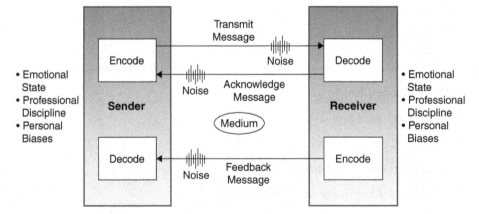

Figure 10-1   A Sender-Receiver Model

In this model, the sender sends a message to the receiver, and the receiver either acknowledges that the message was received or provides feedback to the sender in the form of responding back to the original message.

Encode means that the message is codified into symbols such as words, text, pictures, or sound, depending on the transmission medium.

Transmit Message refers to the medium used, such as talking, writing, typing, or texting.

Decode refers to the receiver interpreting the message that was delivered to them.

Noise refers to any interference or barriers that could affect the understanding of the message, such as

- Physical noise (loud music, machine noise)
- Distractions
- Distance
- Unfamiliar technology
- Cultural differences (for example, a phrase in one part of the world may have a different meaning in another part of the world)
- Lack of interest or knowledge

Feedback Message refers to the receiver responding back to the sender in various forms, such as

- Answering the question that was being asked
- Providing the information that was requested
- Repeating the message (for example, repeating a phone number to ensure the receiver wrote it down correctly)
- Using nonverbal cues, such as nodding your head in agreement or shaking your head in disagreement

This communication model incorporates the idea that the message itself and how it is transmitted and received will be influenced by factors such as the sender's and receiver's emotional state, knowledge of the topic, background, personality, culture, working methods, nationality, age, professional discipline, race, ethnicity, and many other factors.

The sender is primarily responsible for ensuring that the message has been sent in its entirety, is clear, and that the receiver has received and understood the message.

This model shows only two people and the factors that can cause misinterpretation between two people. If you add a third person and a fourth person, you can see how rapidly a message can change going from one person to another.

Communication Requirements Analysis

Project managers must analyze the communication needs of stakeholders to determine the *who*, *what*, *how*, *why*, and *when* and adjust their communication style according to the situation and audience.

There are various ways, mechanisms, and dimensions of communication that impact how you exchange information with stakeholders:

- **Written and Verbal:** You write differently compared to how you speak.

- **Formal and Informal:** A formal project plan is written differently from an informal text message.

- **Internal and External:** Communication with stakeholders within your organization may be different from communication with stakeholders outside of your organization.

- **Official and Unofficial:** Official communication released to the public and other stakeholders may be different from communication internal within the project team.

- **Nonverbal:** This form of communication includes body language, pitch and tone, hand gestures, and facial expression.

- **Media:** This form of communication includes pictures, graphs, and charts.

- **Choice of Words:** Subtle differences in the use of words can change the meaning of the communication.

- **Hierarchical Focus:** You adjust your communication style according to the position or title of the stakeholder:

  - **Upward:** Stakeholders senior to you in ranking

  - **Downward:** Stakeholders junior to you in ranking

  - **Horizontal:** Stakeholders who are your peers within the organization

You need to take all of these factors into consideration when creating an effective communication plan.

Misunderstanding can be reduced (although not eliminated) by using the 5 *C*s of written communication. Although there are few different versions of the 5 *C*s, the following are per PMI:

- Correct grammar and spelling

- Concise expression and elimination of excess words

- Clear purpose and expression directed to the needs of the reader

- Coherent logical flow of ideas

- Controlled flow of words and ideas

Good communicators adjust their communication style according to the audience they are communicating with and consider factors such as

- Personal differences

- Cultural differences

- Political differences

- Diversity and inclusion

- Stakeholders' preferred method of communication

- Active listening (discussed in the "Active Listening" section in this chapter)

Bearing all these factors in mind, you can see why planning communication is an important factor contributing to success of projects. Unfortunately, the reality is that this communication is performed inefficiently and poorly in many organizations. Thus, as project manager, you might need to consider the following factors that can influence communications planning:

- The need for a sponsoring organizational structure

- Your organization's culture (an EEF)

- Results of stakeholder analysis

- Reporting relationships

- Functional areas involved in the project

- Number of people involved in the project

- Physical location of the project stakeholder

- Information needs of each stakeholder

- Experience level of project team members

- Availability of technology

- Immediacy and frequency of information needs

- Desired form of project communications

- Expected length of the project

- Organizational risk level of project

- Expected change impact on end users

- Organizational culture

- Level of external communications needed

- Procurement contracts

- Any constraints advised by legal counsel

Communication Methods

The three types of communication methods are as follows:

- ***Interactive Communication***: Anyone can talk at any time; for example, conversations, telephone calls, team status meetings, video conferencing.

- ***Push Communication***: One-way communication to a specific audience. This method ensures information is distributed but does not verify that the message was actually received and understood by the recipient; for example, voicemails, faxes, memos, reports, letters, emails.

- ***Pull Communication***: Information saved in a central repository so that people can retrieve the information at their discretion; for example, shared drives, web portals, internal databases (such as lessons learned databases).

Communication Technology

Technology is constantly changing, and you will continue to change the way you communicate according to new technological advances. However, you do not just randomly choose the latest new tool available because different tools can be used for different types of communication and collaboration. There are various considerations to make and factors to consider that can affect the choice of technology, such as

- Urgency and frequency of the information

- Availability of the technology, especially if stakeholders are global (some technology may not be available in all regions)

- Reliability of the technology

- Ease of use

- Project environment (face-to-face team members use different tools compared to virtual team members)

- Confidentiality of information

Key Artifact: Communication Management Plan

The communication management plan documents how project communication will be planned, structured, implemented, and monitored throughout the project life cycle to all stakeholders. It includes items such as

- Stakeholders' communication requirements (who needs what information, when do they need it, why is it important to them, how often do they need it, when will it be delivered, and how will it be delivered?)

- Distribution plan of who gets what information, when, and how

- Schedule detailing when information will be updated and available

- Escalation process of issues and unresolved items

- Constraints to communications

- Best practices for meetings

- Person responsible for communicating

- Constraints to communication (for example, stakeholders are located globally across 15 time zones. With no overlap of office hours, how do you handle meetings and conference calls?)

- Methods and technology used to communicate

- Person responsible for authorizing the release of confidential information

- Glossary of project terms

- Templates for status reporting, team meetings, and so on

- Methods and processes for updating this plan

- Resources and budget allocated for project communications

- Organizational change management aspects

- Use of the Project Management Information System (PMIS), team collaboration site, or other project tools for communicating

- Data points to be included in project status reports

This list is not exhaustive but does include some examples of the type of information documented in the communication management plan. As with any of the management plans, you should not try to memorize all the examples that we have listed. Instead, understand the purpose of the management plan; in this case, anything related to the processes and procedures of communicating project information to stakeholders and team members is documented here.

Table 10-2 shows some of the most common project communication types and methods, what each is best used for, and some important notes related to it.

Table 10-2   Common Communication Types and Methods

Communication Option	Best Use(s)	Important Notes
Face-to-Face	Best method to start business relationships and earn trust. Best for sensitive, interpersonal, or difficult messages. Best for communicating emotional and nonverbal messages.	Richest, most efficient method. Only way to do business in many cultures. "Showing up" demonstrates commitment.
Video Conferencing	Best substitute for face-to-face meetings.	Increasing availability through web conferencing tools. Make sure technology works in advance. Reduces meeting participants' ability to multitask during meeting.
Direct Audio (Telephone)	When interactive conversation is needed. When visual communication is not needed. When urgency is important. When privacy is important.	If placed on speaker phone, assume others are in the room.
Voicemail	Short messages. When common message needs to be sent to multiple people. When targeted stakeholder is auditory-oriented or is inundated with email.	If lengthy message, summarize message content up front. Avoid for controversial or sensitive communications. Make sure stakeholder checks voicemail regularly.

Communication Option	Best Use(s)	Important Notes
Electronic Mail	When common message needs to be sent to multiple people. When targeted stakeholder is visually oriented or prefers email communications. When communication record is needed.	Use proper encryption methods for your organization if the message contains protected data. Gauge and clarify the organizational culture for email communications. Clarify how supporting materials should be handled (as attachments, direct links, and so on). Avoid lengthy emails whenever possible, or summarize content up front, and highlight any actions that you are requesting. Use the subject line effectively—ensure it is consistent with topic/focus.
Instant Messaging	For daily interactions of project team. For virtual project teams. Group/team IM tools can facilitate team collaboration.	Helps to build community and project team intimacy. Not appropriate for formal work relationships. Keeps the office quieter. Most group/team IM tools can record discussions. Monitor privacy and confidentiality concerns.
Texting	When brief, one-on-one information needs to be shared between people where informal, friendly relation is established. When immediate response is not needed. When communication does not warrant a phone call or people cannot take or receive a phone call.	Although technology is improving, do not assume the message is always received or received in correct order (if more than 140 characters).

Communication Option	Best Use(s)	Important Notes
Audio Conferencing	When group collaboration is needed and face-to-face meeting is not possible. When a desktop or document does not need to be shared in real time.	More social presence than email or IM. Allows participants to multitask and do other things, which makes level of engagement and meeting quality an ongoing project risk. Most web conferencing tools provide audio, too. Most systems allow conference to be recorded.
Web Conferencing with Audio	When group collaboration is needed and face-to-face meeting is not possible. When data or presentation needs to be shared. Virtual training sessions.	Same challenges as audio conferencing. Invest more prep time on technology readiness and training. Able to record questions. Record and make available for later access.
Web Conferencing with Video	When visible group collaboration is needed and face-to-face meeting is not possible. When facial expressions and/or nonverbal communications need to be visible. When data or presentation needs to be shared.	Participants need enough privacy and environment control to allow for video cameras. Ensures higher level of engagement and participation; reduces multitasking. Invest more prep time on technology readiness and training. Record and make available for later access.
Project/Team Collaboration Tools	When ongoing group collaborations on work products or topic discussions need to be documented.	Builds community and project team intimacy.
Social Networking Tools	When project information needs to be shared outside of core working team. When a sense of community needs to be established or improved, especially for external stakeholders. When quick, real-time feedback is needed from external stakeholders to facilitate project decisions.	Must determine use level of social networking tools by targeted audiences (comfort, frequency, and so on). Enterprise social networking tools (such as Yammer) can be used when access to project information must be secured and limited to authorized users.

Manage Communications

The Manage Communications process refers to updating stakeholders with relevant information regarding the project. It is the process of creating, collecting, distributing, storing, retrieving, managing, monitoring, and disposing of information in a timely manner.

Put simply, this process refers to activities such as sending, receiving, and deleting emails; running and distributing reports; hosting meetings and conference calls; having conversations; and so on—something that you do all the time!

Communication Skills

As mentioned, communication is a vital skill for project managers because you need to ensure tasks are being performed, teams are working together, and team members are collaborating. As a project manager, you will adjust your communication style according to the situation and the audience and will consider factors to improve communication (such as cultural differences, personal differences, and diversity).

Communication is about not just words but also nonverbal cues such as body language, pitch and tone, gestures, and facial expression. They all need to be considered for effective communication.

Active Listening

Communication is not just about talking. Communication is also about listening to the other person. A good communicator is also a good listener and allows the other person to talk. If you are constantly interrupting and talking over the other person, that is not a sign of good communication.

A component of listening is *active listening*, where you are giving feedback to the other person. Some examples of feedback could be in the form of repeating the message, clarifying the message, confirming the message, nodding your head in agreement, or shaking your head in disagreement.

Barriers and Enhancers of Communication

Table 10-3 outlines barriers to and enhancers of communication.

Table 10-3   Barriers to and Enhancers of Communication

Communication Barriers	Communication Enhancers
Distorted perceptions	Active listening
Distrusted sources	Making the message relevant to the receiver
Transmission errors	Reducing the message to its simplest terms
Noise	Organizing the message
Message not clearly encoded	Repeating key points
Hostility	Being timely
Becoming emotional	Being concise and clear
Power games and politics	

Other Types of Communication

Good communicators adjust their communication style according to whether the communication is formal, informal, verbal, or written. Table 10-4 summarizes some examples of these types.

Table 10-4   Types of Communication

Formal Written	Informal Written	Formal Verbal	Informal Verbal
Project plans	Emails	Presentations	Meetings
Project charter	Handwritten notes	Speeches	Conversations
Contracts	Brief notes	Keynote addresses	Ad hoc discussions
Business case	Instant messaging	Product demos	
Progress reports			

Number of Communication Channels

The sender-receiver model shows how information can be misinterpreted along the communication chain. Another major factor that can impact communication in such a way is the number of *lines of communication*, also known as the number of *communication channels* (these terms are used interchangeably).

When a team member communicates with another team member, this represents a line of communication. When a team has several team members, there are several communication channels, denoted by the following formula:

$$\frac{n(n-1)}{2}$$

where *n* represents the number of people on a team.

Let's say there are four people in a team, as denoted in Figure 10-2.

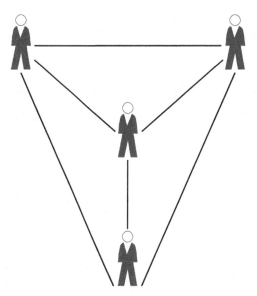

Figure 10-2 Lines of Communication in a Team

In the figure, each line between each person represents a line of communication.

Question: In a four-person team, are there four lines of communication?

Answer: No. There are six (count the lines in the figure).

Let's put this example into the formula. Because there are four people in the team, the formula becomes:

$(4 \times 3) / 2 = 6$

NOTE   There are two considerations to be mindful of in the exam:

1. Read the question carefully to determine whether you are *included* in the team or if you have to add yourself to the team:
   - If the question states "You are managing four people," you need to add yourself to the team, so there are five people on the team.
   - If the question states "You are part of a team of four," you are included in the team, so there are four total team members.

2. Determine whether the question is asking for the total number of communication channels or is asking you to calculate additional communication channels.

Question: You are managing a team of 10 analysts. Two more analysts are added to the team. How many more lines of communication have been added?

Answer: 23

Because you are managing 10 analysts, initially there are 11 people (10 analysts plus you). Therefore,

Initially with 11 people: 11(10) / 2 = **55**

When 2 more people are added, there are 13 people in the team. Therefore,

Addition of 2 people: 13(12) / 2 = **78**

The number of communications channels increased:

78 – 55 = **23**

Creating Project Artifacts

An important aspect of communication is that items such as plans and project status are often communicated via documents (artifacts). The project team, along with the project manager, including the agile team and team facilitator on adaptative projects, create and maintain these artifacts using correct configuration management so that stakeholders can review the latest versions of the artifacts.

The creation, collection, distribution, storage, retrieval, management, monitoring, and disposing of information are performed using the *Project Management Information System (PMIS)*, which is the collection of software tools and processes you use to manage your project. This includes such items as the change management system, configuration management system, archiving system, reporting system, business intelligence tool, plus whichever software tools you use to develop, plan, and manage the project.

Guidelines for Facilitating Meetings

A major factor causing inefficiency and frustration among team members is attending scores of countless nonproductive and unnecessary meetings. A meeting is a good tool to exchange information, share knowledge, collaborate, reach a consensus, provide status, and make decisions. But it is only a good tool when used efficiently and effectively. Otherwise, it can be nonproductive and time consuming.

Imagine a team of 10 team members attending an unnecessary one-hour meeting. They did not need to be there, and they got nothing out of the meeting. That adds up to 10 hours of lost productivity. If they attend these kinds of meetings every day, then over five days, that's 50 hours of lost productivity. Now imagine the whole organization attending such nonproductive meetings, and you can see how companies can end up spending hundreds, if not thousands, of hours of lost productivity every month due to these unnecessary meetings.

Consequently, it is important for an organization to set its own standards and best practices for conducting meetings and for project managers to follow those guidelines and best practices when organizing and facilitating project meetings. Meetings should be productive and efficient. Do you really need to schedule a one-hour meeting for a simple stakeholders' status update? Or will 15 minutes suffice?

Each organization has its own guidelines, but commonly they include

- Ensuring the meeting has a purpose (don't just schedule a meeting for the sake of having a meeting).

- Ensuring the meeting is the appropriate length of time for attendees' engagement and collaboration.

- Ensuring only the appropriate attendees are invited to the meeting.

- Setting and distributing an agenda prior to the meeting start.

- Reviewing an agenda prior to the meeting and sticking to the agenda during the meeting.

- Assigning an attendee to take meeting minutes or notes (or record if permissions are appropriate).

- Keeping the meeting discussions on topic according to the agenda.

- Distributing meeting minutes, notes, or recordings in a timely manner.

Monitor Communications

The Monitor Communications process refers to ensuring the communication needs of stakeholders are being met.

According to the sender-receiver model, it is the sender's primary responsibility to ensure the message has been received as it was intended and that the receiver has understood the message.

Thus, you ensure that the right information has been sent to the right stakeholders at the right time. You follow up with stakeholders to ensure that they received the correct information and have understood the information. You also follow up with stakeholders whom you have not heard from to provide any information you had requested from them. You also follow up with stakeholders to provide any feedback (positive or constructive) about the project or deliverables so far.

A variety of methods may be used, such as

- Customer satisfaction surveys

- Lessons learned

- Observation of stakeholders' reactions and body language

- Review of the issue log

- Emails and meetings

By monitoring communications, you determine engagement levels of stakeholders and adjust communication accordingly to ensure stakeholders are at the appropriate level of engagement.

Osmotic communication is a means of receiving information without any direct communication. For example, when you are sitting in your cube or office doing your work, different groups of conversations may be going on around you that you are not a part of, nor are you necessarily eavesdropping. However, you may inadvertently overhear a conversation that is relevant or of interest to you. This is referred to as osmotic communication.

Osmotic communication can work only in a face-to-face environment (tight matrix). It does not work in a virtual environment if you are sitting by yourself with no one else around.

 ## Agile Approach to Communication

For the most part, communication between predictive and agile approaches are consistent. You still need to ensure the communication is effective and efficient. You still plan the information needs to ensure the appropriate stakeholders are receiving the appropriate information in a timely manner, regardless of the project life cycle approach.

However, the feedback loops in agile are much shorter, meaning there is much more communication and collaboration in agile. Because the team works in short iterations with constant involvement of the customer (via the product owner), agile projects allow for constant communication. The agile team, product owner, and team facilitator are constantly collaborating daily.

The daily standup meeting ensures the team members' status and impediments are communicated daily and any new user stories will be communicated and placed in the product backlog for reprioritization in real time.

The Scrum-of-scrum meetings are regular meetings between agile teams on the same project to share information and status with each other. Agile teams are small, so on a large project, several agile teams will work together. On a regular basis (not necessarily daily), a team member from each team, usually the team facilitator, will attend and participate in these Scrum-of-scrum meetings.

At the end of each iteration, the team has a sprint retrospective ceremony to discuss lessons learned, so continuous improvement is built into the agile ethos.

Also remember that the agile team is given the autonomy to make day-to-day decisions on the project regarding the priorities of the sprint backlog, activities, and user stories. The team facilitator (or Scrum master) acts as a servant leader, encouraging collaboration between team members and ensuring the team has the necessary information and data to perform the work.

In adaptive projects, weekly status meetings with stakeholders are not scheduled. Instead, the use of the *information radiator* eliminates the need for such extensive stakeholder status meetings but still aids in communication of status to stakeholders. The following common charts are used as information radiators:

- **Burnup Chart:** Shows how many story points have been completed based on the definition of done (show the work accomplished).

- **Burndown Chart:** Shows how many story points remain based on the definition of done (shows the work that is left).

- **Cumulative Flow Diagram:** Shows how many story points have not started, are being worked on, and have been completed.

- **Kanban Board (Task Board):** Shows the user stories or tasks that have not started, are being worked on, and have been completed.

These charts are discussed in detail in Chapter 14.

It is worth noting, however, that hybrid projects often involve periodic status reports and regular stakeholders' status meeting. Remember that hybrid projects have elements of both predictive and agile, so status reports and weekly status meetings may be performed alongside daily standup meetings and Scrum-of-scrum meetings.

Exam Preparation Tasks

As mentioned in the section "How to Use This Book" in the Introduction, you have a couple of choices for exam preparation: the exercises here, Chapter 18, "Final Preparation," and the exam simulation questions on the Pearson Test Prep practice test software.

Review All Key Topics

Review the most important topics in this chapter, noted with the Key Topic icon in the outer margin of the page. Table 10-5 lists a reference of these key topics and the page numbers on which each is found.

Table 10-5   Key Topics for Chapter 10

Key Topic Element	Description	Page Number
Section	Communication Model	340
Section	Communication Requirements Analysis	342
Section	Communication Methods	344
Paragraph	Osmotic communication	354
Section	Agile Approach to Communication	354

Define Key Terms

Define the following key terms from this chapter and check your answers in the glossary:

effective communication, efficient communication, interactive communication, push communication, pull communication, active listening, osmotic communication, information radiator

Review Questions

1. You are attending a stakeholders' status meeting and presenting the project results to key stakeholders. One stakeholder mentions to you that they would now like an email summary of the project every Friday morning. What should you do next?

   a. Inform the team facilitator of this new requirement.

   b. Update the communication management plan.

    c. Refer the key stakeholder to the information radiator for updated status.

    d. Inform the team of this new requirement.

2. Based on the sender-receiver model, who has the primary responsibility when sending the message, to ensure the receiver has received and understood the message?

    a. The receiver by correctly decoding the message

    b. The sender by ensuring the message has been encoded and transmitted in a way the receiver can understand

    c. The sender by correctly decoding the message

    d. The receiver by ensuring the message has been decoded and understood

3. Two team members from different parts of the world are having a conversation, but both are misinterpreting gestures and phrases due to cultural differences and accents. This is an example of which of the following?

    a. Noise

    b. Lack of communication skills

    c. Lack of communication styles assessment

    d. Intolerance

4. Which of the following are not among the 5 *C*s of written communication? (Choose two.)

    a. Clear purpose and expression directed to the needs of the reader

    b. Coherent logical flow of ideas

    c. Compilation of information from available sources

    d. Communicating relevant information

    e. Correct grammar

5. You have created a shared drive to ensure the latest versions of project documentation are available to all team members. The communication method described here is which of the following?

    a. Push

    b. Formal written

    c. Pull

    d. Internal

6. David is managing a high-visibility project, but there is much confusion between stakeholders on the progress and status of the project. He has been careful to ensure that all possible information about the project has been available to all the stakeholders, but many stakeholders are unable to interpret the results that don't pertain to them. How could David have avoided this situation?

   a. David should have updated the stakeholder engagement plan to ensure stakeholders are engaged on the project.

   b. Stakeholders should have been briefed on how to read and interpret the information.

   c. David should have understood the information needs of the stakeholders and should have sent them only the relevant information they need.

   d. Based on the sender-receiver model, David should have followed up with the stakeholders after sending them the information to ensure they understood it.

7. One of your team members has not been very responsive in emails and work requests recently, and has not been timely in resolving issues assigned to her. As the PM, you want to understand what the problem is. What type of communication should you initially utilize in this situation?

   a. Formal written

   b. Informal verbal

   c. Formal verbal

   d. Informal written

8. Which of the following are enhancers of communication? (Choose two.)

   a. Noise

   b. Active listening

   c. Formal verbal

   d. Pull communication

   e. Timely

9. Your team member Cathy phones you after a brief meeting from one of the stakeholders' offices. She informs you that she has encountered some resistance in collecting important project information needed. As the PM, you give Cathy some detailed instructions on how to get the necessary information. To ensure Cathy has fully understood the instructions, you should do which of the following?

   a. Follow up with an email clearly outlining the instructions discussed.

   b. Focus on nonverbal clues such body language and paralingual communication.

   c. Ask Cathy to confirm that she understood the message.

   d. Ask Cathy to repeat the instructions back to you.

10. You are a team facilitator, and a key stakeholder is requesting regular status updates of your project. What should you do?

   a. Give them access to the information radiator.

   b. Add them to the email distribution list.

   c. Invite them to the weekly status meetings.

   d. Invite them to the daily standup meetings.

This chapter covers the following topics regarding quality management:

- **Introduction to Quality:** Review quality and learn why quality is an important constraint on a project.

- **Plan Quality Management:** Review the common tools and artifacts for planning the quality management process.

- **Manage Quality:** Review the procedures for quality assurance.

- **Control Quality:** Review the procedures for quality control.

- **Other Quality Terms:** Review key quality terms you need to know for the exam.

- **Quality Theories:** Review key quality theories and pioneers you need to know for the exam.

## CHAPTER 11

Project Quality

In this chapter, we discuss in detail the quality management approach of projects as needed for the PMP exam and discuss the common process tools and artifacts needed to successfully deliver a quality product or service. We also discuss the principles related to the *PMBOK® Guide*, Sixth Edition; the *PMBOK® Guide*, Seventh Edition; and the Exam Content Outline (ECO).

This chapter addresses the following objectives from the PMP Exam Content Outline:

Domain	Task #	Exam Objective
People	Task 4	Empower team members and stakeholders
People	Task 7	Address and remove impediments, obstacles, and blockers for the team
People	Task 10	Build shared understanding
Process	Task 1	Execute project with the urgency required to deliver business value
Process	Task 7	Plan and manage quality of products/deliverables
Process	Task 9	Integrate project planning activities
Process	Task 10	Manage project changes
Process	Task 11	Plan and manage procurement
Process	Task 15	Manage project issues
Process	Task 16	Ensure knowledge transfer for project continuity
Business Environment	Task 1	Plan and manage project compliance
Business Environment	Task 2	Evaluate and deliver project benefits and value
Business Environment	Task 3	Evaluate and address external business environment changes for impact on scope

"Do I Know This Already?" Quiz

The "Do I Know This Already?" quiz allows you to assess whether you should read this entire chapter thoroughly or jump to the "Exam Preparation Tasks" section. If you are in doubt about your answers to these questions or your own assessment of your knowledge of the topics, read the entire chapter. Table 11-1 lists the major headings in this chapter and their corresponding "Do I Know This Already?" quiz questions. You can find the answers in Appendix A, "Answers to the 'Do I Know This Already?' Quizzes and Review Questions."

Table 11-1 "Do I Know This Already?" Section-to-Question Mapping

Foundation Topics Section	Questions
Introduction to Quality	1–2
Plan Quality Management	3–4
Manage Quality	5
Control Quality	6–8
Other Quality Terms	9
Quality Theories	10

CAUTION The goal of self-assessment is to gauge your mastery of the topics in this chapter. If you do not know the answer to a question or are only partially sure of the answer, you should mark that question as wrong for purposes of the self-assessment. Giving yourself credit for an answer you correctly guess skews your self-assessment results and might provide you with a false sense of security.

1. One of the machines your team uses to test deliverables has broken down and needs to be fixed. This action would be best referred to as which of the following?

    a. Corrective action

    b. Defect repair

    c. Preventive action

    d. Cost of conformance

2. Of the following, which would be considered a defect?

    a. You deliver a product according to the customer's requirements, but the product does not work correctly.

    b. You are analyzing a control chart and see seven data points below the mean.

    c. One of the machines that you are using to test the product suddenly breaks down and grinds to a halt.

    d. You deliver a product that works perfectly but it is not what the customer requested.

3. How would you classify the cost of product recalls?

   a. Cost of conformance

   b. External failure cost

   c. Internal failure cost

   d. Appraisal cost

4. After a lengthy discussion and debate with your stakeholders, you have finally agreed on the quality standards that the team must abide by for the next project. What should you, as the project manager, do next?

   a. Notify the team.

   b. Update the quality management plan.

   c. Notify the sponsor.

   d. Schedule the kickoff meeting.

5. Your team is in the testing phase of a project, and they have identified test cases and scenarios and are now performing tests to ensure the system is working correctly. Another group is conducting a review of your team's work to ensure project procedures are being followed. What tool is being employed by this other group?

   a. Statistical sampling

   b. Audit

   c. Quality assurance

   d. Quality control

6. You are working with your team to resolve a perplexing issue and need to get to the primary cause. Which tool will you most likely use?

   a. Ishikawa diagram

   b. Pareto chart

   c. Statistical sampling

   d. Scatter diagram

7. Many issues on your project need to be resolved, and you want to identify a way of prioritizing these issues so that the team can fix the root causes that are creating the greatest number of issues. What tool will you most likely use?

   a. Ishikawa diagram

   b. Statistical sampling

    c. Pareto chart

    d. Scatter diagram

8. Which of the following is an out-of-control situation?

    a. You see seven data points above the mean.

    b. You see one data point above the upper control limit.

    c. You see one data point above the lower control limit.

    d. You see a common cause variance.

9. One of the characteristics of an agile project is that the team is continuously trying to find ways of improving efficiency. Which of the following ceremonies would be most closely aligned to Kaizen?

    a. Backlog grooming

    b. Daily standup meeting

    c. Sprint retrospective

    d. Sprint review

10. Which of the following quality concepts were promoted by Crosby and Juran, respectively?

    a. 80:20 rule, 14 points of TQM

    b. Fitness for use, zero defects

    c. 14 points of TQM, fitness for use

    d. Zero defects, fitness for use

Foundation Topics

Introduction to Quality

The Quality Management knowledge area of the *PMBOK® Guide*, Sixth Edition, addresses the processes for incorporating the organization's quality policies for the product and the project process.

You've probably heard the common phrase "build quality in." Here, we delve a little deeper into the meaning of that phrase. First, we want to emphasize that quality refers to both the product as well as the process. To build quality into the product (or service), you have to build quality into the entire product process.

Definition of Quality

There are various definitions of *quality*, but the one PMI has chosen to adopt as its standard is the ISO 9000 definition, which states

Quality is the degree to which a set of inherent characteristics fulfills requirements.

Notice the definition specifically relates to the product meeting requirements, not that the product actually has to work (although in many cases this would be implied). Let's break this down into simple terms.

A product or service that meets the customer's requirements but does not work is not considered a defect. As an example, suppose you hired a painter to paint a room in your house, and you instructed them to paint one wall bright blue, one wall bright pink, another wall fluorescent yellow, another wall green, and the ceiling purple. Those are your requirements. If the builder painted the room exactly according to those requirements, but you didn't like the final product because the colors clashed too much, you cannot state that the painter did poor quality work. You also cannot tell the painter that this work is defective because the colors do not complement each other. You gave the painter a bad set of requirements in this case.

Conversely, you could deliver a perfectly working product to a customer, but if it doesn't meet their requirements, this would be considered a defect. For example, if you built and delivered a perfectly working bicycle to your client, but they had asked for a tricycle, this would be a defect because you failed to deliver what the client asked for (even though the bicycle works perfectly).

EXAM TIP! For the PMP exam, always be cognizant of this definition of quality.

From the project manager's perspective, the basic theme regarding quality is that this should be a proactive process with an emphasis on preventing issues over fixing issues. Of course, issues will be found and need to be fixed, but preventing an issue is better than fixing an issue.

Continuous improvement is another key theme. You should always strive to learn from your mistakes and put processes in place to make small but constant incremental changes to the quality management process. Simply fixing an issue is not always enough. You also need to ensure it does not reoccur.

EXAM TIP!   For the exam, always look for option choices that are proactive rather than reactive, that prioritize prevention over inspection, and that promote continuous improvement.

Five Levels of Increasing Effective Quality Management

Quality has costs associated with it, and building quality into your project process and product is an investment. If it's a big investment, however, you might decide not to spend the money initially, in which case you might end up having to spend even more money in fixing defects afterward. The following are some approaches to quality management in descending order from the most expensive approach to the least expensive.

1. The most expensive approach to quality management is letting the customer find the defect. This results in additional costs to fix the issue, frustration from the customer, which can lead to loss of business, loss of reputation, loss of customers, litigation claims, recall of the product, among many others. This is also known as an *external failure cost* (discussed later).

2. Focus on quality control to detect and correct defects before the deliverables are sent to the customer. Although a better approach than allowing the customer to find the defect, focusing on quality control has costs associated with it, too, and can be an expensive approach if many defects are found that need to be fixed. This is also referred to as an *internal failure cost* (discussed later).

3. Focus on quality assurance to correct the process itself. If the process is working perfectly, the output of each process should be defect-free, leading to a defect-free final product. In this case, testing the final product should be at a minimum.

4. Incorporate quality into the planning and design of the project and product. Having procedures in place to identify and deal with potential failures is a more proactive approach than identifying and fixing issues after they have occurred.

5. Create a quality culture throughout the organization so that everyone is aware and committed to quality in processes and products. This is always considered the best approach; however, the reality is that not every organization gets to this stage.

Grade versus Quality

A term that is often confused with *quality* is *grade*. The official definition of **grade** is "a category assigned to deliverables having the same functional use but different technical characteristics."

Let's translate this into plain English. Grade refers to things like the number of features a product has, the types of features a product has, and a customer's perception of the product, whereas quality refers to whether the product actually does what it's supposed to do (meet the customer's requirements).

For example, you could purchase the base model of a car, or you could purchase the top-of-the-range version of the same model. The base model does not have many features, whereas the top-of-the-range model has all the "bells and whistles." Thus, the base model is considered lower grade, and the top-of-the-range model is considered higher grade. Let's say you purchased the top-of-the-range model with all the features you could possibly ask for, but those features keep breaking down. Then that would be poor quality.

There is nothing wrong in having a low-grade product. A low-grade product has fewer features but is less expensive and marketed toward a different set of customers than those of a high-grade product. Regardless, in either case, poor quality should never be acceptable. It is possible to have a high-grade product that is low quality (many product features, but those features do not work correctly), or a low-grade product that is high quality (fewer features, but the product works as it is supposed to).

Building Quality into Processes and Deliverables

The project team measures the quality of a product and process using metrics and acceptance criteria based on the requirements. Remember from Chapter 6, "Project Scope," that there are many types of requirements, including quality requirements and compliance requirements, both of which are relevant here. Quality has several dimensions, for example:

- **Performance:** Does the product function as it is supposed to? For example, does the high-speed wireless router provide the speed it was designed for?

- **Conformity:** Does the product meet the needs of the customer?

- **Reliability:** Does the product function consistently?

- **Resilience:** How quickly can the product recover in case of a failure?

- **Satisfaction:** Is the customer happy with the product?

- **Uniformity:** How does the product compare with its competitors?

- **Efficiency:** Is the product designed to be user friendly so that it can produce the same results with minimum effort from the end user?

- **Sustainability:** Does the product produce a positive impact externally (economic, social, environmental, and so on)?

Project teams need to plan for three types of actions:

- *Corrective Action*: An intentional activity that realigns the work with the project management plan

- *Defect Repair* **(a.k.a Rework)**: An intentional activity to modify a nonconforming product to ensure it meets requirements

- *Preventive Action*: An intentional activity that ensures future performance of the work aligns with the project management plan

Let's expand on these terms. A *corrective action* refers to fixing the process or the machinery. For example, if a machine in a production line breaks down, fixing or replacing that machine is a corrective action. Likewise, fixing any deviations from the baseline to try to get back in line with the plan is also a corrective action. If you see the project going over budget or behind schedule, taking action to bring the project back to the original budget or schedule would be a corrective action.

A *defect* refers to issues with the product itself (the deliverable of the project). If you are testing the product or service, and it is not doing what it is supposed to be doing (it is not meeting requirements), this would be considered a defect. Fixing the defect is naturally known as a "defect repair," also known as "rework."

A *preventive action* refers to trying to prevent a corrective action and/or a defect repair from occurring in the first place. For example, regular maintenance of machines would be a preventive action because you are trying to prevent a corrective action. Using good-quality raw materials would be a preventive action because you are trying to prevent a defect repair.

Also note that a corrective action and defect repair both refer to fixing an issue that has arisen. It is not enough just to simply fix this issue, however; the team also needs to ensure that the issue does not occur again. Root cause analysis (discussed later in the chapter) is a common tool for this activity.

Continuous Improvement

To continue the discussion on preventive actions, another key theme regarding quality is continuous improvement. You should always try to continuously improve project processes to try to prevent any potential future failures. The Plan-Do-Check-Act (PDCA) cycle, also referred to as the Plan-Do-Study-Act (PDSA) cycle forms the basis for many continuous improvement methodologies, such as Six Sigma, Lean, and Kaizen. The basic concept, as defined by Shewhart and Deming, is that organizations should make small incremental changes to continuously improve their processes rather than try to make one huge change that will often be mismanaged and difficult to implement. The four basic stages (illustrated in Figure 11-1) are

1. **Plan:** Define the objective, processes, and procedures.

2. **Do:** Execute the plan and obtain data.

3. **Check:** Analyze the data and compare to the plan.

4. **Act**: Act accordingly based on the results; that is, identify root causes of issues, try to get back onto plan, reevaluate the plan, modify the plan, and so on.

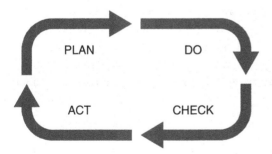

Figure 11-1 Plan-Do-Check-Act Cycle

Quality Control versus Quality Assurance

Two terms that are often confused and sometimes used interchangeably are *quality control* and *quality assurance*. It is important to understand the difference between these terms.

- *Quality Control*: Refers to testing the product or the deliverable to ensure it meets the requirements and functioning as it is supposed to

- *Quality Assurance*: Refers to ensuring the processes and procedures are being followed. It means ensuring that the team is doing what they are supposed to be doing

For example, assume your team has 50 scenarios that need to be tested. Testing each individual scenario to ensure the results are a pass would be quality *control*, whereas ensuring your team has actually tested all 50 scenarios would be quality *assurance*. Your team might have tested only 30 scenarios, and if everything has passed so far, they stop testing because they might incorrectly assume that the other 20 scenarios will also pass. This behavior is unacceptable to you. The team did not follow procedures.

Thus, ensuring that the team is following project policies, processes, and procedures is quality assurance. This refers to following *all* the project policies, processes, and procedures (not *just* the process of testing the product). You want to ensure that procedures such as change control, documentation, stakeholder approval of interim deliverables, and so on are all followed correctly.

We also want to stress that quality is a function of all team members, and success requires the participation of all team members. Although specific teams and/or team members might be responsible for measuring quality compliance and gaps, the whole team needs to work together to create success. This cooperation includes working with vendors and third parties too. An organization and its suppliers are interdependent on one another. Receiving poor-quality product from a supplier has consequences on the product. Constant delays from the supplier has consequences on the project process. So, a partnership with a vendor should always aim to be a mutually beneficial relationship. A long-term relationship is preferred to short-term gains (of course, that depends on the nature and size of the project, the industry, and the situation).

The *PMBOK® Guide*, Sixth Edition, processes relating to quality management are as follows:

- Plan Quality Management

- Manage Quality

- Control Quality

We discuss each process as it relates to the Exam Content Outline (ECO) and the PMP exam.

Agile Approach to Quality Management

The principles of quality management are the same regardless of the project life cycle approach. The nature of the agile/adaptive approach, however, has some key quality management aspects built into the process itself.

Here are a few key aspects of the agile quality management approach you will want to know for the exam:

- **Retrospectives:** In agile, continuous improvement and lessons learned are built into the whole agile process. At the end of each sprint, the teams hold the iteration retrospective ceremony to discuss what went well and what needs to be improved. These recurring retrospectives regularly check on the effectiveness of the quality processes. The team members investigate the root cause and suggest new approaches to quality improvement.

- **Frequent, Small Iterations:** An agile sprint is only one to four weeks, so quality management is much more manageable in short iterations rather than, say, predictive phases, which could last many months. These small batches of work aim to identify inconsistencies and issues early so that they can be fixed early, which means continuous improvement along the way.

- **Definition of Done:** Early in the project, the agile team, the team facilitator, and the product owner determine the detailed acceptance criteria for the work (the definition of done), which will clearly identify whether the work is complete. Having this level of detail on small work increments of work clearly identifies whether the increment meets the requirements.

- **Identification of Impediments:** The daily stand-up meeting serves as a basis for the team to identify issues and impediments that are slowing down the team or blocking their work.

Plan Quality Management

The first process of Quality Management is Plan Quality Management; it refers to the procedures for both quality control as well as quality assurance. The purpose is to provide guidance and direction on testing the product and ensuring the project policies, procedures, and standards are being adhered to. These procedures are documented in the quality management plan.

As with all planning processes, Plan Quality Management should be performed in parallel with other planning processes because all knowledge areas impact one another. Quality impacts every area of a project, so planning should start as early as possible.

Compliance

When planning quality, the project manager and project team must also consider the standards and regulations that govern the development, testing, and delivery of the product. Make sure you understand the difference between a standard and a regulation:

- *Standard*: This is usually a best practice and generally established by the industry or the organization.

- *Regulation*: This is usually imposed by a government body. There are many types of regulations, but some regulations (such as laws) can lead to financial penalties and other punishments for noncompliance.

Most projects need to abide by standards and/or regulations, which are considered constraints on the project. Requirements for such compliance need to be identified, tracked, and managed throughout the project life cycle. For example, on a construction project, you need to understand the zoning laws and building codes that affect what and how your building will be constructed.

Compliance requirements are considered nonfunctional requirements, but abiding by the compliance requirements and satisfying them are part of the quality activity of a project.

Some risks might be involved in compliance, such as

- Being unaware of regulations related to the project

- Being unaware of changes to laws, regulations, and standards that could impact your project

- Misunderstanding the compliance requirement, leading to confusion on how it needs to be implemented, tested, and delivered

Consequences of noncompliance to regulations vary greatly depending on the regulation itself and can lead to financial penalties and even jail time for serious offenses.

The organization needs to identify the person who will be accountable in the event of noncompliance; normally, it is someone at a senior management level.

Key Artifact: Quality Management Plan

The quality management plan documents how policies, procedures, and guidelines will be implemented and refers to procedures for both quality control and quality assurance. The type of information documented in the quality management plan includes

- Quality standards for the project
- Quality objectives
- Roles and responsibilities as they relate to quality control and quality assurance
- Procedures for testing the product (quality control)
- Quality tools that will be utilized
- Procedures for nonconformance of items
- Sign-off procedures for senior stakeholders and management

Key Artifact: Quality Metrics

Quality metrics describe how to measure the quality of the product/service and the project process. Early on during the planning stages of the project, the project manager and/or the team set certain metrics in place to determine whether the project management processes are working well. Examples of quality metrics include failure rates, number of defects over time, total downtime, percentage of tasks completed on time, and cost performance. Every industry, organization, and project determines its own set of metrics.

Key Tool and Technique: Cost of Quality

Costs associated with quality management are a direct cost to your project. Costs related to building quality in (such as using good-quality raw materials and regular maintenance of machines) are all included in the cost baseline. Likewise, the costs of fixing defects, issues, and failures are direct costs to your project. Thus, a key tool for planning quality is the cost of quality.

There are various categories of cost of quality as follows:

1. *Cost of Conformance*: Refers to money spent to *avoid* failures.

   ■ **Prevention Costs:** Refers to building quality into the product or process and describes the money spent to anticipate failures and prevent failures from occurring. Some examples are

   — Regularly maintaining machines to reduce equipment failures

   — Using good-quality raw materials to reduce product failures

   — Sending team members on appropriate training at the right time to reduce human errors

   — Using the right machine for the right job to reduce wastage and increase productivity

   — Documenting processes to reduce human errors

   ■ **Appraisal Costs:** Refers to any kind of testing such as

   — Testing the product (includes all the different types of tests such as unit testing, system testing, and regression testing on IT projects)

   — Testing the process

   — Inspecting raw materials before they are input into a machine

   — Testing to ensure the product is meeting safety requirements (destructive testing losses)

2. *Cost of Nonconformance*: Refers to money spent *due to* failures.

   ■ **Internal Failure Costs:** Costs to fix issues during the project such as

   — Defects (need to fix/rework the product to meet requirements)

   — Scrap (need to abandon the deliverables created so far)

   — Downtime (a machine fails and no one can do any work until it is fixed)

   — Failure analysis

   — Low team morale (an intangible factor but an internal failure nonetheless)

   ■ **External Failure Costs:** Costs to fix issues found after the product has reached the customer. Some examples are

   — Warranty work

   — Liabilities

   — Product recalls

— Product returns

— Customer complaints

— Loss of business/reputation

— Litigation claims

Manage Quality

The Manage Quality process refers to quality assurance. It means ensuring teams are following the quality standards, policies, and procedures. It ensures that the team members are doing what they are supposed to be doing and that procedures are being followed. One of the key goals of quality assurance is to identify any potential failures in the process and determine areas of process improvement to increase efficiency, effectiveness, and ultimately, stakeholder satisfaction.

Key Tools and Techniques of Manage Quality

Some of the tools used for quality assurance are as follows:

- *Quality Audit*: A structured independent review of the entire project process to ensure project activities comply with the organization's processes, policies, and procedures. A quality audit is normally performed by a team outside the project team, such as the internal audit department, or an external auditor. Some objectives of an audit include

    - Ensuring that best practices and procedures are being followed

    - Identifying any gaps and shortcomings in the process

    - Sharing best practices if they are deemed not to have been followed

    - Providing recommendations for any improvements to the project processes and procedures

- **Matrix Diagram:** Used for analyzing the relationship between data sets to determine all the factors that could impact quality.

- **Design for X:** Also known as Design for Excellence, a systematic approach to achieve an objective. X is a variable factor that can have many considerations, such as cost, reliability, quality, and recyclability, to name just a few

The tools discussed in the "Control Quality" section are also relevant here in "Manage Quality."

Key Artifact of Manage Quality: Quality Report

Because the Manage Quality process refers to quality assurance, the summary of findings is documented in a report. The auditors create a report of their findings, as does the project manager or others involved in quality assurance. This report includes quality management issues and recommendations for corrective actions.

Control Quality

The Control Quality process refers to quality control, which is the team's testing of the product to ensure the deliverable is meeting the requirements. The team members verify the completeness, compliance, and conformance to ensure the product is fit for the customer's use.

The team members are not just testing the final product. Quality control must be performed throughout the project to ensure that each deliverable at each stage of the project is meeting all requirements.

Key Tool and Techniques of Control Quality

Although the tools are discussed here in the "Control Quality" section, they equally apply to "Manage Quality" because the same tools can be used to test the process as well as the product.

Inspection

Arguably the most common technique for quality control and quality assurance is inspection, also referred to as testing or product evaluation (for quality control). Simply put, the team needs to test the product, service, and processes to ensure the correct grade and quality of the product are being delivered according to requirements, and project policies and procedures are being followed. Additionally, the customer needs to inspect and test the product to ensure it is meeting their requirements and expectations (sometimes referred to as user acceptance testing).

As an example, if you hire contractors to remodel your home, you, as the customer, continuously inspect their progress to ensure they are remodeling your home according to your expectations. Likewise, when an IT team delivers software to a client, they perform various stages of testing, such as unit testing, function testing, regression testing, and stress testing (to name a few) before going live. However, it is important to note that teams should be testing the product and the process at every stage of the project, not wait until the end.

Pareto Chart

A *Pareto chart* is a specialized type of histogram that shows critical issues (or the causes of an issue) in descending order of frequency. Figure 11-2 shows a sample Pareto chart.

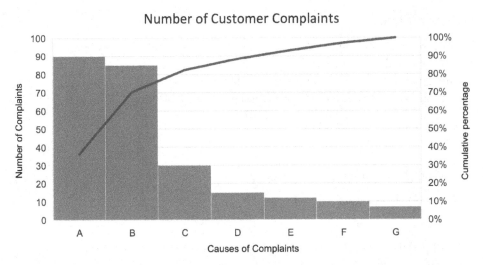

Figure 11-2   A Pareto Chart

Notice there are two y-axes:

- The one on the left refers to the bar chart.

- The one on the right is a cumulative percentage that refers to the cumulative percentage line across the top.

In this example, factor A is the cause of the highest number of complaints (hence the largest bar) and accounts for approximately 35 percent of all the complaints. Factor B is the cause for the next highest number of complaints. Factors A and B together account for approximately 70 percent of all complaints. Factors A, B, and C together account for approximately 80 percent of all complaints, and so on, until we get to 100 percent.

The guiding factor behind the Pareto chart is the "80:20" rule, which states that 80 percent of the issues are a result of 20 percent of the causes. So, by fixing the 20 percent of the causes, you can fix 80 percent of the issues.

Of course, it does not always have to be a straight 80:20, but the principle is that a small number of factors causes the greatest number of issues. So, those are the factors that need to be resolved first. In this case, factors A and B should be the ones that you would look at resolving first. Fixing those factors will fix more than 70 percent of all the customer complaints.

In this way, a Pareto chart is used to prioritize issues and identify which issues need to be resolved first.

Root Cause Analysis

Root cause analysis is used to determine the underlying cause of a problem and solve it. It is used to identify the root cause of an issue so that it can be fixed, thereby preventing any further issues from occurring. The main tool used for root cause analysis has four names that are used synonymously in the PMP exam. They are

- Cause and Effect Diagram

- Ishikawa Diagram

- Fishbone Diagram

- Why-Why diagram

EXAM TIP!   Make sure you know all these four names relating to root cause analysis. They are the same tool but with four synonymous names.

Figure 11-3 shows a simple *Ishikawa diagram*.

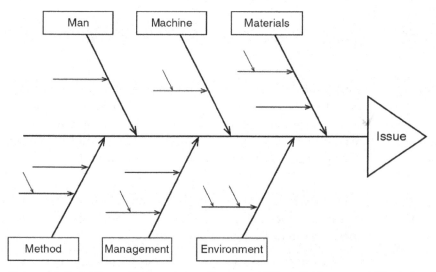

Figure 11-3   Ishikawa Diagram (a.k.a. Cause and Effect, Fishbone, and Why-Why diagram)

The basic principle is as follows:

1. The issue is identified on the right side (in this case, in the triangle although it does not necessarily need to be a triangle).

2. List all possible causes of the issue in the boxes above and below (in this case, Man, Machine, Materials, Method, Management, and Environment).

3. Then, for each possible cause, drill down and ask a certain number of "whys," which should eventually lead you to the root cause.

Each industry and organization uses the Ishikawa diagram in its own way, but when Professor Kaoru Ishikawa developed this, it was commonplace to use the "5 why" analysis, which states that by asking subsequent questions and drilling down five times, you should get to the root cause of the issue.

Scatter Diagram

A *scatter diagram* is used to show a correlation between two variables. Figure 11-4 shows a simple scatter diagram.

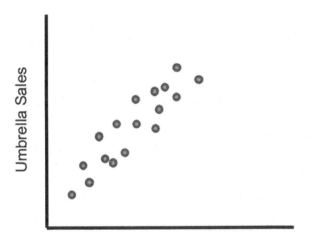

Figure 11-4   Scatter Diagram

This example shows whether there is a direct correlation between the number of rainy days and sales of umbrellas. When scatter points trend in one direction, as shown in Figure 11-4, and you can see there might be a line of best fit, this signifies that there is a direct correlation between these variables. Instead, if these points were randomly scattered all over the chart, there would be no correlation between the two variables.

Control Charts

Key Topic

A *control chart* is used to show whether a process is stable and predictable; this type of chart is used extensively in manufacturing (among other industries). Figure 11-5 shows a simple control chart.

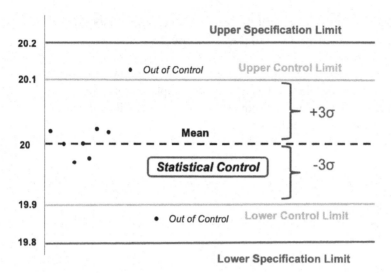

Figure 11-5   Control Chart

Suppose you are in a manufacturing environment, and you are producing glass bottles that need to be 20 centimeters in height. As these batches of bottles come out of the production line, you will take a laser measure of the height of these bottles. As long as they are 20 cm, that will be perfect. However, due natural variations in the production process, not all batches will be exactly 20 cm. Some will be slightly larger and some slightly smaller. As long as this variation falls within an acceptable range, the process is within statistical control.

You can plot these results on a control chart. Because the bottles need to be 20 cm in height, this would be the mean line shown in Figure 11-5. You will see some data points on the mean (implying they are exactly 20 cm), some above, and some below.

The acceptable variations are known as *control limits*, and there is an upper control limit and a lower control limit. In Figure 11-5, the upper control limit is 20.1 cm, and the lower control limit is 19.9 cm. As long as the batches of bottles are within 19.9 cm and 20.1 cm, the process is within statistical control.

The moment you see one data point either above the upper control limit or below the lower control limit, the process has gone out of control. The machine operator is responsible for investigating and fixing the issue. A common reason for an out-of-control situation is that the machine needs recalibrating, hence the operator being the first point of contact.

There is also a specification limit (upper and lower) that is set by the customer, which represents the customer's requirements. The control limits, however, are set by the process itself, and the standard precision level for the purpose of the PMP exam is 3 standard deviations (+/– 3 sigma).

Let's expand on this topic. As mentioned, any data points that are between the upper and lower control limits are generally referred to as being within statistical control. However, there are many exceptions known as *zone tests*. You need to know only one zone test for the PMP exam; it is known as the ***Rule of*** 7, as depicted in Figure 11-6.

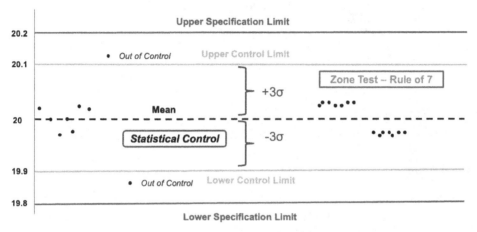

Figure 11-6   Rule of 7

The Rule of 7 states that seeing either seven *consecutive* data points above the mean *or* seven *consecutive* data points below the mean also signifies an out-of-control situation, and the team members need to investigate. In the example, the manufacturing process has created seven batches of bottles in a row that are greater than 20 cm. You need to investigate why. If the process continues this trend, it may start making bigger and bigger bottles until they have breached the control limit.

Two other important terms related to control charts are

- **Common Cause Variance (a.k.a. Random Cause):** These are data points that are in control within the upper and lower control limits.

- **Special Cause Variance (a.k.a. Assignable Cause):** These are out-of-control data points that are either above the upper control limit or below the lower control limit.

Figure 11-7 summarizes all the control chart terms discussed in one diagram.

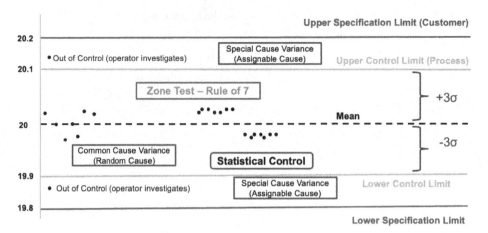

Figure 11-7   Full Control Chart

Statistical Sampling

Statistical sampling is used to test a representative sample of the population, so the team does not need to test every single data point. The purpose is to reduce the number of tests without reducing the quality or the scope of the test. For example, let's say you are implementing a payroll system and want to ensure that all employees get paid correctly and on time with the appropriate deductions and taxes taken correctly. The team needs to test to ensure all employees' payroll and deductions are working. Suppose there are 100,000 employees; in this case, the team will not repeat this test on all 100,000 employees. Instead, team members will identify all the different populations of employees and select a handful from each population to test. Instead of doing 100,000 tests, now team members need to perform only a few hundred tests to ensure all employee populations are working correctly.

Value Stream Map

A value stream map is a process improvement tool showing a detailed visualization of all steps in a process and used to identify bottlenecks and inefficiencies. Figure 11-8 shows a sample value stream map. On the time ladder at the bottom of the diagram, the top bar labeled "Wait" represents non-value-added time, and the bottom bar labeled "Process Time" represents value-added work. If you are looking for areas of efficiency, you should first look at reducing the non-value-added time in the top bar.

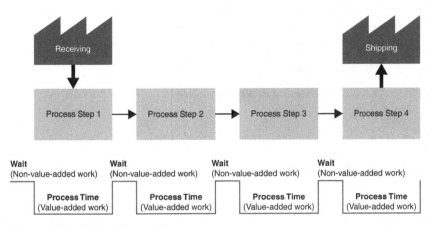

Figure 11-8 Value Stream Map

Checklist and Check Sheet

A checklist is list of items, actions, or points to be considered and is often used as a reminder for individuals and teams. By creating and following checklists, team members can ensure that all required steps have been performed and all tasks completed. Many people simply refer to this as a "to-do" list. These lists can be developed using historical data (OPA, such as prior project files) and expert judgment.

A check sheet, also known as a tally sheet, is a way of organizing a list of defects of the product.

Other Quality Terms

The exam also often covers a few additional terms related to quality. You need to understand the terms described in the sections that follow.

Validate versus Verify

The two terms *validate* and *verify* sound similar to one another, and people often use them synonymously; however, there is a difference, and you need to distinguish between the two terms for the exam:

- **Validate** means the product or service is being produced and delivered according to the customer's requirements.

- **Verify** means that the product or service is being produced correctly according to standards and regulations.

For example, when you're building a house, validate would mean the house is being built according to the architectural plans, built to the correct design, the right number of rooms, the correct size, and so on. Verify would mean that the house is being built according to the building codes and regulations of the locale.

- The project team will validate and verify the deliverables (quality control).

- The customer will validate and accept the deliverable (validate scope).

Kaizen

Kaizen means "continuous improvement" and is a quality management methodology that uses the Plan-Do-Check-Act (PDCA) cycle to make small but consistent steps to improve quality. One of the key activities of continuous improvement is lessons learned, which should be conducted throughout the project to understand what went well and what can be improved to prevent future failures and inefficiencies.

The basic principles behind Kaizen are as follows:

- Changes should be small and easy to manage.

- Ideas should come from the workers who are performing the work on a daily basis.

- Employees should continuously aim to improve their own performance and take ownership of their responsibilities. This will also aid in motivation and engagement.

- Employees should always reflect on what went well and what could be improved.

In agile, lessons learned and continuous improvement are built into the whole agile ethos and are conducted during the sprint retrospective meetings. Unfortunately, it is not on predictive projects, so the project manager must identify time for this task.

Precision versus Accuracy

Similar to validate and verify, the terms *precision* and *accuracy* are used interchangeably by many people. However, there is a difference, and you need to distinguish the two terms for the exam:

- *Precision* means data points are clustered together and have little scatter.

- *Accuracy* means the data points are on or close to the mean.

Figure 11-9 depicts the differences between the two terms. When you're shooting darts at a target board, if a dart lands right in the center, it is accurate. If all the darts land in one section, not necessarily in the center, that is precise.

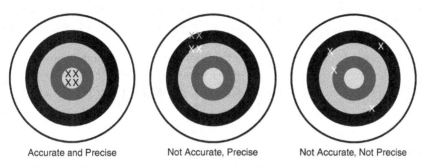

Accurate and Precise   Not Accurate, Precise   Not Accurate, Not Precise

Figure 11-9   Precision versus Accuracy (Credit: darrenwhi/123RF)

Quality Theories

For the PMP exam, you need to be aware of some quality pioneers, but you do not need to study them in detail. The following is a summary:

- **W. Edwards Deming**
  - Developed the 14 points of total quality management.
  - Observed that 85 percent of quality issues are management related. The worker causes quality issues only 15 percent of the time.
  - Together with Walter Shewhart, developed the Plan-Do-Check-Act cycle.

- **Joseph M. Juran**
  - Defined quality as "fitness for use."
  - Promoted the distinction between grade and quality.
  - Developed the Juran Trilogy, which breaks quality management into quality planning, control, and improvement.

- **Philip B. Crosby**
  - Wrote the book *Quality Is Free* with the notion that in a good quality process, although it may be a big initial investment, the savings due to increased productivity, decreased rework, and increased customer satisfaction will offset the initial investment.
  - Promoted the concept of zero defects.

- **Genichi Taguchi**
  - Attempted to establish financial measures related to quality and emphasized quality should be designed into the product.

- **William (Bill) Smith, Jr.**
  - Developed the Six Sigma process improvement concept.

Exam Preparation Tasks

As mentioned in the section "How to Use This Book" in the Introduction, you have a couple of choices for exam preparation: the exercises here, Chapter 18, "Final Preparation," and the exam simulation questions on the Pearson Test Prep practice test software.

Review All Key Topics

Review the most important topics in this chapter, noted with the Key Topic icon in the outer margin of the page. Table 11-2 lists a reference of these key topics and the page numbers on which each is found.

Table 11-2   Key Topics for Chapter 11

Key Topic Element	Description	Page Number
Section	Definition of Quality	365
Section	Grade versus Quality	367
List	Three types of quality actions	368
Section	Quality Control versus Quality Assurance	370
Section	Key Artifact: Quality Management Plan	373
List	Categories of quality cost	374
Section	Inspection	376
Section	Pareto Chart	376
Section	Root Cause Analysis	378
Section	Control Charts	379

Define Key Terms

Define the following key terms from this chapter and check your answers in the glossary:

quality, grade, corrective action, defect repair, preventive action, quality control, quality assurance, standard, regulation, cost of conformance, cost of nonconformance, quality audit, Pareto chart, Ishikawa diagram, scatter diagram, control chart, Rule of 7, precision, accuracy

Review Questions

1. You notice that one of the machines on the production line is working inefficiently and has produced several defects. Some of the defects need to be scrapped, but some can be repaired. You issue a change request to have the machine fixed, which is approved. This action would be referred to as

   a. Defect repair

   b. Preventive action

   c. Rework

   d. Corrective action

2. You have been reassigned to an existing project replacing the current project manager who has left the organization. You want to determine the quality goals and objectives for the project. What should you do?

   a. Reach out to the team.

   b. Review the organizational process assets because they are standard operating procedures.

   c. Review the project charter.

   d. Review the quality management plan.

3. You managed a project to remodel a customer's house. After only a month, the customer calls you complaining that the internal doors are not aligned correctly and do not close properly. When you check, you realize that the wrong size doors were installed, and you need to replace them all. The costs incurred in replacing the doors would be considered which of the following?

   a. Internal failure cost because this should have been caught during the final inspection

   b. External failure cost because the product has been delivered to the customer

   c. Internal failure cost because this is a defect

   d. External failure cost because this is rework

4. You are in a meeting with your team members and are discussing the acceptable tolerance levels regarding the quality of deliverables. One team member states that the acceptable range should be within 2.5 percent, whereas others state 3-sigma. What should you advise?

   a. They should follow the industry standards.

   b. They should follow the organization's standards.

c. They should consult with the PMO.

d. They should consult the quality management plan.

5. The quality assurance team is reviewing documentation to ensure your team has followed procedures and to identify any abnormal variations. What are they doing?

a. Audit

b. Quality control

c. Managing quality

d. Verifying deliverables

6. The upper control limit is set to 400, and the lower control limit is set to −300. The upper specification limit is set to 280, and the lower specification limit is set to −280. You have a data point that is at 375. Which of the following is true?

a. The process is within statistical control within the customer's requirements.

b. The process is within statistical control, and the customer's requirements are being met.

c. The process has gone out of control but is within the customer's requirements.

d. The process has gone out of control and is not within the customer's requirements.

7. There are different factors causing a particular issue, and you want to find the root cause. You look at a chart that lists all possible causes of the issue and drills down each possible cause asking a certain number of "whys." Which tool and technique would be best suited to test a representative sample of the population?

a. Ishikawa diagram

b. Pareto chart

c. Statistical sampling

d. Value stream map

8. Iteration retrospectives can be used for continuous improvement. True or False?

a. True

b. False

9. You are looking at a control chart and notice that a few data points are falling on the mean, some data points are grouped together above the mean but below the upper control limit, and some are grouped together below the mean but above the lower control limit. Which of the following statements is true?

   a. One data point above the upper control limit is accurate, but seven consecutive data points above the mean violate the Rule of 7.

   b. The data points grouped together are accurate, but the data points on the mean are precise.

   c. Seven consecutive data points above the mean would be precise, and one data point below the lower control limit is accurate.

   d. The data points that are grouped together are precise, but the data points on the mean are accurate.

10. Match the terms on the left to the scenarios on the right.

1. Low grade	a. Your customer asked for 24-inch monitors, but you built and delivered 20-inch monitors.
2. Poor quality	b. The customer called stating that the camera's functionality does not work, so now you need to fix it.
3. Appraisal cost	c. Your cell phone has an 8-megapixel camera, whereas your competitors have a 10-megapixel camera.
4. External failure cost	d. Your team is testing the project component after each completed process.

This chapter covers the following topics regarding procurement management:

- **Plan Procurement Management:** Review the common tools and artifacts for planning the procurement procedures for a project.

- **Conduct Procurements:** Review the common tools and artifacts for getting bids from vendors, selecting vendors, negotiating contracts, and signing the contract.

- **Control Procurements:** Review the common tools, procedures, and artifacts for monitoring the work of vendors and closing out the contract with vendors.

## CHAPTER 12

Project Procurement

In this chapter, we discuss the various types of contracts and procurement processes to successfully manage vendors and contractors during a project. We discuss the principles related to the *PMBOK® Guide*, Sixth Edition; the *PMBOK® Guide*, Seventh Edition; and the Exam Content Outline (ECO).

This chapter addresses the following objectives from the PMP Exam Content Outline:

Domain	Task #	Exam Objective
People	Task 8	Negotiate project agreements
People	Task 9	Collaborate with stakeholders
People	Task 10	Build shared understanding
Process	Task 2	Manage communications
Process	Task 3	Assess and manage risk
Process	Task 5	Plan and manage budget and resources
Process	Task 6	Plan and manage schedule
Process	Task 7	Plan and manage quality of products/deliverables
Process	Task 8	Plan and manage scope
Process	Task 9	Integrate project planning activities
Process	Task 10	Manage project changes
Process	Task 11	Plan and manage procurement
Process	Task 12	Manage project artifacts
Process	Task 15	Manage project issues
Process	Task 16	Ensure knowledge transfer for project continuity

"Do I Know This Already?" Quiz

The "Do I Know This Already?" quiz allows you to assess whether you should read this entire chapter thoroughly or jump to the "Exam Preparation Tasks" section. If you are in doubt about your answers to these questions or your own assessment of your knowledge of the topics, read the entire chapter. Table 12-1 lists the major headings in this chapter and their corresponding "Do I Know This Already?" quiz questions. You can find the answers in Appendix A, "Answers to the 'Do I Know This Already?' Quizzes and Review Questions."

Table 12-1   "Do I Know This Already?" Section-to-Question Mapping

Foundation Topics Section	Questions
Plan Procurement Management	1–4
Conduct Procurement	5–7
Control Procurement	8–10

CAUTION   The goal of self-assessment is to gauge your mastery of the topics in this chapter. If you do not know the answer to a question or are only partially sure of the answer, you should mark that question as wrong for purposes of the self-assessment. Giving yourself credit for an answer you correctly guess skews your self-assessment results and might provide you with a false sense of security.

1. Which of the following is not an advantage of centralized contracting?

   a. Departmental expertise

   b. Standardized procedures

   c. Project dedicated procurement resources

   d. PM spends less time on procurement activities

2. You are trying to determine whether to outsource an activity to a vendor by considering the cost implications, availability of resources, and the schedule. What are you performing?

   a. Cost benefit analysis

   b. Make or buy analysis

   c. Conduct procurement

   d. Procurement strategy

3. You have decided to outsource an activity to a preferred vendor. Which of the following is true?

   a. This is known as sole source contracting.

   b. This is a make or buy analysis.

   c. This is known as single source contracting.

   d. This is a proposal evaluation.

4. You are managing a construction project for an office building and need 10,000 square feet of carpeting. The customer prefers a standard design that is available from several suppliers. Which of the following is the best bid document to use?

   a. RFP

   b. RFI

   c. FP-EPA

   d. RFQ

5. A potential customer is interested in purchasing a significant number of batches of your flagship product, which will require you to procure additional equipment to fulfill this order. The potential customer sends you a letter of intent so that your company can get a bank loan to procure the additional equipment, but the bank rejects the loan application. What is the most likely reason for the rejection?

   a. Your company may have had financial problems and credit issues within the past year.

   b. You may not have the authority to request loans for your company.

   c. A letter of intent is not a legal document.

   d. There may be serious credit issues and financial problems with the potential customer.

6. You are in a meeting with several potential sellers for an agile project. Most likely, which meeting is this?

   a. Release planning

   b. Bidder's conference

   c. Iteration review

   d. Stakeholders' status meeting

7. Which of the following tools would you utilize to look for potential vendors to discuss the project and receive proposals from?

   a. RFP

   b. Proposal evaluation

   c. Procurement management plan

   d. Advertising

8. You have hired a vendor to perform certain activities on your project. Which of the following is not true regarding early termination?

   a. Your vendor can terminate the contract for cause.

   b. Your vendor can terminate the contract for convenience.

   c. You can terminate the contract for convenience.

   d. You can terminate the contract by mutual agreement.

9. You have a dispute with one of your vendors regarding the work they completed and the work that was agreed to. What should you do to determine the next steps to resolve this dispute?

   a. Refer to the procurement management plan.

   b. Refer to the legal department of your organization.

   c. Refer to the procurement manager of your project.

   d. Refer to the contract with the vendor.

10. You have an FFP contract with your vendor. What will be your biggest concern as you are monitoring their work?

   a. Bait and switch

   b. More resources used than originally planned

   c. A schedule slowdown resulting in increased cost

   d. Increased cost of raw materials

Foundation Topics

Procurement is all about getting goods and services from outside of the organization. The project manager and team determine whether to perform the work in-house or outsource the work. They plan and manage agreements and contracts and ensure the vendor is performing the work that they were hired to perform. There can be significant legal obligations and penalties tied to the procurement process, so it is important to perform these processes correctly for project success.

EXAM TIP   There are a couple of considerations that you need to make for the PMP exam:

1. Most of the activities and processes for the other knowledge areas of a project refer to the project manager and the team performing the work for the customer. In procurement management, the project manager and the team are now the customer. They hire the vendor to perform the work. Thus, the project manager and the team give their requirements to the vendor, from which will be developed the scope of the project (or the statement of work), the schedule, and the budget. This is documented in a legal contract.

2. Unless stated otherwise, the questions are from the buyer's perspective. If a question does not state whether you are the buyer or the seller, always assume you are the buyer.

3. Unless the question states otherwise, assume that the project has a procurement resource with whom the project manager works on procurement activities. However, the project manager should be familiar enough with procurement processes to make intelligent decisions about contracts.

The *PMBOK® Guide*, Sixth Edition, processes related to procurement management are as follows:

- Plan Procurement Management

- Conduct Procurements

- Control Procurements

We discuss each process in detail as it relates to the Exam Content Outline and the PMP exam.

Plan Procurement Management

The Plan Procurement Management process refers to determining the procedures for acquiring goods and services from outside of the organization. It addresses the procedures for making purchasing decisions and identifying potential sellers. We determine the steps required during procurement and the types of contracts that need to be negotiated.

Centralized vs. Decentralized Contracting

In a *centralized contracting* environment, all procurement activities must go through a central procurement department within the organization. Standard procedures must be followed, and the procurement department is responsible for all procurements.

In a *decentralized contracting* environment, the organization does not have a procurement department, but instead a single dedicated procurement manager oversees each project.

Table 12-2 shows some advantages and disadvantages of centralized and decentralized contracting.

Table 12-2   Centralized vs. Decentralized Contracting

Centralized		Decentralized	
Advantages	**Disadvantages**	**Advantages**	**Disadvantages**
Department of contracting expertise.	Procurement staff is not dedicated to project.	Procurement staff is dedicated to project.	Limited to the procurement staff's experience.
Standardized procedures and contract documentation.	Procurement resources are not always available when you need them.	Project manager has more control over procurement activities.	Must develop contracting expertise.
Project manager doesn't need to spend as much time on procurement activities.			

Components of a Contract

A contract must contain these five elements at a minimum:

- **Offer:** This component documents the good or service that the seller is offering.

- **Acceptance:** This component documents the good or service that the buyer is accepting.

- **Capacity:** This component ensures the seller can perform the work and the contract signers are of sound mind and legal age.

- **Consideration:** This component is also known as "quid pro quo," which states that the seller is providing the good or service for something in return. Usually, it's money, but it doesn't have to be.

- **Legal Purpose:** This component ensures that the good or service that is being delivered must be a legal good or service in the locale it is being delivered. For example, if it is illegal to build a 200-foot tower next to your office building, you cannot have a contract to do so.

Typically, a contract has many more components than just the ones listed here, but these are the minimum for a contract. Other components of a contract include

- Delivery date and schedule

- Description of the work

- Responsibilities of both parties

- Guarantees and warrantees if applicable

- Identification of authority

- Provision for termination

- Terms and conditions

This is not an exhaustive list by any means, but it represents a few components typically found in a contract.

Types of Contracts

For the PMP exam, you need to understand just a few types of contracts (and some variations). In reality, there are many types of contracts, and a contract itself can be a hybrid of other contract types.

Contracts in a Predictive Environment

For the PMP exam, you need to know three basic types of contracts for predictive projects and a few variations on two of them. In the real world, there are many types of contracts, which can be a mix of several other types of contracts. The contract types you need to know for the PMP exam are as follows:

1. *Fixed Price Contract*

   - In a fixed price contract, the entire procurement work is completed at a predetermined fixed price to the buyer, and if the buyer does not change the scope of work after the contract is signed, they just pay this one fixed price to the seller.

   - In this type of contract, the seller assumes all risks of the contract (therefore, the seller must control costs). Remember that risk means uncertainty, so the seller has all the uncertainty on this kind of contract. The buyer knows exactly how much they will pay for the work.

   - A fixed price contract should have a very detailed statement of work because both buyer and seller need to agree to the exact parameters of the work and agree on what will be delivered and what will not.

EXAM TIP   The buyer prefers a fixed price contract when

- Requirements are well defined.

- It is a well-understood project with minimum risk.

- The buyer wants to reduce the risk to their organization.

- The buyer wants an easier contract to administer (for example, the buyer will receive a single invoice and will not need to verify receipts against materials delivered and work done).

- **Variations of a Fixed Price Contract:**

  - **Firm Fixed Price (FFP):** This is the most common type of fixed price contract and preferred by most buyer organizations because the price for the goods or service is set at the beginning and not subject to change unless the scope of work changes.

  - **Fixed Price Incentive Fee (FPIF):** An incentive is added to the fixed price and could be in the form of a bonus, a penalty, or a cost share.

    - In the case of a penalty, the seller has an incentive to meet a certain predetermined goal; otherwise, they may need to pay penalties.

    - In the case of a cost share, a ceiling price is established, and any expenses above the ceiling price are covered by the seller.

  - **Fixed Price with Economic Price Adjustments (FPEPA):** This fixed price contract has adjustments for factors such as inflation, price volatility, exchange rate volatility, or other economic conditions.

2. *Cost Reimbursable Contract*

- In a cost reimbursable contract, the seller is reimbursed for all costs and expenses and may receive a fee based on certain factors.

- In this type of contract, the buyer assumes all risks of the contract because the final cost is unknown until the end of the project. The seller has no incentive to control costs because the buyer is paying, so the seller might not care about wastage or using additional resources. Therefore, the buyer might try to control costs.

EXAM TIP   The buyer prefers a cost reimbursable contract when
- The scope is expected to change significantly throughout the project.
- There is high risk (uncertainty) where you cannot determine scope, budget, or schedule easily at the beginning (such as research and development projects).

- **Variations of Cost Reimbursable Contracts:**
    - **Cost Plus Percentage of Cost (CPPC):** Here, the seller is reimbursed for costs plus receives a predetermined percentage of the cost. For example, if the contract states "Cost +10%," the seller is reimbursed for all their expenses plus an additional 10 percent of those expenses that represent the profit that they will be making. In this type of contract, the seller may have an incentive to increase cost, because the higher the cost, the more remuneration they receive.

    - **Cost Plus Fixed Fee (CPFF):** Here, the seller is reimbursed for all expenses and receives a fixed fee regardless of how much the costs are.

    - **Cost Plus Incentive Fee (CPIF):** Here, the seller is reimbursed for costs and receives an incentive fee if they meet a certain condition.

    - **Cost Plus Award Fee (CPAF):** The seller receives a fixed fee and a subjective award at the discretion of the buyer (think of it as a "tip").

3. *Time and Material (T&M) Contract* (a.k.a. Time & Means)

- In a T&M contract, the seller is remunerated for their time and reimbursed for materials.

- Each unit of time has the seller's profit built in. For example, if the seller charges $200 an hour and their expenses are $120 an hour, they make $80 an hour in profit. Plus, they are reimbursed for expenses.

- This type of contract is often set up with a "known cost" or "not to exceed" clause (also known as a ceiling price) where the risk of the contract is initially with the buyer until the ceiling price is reached, in which case it then transfers to the seller.

EXAM TIP   The buyer prefers a time and materials contract when
- A precise statement of work cannot be quickly described or agreed to.
- It is used for short-term staff augmentation–type projects.

4. **Indefinite Delivery Indefinite Quantity Contract:** This type of contract provides for an indefinite quantity of goods and services with a stated lower and upper limit for fixed time period.

Contracts in an Adaptive Environment

The following are basic types of agile contracts you need to know for the PMP exam:

- **Capped Time and Materials Contract:** This is similar to the traditional T&M contract with an upper limit set for the customer; however, the seller can receive a benefit if the project finishes early.

- **Target Cost Contract:** The buyer and seller agree to a final cost and share any cost overruns or underruns.

- **Incremental Delivery Contract:** The price is negotiated per iteration, but the contract can be reviewed and adjusted at prenegotiated points on the project.

Two other types of contracts you need to be aware of:

- **Completion Contract**
  - Most contracts are considered a completion contract.
  - The seller is remunerated for delivering a specific good or service.
  - It requires the seller to complete and deliver the specified product.

- **Term Contract**
  - It refers to the scope in more general terms when the scope, timeline, and budget are not established and there is no guarantee of any outcome.

- It is used for a specified level of effort for a specified time period rather than a deliverable.

- For example, you hire a vendor on a research and development project to perform 1,000 hours' worth of work. The vendor sends a team to you, and you delegate tasks to the team. They collectively perform a total of 1,000 hours of work, and then the contract is closed. However, there is no guarantee that this team will deliver something.

Key Tools and Techniques of Plan Procurement Management

The project manager and the team need to plan the procurement process carefully during the project to ensure they have selected the right vendors for the appropriate work and negotiated contracts correctly. The following sections describe some common methods and tools they might apply.

Make or Buy Analysis

A *make or buy analysis* simply refers to determining whether to hire vendors to perform the work or to perform the work in-house. There are many considerations when making this decision, such as

- **Cost:** Is it more cost-effective for a vendor to perform the work? The project manager and the team perform a cost-benefit analysis to determine whether it is cost-effective to outsource the work versus perform it in-house. You might need to consider return on investment (ROI), net present value (NPV), payback period, internal rate of return (IRR), and benefit cost ratio (BCR), among others.

- **Schedule:** If the project is running behind schedule and you have a fixed deadline, you may decide to outsource some activities to a vendor to try to get back on track. This would be an example of a corrective action.

- **Risk:** You want to reduce the risk to your organization or transfer a risk.

- **Resources:** You do not have the resources to perform the work (such as a specialized machine or a specialized skill set), so you outsource to a vendor who does.

- **Requirements:** You do not have the expertise to meet the requirements.

- **Quality:** The quality of the work might not be up to standard.

Some reasons why you may prefer to keep the work in-house include

- **Control:** You have more control of the work if you perform it yourself. When you outsource, you are at the mercy of the vendor.

- **Proprietary Information:** You want to keep confidential information secure.

- **New area of business:** If your business is expanding into new areas, you want to grow expertise in this area and may decide to perform the work in-house by hiring new employees with new skill sets instead of outsourcing to a vendor.

Source Selection Analysis

The buyer needs to evaluate and determine the types of vendors they prefer to hire when deciding to outsource the work. The vendor must meet the minimum criteria to be considered for a contract, which must be determined before submitting a request for proposal. This evaluation method refers to the source selection analysis, and the decision is referred to as the source selection criteria.

As a simple example, suppose you need to do some remodeling work in your house. For this kind of project, you do not reach out to large multinational construction firms for a bid. Instead, you reach out to small local contracting companies to do the work. This is your source selection criteria.

Other common examples of source selection criteria include

- **Lowest Cost Vendor:** Your company decides you need to select the vendor with the least cost, regardless of quality or any other factor.

- **Qualifications/Certifications:** For example, a criterion might be "the project manager has to be PMP certified."

- **Size and Experience of the Vendor:** For example, you might consider only large organizations. Conversely, you might decide that you will consider only small organizations to bid on this contract.

- **Classifications:** You consider only organizations that fall within a certain category. For example, you might choose a veteran-owned small business or woman-owned small business, which is common for U.S. federal government contracting.

- **Financial Capability:** You need to determine whether the vendor is a solvent organization.

- **Technical Capabilities:** You consider how much technical expertise the vendor has in providing the good or service.

- **Management Approach:** You consider whether the vendor's management approach is compatible with your organization's management approach.

- **Warranty:** You might consider what type of warranty the vendor is providing.

- **Past Performance:** You review how the vendor has performed on past projects or what kind of performance reviews the vendor has received from other customers (for example, online reviews).

- **Risks:** You might consider risks involved in outsourcing to a vendor. For example, you might determine there is a higher risk of delay in receiving raw materials from a vendor located 500 miles away compared to a local vendor.

- **References:** Your organization may require references from the vendors' prior customers.

- **Fixed Budget:** As the buyer, you have a fixed budget, and potential sellers propose the work they can perform within that fixed budget.

These are just some examples, not an exhaustive list. Each organization has its own set of considerations when trying to determine which vendors to work with.

The analysis is known as the *source selection analysis*. The decision is known as the source selection criteria.

Two types of source selection analyses are noncompetitive:

- *Sole Source*

  - In this case, only one vendor can perform the good or service, so you have no choice but to choose this vendor.

  - This situation could arise due to a monopoly, or the vendor has exclusive rights due to a patent.

- *Single Source*

  - This refers to a preferred vendor.

  - In this case you have the option to reach out to other vendors if you want, but because the preferred vendor has already been vetted by the organization and proved their competence, most project managers simply hire the preferred vendor.

Key Artifacts of Plan Procurement Management

The artifacts covered in the sections that follow are created as part of procurement planning.

Procurement Management Plan

The procurement management plan documents how the team will acquire goods and services from outside the organization. It documents items such as

- How procurements will be coordinated
- The stakeholder's roles and responsibilities related to procurement
- The risk management procedures regarding procurements
- The process for obtaining bids
- How multiple vendors will be managed
- The timetable of key procurement activities
- Legal jurisdictions and currency

This is not an exhaustive list, but just some examples of the types of items documented in the procurement management plan.

Procurement Strategy

After it has been determined that the work will be outsourced, a strategy is developed for the activity that is being outsourced. The three basic components to the procurement strategy are

- **Delivery Methods:** For example, will you allow the vendor to use a subcontractor? Will this be a joint venture? Will this be a custom build? There are different delivery methods based on the industry, project, and situation.
- **Contract Payment Types:** What type of contract do you prefer to negotiate? At what stages of the project will the seller be paid?
- **Procurement Phases:** The strategy documents how the procurement will move through the various phases of the project if applicable.

Bid Documents

Bid documents are used to solicit proposals from vendors. For the exam, you should know three basic types of bid documents:

- **Request for Information (RFI)**

  - The buyer or seller needs additional information.

  - It is sometimes used before sending out an RFP.

  - It is sometimes used after an RFP has been submitted.

- **Request for Quote (RFQ)**

  - It usually focuses on pricing only.

  - It is generally used for standard items that require no customization.

  - For example, you need to purchase 1,000 rolls of 100 feet of copper wiring. This is a standard product; you are not customizing the product. You just need to know the bottom-line: how much will it cost?

- **Request for Proposal (RFP)**

  - It focuses on the needs and requirements of the customer.

  - The seller cannot give a quote until they collect requirements and scope out the project.

  - For example, you need to implement a business intelligence system that is specifically designed for your business process. This is a custom product, so requirements need to be gathered and understood before the vendor is able to provide a quote.

Procurement Statement of Work

The procurement statement of work is often referred to as term of reference (TOR) for the procurement of services. It is developed from the scope statement and contains details such as

- Tasks that need to be performed by the seller

- Standards that seller must abide by

- Data that needs to be submitted for reviews

- Scope, schedule, budget, and other constraints

The procurement statement of work is a detailed document that will become part of the contract. The exact level of detail depends on the type of contract, but it must be written in sufficient detail so that both buyer and seller can understand and agree on what is to be delivered and what is not. Table 12-3 provides a summary of the procurement documents we have just discussed.

Table 12-3 Summary of Procurement Documents

Procurement Management Plan	Procurement Strategy	Statement of Work	Bid Documents
How procurement work will be coordinated and integrated with other project work, particularly with resources, schedule, and budget	Procurement delivery methods	Description of the procurement item	Request for information (RFI), Request for quote (RFQ), Request for proposal (RFP)
Timetable for key procurement activities	Types of agreements	Specifications, quality requirements, and performance metrics	
Procurement metrics to manage the contract	Procurement phases	Description of collateral services required	
Responsibilities of all stakeholders		Acceptance methods and criteria	
Procurement assumptions and constraints		Performance data and other reports required	
Legal jurisdiction and currently used for payment		Quality	
Information on independent estimates		Period and place of performance	
Risk management issues		Currency; payment schedule	
Prequalified sellers, if applicable		Warranty	

Conduct Procurement

The Conduct Procurement process refers to discussing the project with sellers, receiving their proposals, selecting the seller, negotiating agreements and contracts with the sellers, and finally signing the contract, or making agreements. Agreements can be documented in many forms, such as

- Service-Level Agreements (SLAs)
- Nondisclosure Agreements (NDAs)
- Supplemental Agreements

- Memorandum of Understanding (MOA)

- Contracts

Key Tools and Techniques of Conduct Procurement

The sections that follow describe some of the common methods and tools for conducting procurement activities.

Advertising

Based on your selection criteria you need to look for potential vendors to submit an RFP or RFQ. One of these methods is advertising so that potential vendors can reach out to you. You do not need to use this method in a sole source or single source situation.

Bidder's Conferences

A *bidder's conference* is a single meeting with all the potential sellers to ensure that all sellers have a clear and common understanding of the procurement process. It could be a face-to-face meeting, a conference call, or a video conference meeting. The primary characteristics of a bidder's conference are as follows:

- It is conducted by the buyer prior to submission of any bids.

- The purpose is to ensure fairness and an even playing field so that no seller receives preferential treatment.

- It generally starts with the buyer sending an RFP to the sellers, inviting them to the bidder's conference. The sellers are given a deadline by which to submit any questions, and all questions are answered and available to all the potential sellers.

- The meeting itself is an open dialogue where the buyer discusses the project openly with all the potential sellers and all potential sellers may ask questions openly.

- The process is transparent and attempts to prevent favoritism toward a particular vendor and prevent collusion between the buyer and a seller organization.

- From a buyer's perspective, one of the main advantages of using a bidder's conference is that the buyer needs to organize only one meeting. Otherwise, they would organize individual meetings with each seller to discuss the same project, which is more time consuming. Imagine if you have 20 potential sellers.

You could either organize 20 separate meetings, one with each vendor, to discuss the same project, or organize one bidder's conference inviting them all.

There are variations of bidder's conferences based on the industry and organization, but the points previously listed are the basic principles. Not every industry uses a bidder's conference. In the United States, for example, bidder's conferences are common among federal government agencies, but private industries rarely use this approach.

Proposal Evaluation

After you, as the buyer, have received bids from the potential sellers (either after a bidder's conference or otherwise), you need to evaluate those proposals and rank them to determine which one to select. There are many ways of evaluating and proposals, and all organizations and individuals have their own approaches. Based on the proposal evaluations, you select your highest-ranking vendor and start contract negotiations with them.

The key interpersonal skill set needed here is negotiation. Remember, for the PMP exam, it is assumed that a project manager will always have access to a procurement resource when negotiating contracts. Although the project manager might not be the lead negotiator, the PM could still be involved in the contract negotiations regardless.

EXAM TIP   PMI assumes the project manager will always have access to a procurement resource when negotiating contracts.

Other Important Procurement Terms

The following are some additional procurement terms you need to be aware of for the PMP exam:

- **Qualified Vendors List:** These vendors meet the source selection criteria and are approved to provide the goods or services. They have not necessarily been hired yet. These are the vendors to whom the buyer will send out RFPs or RFQs to receive their bids.

- **Letter of Intent (LOI):** This document outlines the preliminary intention of one party to do business with another. It can be used in many ways; however, it is not a legal document.

- *Privity:* This term refers to the contractual obligations between the buyer and seller. If you have a contract with a vendor, you are in privity with this vendor, and the vendor is in privity with you. You both have a legal obligation over one another; however, if the vendor decides to outsource part of their work to a subcontractor, you are not in privity with their subcontractor because you do not have a contract with them. Thus, you cannot delegate any work or even communicate with the subcontractor. All your delegation and communication need to go through the vendor that you are in privity with.

- **Force Majeure:** This clause on a contract refers to an "act of God," a negative and sudden event that you are not in control of, nor can you predict well in advance. This includes natural disasters such as flooding and hurricanes as well as human-caused situations such as rioting and war. This clause states that neither party can be held liable for nonperformance of work due to factors beyond their control.

Control Procurement

The Control Procurement process refers to contract administration and monitoring the work of the hired vendor. It is the process of managing the procurement relationship, identifying success and failures of the procurement, controlling any changes, and closing out the contract with the vendor.

Because the buyer and seller are both in privity with one another, each party has a legal obligation over the other, so both parties ensure the other party is meeting their contractual obligation. If either party wants to change or modify the contract, there must be a contract Change Control process in place.

As a buyer, you conduct regular performance reviews of the vendor to ensure they are performing the work as agreed to in the contract, and you observe how efficiently they are performing the work. You determine, for example, whether they are delivering good quality work timely or whether there are constant defects that you and your team are pointing out to them. You regularly test and inspect their work to ensure they are delivering the product or service they were hired to deliver.

The approach to monitoring the work of the vendor may be determined by the type of contract, too. For example:

- **Fixed Price:** Because the seller has the uncertainty about cost, you might need to watch out for a "bait and switch," a practice through which the vendor has promised (and you are paying for) high-grade and high-quality raw materials, but they instead use a lower grade and quality to lower their expenses.

- **Cost Reimbursable:** Because the buyer is paying for all the costs, you, as the buyer, might want to monitor the seller's costs and ensure that the resources utilized are actually adding value to the project. For example, are the five additional team members that the vendor brought on board really needed? Or could they just need three instead?

- **Time and Materials:** Because you are paying for seller's time, you might want to observe the vendor's work and monitor their invoices to ensure they are not padding the schedule. For example, if they charged you for 100 hours of work, you want to ensure that they actually performed 100 hours of productive work and not that they took long breaks and purposely worked slowly to extend the time, all the while charging you.

Key Tools and Techniques of Control Procurement

The sections that follow describe some of the common tools and techniques that you can use for monitoring and controlling the work of the vendor.

Performance Reviews and Inspections

The buyer tests and inspects the work of the seller to ensure the work is being performed according to the contract. Before the contract is closed, the buyer may perform user acceptance testing, do walkthroughs, or inspect the deliverables. The exact procedures and activities depend on the industry and nature of the project.

In addition, the buyer determines the performance of the work of the vendor and how efficiently they are performing. For example, are they ahead of schedule or behind schedule, over budget, or under budget? Are there quality issues with the product?

Audit

An audit is an independent review to ensure processes and procedures are being followed on a project. An independent team verifies that the project team members are following the organization's policies, procedures, and standards and identifies any gaps.

Contract Change Control System

Any changes to the contract must go through a formal Change Control process. Because contracts are legal documents, the contract Change Control process might be more complex than a regular internal Change Control process because external parties are involved. One party might not understand why the other party needs the change, so there could be more back and forth before an agreement is made.

There are different types of contract changes, as follows:

- **Administrative Changes:** These are simple nonsubstantive changes and the most common type of changes. They are usually easy to make with minimum effort, such as changes to personnel, contact information, and misspellings. There are no changes to the actual scope of the project or the budget or timeline.

- **Contract Modifications:** These changes refer to substantive changes to the contract, such as changes to scope, functionality, or deadline.

- **Supplemental Agreements:** These changes refer to additional agreements that relate to the contract but are negotiated separately.

- **Constructive Changes:** These changes are caused by the action or inaction of the buyer. For example, the schedule needs to change because the buyer failed to deliver information needed for the seller to continue their work. The work was held up due to the inaction of the buyer.

- **Termination of the Contract:** These changes are discussed in the section "Closing Procurements."

Claims Administration

If there is a dispute or disagreement, the buyer and seller must work to resolve the dispute, and the procedures for claims administration are documented in the contract itself.

Some common areas of dispute are

- **Warranty:** The product or service fails before the end of the warranty period.

- **Waivers:** This means giving up certain rights.

- **Breach of Contract:** There is a failure to meet the obligation.

- **Cease & Desist:** There is a call to stop an illegal activity and not perform it again.

A negotiated settlement, following the procedures outlined in the contract, is the preferred approach, but if this fails, there might be an alternate dispute resolution (ADR), which is also documented in the contract, such as mediation and arbitration.

Closing Procurements

Procurement can be closed in one of two ways:

- **Completion of the Contract**

    - The work has been completed by the seller, and the product or service has been successfully delivered to the customer.

    - This is the best way to close the contract.

    - Usually, the final payment of outstanding invoices signifies the contract is closed.

    - On larger projects, the completion can be followed by a written notice from the buyer to the seller confirming the contract is now closed.

- **Early Termination of the Contract**

    - **For Convenience**

        – For the PMP exam, only the buyer has the right to terminate, and it must be negotiated in the contract. It is not automatically implied.

        – This termination clause states that the buyer can cancel the contract early due to business reasons.

        – For example, the buyer may terminate the contract with the seller early if senior management cancels the project.

    - **For Cause**

        – This termination is an implied right for both the buyer and seller that refers to a cardinal breach of the contract.

        – Either party can take legal action due to the default of the contract by the other party.

    - **By Mutual Agreement**

        – The contract can be canceled early by mutual consent of both parties.

        – This a right for both the buyer and seller.

Exam Preparation Tasks

As mentioned in the section "How to Use This Book" in the Introduction, you have a couple of choices for exam preparation: the exercises here, Chapter 18, "Final Preparation," and the exam simulation questions on the Pearson Test Prep practice test software.

Review All Key Topics

Review the most important topics in this chapter, noted with the Key Topic icon in the outer margin of the page. Table 12-4 lists a reference of these key topics and the page numbers on which each is found.

Table 12-4   Key Topics for Chapter 12

Key Topic Element	Description	Page Number
Exam Tip	Procurement	395
Section	Types of Contracts	397
Section	Make or Buy Analysis	401
Section	Source Selection Analysis	402
List	Noncompetitive forms of procurement	403
Paragraph	Bidder's Conference	407
Paragraph	Privity	409
Section	Closing Procurements	412

Define Key Terms

Define the following key terms from this chapter and check your answers in the glossary:

fixed price contract, cost reimbursable contract, time and material (T&M) contract, make or buy analysis, source selection analysis, sole source, single source, bidder's conference, privity

Review Questions

1. You are an IT project manager for an organization where senior management is risk averse. Partway through an implementation project, you decide that some activities need to be outsourced to a vendor due to lack of resources in your company. Which type of contract should you negotiate?

   a. T&M

   b. FFP

   c. CPFF

   d. CPIF

2. In which of the following scenarios would you most likely use an RFP?

   a. You need 200 feet of copper piping.

   b. You need 35 chairs for a conference room.

   c. You need a custom solution for your IT system.

   d. You need 50 standard laptops for the office.

3. Your senior stakeholders want you to select a small local vendor to perform an activity that you are planning to outsource. Which of the following is true?

   a. This is source selection criteria.

   b. This is a make or buy analysis.

   c. This is a requirement.

   d. This is a procurement strategy.

4. You have decided to outsource the work and sign a CPPC contract with a vendor. What will be your biggest concern throughout the project?

   a. Schedule

   b. Vendor's access to proprietary information

   c. Vendor's expertise

   d. Cost

5. You need to purchase 500 windows of equal size for a hotel construction project. What type of bid document should you submit to the vendor so that they can send you a quote?

   a. RFQ

   b. RFP

   c. RFI

   d. FFP

6. Your vendor hired one of their subcontractors, who has severely underperformed. You have reached out to the subcontractors several times, but they have completely ignored you. Which of the following is true?

   a. The subcontractor is within their right not to respond to you.

   b. You should cancel the contract for cause due to their underperformance.

   c. You should take legal action against the subcontractor.

   d. You should take legal action against your vendor.

7. In which of the following situations will a force majeure clause apply? (Choose two.)

   a. The area deals with poor economic conditions.

   b. A sudden tornado touches down in the area.

   c. The country has gone into a recession.

   d. Material prices have increased in the area.

   e. There is rioting in the area.

   f. The vendor's subcontractor delays shipment of raw materials, which you have no control over.

8. Your vendor requests a change to the contract. They were waiting for important data and details on requirements from one of your teams before they could start work on their activity. However, it has been several weeks since the request, and they still have not received the information they need, which will now jeopardize the deadline. They are asking for an extension to the deadline. What should you do?

   a. Terminate the contract for cause.

   b. Extend the deadline due to a contract modification.

   c. Add this entry to the risk register.

   d. Extend the deadline due to a constructive change.

9. Which of the following would be an example of an administrative change to the contract?

   a. The contract is terminated for cause.

   b. The deadline is extended due to the buyer failing to provide the raw materials that the vendor needed to start the work.

   c. The phone number for the contact person has changed.

   d. Due to a new discovery, the costs negotiated on the contract need to change.

10. Match the contract types on the left to the scenario on the right.

1. FFP	a. You need to hire three technical analysts for two weeks to complete some tasks on the project.
2. CPFF	b. You need to know in detail what the final cost will be.
3. T&M	c. The outcome of the project is uncertain in terms of scope, time, and cost.
4. FPEPA	d. This a five-year contract and you want to reduce the risk to your organization, but you have agreed to adjust for inflation.

This chapter covers the following topics regarding the Uncertainty performance domain and the Project Risk Management knowledge area.

- **Uncertainty and Risk Management Overview:** Review the key concepts and terms involved in uncertainty and risk management to provide the foundation for further discussion.

- **Risk Management Planning:** Review the artifacts, tools, and techniques used for risk management planning.

- **Key Risk Management Artifacts:** Review the key risk management artifacts that are used by all the risk management processes.

- **Risk Identification and Analysis:** Review the key tools and techniques involved with risk identification, plus qualitative and quantitative risk analysis.

- **Risk Response Planning:** Review the key strategies used to manage threats, opportunities, and the different flavor of uncertainty.

- **Risk Response Implementation and Monitoring:** Review the key concepts used in risk response implementation and risk monitoring.

## CHAPTER 13

Uncertainty

This chapter reviews the activities and functions involved with managing uncertainty and risk on a project. This review highlights the key fundamentals, processes, tools, concepts, and terms that are emphasized by PMI to better prepare you for the PMP exam.

In the *PMBOK® Guide*, Sixth Edition, risk management is covered in the Project Risk Management knowledge area, which includes these processes:

- Plan Risk Management
- Identify Risks
- Perform Qualitative Risk Analysis
- Perform Quantitative Risk Analysis
- Plan Risk Responses
- Implement Risk Responses
- Monitor Risks

In the *PMBOK® Guide*, Seventh Edition, one of eight project performance domains is the Uncertainty performance domain. *This demonstrates that PMI recognizes the importance that this project management area has on project success.*

Per *PMBOK® Guide*, Seventh Edition, if the Uncertainty performance domain is effectively executed, the project will demonstrate these outcomes:

1. An awareness of the project environment, including the technical, social, political, market, and economic environments
2. A proactive exploration and response to uncertainty
3. An awareness of the interdependence of the multiple variables on the project
4. A capacity to anticipate threats and opportunities and understand the consequences of issues

5. Project delivery with little to no impact from unforeseen events or conditions

6. The realization of opportunities to improve project performance and outcomes

7. The effective utilization of cost and schedule reserves to maintain alignment with project objectives

In this chapter, we discuss the principles from the respective *PMBOK® Guide*, Sixth Edition, and *PMBOK® Guide*, Seventh Edition, sections mentioned and address the following objectives from the PMP Exam Content Outline:

Domain	Task #	Exam Objective
People	Task 2	Lead a team
People	Task 3	Support team performance
People	Task 7	Address and remove impediments, obstacles, and blockers for the team
People	Task 8	Negotiate project agreements
People	Task 9	Collaborate with stakeholders
People	Task 13	Mentor relevant stakeholders
People	Task 14	Promote team performance through the application of emotional intelligence
Process	Task 3	Assess and manage risks
Process	Task 4	Engage stakeholders
Process	Task 5	Plan and manage budget and resources
Process	Task 6	Plan and manage schedule
Process	Task 7	Plan and manage quality of products/deliverables
Process	Task 8	Plan and manage scope
Process	Task 9	Integrate project planning activities
Process	Task 10	Manage project changes
Process	Task 13	Determine appropriate project methodology/methods and practices
Process	Task 15	Manage project issues
Business Environment	Task 1	Plan and manage project compliance
Business Environment	Task 2	Evaluate and deliver project benefits and value
Business Environment	Task 3	Evaluate and address external business environment changes for impact on scope

"Do I Know This Already?" Quiz

The "Do I Know This Already?" quiz allows you to assess whether you should read this entire chapter thoroughly or jump to the "Exam Preparation Tasks" section. If you are in doubt about your answers to these questions or your own assessment of your knowledge of the topics, read the entire chapter. Table 13-1 lists the major headings in this chapter and their corresponding "Do I Know This Already?" quiz questions. You can find the answers in Appendix A, "Answers to the 'Do I Know This Already?' Quizzes and Review Questions."

Table 13-1   "Do I Know This Already?" Section-to-Question Mapping

Foundation Topics Section	Questions
Uncertainty and Risk Management Overview	1–2
Risk Management Planning	3
Key Risk Management Artifacts	4
Risk Identification and Analysis	5–7
Risk Response Planning	8–9
Risk Response Implementation and Risk Monitoring	10

CAUTION   The goal of self-assessment is to gauge your mastery of the topics in this chapter. If you do not know the answer to a question or are only partially sure of the answer, you should mark that question as wrong for purposes of the self-assessment. Giving yourself credit for an answer you correctly guess skews your self-assessment results and might provide you with a false sense of security.

1. What is the difference between a threat and an opportunity?

    a. There is no difference. They are both risks that need to be managed.

    b. Opportunities are escalated to senior management because they need more authority to take advantage of.

    c. There is no difference. They can both have a negative impact on the project objectives.

    d. Threats are risks that can negatively impact project objectives. Opportunities are risks that can positively impact project objectives

2. What is the difference between risk appetite, risk threshold, and risk tolerance?

    a. There is no difference. These three terms are interchangeable.

    b. Risk appetite describes the general attitude of the organization regarding risk. The other two terms mean the same thing.

    c. Risk appetite describes the general attitude of the organization regarding risk, risk tolerance defines how much impact the organization will accept, and risk threshold defines the impact point where the risk will no longer be accepted.

    d. Risk appetite and risk tolerance mean the same thing; both define the general attitude of the organization regarding risk. Risk threshold defines the impact level where the risk must be avoided.

3. Which of the following statements are true about the risk management plan? (Choose two.)

    a. It contains the risks the project is managing.

    b. It often contains sections describing the risk strategy, the risk categories to be used, and the definitions for risk probability and impact to be used.

    c. It often contains sections describing the risk register to be used, the risk report to be used, and the initial list of defined risks.

    d. It documents how risks will be managed and controlled for the project.

4. Which risk management processes use the risk register and the risk report?

    a. The risk register is used during risk identification, and the risk report is used during risk monitoring.

    b. They are used by all the risk management processes throughout the project.

    c. They are both used during risk identification and risk monitoring.

    d. The risk register is used during risk identification and risk response planning. The risk report is used during risk response implementation and risk monitoring.

5. What are common acronyms used to describe common sources of project risks?

    a. RBS, WBS, and RISKS

    b. PETO and UVCA

    c. PESTLE and TECOP

    d. PESTLE, TECOP, and VUCA

6. What is the objective of qualitative risk analysis?

   a. To determine the probability each identified risk will occur

   b. To prepare for quantitative risk analysis

   c. To determine the strategy to handle each risk

   d. To prioritize and rank the identified risks so the project can focus on the high-priority risks

7. What are some examples of quantitative risk analysis tools?

   a. Simulation, probability and impact matrix, and SWOT analysis

   b. Delphi technique, RBS, and expected monetary value

   c. Simulation, sensitivity diagrams, and influence diagrams

   d. Decision trees, simulation, and risk breakdown structures

8. What are the response options for dealing with threats?

   a. Escalate, Transfer, Accept, Avoid, and Mitigate

   b. Escalate, Share, Accept, Exploit, and Enhance

   c. Gather information, prepare for multiple outcomes, and build in resilience

   d. Progressive elaboration, experiments, and prototypes

9. What is secondary risk?

   a. Those risks that are deemed to be low priority

   b. Any risks left over after all the risk response strategies are implemented

   c. A new risk resulting from the implementation of a risk response plan

   d. Those risks that will be addressed after the primary risks are handled

10. Which of the following is NOT an objective of the risk monitoring process?

   a. Identify new and/or secondary risks

   b. Implement the agreed-upon risk response plans

   c. Assess if overall project risk level has changed

   d. Track status of contingency reserves

   e. Monitor implementation status of risk response plans

Foundation Topics

Uncertainty and Risk Management Overview

Through the management of uncertainty and risk on a project, an effective project manager really provides value. All projects, by their nature, have elements of uncertainty, and there are always events that can happen outside the control of the project team and organization that can impact the project's ability to achieve the desired objectives.

As highlighted by the Uncertainty performance domain outcomes by PMI, the keys are to take a holistic view of the project environment, anticipate and plan responses for as many potential risk events as possible, and leverage project approaches that make your project resilient to both the known and unknown risks that can occur.

For decades, PMI simply referred to this area of project management as *project risk management*, and you could make the argument they could still use this reference. In the *PMBOK® Guide*, Sixth Edition, PMI introduced the elements of variability risk and ambiguity risk when discussing nonevent risks, and now in the *PMBOK® Guide*, Seventh Edition, they have taken it a step further by dedicating one of the eight performance domains to uncertainty.

For the discussion of uncertainty, PMI includes *uncertainty* itself, which is a state of not knowing; *ambiguity*, which is a state of being unclear; *complexity*, which is a characteristic of something that is difficult to manage due to human behavior, system behavior, or the number of interdependencies; *volatility*, which is the possibility of rapid and unpredictable change; and, of course, *risk*, which is an event that may or not occur.

At the end of the day, all these aspects of uncertainty are potential risks to your project, and your focus as the project manager is to reduce any elements of uncertainty and ambiguity, break down the complex into smaller and more manageable pieces, prepare for any volatility, and have responses ready for any risk events that actually occur.

This wider focus on uncertainty helps ensure the project manager and project team are considering the complete project environment when assessing risks and placing proper attention on the factors that impact the project team's ability to deliver a quality solution that meets or exceeds stakeholder expectations—and that primarily is on any ambiguity and complexity that exists with the targeted project solutions.

This focus on **uncertainty**, **ambiguity**, and **complexity** involved with the targeted deliverables emphasizes the importance of the development approaches and the quality management approaches to be considered during project planning. In fact, the development approach can be one of the key risk responses to deal with uncertainty, *volatility*, or complexity in the targeted solution. This is one of the main drivers behind the rising adoption of the adaptive development approach, because it has both risk management processes and project resilience inherently built into it. In addition, this is why an effective quality management approach is essential to managing risks on a project, especially the unforeseen ones inherent in the development of the project solution. The ability to identify potential failures and defects as early as possible provides the project team the time to respond, take corrective action, and still deliver a solution that meets stakeholder expectations.

In addition, like other project management processes, managing uncertainty and risk is not a one-time activity. It is continuous until the project is completed. But it is critical to determine how your project will manage risks up front. We cover this topic in more detail later in the chapter. And on that note, how risks will be managed and how much time and effort will be invested into the formality of risk management vary depending on your organization, industry, project size, project complexity, and project importance.

Before we review the formal risk management processes from the *PMBOK® Guide*, Sixth Edition, that you need to be familiar with for the exam, let's take a step back and review some key risk management terms and concepts you need to understand both for that review and for the exam.

Risk Definition and Sources of Risk

First, let's cover the official definition of a *risk*. Per PMI, a risk is an uncertain event or condition that, if it occurs, has a positive or negative effect on one or more project objectives. The sources of risks for your project will vary depending on the type of project, project environment, and industry; however, common environmental factors can impact uncertainty on any project. Those factors include, but are not limited to, the following:

- **Economic factors:** Examples include overall economic conditions, volatility in prices, volatility in exchange rates, availability of physical resources, supply chain conditions, ability to borrow funds, inflation, and deflation.

- **Legal or legislative requirements and constraints:** Potential changes in legislation or legal requirements can impact the level of compliance to be met, the work processes to be used, or the documentation to be generated.

- **Political influences:** These influences can be either internal or external to the organization.

- **Technical considerations:** These factors pertain to new, emerging, or complex technologies.

- **Market influences:** Examples include shifts in market conditions and potential actions from the primary competition.

- **Social influences:** These influences include shifts in cultural or media opinion.

- **Physical environment:** These factors pertain to safety, working conditions, and weather.

- **Ambiguity:** This factor relates to being unclear about current or future conditions.

Risks Versus Issues

Next, let's clarify the differences between risks and issues on a project. The main difference is that a risk is a potential issue. If the risk happens, it is now an issue. When it is an issue, then a workaround or corrective action is needed to protect the project objective(s). In addition, risks are documented in the project's risk register (we cover this register later) and issues are documented in the project's issue log. See Table 13-2 for a quick summary of the differences between risks and issues.

Table 13-2   Differences Between Risks and Issues

	Risks	**Issues**
Definition	Negative risks are potential issues	A threat risk that actually occurs
Response strategy	Risk response plan	Corrective action or workaround
Documented	Risk register	Issue log

In agile, issues are commonly referred to as *impediments*, *obstacles*, or *blockers*. Generally, these terms are synonymous; however, there are subtle differences between them, as follows:

- **Impediment:** Refers to a situation or action that slows down or hinders the progress of the work or the team. For example, senior management might ask the team to constantly run reports and provide status updates during a sprint. This would be considered nonvalue-added work that could hinder the team's performance. In such cases, the team facilitator could run these reports instead, thereby shielding the team from such nonvalue-added work.

- **Obstacle:** Refers to a barrier that can prevent the work from starting and needs to be moved or avoided before work can start. For example, building work cannot start until a permit is received.

- **Blocker:** Refers to events or conditions that cause the work to stop once it has started. For example, a software license has expired and the team cannot continue.

Planning and estimating the product backlog items can help identify certain impediments; for example, a large user story that cannot be broken down into smaller user stories based on the current level of information provided. Risk reviews are another common tool for identifying impediments.

For the exam, know that impediments should first be communicated to the team facilitator at the daily standup ceremony, but the detailed discussion should be taken offline after the meeting (remember, the daily standup meeting should last no more than 10 to 15 minutes). The team facilitator should then work with the appropriate stakeholders to try to remove these impediments, obstacles, or blockers. The team facilitator may use an impediment task board to keep track of and communicate the status of impediments.

Threats and Opportunities

If you are new to project risk management, you might have assumed all risks are negative. This is not necessarily the case. Negative risks are referred to as *threats*. Positive risks are referred to as *opportunities*. The goal of the project manager and project team is to minimize the impact of any threats to the project objectives and to exploit any opportunities that can enhance the project objectives.

Because most people are accustomed to negative risks, and most projects and organizations focus on these threats to project objectives, people are often unsure what a positive opportunity risk even is. In summary, the sources of both types of risk are the same. It is the potential event or condition that determines whether it will have a positive or negative impact on your project. See Table 13-3 for examples of positive and negative risks to further clarify the difference.

Table 13-3 Examples of Threats and Opportunities

Risk Source Category	Negative Risk (Threat) Example	Positive Risk (Opportunity) Example
Government/ political climate	Change in government could result in tariff increases, more restrictions for exporting your product, and more regulation.	Change in government could result in tariff decreases, less restrictions for exporting your product, and less regulation.
Economy	Increasing inflation rates could reduce demand for your product.	Improving economic conditions might increase demand for your product.
Technology	Use of new technology might be prone to more defects.	Use of new technology might increase team productivity and reduce costs.

Risk Source Category	Negative Risk (Threat) Example	Positive Risk (Opportunity) Example
Resources	Potential foreign exchange rate increases might impact cost of key materials by 25 percent.	Potential foreign exchange rate decreases might reduce cost of key materials by 25 percent.
Legislative/legal	New legislation might increase compliance and reporting requirements.	New legislation might create tax incentives for customers to purchase your product.
Market conditions	Competitors might release a more advanced product ahead of your schedule.	Minimal competition in the market provides an opportunity to take significant market share.
Physical environment	Prolonged subzero weather conditions could impact the construction schedule.	Unseasonably warm weather might allow for an accelerated construction schedule.
Social trends	Shifting social trends could reduce demand for your product.	Directed marketing campaign in support of priority social causes might increase goodwill in your customer base.

Risk Classifications and Types

Now that we've covered what risks, threats, and opportunities are and where they can originate, let's review the common ways to organize project risks.

The reason to organize risks is to improve your view of the entire playing field, improve the effectiveness of the strategies developed to manage the risks, avoid duplication and/or contradictory risk response strategies, and help determine where to focus budget and resources in response to these risks. In addition, when you have a better picture of all the risks and have them organized logically, you can better implement an integrated risk management approach. An integrated risk management approach here refers to the process of determining which risks can be managed by the project team itself and which ones need to be delegated or escalated to appropriate levels within the organization. The process of doing this is called *risk categorization*. Specifically, risk categorization is the process of organizing project risk sources by the project area affected, or other useful category, to determine the project areas most exposed to the effects of uncertainty.

See Table 13-4 and Table 13-5 for a summary of the risk types and risk classifications you need to be familiar with for the PMP exam.

Table 13-4   Risk Types

Risk Type	Description	Notes
Event	Uncertain future events that might or might not occur	These are the "traditional" risk types. Event risks can be triggered by natural forces, suppliers, clients, government regulations, or even internal resource changes.
Nonevent	The uncertain aspect of a planned situation and/or the uncertainty from lack of knowledge or understanding	This type includes all variability and ambiguity risks.
Business	Risks that are inherent to the business and have the potential for financial loss	These are risks that insurance companies will not cover. Some examples include failed projects and failed business ventures.
Insurable	Risks that insurance companies will cover	Common types include personal risk (accident, death), property risk (fire, theft, floods, and so on), and litigation risk (lawsuits).

Table 13-5   Risk Classifications

Risk Classification	Description	Notes
Effect-based	Classifying risks by their impact on inherent project constraints	Typical effect-based categories include schedule, scope, cost, quality, and resources.
Source-based	Classifying risks based on their origin	This classification uses the same list as sources of project risks (that is, technical, external factors, internal factors, industry-specific).
Individual	Risk that impacts one or more project objectives	These are the risks the project manager is focused on.
Overall	Risks that impact the entire project	This is not the same as the sum of all the individual risks. These are project risks that represent the exposure the stakeholders have to the implications and/or variations of the project outcomes.

Risk Appetite, Risk Threshold, and Risk Tolerance

Before we get into the formal risk management process, let's review three additional terms that are paramount to determining what the overall risk management approach will be for a given project. These three terms are routinely confused and used interchangeably when they should not be.

At the highest level, we start with risk appetite. ***Risk appetite*** is defined as the degree of uncertainty an organization or individual is willing to accept in anticipation of a reward or benefit. In most cases, the appetite level is expressed in general terms: high, medium, or low. An organization with a high risk appetite is willing to handle higher degrees of risk for the high rewards the project outcomes can bring. A given organization's risk appetite can vary based on factors such as

- Industry

- Company culture

- Organizational objectives

- Financial strength of the organization

- Competitors

- Specific project's importance and benefit opportunities

In some environments, the risk appetite may be expressed as either risk-seeking, risk-neutral, risk-tolerant, or risk-averse. Table 13-6 provides a summary of these risk appetite classifications.

Table 13-6   Risk Appetite Classifications

Risk Appetite	Description	Notes
High Risk-seeking	The organization welcomes risks and uncertainty.	Risks are intentionally accepted due to the high reward the project benefits offer.
Medium Risk-tolerant	The organization is comfortable with most uncertainty and accepts risk as a normal part of business and projects.	Risks do not significantly impact behavior or the project approach.
Medium Risk-neutral	The organization deliberately takes reasonable risks for a short period of time to generate long-term benefits.	There is a clear trade-off between risk and reward.
Low Risk-averse	The organization is uncomfortable with uncertainty.	The approach is to take as few risks as possible and to avoid and prevent risks.

After you understand the general risk appetite of the organization and for your project specifically, you can move to establishing the risk tolerance. ***Risk tolerance*** is the maximum potential impact of a risk that the stakeholder or organization is willing to accept for a given risk. The risk tolerance is normally expressed in a range. For example, a cost variance of +/–10 percent of budget or a schedule slippage of 5–10 days. In other words, as long as the impact of the given risk stays within these boundaries, the organization will accept the risk.

However, there is point of impact at which the organization or stakeholder will no longer accept the risk and action must be taken. This point is called the *risk threshold*. The risk threshold is formally defined as the measure of acceptable variation around a project objective that reflects the risk appetite of the organization and stakeholders. Below this level, the organization will accept the risk; above it, it will not be accepted.

So in our previous examples of risk tolerance, the risk threshold for cost overruns is 10 percent, and the risk threshold for schedule slippage is 10 days. As mentioned in the definition of risk threshold, the greater the risk appetite of the organization, the higher the risk tolerance range and risk thresholds normally are for the impact to project objectives.

Now that we've reviewed the key concepts and terms involved with risk management, let's turn our attention to the seven formal processes involved in project risk management:

1. Plan Risk Management

2. Identify Risks

3. Perform Qualitative Risk Analysis

4. Perform Quantitative Risk Analysis

5. Plan Risk Responses

6. Implement Risk Responses

7. Monitor Risks

Risk Management Planning

The first step in the risk management process is to determine how risks will be managed and controlled on your project. The methodology and approach you will use is captured in the risk management plan. This step is called Plan Risk Management in the *PMBOK® Guide*, Sixth Edition. The primary objective of this process is to ensure the approach used is consistent and proportionate to the impact of individual risks identified and to the importance of the project to the organization and key stakeholders.

Like other subsidiary project management plans, the risk management plan is a component of the overall project management plan, and it is developed through a combination of expert judgment, stakeholder interviews, meetings, and organizational process assets (OPAs) and enterprise environmental factors (EEFs) inputs.

Although risk management planning is performed at the beginning of the project, it is not a one-time task. The effectiveness of the risk management plan should be evaluated at periodic intervals throughout the project and adjusted if needed.

NOTE The risk management plan does *not* capture the specific risks of the project. It describes *how* risks will be managed and controlled. The actual project risks are captured in the risk register (or risk list).

As mentioned previously, the key output or artifact from this process step is the risk management plan. Let's next review the common elements of a ***risk management plan***.

- **Risk strategy:** This section describes the general approach to managing risk on the project. This is influenced greatly by the risk appetite of the organization and key stakeholders.

- **Methodology:** This section defines the specific approaches, tools, and data sources that will be used to perform risk management on the project.

- **Roles and responsibilities:** This section defines the lead, support, and risk management team members for each type of activity described in the risk management plan and their responsibilities.

- **Budgeting:** This section identifies the funds needed to perform the risk management activities and establishes the protocols for determining contingency and management reserves.

- **Timing:** This section defines when and how often the risk management activities are performed throughout the project. These process events should be incorporated into the project schedule.

- **Risk categories:** This section provides the list of classifications to help organize the risks of the project. We discussed this issue earlier in the chapter.

- **Stakeholder risk thresholds:** This section captures the risk appetite of the key stakeholders. Specifically, the measurable risk threshold levels around each project objective should be noted, because they drive the definitions of probability and impacts used to assess and prioritize individual risks. In addition, these risk threshold levels determine the acceptable level of overall project risk exposure and drive the risk management approaches to be implemented.

- **Definitions of risk probability and impact:** This section defines the levels of probability and impact that will be used for your project. Most projects have at least the three basic levels of high, medium, and low. However, projects that require a more detailed risk management approach may have additional levels. The key is that each level is defined for the probability levels and the impact levels, and these definitions are used in the probability and risk matrix. In many cases, these definitions are predefined by the organization and are part of the organizational process assets (OPAs). Either way, they may still need to be customized for your specific project. See Table 13-7 for an example of probability and impact definitions across three project objectives.

Table 13-7 Probability and Impact Definitions Example

Scale	Probability	Impact on Project Objectives (+/−)		
		Time	**Cost**	**Quality**
High	>70%	> 3 months	> $250K	Significant impact to key functions
Medium	30%–69%	4–12 weeks	$50K–$250K	Some impact to key functions
Low	<30%	< 4 weeks	< $50K	Minor impact to key functions

- **Probability and impact matrix:** This section depicts the scoring matrix used to assign a relative value to individual risks (threats and opportunities) during the Perform Qualitative Risk Analysis process. This score is used to determine the priority of each individual risk in relation to the others.

- **Reporting formats:** This section defines how the outputs of the risk management process are documented, analyzed, and communicated. Specifically, the content and format of the risk register and risk report are defined here.

- **Tracking:** This section defines how the risk activities are recorded and how the risk management processes are audited for the project.

Key Risk Management Artifacts

Because we just covered the risk management plan artifact, let's review the other two key artifacts you need to be familiar with when it comes to risk management: the risk register and risk report.

The structure for both the risk register and the risk report is drafted as part of the risk management planning process, and they are used (updated) throughout all the risk management processes.

Risk Register

The *risk register* serves as the central repository (the logical database) for all risk management activities as they are conducted throughout the project. This is the place where each identified risk is logged. The specific data captured in the risk register varies depending on the normal factors (organization policies, industry, project complexity and size, risk management rigor required, and so on). Common data elements captured in a risk register include, but are not limited to, the following:

- **Risk ID Number:** A unique identification for each risk logged.

- **Risk Name/Title/Description:** The name, title, and/or description of the risk.

- ■ **Risk Category:** The assigned category for the individual risk. The specific value list depends on the risk classifications used for the project.

- ■ **Risk Trigger:** The specific event or risk threshold that will trigger the risk to actually occur.

- ■ **Date Identified:** The date the risk was identified and logged into the risk register.

- ■ **Priority:** The priority level assigned to the individual risk.

- ■ **Probability:** The probability rating assigned to the individual risk.

- ■ **Impact:** The impact level assigned to the individual risk.

- ■ **Risk Score:** The final risk score determined for this individual risk.

- ■ **Risk Owner:** The person who owns the risk response strategy for this individual risk.

- ■ **Response Strategy:** The agreed-upon response strategy for this individual risk.

- ■ **Response Due Date:** The date the response strategy execution is expected.

- ■ **Risk Status:** The current status of the risk. At a minimum, the value list here includes Open and Closed.

- ■ **Risk Update Date:** The date of the last update to this entry in the risk register.

In short, the risk register can be customized to capture the level of risk analysis performed and level of risk management required for the project. See Figure 13-1 for an example of a risk register.

Project ID					Project Manager				
Project Name					Sponsor				
Risk ID	Description	Probability	Impact	Risk Score	Category	Trigger	Response Strategy	Contingency Reserve	Risk Owner

Figure 13-1   Risk Register Template

NOTE   On adaptive projects, this artifact might be called a risk list, but it serves the same function as the risk register.

Risk Report

The other key artifact that originates from the risk management process is the *risk report*. Like the risk register, the template is drafted as part of the risk management plan and then used throughout the project as risk management activities are conducted.

If you're not using a template from the organization's process assets, the structure for both the risk register and the risk report are drafted as part of the risk management planning process and then used (updated) throughout all the risk management processes.

The purpose of the risk report is to provide a management summary of the project's risk profile. This project document summarizes the level of overall project risk and individual project risks at any point in time on the project.

Like the risk register, the risk report has no set format or content. The key is to provide an accurate and informative summary to the key project stakeholders regarding the project's risk status at regular points throughout the project. You can think of it as an analysis summary of the risk register. Most risk reports are divided into a minimum of two sections: an overall project risk summary section and a list of high-priority individual risks. Common elements captured in a risk report include, but are not limited to, the following:

- Overall project risk status
- Source(s) of overall project risk
- Planned risk responses for overall project risk
- Summary information on individual project risks
- List of the key prioritized risks with planned risk responses
- Total threats versus opportunities
- Totals by risk categories
- Key metrics
- Contingency reserves status
- Key trends
- Summary conclusion

Risk Identification and Analysis

Before you can determine how you are going to respond to project risks, you first need to identify them and then assess them for their potential impact to your project objectives. Let's first look at the techniques used to identify risks, and then we'll dive into the different methods used for risk analysis.

Identifying Risks

The first step is identifying your project risks. We covered a lot of this topic when discussing the sources of project risk during the earlier overview section in this chapter. In this section, we touch on those risks again and highlight the key tools commonly used.

TIP   Risk identification is an iterative process that is ongoing until project completion. The project manager and project team should remain diligent to protect and/or enhance the project objectives.

There are common sources of external and internal project risk. In fact, there are acronyms to help you remember them:

- **PESTLE:** Political, Economic, Social, Technical, Legal, and Environmental

- **TECOP:** Technical, Environmental, Commercial, Operational, and Political

- **VUCA:** Volatility, Uncertainty, Complexity, and Ambiguity

Many organizations capture these common risk sources in prompt lists, checklists, or in a *risk breakdown structure (RBS)* to use a tool for the risk identification process. These templates (prompt lists, checklists, RBS) can be used as frameworks and starting points when conducting interviews or group meetings as part of the risk identification process. See Figure 13-2 for an example of an RBS using a TECOP framework.

RBS Level 0	RBS Level 1	RBS Level 2
All Project Risk Sources	1.0 Technical	1.1 Scope definition
		1.2 Requirements definition
		1.3 Estimates
		1.4 Assumptions and constraints
		1.5 Technical complexity
		1.6 Technical maturity
		1.7 Technical interfaces
	2.0 Environmental	2.1 Competition
		2.2 Exchange rates
		2.3 Sites and Facilities
		2.4 Weather conditions
		2.5 Environmental impacts
	3.0 Commercial	3.1 Contract terms and conditions
		3.2 Market conditions
		3.3 Suppliers and vendors
		3.4 Subcontractors
		3.5 Customer stability
	4.0 Operational	4.1 Operations management
		4.2 Program and portfolio management
		4.3 Organizational culture
		4.4 Resourcing
		4.5 Internal procurement
	5.0 Political	5.1 Pending legislation
		5.2 Current regulations
		5.3 Political climate
		5.4 Pending trade agreements

Figure 13-2   Risk Breakdown Structure Example

Like other aspects of project management, the methods for gathering inputs for risk identification are similar. Let's review the common methods and tools used in the risk identification process.

- **Expert judgment:** Leveraging the experience and expertise of individuals who have worked previously on similar projects and/or in the business area.

- **Interviews:** Meeting one-on-one with experienced team members, stakeholders, and subject matter experts.

- **Brainstorming/team meetings:** Conducting team meetings and/or brainstorming sessions to identify risks.

- **Delphi technique:** Gaining consensus among a group of experts. The process requires a facilitator that successively collates the inputs from the experts using questionnaires until a consensus is reached. The method also allows the experts to share their thoughts anonymously and without influence from others.

- **SWOT analysis:** Reviewing the SWOT analysis performed on the project and/or organization to look for additional threats (from the Weakness and Threats sections) and opportunities (from the Strengths and Opportunities section).

- **Assumption and constraint analysis:** Reviewing any assumptions and constraints that have been identified in the planning process. There are often risks around these assumptions and constraints.

- **Document analysis:** Reviewing the project documents for potential risks, including, but not limited to, contracts, agreements, historical project records, especially past risk registers from similar projects, technical documentation, project schedule, project budget, and quality management plan.

- **Root cause analysis:** Identifying the underlying causes of a problem so that preventive or corrective action can be taken. In the context of risk identification, this analysis can be used to proactively identify potential threats and opportunities. The common method would involve starting with a problem statement like "the project might be delayed" and exploring what threats could cause that to happen. And vice versa, a benefit statement is proposed like "the project is delivered under-budget" and exploring what opportunities could cause that to happen.

Qualitative Risk Analysis

After the risks are identified, they need to be prioritized and ranked so the project can focus on the high-priority risks. This process is called qualitative risk analysis. The two key aspects of a risk that need to be assessed are the probability it will occur and the impact to the project if it does occur. As you can imagine, the challenge with this process is threefold:

- This is subjective judgment open to perception bias.

- The analysis is dependent on the quality of the data and information about the risk.

- Stakeholders may not have the same perception for the probability nor the impact of a given risk.

When the qualitative risk analysis process is completed, the risks are scored relative to each other; the high-priority risks are identified; an owner who is assigned to each risk is responsible for developing and implementing the corresponding risk response plan; the risk register is updated with the assessment results; and the foundation is in place to either perform quantitative risk analysis or to move forward with risk response planning.

The process of determining the priority for each individual risk involves gaining consensus from the relevant project stakeholders on the probability the risk will occur and on the impact to one or more project objectives if it does occur. Two tools that are frequently used in the process were mentioned as part of the risk management plan: the risk probability and impact assessment and the risk probability and impact matrix. The idea for both is that criteria are established for a risk to be determined a specific value on your priority scale. Refer to Table 13-7 for an example of a risk probability and impact assessment and see Figure 13-3 for an example of a risk probability and impact matrix. In a risk probability and impact matrix, the values in each cell represent the relative score assigned to the risk, which is the product of the probability and impact values assigned to the risk.

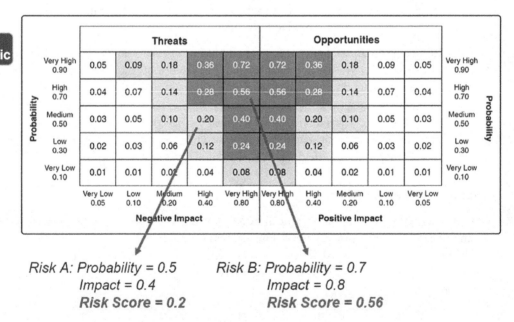

Figure 13-3   Risk Probability and Impact Matrix

A simple formula is used to calculate the risk score as follows:

Probability * Impact = Risk Score

Table 13-8 provides an example where a project uses a numerical scale of 1–10 (1 being the lowest value, 10 being the highest value) for probability and impact to determine a final score and ranking for each risk.

Table 13-8 Qualitative Risk Analysis

Risk	Probability	Impact	Risk Score	Ranking
Risk 1	8	7	56	1
Risk 2	5	10	50	3
Risk 3	6	9	54	2
Risk 4	7	5	35	4
Risk 5	2	2	4	5

NOTE   In some organizations, the low-ranking risks may be placed on a separate risk watchlist.

In addition to probability and impact, there may be other factors evaluated before assigning a final priority to a risk, including the following:

- **Urgency:** The time period a response would need to be implemented to be effective. The shorter the time, the higher the urgency level.

- **Proximity:** The time period before the risk could impact one or more project objectives. The shorter the time, the higher the proximity level.

- **Dormancy:** The time period that may elapse after the risk has occurred but before its impact is detected on one or more project objectives. The longer the time, the higher the dormancy level.

- **Manageability:** The ease of the risk owner to manage the occurrence and/ or impact of the risk. The easier the management level, the higher the manageability.

- **Controllability:** The degree in which the risk owner can control the risk's outcome. The easier it can be controlled, the higher the controllability.

- **Detectability:** The ease with which the risk occurring or about to occur can be detected and recognized. The easier to detect, the higher the detectability.

- **Connectivity:** The extent the risk is related to other individual project risks. The higher the number of related risks, the higher the connectivity.

- **Strategic impact:** The potential for the risk to have a positive or negative effect on the organization's strategic goals. The higher the effect, the higher the strategic impact.

- **Propinquity:** The degree to which a risk is perceived to be significant by one or more stakeholders. The higher the significance, the higher the propinquity.

Quantitative Risk Analysis

The next type and level of risk analysis is called quantitative risk analysis, which analyzes risks based on numeric values such as cost, time, or resources. More commonly for the exam, quantitative risk analysis is based on a monetary value.

The purpose of quantitative risk analysis is to assess the combined effect of all individual project risks and other sources of uncertainty on overall project objectives. In other words, it quantifies overall project *risk exposure*. The other benefits of quantitative risk analysis are that it reduces the bias and combats the static nature of qualitative risk analysis.

Sounds like a great thing to do, right? So why is it not common to see this analysis performed? There are several reasons, including, but not limited to, the following:

- It requires high-quality data about the individual project risks.

- It requires a solid baseline for scope, schedule, and cost.

- It requires additional time and investment.

- It frequently requires the use of specialized risk modeling tools and expertise.

The use of quantitative risk analysis is more common in industries that have high-quality data points readily available, such as financial, manufacturing, and military defense. In addition, the use of quantitative risk analysis is normally reserved for large, complex, strategically important or contractual-based projects.

Despite the lack of common usage, you do need to be familiar with the process and the key tools that can be used as part of quantitative risk analysis for the exam. Per PMI, quantitative risk analysis is not required for all projects.

The sections that follow describe some tools, techniques, and models that come into play with quantitative risk analysis.

Expected Monetary Value

One powerful technique to help align the contingency reserves for your project with the actual identified risks is to assign an expected monetary value (EMV) to each identified risk. The process involves taking the product of the probability the risk will occur by the expected monetary impact if it does occur.

The formula for expected monetary value is as follows:

Probability * Monetary Impact = Expected Monetary Value (EMV)

See Table 13-9 for an illustration. In this illustration, the total EMV calculated can be used to adjust the contingency reserves accordingly.

Table 13-9   Expected Monetary Value

Risk	Probability (%)	Impact ($)	EMV (Probability * Impact)
Threat 1	50%	–$75,000	–$37,500
Threat 2	35%	–$100,000	–$35,000
Threat 3	70%	–$30,000	–$21,000
Threat 4	20%	–$15,000	–$3,000
Opportunity 1	40%	$80,000	$32,000
Opportunity 2	55%	$20,000	$11,000
Total EMV			**–$53,500**

In this example, an adjustment of $53,500 will be made to the contingency reserve.

However, there are various other methods of calculating contingency reserves amounts that you do not need to know for the exam. This example shows just one method of adjusting contingency reserves that you need to be aware of for the exam.

Simulation

Simulation models can be used to show the combined effects of individual project risks and other sources of uncertainty, especially work task estimate durations and cost estimates. These specialized computer models commonly employ Monte Carlo analysis, which performs random iterations using probability distributions for cost and/or duration estimates. See Figure 13-4 for sample output from a Monte Carlo analysis.

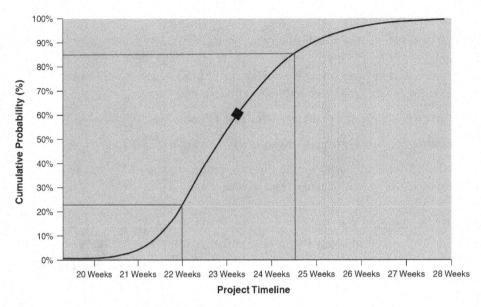

Figure 13-4   Monte Carlo Analysis Simulation

In the example shown in Figure 13-4, the black box indicates the target completion duration of the project (23.5 weeks). What is the probability the project completes in this time per the Monte Carlo analysis results? It is 60 percent. Also, two sets of lines forming right angles indicate the project has a 22 percent chance of completing in 22 weeks and an 85 percent chance of completing in 24.5 weeks.

In addition, these simulation tools allow a project to analyze which identified risks have the greatest impact on the project's critical path. This information can direct and focus efforts during the risk response planning stage.

Sensitivity Diagrams

Sensitivity analysis helps determine the individual project risks or other sources of uncertainty that have the greatest potential impact on project objectives. It correlates variations in project outcomes with variations in elements of the quantitative risk analysis model. These elements can include individual project risks, project work elements with a high degree of variability, or specific sources of ambiguity. A common technique to show results is to use a tornado diagram where elements are ordered by descending correlation strength. This technique results in a visual that looks like a tornado. See Figure 13-5 for a sample sensitivity analysis tornado diagram.

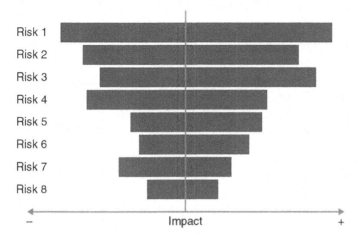

Figure 13-5 Sensitivity Tornado Diagram

Influence Diagrams

Influence diagrams are graphical tools used to assist decision-making when uncertainty exists. The diagrams can be created for the entire project or for a portion of a project to show all the factors that lead to a given outcome and the relationship among those factors. An influence diagram captures the entities, events, influences, and outcomes and the relationship between them. Simulation models, like Monte Carlo analysis, can take the diagram along with the ranges and/or probability distributions for any elements within the diagram that have uncertainty to indicate which elements have the greatest influence on project outcomes. This information can then help direct the team's risk response planning. For an example of an influence diagram, see Figure 13-6.

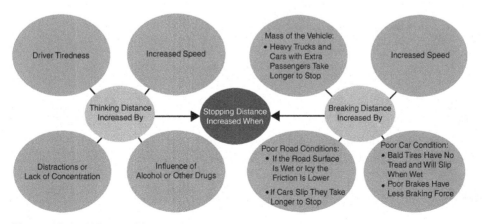

Figure 13-6 Influence Diagram

Decision Tree

Decision trees are effective tools when a project team needs to decide between alternative options. The alternatives are depicted in the tree diagram using branches that represent the various decision options and events to be considered. For each decision or event, associated costs and project risks can be accounted for as additional branches in the tree. Then the decision tree is evaluated by calculating the expected monetary value for each individual branch. The branch with the highest EMV value represents the optimal decision and path to take.

This tool is better understood by looking at an example. Let's consider a project that needs to decide whether to build a new plant or upgrade an existing plant. The cost to build the new plant is $200 million. The cost to upgrade the plant is $80 million. Regardless of the build versus upgrade decision, the sales forecast indicates a 65 percent chance of strong demand and a 35 percent chance of weak demand. If you build a new plant and get a strong demand, the company expects to make $320 million, If there is weak demand, the profit expectations are only $150 million. If the plant is upgraded and there is strong demand, the company expects to make $190 million. If there is weak demand, the profit expectations are $95 million. What are the EMVs to build and upgrade, and which option should you choose?

See Figure 13-7 for an example of an accompanying decision tree and the related EMV calculations.

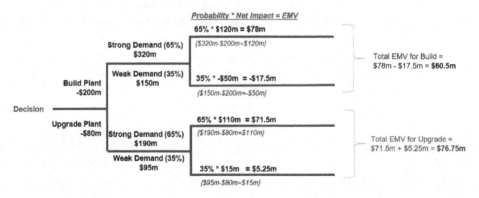

Figure 13-7   Decision Tree

In this example, you would choose to upgrade the plant because the total EMV for Upgrade is greater than the total EMV for Build.

Risk Response Planning

After overall project and individual risks have been identified, analyzed, and prioritized, it is now time to plan the appropriate risk responses. Risk response planning is focused on gaining agreement on what actions and strategies to take to address overall project risk and individual project risks. Effective risk responses reduce overall project risk exposure, minimize threats, and maximize opportunities. In this section, we review the common strategies used to address the different types of risks (threats and opportunities) and the different types of uncertainty (general uncertainty, ambiguity, complexity, and volatility).

Strategies for Addressing Threats

There are five strategies to consider when dealing with *threats* (risks that can have a negative impact on one or more project objectives):

- **Escalate:** Ownership of the risk is escalated to a higher level or authority within the organization. *Risk escalation* is used when the risk is outside the scope of the project and/or the authority of the project manager. Normally, these risks are managed at the program or portfolio level within the organization. After it is confirmed that the risk ownership is accepted by the escalated party, this risk is no longer monitored by the project team.

- **Transfer:** Ownership of the risk is transferred to a third party. The third party typically receives a premium (payment) for managing the risk and dealing with the impact if it does occur. Often, a formal agreement is in place to handle a *risk transference* arrangement. Typical examples include insurance, warranties, guarantees, and performance bonds.

- **Accept:** *Risk acceptance* is the act of recognizing the threat but taking no proactive action to either reduce the probability or lessen the impact if it does occur. An organization with a higher risk appetite is likely to accept more risks. Risk acceptance is commonly used in two scenarios. One, it is used on low-priority risks, and two, it is used on risks that cannot be managed in a cost-effective way. There are two flavors of risk acceptance: passive and active. Passive acceptance is literally taking no action at all regarding the risk outside of the periodic reviews to ensure there are no changes pertaining to the risk. Active acceptance involves accounting for the potential impact by adding to the contingency reserves (budget, time, and/or resources).

- **Avoid:** *Risk avoidance* is the act of eliminating the threat entirely and/or protecting the project from its potential impact. This strategy is normally reserved for a high-priority risk that has a high probability of occurring and a high degree of negative impact if it does occur. A threat can often be eliminated if the quality of the information about it is improved, which may entail doing further research, clarifying requirements, or acquiring more expertise on the matter. Other examples of risk avoidance include, but are not limited to, altering the project strategy, altering the development approach, reducing the scope, and modifying one or more project objectives (like extending the schedule).

> **TIP**   Exam takers commonly confuse risk avoidance and risk acceptance because they think "avoiding" means "ignoring." Instead, when you read "risk avoidance," think "unacceptable," "eliminate," and "highest proactive response possible."

- **Mitigate:** *Risk mitigation* is the act of reducing the probability of occurrence and/or reducing the potential impact for a given threat. We review examples of mitigation approaches when we review strategies for dealing with the different types of uncertainty.

> **NOTE**   The threats that the project team will invest most of their efforts on are those using a risk avoidance or risk mitigation response strategy.

Strategies for Addressing Opportunities

There are five strategies to consider when dealing with *opportunities* (risks that can have a positive impact on one or more project objectives):

- **Escalate:** This strategy is identical to the escalate strategy for threats. Ownership of the risk is escalated to a higher level or authority within the organization. This strategy is used when the risk is outside the scope of the project and/or the authority of the project manager. Normally, these risks are managed at the program or portfolio level within the organization. After it is confirmed that the risk ownership is accepted by the escalated party, this risk is no longer monitored by the project team.

- **Share:** The share strategy is like the transfer strategy used for threats. But rather than a complete transfer of the risk opportunity to a third party, the risk is shared with a third party. This strategy is employed when there is reason to believe that a third party is better positioned to take advantage of the opportunity. The third party typically receives a premium (payment) for sharing the risk. Typical examples of *risk sharing* include joint ventures (teaming agreements), partnerships, special teams, and companies with a specific expertise.

- **Accept:** This strategy is identical to threat risk acceptance. Risk opportunity acceptance is the act of recognizing the opportunity but taking no proactive action. Risk acceptance is commonly used in two scenarios. One, it is used on low-priority opportunities, and two, it is used when the opportunity cannot be addressed in a cost-effective way. There are two flavors of risk acceptance: passive and active. Passive acceptance is literally taking no action at all regarding the risk outside of the periodic reviews to ensure there are no changes pertaining to the risk. Active acceptance involves accounting for the opportunity by managing the contingency reserves (budget, time, and/or resources).

- **Exploit:** The exploit strategy is the inverse of the risk avoidance strategy used for threats. Rather than eliminating the threat entirely, the team wants to remove any uncertainty and make sure the opportunity definitely happens. This strategy is normally reserved for the high-priority opportunities that have a high degree of positive impact if they do occur. Some examples of *risk exploitation* include, but are not limited to, assigning the most talented resources or acquiring highly skilled consultants to ensure a quality product is delivered on a shorter time schedule and using new technology and/or streamlined work processes to reduce project cost and duration.

- **Enhance:** The risk enhancement strategy is the inverse of the risk mitigation strategy used for threats. *Risk enhancement* is the act of increasing the probability of occurrence and/or increasing the potential impact for a given opportunity. The actions taken for a risk enhancement response are often like those taken for risk exploitation, just less aggressive. The actions are not going to guarantee absolutely that the opportunity occurs. For example, let's say your project receives a significant bonus if the product is delivered within one year. You could require paid overtime or procure the best resources, but this would drive up your costs. Instead, you decide to focus on strong team-building measures and offer a bonus to the team if the project does complete within one year.

To summarize the threat and opportunity risk response strategies and to help you remember the symbiotic relationships between them, see Table 13-10.

Table 13-10   Threat and Opportunity Risk Response Strategies Summary

Threat Strategy	Brief Description	Opportunity Strategy	Brief Description
Escalate	Escalate to higher authority	Escalate	Escalate to higher authority
Transfer	Deflect risk to third party	Share	Partner with third party

Threat Strategy	Brief Description	Opportunity Strategy	Brief Description
Accept	Acknowledge	Accept	Acknowledge
	Passive: take no action		Passive: take no action
	Active: add additional funds to contingency reserves		Active: add additional funds to contingency reserves
Avoid	Eliminate the risk	Exploit	Ensure risk occurs
Mitigate	Reduce the probability and/ or impact	Enhance	Increase the probability and/or impact

One reason PMI has a performance domain focused on uncertainty is the importance of taking a holistic view of the project and addressing the most prevalent reasons that projects do not meet their intended objectives and not just focusing on individual risks. These reasons are centered around general uncertainty, ambiguity, complexity, and volatility; and they are commonly the largest sources of risk for any project. Let's look at each category individually and discuss some common risk response strategies for each.

Strategies for Addressing General Uncertainty

When you are faced with general uncertainty, especially around the solution the project is to deliver, here are key strategies to consider:

- **Gather information:** This is the most basic and intuitive strategy when dealing with uncertainty, especially when it is caused from a general lack of information and knowledge. When you gather more information from research and/or interviewing experts, you can greatly reduce the uncertainty level.

- **Prepare for multiple outcomes:** In situations where the optimal solution to be delivered can vary depending on whether some event occurs (a risk), and the possible outcomes are limited, the project team can plan on a backup or contingency solution if the primary solution proves not to be viable or effective. If the possible outcomes are numerous, then the project team would need to analyze the potential events and/or causes in greater detail to determine the most likely outcomes and then focus on those as part of the contingency plans.

- **Leverage set-based design:** In situations where there is a large amount of uncertainty around the solution design and no clear priority has been set around the typical project constraints (schedule, budget, quality, risk), the project team can investigate multiple designs and alternatives for the solution and evaluate the trade-offs on the project constraints early in the project. Then from this evaluation, the project team determines which approach(es) to take. In this situation, some type of adaptive project approach would be invaluable.

- **Build in resilience:** In situations where there is a high probability of changes, using a project and development approach that has built-in resiliency is invaluable and can be the best response plan for this type of uncertainty.

Strategies for Addressing Ambiguity

Much like general uncertainty, when you're dealing with ambiguity around the solution the project is to deliver, the response strategies are similar and place an emphasis on taking a more adaptive approach to the project. Here are key strategies to consider:

- **Progressive elaboration:** Progressive elaboration can be used for plans, solution requirements, and the solution itself. It is the process of continuing to refine details as more accurate information is received. Rolling wave planning is an example of progressive elaboration, and agile/adaptive project approaches use progressive elaboration to refine the product requirements and the product through each iteration.

- **Experiments:** In situations where the ambiguity is caused by a lack of information around the specific cause-and-effect relationships, a set of well-designed experiments can be conducted to gain better information and reduce the ambiguity involved. This situation is very common in adaptive methodologies and often referred to as a risk spike.

- **Prototypes:** Another tool to reduce ambiguity around solution options or aspects of a solution option or even solution requirements is to prototype a possible option. From the prototype, stakeholders have something tangible to evaluate and provide feedback on, which can help bring clarity to the desired solution and reduce ambiguity.

Strategies for Addressing Complexity

Before we review the common strategies to deal with the different types of complexity, let's discuss a popular complexity model you may see on the exam.

Stacey Complexity Model

The Stacey complexity model, developed by Ralph Stacey, is used to guide management approaches by accounting for two general sources of uncertainty: what to do (requirements) and how to do it (technology). See Figure 13-8 for an example.

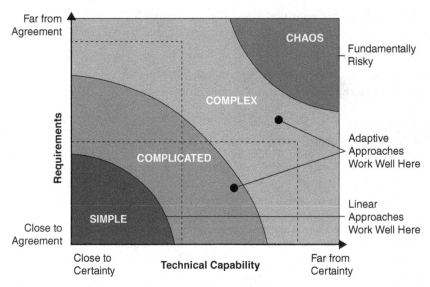

Figure 13-8   Stacey Complexity Model

For the purpose of the PMP exam, the key is to understand which project development approach is best suited for your project depending on these two uncertainty factors. When requirements are fairly clear and there is an agreement among the stakeholders and the team is confident in how they are going to do it (they have done this before; the technology is stable), then a more predictive linear project approach fits well. Otherwise, if the two uncertainty factors map into the Complicated or Complex regions, then an adaptive project approach is better suited to manage these aspects. If your project maps into the Chaos region, then you have a very high-risk project, and in many cases, the project should be abandoned until more certainty on one of the aspects can be achieved.

Now let's look at the key risk response strategies for dealing with the different kinds of complexity.

Systems-Based Complexity

To deal with systems-based complexity, there are two common approaches:

- **Use decoupling:** Decoupling is the process of breaking down the whole system into separate parts where each part has a primary function. This process helps to simplify the work process, reduces the number of interconnections, allows each part to be modified without impacting the other parts of the system, allows each part to be tested on its own, and reduces the overall size of the problem. This design approach is a best practice in iterative and incremental development.

- **Use simulation:** The use of simulation to manage systems-based complexity has several layers. Simulation tools can be used during testing for any component or combinations of components of the system. In addition, if the system is more about people behavior, then information about the targeted behavior in a similar situation or environment can be used for simulating the expected behavior in this new environment.

Reframing Complexity

In some situations, the complexity is due to your perception or due to reliance on specific data. In these cases, looking at the problem differently and/or acquiring better data can reduce the perceived complexity. The two common approaches for managing reframing complexity are as follows:

- **Seek diverse perspectives:** The technique of leveraging different perspectives to view a complex problem or system. This approach can include brainstorming with the project team to open up divergent ways of looking at the situation. In this situation, having a diverse project team with different backgrounds and experiences can be invaluable.

- **Use balanced data:** The use of balanced data sources helps provide a broader perspective on the situation and can help counteract the negative effects on relying just on source. An example would be to use a combination of historical data and forecasting data and/or to use multiple sources of data.

Process-Based Complexity

To deal with process-based complexity, here are three common approaches:

- **Build iteratively and/or incrementally:** Building the solution iteratively and/or incrementally is a hallmark of the adaptive approach. This approach allows the team to focus on specific features on each iteration and get immediate feedback from the stakeholders. In each iteration, the team learns what is working and what is not working and adjusts from there.

- **Engage stakeholders often:** Get feedback from the stakeholders early and often. This approach reduces assumptions, builds stakeholder engagement and ownership, and provides continuous learning throughout the project. Again, this is another hallmark of the adaptive approach but can also be incorporated into hybrid and predictive approaches.

- **Build in redundancy:** For critical system elements, build in redundancy or include the ability to gracefully degrade functionality in case any critical component of the system fails.

Strategies for Addressing Volatility

In the Uncertainty performance domain section of *PMBOK® Guide*, Seventh Edition, PMI focuses on two aspects of project volatility: fluctuations in available materials and in available resource skill sets. Although these are certainly two flavors of volatility, they seem to omit the most common source of volatility—changes in scope and in requirements—when reviewing common approaches to responding to volatility risk. So we add that to our strategy list for responding to volatility risk. To deal with volatility, here are the common approaches:

- **Leverage an adaptive approach:** As discussed in Chapter 3, "Development Approach and Life Cycle Performance," one of the common reasons an adaptive approach is used is to deal with project environments where there is likely to be scope and requirements volatility. The approach is resilient and is set up to handle frequent and sudden changes.

- **Analyze alternatives:** If there is volatility risk around the availability of materials and/or skill sets, the project team can proactively analyze alternative approaches to accomplish the event or work that is at risk. Examples would include resequencing work, outsourcing work, and leveraging a different mix of skill sets.

- **Allocate reserves:** This would be an example of accepting the risk involved around materials and resource price volatility and/or schedule availability. As we mentioned in that section, the risk is actively accepted by allocating a cost reserve to the budget to deal with price fluctuations and allocating a schedule reserve to deal with delays due to resource or material availability.

Because we have discussed several types of reserves throughout this book, see Table 13-11 for a quick summary of the reserve types and their definitions.

Table 13-11 Summary of Reserve Types

Reserve Type	Description
Cost	Budget amount to deal with budget line-item price fluctuations.
Schedule	Duration period on the schedule to deal with delays due to resource and/or material availability.
Contingency	Planned reserve to handle project risks. This always includes a budget amount, but it can also include a schedule and resource reserve.
Management	Budget category to handle unexpected events like unplanned in-scope work.

NOTE Contingency reserves are for known risks (known unknowns) and are the responsibility of the project manager.

Management reserves are for unknown risks (unknown unknowns) and are the responsibility of senior management.

For the PMP exam, assume that the project manager is aware of how much money is in the management reserves but has no authority to make any decisions regarding management reserves. The project manager's authority is strictly limited to contingency reserves.

Other Risk Response Planning Notes and Terms

Before risk response planning is complete, the project team needs to review all the planned risk responses to ensure all the priority risks are addressed and that there are no apparent discrepancies or conflicts between the various planned risk responses. If there are conflicts, the impacted risk response plans need to be reevaluated.

When risk response planning is complete, the set of risk response strategies to address the high-priority overall project risks and individual risks is known as the contingency plan. In addition, it is best practice to have a fallback plan (a Plan B) ready if the contingency plan proves not to be effective.

In addition, there is a possibility of new risks from the implementation of any of the primary response strategies. This type of risk is called a secondary risk. An example of a secondary risk would be when a project team decides to work overtime for the next month to reduce the risk of missing an important deadline (the risk response plan). However, this action could increase the risk of more work errors in the product (secondary risk).

Also, it is common that risk response strategies are not implemented for every identified risk. The risks that are left over after all risk responses have been implemented are called residual risks. See Table 13-12 for a quick summary of these terms.

Table 13-12 Summary of Other Risk Response Planning Terms

Term	Description
Contingency plan	Primary risk response strategy.
Fallback plan	Backup plan if the contingency plan proves to be ineffective.
Secondary risk	"New risk" resulting from any of the response strategies.
Residual risk	Any risks left over after all risk response strategies are implemented. The risk response strategy is always a passive acceptance and per PMI should be limited to low-probability, low-impact risks.

Risk Response Implementation and Risk Monitoring

The last two processes for risk management are the "follow-through" elements: risk response implementation and risk monitoring. Let's review the highlights of each element that you need to know for the exam.

Implementing Risk Responses

Risk response implementation is what you think it is. It is the process of actually implementing the agreed-upon risk response plans to reduce overall project risk exposure, minimize individual threats, and maximize opportunities. One key note: In reality, this step is commonly neglected in the risk management process. In this situation, the project manager needs to work with the risk owners to make sure the plans are being implemented and moving forward.

Risk response implementation is done throughout the project and involves updates to the related tracking and reporting documents, especially the risk register and the risk report. In addition, change requests might be needed as part of some of your risk response plans, especially if they impact the cost and schedule baselines. Also, a regular periodic review of risks includes tracking the status and effectiveness of the risk response plans.

Monitoring Risks

Risk monitoring is the process in which the project manager and project team spend most of their efforts after the initial risk identification and risk response planning are completed. This process involves tracking existing risks, monitoring implementation of risk response plans, identifying and analyzing new and/or secondary risks, reevaluating risks, reevaluating strategies, and evaluating risk process effectiveness.

Most importantly, by staying on top of the evolving project risk landscape, this process enables project decisions to be based on current information regarding overall project risks and individual risks. To make this happen, it is vital to establish frequent and periodic review and/or feedback sessions and include *risk review* as part of that process. It is worth noting that this is one of the advantageous elements of the adaptive project approach because frequent and regular review sessions and feedback loops are part of the process, including daily stand-up meetings, sprint/iteration reviews, and retrospectives. However, these same frequent reviews can be implemented in more predictive and hybrid projects, too.

In addition, the risk monitoring process includes tracking the reserves that were set up to manage risks. As the project progresses and reserves are utilized, the project manager needs to continuously assess whether the remaining reserves are still sufficient to handle the current remaining risks.

The other aspect of risk monitoring mentioned before is the periodic evaluation of the effectiveness of the overall risk management process. This evaluation can be done as part of the project review meetings, the risk review meetings, or via a more formal risk audit process. The risk management plan would document the format and objectives of the risk audit process.

To recap the activities and objectives of the risk monitoring process, here is a summary checklist to assist your exam preparations:

- Assess whether the overall project risk level has changed.

- Determine whether implemented risk responses are effective.

- Determine whether the status of existing risks has changed.

- Identify new and/or secondary risks.

- Assess whether project assumptions are still valid.

- Confirm whether the overall project strategy is still appropriate.

- Monitor whether reserves are still sufficient to cover remaining risk levels.

- Ensure the risk management policies and procedures are being adhered to.

- Evaluate whether the overall risk management approach is appropriate.

Exam Preparation Tasks

As mentioned in the section "How to Use This Book" in the Introduction, you have a couple of choices for exam preparation: the exercises here, Chapter 17, "Final Preparation," and the exam simulation questions on the Pearson Test Prep software online.

Review All Key Topics

Review the most important topics in this chapter, noted with the Key Topic icon in the outer margin of the page. Table 13-13 lists a reference of these key topics and the page numbers on which each is found.

Table 13-13   Key Topics for Chapter 13

Key Topic Element	Description	Page Number
Paragraph	Uncertainty performance domain	419
Section	Uncertainty and Risk Management Overview	424
Section	Risk Definition and Sources of Risk	425
Section	Risks Versus Issues	426
Section	Threats and Opportunities	426
Section	Risk Classifications and Types	427
Section	Risk Appetite, Risk Threshold, and Risk Tolerance	429
Section	Risk Management Planning	431
Section	Risk Register	433
Section	Risk Report	434
Section	Identifying Risks	435
Section	Qualitative Risk Analysis	437
Figure 13-3	Risk Probability and Impact Matrix	438
List	Other risk factors	439
Section	Quantitative Risk Analysis	440
Section	Risk Response Planning	445
Section	Strategies for Addressing Threats	445
Section	Strategies for Addressing Opportunities	446
Section	Implementing Risk Responses	454
Section	Monitoring Risks	454

Define Key Terms

Define the following key terms from this chapter and check your answers in the glossary:

uncertainty, ambiguity, complexity, volatility, risk, risk categorization, risk appetite, risk tolerance, risk threshold , risk management plan, risk register, risk category, risk report, risk breakdown structure (RBS), risk exposure, threat, risk escalation, risk transference, risk acceptance, risk avoidance, risk mitigation, opportunity, risk sharing, risk exploitation, risk enhancement, risk review

Review Questions

1. Due to the potential impact to multiple project objectives, the project team has decided to take action to eliminate a particular risk. Which risk response strategy have they selected?

   a. Risk acceptance

   b. Risk mitigation

   c. Risk avoidance

   d. Risk escalation

   e. Risk transfer

2. When the project team is dealing with threats, which risk response strategies will require more effort?

   a. Risk mitigation and risk acceptance

   b. Risk avoidance and risk escalation

   c. Risk avoidance and risk mitigation

   d. Risk escalation and risk mitigation

3. By considering the uncertainty level of both the requirements and the technical solution for the project, the project manager refers to the Stacey complexity model and determines the project falls into the Complicated range. What project approach does the Stacey complexity model recommend in this situation?

   a. Predictive approach

   b. Adaptive approach

   c. Hybrid approach

   d. Prototyping approach

   e. Resilient approach

4. Which risk analysis tool is used to determine which risks have the greatest impact on the project's critical path?

   a. Decision trees

   b. Tornado diagrams

   c. Influence diagrams

   d. Probability and impact matrix

   e. Monte Carlo simulation

5. What are some of the reasons organizations do not leverage quantitative risk analysis during the risk analysis process? (Choose three.)

   a. It requires additional time and investment.

   b. It requires high-quality data for each individual project risk.

   c. It requires responsibility and accountability for the project.

   d. It requires a solid baseline for scope, schedule, and cost.

   e. It is used only on projects in the financial industry.

6. What are some other factors besides probability and impact that should be evaluated before assigning a final priority level to a given risk?

   a. Political, economic, and urgency

   b. Controllability, connectivity, and social impact

   c. Dormancy, manageability, and resource availability

   d. Urgency, proximity, and propinquity

   e. Strategic impact, detectability, and technical

7. During risk identification, the project team discovered an opportunity to reduce the project cost by 30 percent. Due to this potential savings, the project team decided to make sure this opportunity occurs. What risk response strategy are they employing in this scenario?

   a. Risk exploitation

   b. Risk avoidance

   c. Risk enhancement

   d. Risk mitigation

   e. Risk sharing

8. Risk A has a probability of 50 percent and an impact score of 9. Risk B has a probability of 60 percent and an impact score of 8. Risk C has a probability of 90 percent and an impact score of 6. Risk D has a probability of 30 percent and an impact score of 10. Which risk will be ranked the highest?

   a. Risk A

   b. Risk B

   c. Risk C

   d. Risk D

9. The project team documents in the risk management plan that it will use risk classifications of scope, schedule, cost, and quality. What type of risk classification is this?

    a. Source-based

    b. Event

    c. Nonevent

    d. Effect-based

    e. Project objectives

10. If an organization is comfortable with most uncertainty and accepts risk as a normal part of doing business and projects, how you would describe the risk appetite of the organization?

    a. Risk-tolerant

    b. Risk-seeking

    c. Risk-neutral

    d. Risk-accepting

    e. Risk-adverse

    f. Risk-savvy

This chapter covers the following topics of the measurement performance domain and the monitoring and controlling of a project:

- **Performance Measurement and Monitoring and Controlling:** Learn PMI's approach to measuring performance and monitoring and controlling a project.

- **Performance Tracking Tools and Artifacts:** Review the common tools and artifacts for measuring project and team performance.

- **Earned Value Management (EVM):** Review the earned value management formulas that you need to understand for the PMP exam.

## CHAPTER 14

Project Measurement

In this chapter, we discuss monitoring and controlling a project and taking measurements to assess and report on the performance of a project. We discuss the principles related to the *PMBOK® Guide*, Sixth Edition, the *PMBOK® Guide*, Seventh Edition, and the Exam Content Outline (ECO).

This chapter addresses the following objectives from PMP Exam Content Outline:

Domain	Task #	Exam Objective
People	Task 3	Support team performance
People	Task 9	Collaborate with stakeholders
People	Task 10	Build shared understanding
Process	Task 1	Execute project with the urgency required to deliver business value
Process	Task 2	Manage communications
Process	Task 3	Assess and manage risk
Process	Task 4	Engage stakeholders
Process	Task 5	Plan and manage budget and resources
Process	Task 6	Plan and manage schedule
Process	Task 7	Plan and manage quality of products/deliverables
Process	Task 8	Plan and manage scope
Process	Task 9	Integrate project planning activities
Process	Task 10	Manage project changes
Process	Task 11	Plan and manage procurement
Process	Task 12	Manage project artifacts
Process	Task 15	Manage project issues
Process	Task 16	Ensure knowledge transfer for project continuity

Domain	Task #	Exam Objective
Process	Task 17	Plan and manage project/phase closure or transitions
Business Environment	Task 2	Evaluate and deliver project benefits and value
Business Environment	Task 3	Evaluate and address external business environment changes for impact on scope

"Do I Know This Already?" Quiz

The "Do I Know This Already?" quiz allows you to assess whether you should read this entire chapter thoroughly or jump to the "Exam Preparation Tasks" section. If you are in doubt about your answers to these questions or your own assessment of your knowledge of the topics, read the entire chapter. Table 14-1 lists the major headings in this chapter and their corresponding "Do I Know This Already?" quiz questions. You can find the answers in Appendix A, "Answers to the 'Do I Know This Already?' Quizzes and Review Questions."

Table 14-1 "Do I Know This Already?" Section-to-Question Mapping

Foundation Topics Section	Questions
Performance Measurement and Monitoring and Controlling	1–3
Performance Tracking Tools and Artifacts	4–7
Earned Value Management (EVM)	8–10

CAUTION The goal of self-assessment is to gauge your mastery of the topics in this chapter. If you do not know the answer to a question or are only partially sure of the answer, you should mark that question as wrong for purposes of the self-assessment. Giving yourself credit for an answer you correctly guess skews your self-assessment results and might provide you with a false sense of security.

1. Which of the following are types of key performance indicators (KPIs)? (Choose two.)

   a. Schedule indicators

   b. Lagging indicators

   c. Leading indicators

   d. Cost indicators

   e. Quality assurance indicators

2. Which of the following is not a reason for taking performance measurements on a project?

   a. Determining whether you are on schedule

   b. Performing an impact analysis of changes

   c. Tracking costs

   d. Tracking resource utilization

3. Which of the following does not represent the SMART criteria?

   a. Attainable

   b. Realistic

   c. Analytical

   d. Measurable

4. The team facilitator is discussing with key stakeholders the status of the project and showing them the tasks that are remaining, the tasks that are currently being worked on, and the ones completed. Most likely, which chart is the team facilitator referring to?

   a. Information radiator

   b. Burnup chart

   c. Cumulative flow diagram

   d. Kanban board

5. Which of the following tools do you use to show the number of story points that have been accomplished by the team?

   a. Information radiator

   b. Burndown chart

   c. Burnup chart

   d. Cycle time

6. Which of the following would not be examples of a chart or report that you would use to track performance? (Choose two.)

   a. Cumulative flow diagram

   b. Ishikawa diagram

   c. Net promoter score

   d. Scrum board

   e. Pareto chart

7. Which of the following would you not find on an information radiator for an agile team?

    a. Burnup chart

    b. Scrum board

    c. Velocity chart

    d. Gantt chart

8. Which of the following terms measures the cost efficiency you have achieved so far?

    a. CV

    b. SPI

    c. CPI

    d. TCPI

9. Which of the following metrics shows that the project is on budget and on schedule?

    a. SV is negative, and CV is negative.

    b. CPI is greater than 1, and SPI is greater than 1.

    c. BAC is less than EAC.

    d. CPI is 1, and SPI is 1.

10. The planned value for your project is $2,000 per week, and you are told that SV= –$2,000. How would you interpret this?

    a. You are over budget.

    b. You have $2,000 worth of work left to do.

    c. You are behind schedule.

    d. You have completed $2,000 worth of work.

Foundation Topics

Project Measurement

The measurement performance domain of the *PMBOK® Guide*, Seventh Edition, addresses the activities required to assess the performance of the project and take appropriate action to maintain optimal performance.

The equivalent process group of the *PMBOK® Guide*, Sixth Edition, is monitoring and controlling, which PMI describes as the processes required to track, review, and regulate the progress and performance of the project; identify areas on which changes to the plan are required; and initiate the appropriate changes.

In short, they both refer to comparing actual results with the plan, identifying deviations from the plan, and working toward getting back onto the plan (corrective actions). We discuss the principles and processes detailed in both the *PMBOK® Guide*, Sixth Edition, and the *PMBOK® Guide*, Seventh Edition.

Performance Measurement and Monitoring and Controlling

A common notion for a successful project is that you need to adequately plan the project. You often hear that a good plan leads to a good execution. However, is that always true?

Often the most well-thought-out plans can go awry due to many factors and risks that were not anticipated. Just as important as planning is monitoring and controlling the project, taking appropriate performance measurements, and making decisions to adjust to any deviations as appropriate.

Per PMI, *monitoring* is referred to as collecting performance data, producing performance measures, and reporting performance information. *Controlling*, on the other hand, is referred to as comparing actual performance with the plan, analyzing variances, and recommending corrective actions as needed.

Effective Measurements and Metrics

There are many reasons why you would want to take performance measurements on a project; they include

- Tracking resource utilization
- Determining whether you are on budget, over budget, or under budget

- Determining whether you are on schedule, ahead of schedule, or behind schedule

- Tracking work completed and funds utilized

- Providing information to stakeholders

- Demonstrating accountability

- Determining the level of value the product or service will deliver to the customer, compared to the initial plan

- Ensuring the final product or service will meet the acceptance criteria

However, just taking measurements by itself is not necessarily adding value to the project. It's what you do with these measurements that count. After you have these measurements, you need to engage stakeholders and make appropriate decisions based on those results.

It is important early in the project to determine effective measures and metrics to ensure you are appropriately tracking, evaluating, and reporting project performance. This step can often be established during the development of the project charter and progressively elaborated as needed. These measures and metrics are documented in the project management plan. Many of these metrics are listed in the appropriate subsidiary plans. Every project manager should tailor the measurement metrics based on the situation, but it is important to measure only what matters. It is easy to overanalyze and measure too many metrics that do not add value and simply waste time.

Establishing key performance indicators (KPIs) to evaluate success and failures during a project is imperative. The two types of KPIs are as follows:

- **Leading indicators:** These KPIs predict changes or trends in the project. This information can reduce performance risk on a project by identifying any unfavorable trends before they reach a tolerance threshold. For example, you can use the current number of work-in-progress tasks to determine whether you are going further and further behind schedule before you hit your tolerance limit. Leading indicators can also be nonquantifiable, such as poor risk management processes or a key stakeholder who is not available or engaged on the project.

- **Lagging indicators:** These KPIs measure deliverables or events after the events have occurred, and they also look at past performance. For example, they look at the number of deliverables completed or the amount of resources consumed. They can often be used to show correlation between certain factors; for example, the reason that a project has a negative schedule variance (behind schedule) could be low team morale.

Any metrics or measurements should always follow the *SMART* criteria, which stands for

Specific

Measurable

Achievable

Relevant

Time-bound

There also are variations of SMART, for example:

■ Meaningful instead of Measurable

■ Agreed or Attainable instead of Achievable

■ Realistic or Reasonable instead of Relevant

■ Timely instead of Time-bound

Understand that running reports, analyzing results, and discussing actions are often time consuming and considered non-value-added work for technical teams, so it is important to measure only what falls within the SMART criteria.

Key performance indicators and measurements vary by project and industry, but some of the common ones include

■ Cost variance (CV)

■ Schedule variance (SV)

■ Cost performance index (CPI)

■ Schedule performance index (SPI)

■ Earned value (EV)

■ Number of tasks complete

■ Number of defects

■ Planned hours versus actual hours

Monitoring and Controlling a Project

The Monitoring and Controlling process group of the *PMBOK® Guide*, Sixth Edition, consists of the processes required to track, review, and regulate the performance of the project. It compares the actual results of the project to the plan and identifies any deviations for further discussion and decision-making. For example, are you ahead of schedule or behind schedule, over budget, or under budget?

The *PMBOK® Guide*, Sixth Edition, processes related to monitoring and controlling are as follows:

- Monitor and Control Project Work

- Perform Integrated Change Control (discussed in Chapter 4, "Starting a Project and Integration")

- Validate Scope (discussed in Chapter 6, "Project Scope")

- Control Scope (discussed in Chapter 6)

- Control Schedule (discussed in the "Earned Value Management [EVM]" section of this chapter)

- Control Costs (discussed in the EVM section of this chapter)

- Control Quality (discussed in Chapter 11, "Project Quality")

- Control Resources (discussed in Chapter 9, "Managing Resources and the Team")

- Monitor Communications (discussed in Chapter 10, "Project Communications")

- Monitor Risks (discussed in Chapter 13, "Uncertainty")

- Control Procurements (discussed in Chapter 12, "Project Procurement")

- Monitor Stakeholder Engagement (discussed in Chapter 5, "Stakeholder Engagement")

As noted, many of these topics are discussed in detail in their appropriate chapters. Here, we provide an overview of monitoring and controlling from the perspective of the Process domain of the Exam Content Outline (ECO).

Regardless of the knowledge area, the principles of monitoring and controlling are the same. You compare the ***work performance data*** (WPD) to the plan and calculate the variance. You then analyze the variance to determine the ***work performance***

information (WPI), which is the interpretation of the variance. A representation of the work performance information is presented in the *work performance report* (WPR); some examples are discussed later in this chapter.

As an example, Control Schedule refers to comparing the actual timeline (WPD) to the planned schedule to determine whether you are on schedule, ahead of schedule, or behind schedule (WPI). You may use earned value analysis (EVA, discussed later in the chapter) to determine this. Likewise, Control Costs refers to comparing actual cost or budget so far (WPD) to the planned cost or cost baseline to determine whether you are on budget, under budget, or over budget (WPI). Again, you can use the EVA to determine this. Control Resources refers to comparing actual physical resources utilized (WPD) to what was originally planned.

Thus, for every process in the Monitoring and Controlling process group of the *PMBOK® Guide*, Sixth Edition, from scope management down to stakeholder management, the following rules apply:

- The start point (or the input) is always the WPD plus the appropriate plan(s) or baseline(s).

- One of the tools and techniques is the variance analysis because you are comparing the actual results to the plan.

- The artifact that is created from each of these processes (or the output) is the WPI, which is the interpretation of the variance.

The first process, Monitor and Control Project Work, integrates all the monitoring and processes together to create the work performance report. Remember (from Chapter 4) that integration management refers to performing all the processes simultaneously and is the master knowledge area that can be performed only by the project manager. Thus, *Monitor and Control Project Work* refers to collecting the work performance information for each knowledge area and presenting the results in the form of charts, graphs, reports, and commentaries (work performance reports).

Performance Tracking Tools and Artifacts

Project managers might use many tools, charts, graphs, and reports to take measurements to determine project performance. In the sections that follow, we look at some of the common ones that you should know for the PMP exam. Some of these are used in both predictive and adaptive projects, some are unique to predictive, and some unique to agile.

First, let's discuss what it is that you need to measure. Although every project and situation is unique, and every project will have unique measures, some common metrics can be applied across many projects. For example, you might apply

- **Technical performance measures:** You can test the product to ensure it meets technical requirements and identify any variances if it does not.

- **Nontechnical performance measures:** These measures include size, accuracy, reliability, and efficiency related to the operation of the system or machine.

- **Errors and defects:** You can identify the root cause of the defect and the number of defects identified versus the number of defects resolved.

- **Work in progress (WIP):** You can measure the number of work components currently being worked on.

- **Queue size:** You can measure the number of items in a queue and see the WIP compared to work remaining.

- **Schedule variance (SV) and schedule performance index (SPI):** Using the planned start and end dates versus actual start and end dates, the SV and SPI determine whether the project is on schedule, ahead of schedule, or behind schedule. The "Earned Value Management (EVM)" section of this chapter explains this metric in further detail.

- **Cost variance (CV) and cost performance index (CPI):** Comparing planned cost to actual cost, the CV and CPI determine whether the project is on budget, under budget, or over budget. The "Earned Value Management (EVM)" section of this chapter explains this metric in further detail.

- **Resource utilization rates:** You also can compare the planned resource utilization to the actual resource utilization.

The sections that follow describe some common tools and artifacts used for analyzing and displaying measurements.

Kanban Board

The *Kanban board* is used extensively in agile. Also known as the task board, agile board, or scrum board, it shows the status of the team's deliverables during a sprint. At a glance, it can show which stories have not started, which are in progress, and which are complete. Figure 14-1 shows an example of a Kanban board.

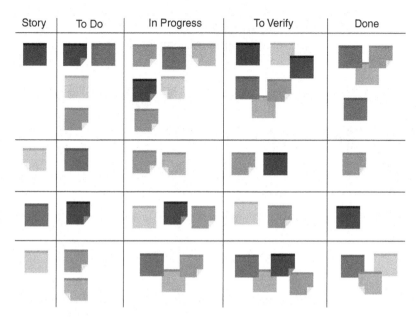

Story	To Do	In Progress	To Verify	Done

Figure 14-1   Kanban Board

The board may also show other types of status such as Testing Started, Testing Complete, and Signed Off. The team chooses to show the status categories that will be helpful to other stakeholders to track the team's status.

The team also needs to determine the optimum work-in-progress (WIP) items that they can be working on at any one time.

- If the team has too many WIP items open, they may not complete them all by the end of the sprint, so those incomplete user stories get placed back into the product backlog. For example, say the team planned to deliver 10 user stories this sprint and started working on all of them simultaneously. By the end of the sprint, if only two were complete based on the definition of done and eight were 95 percent complete, then all eight of those incomplete user stories would return back to the product backlog.

- If the team works on too few items at any one time, some user stories may not even get started by the end of the sprint. For example, say this team decides to just work on one user story at time and will not start another story until the previous is 100 percent complete. By the end of the sprint, they may have completed six user stories and not even started on four of them. Again, these four go back into the product backlog.

The team needs to determine how many user stories they can work on at any one time so that all user stories can delivered 100 percent complete by the end of the sprint.

Burndown Chart

Primarily used for agile projects, the **burndown chart** shows how much work remains to be completed based on the definition of done. Figure 14-2 shows a sample burndown chart.

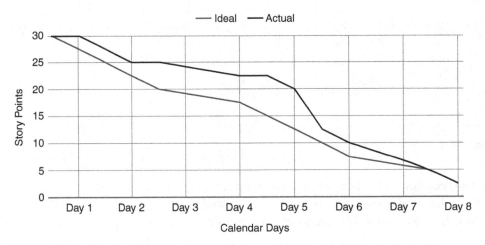

Figure 14-2 Burndown Chart

The Y-axis shows the number of story points, and the X-axis shows the timeline. The *Ideal* line (sometimes referred to as the "plan" line) shows how many story points are expected to remain at a point in time. The *Actual* line indicates how many story points actually remained at that point in time.

Burnup Chart

Primarily used for agile projects, a **burnup chart** shows how much work has been accomplished based on the definition of done. It also shows the work that has been added. Figure 14-3 shows a sample burndown chart.

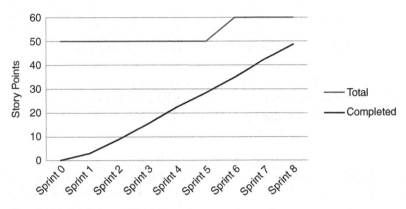

Figure 14-3 Burnup Chart

The Y-axis shows the number of story points, and the X-axis shows the timeline. The *Total* line is the plan and shows how many story points are expected to have been completed at a point in time. It also shows how many story points have been added over time.

The *Completed* line shows the actual results, or how many story points were actually completed at that point in time.

Cumulative Flow Diagram

The ***cumulative flow diagram*** is another Kanban tool that is used extensively in agile, and it shows how many story points (or user stories) have not started, are WIP, and are complete. Figure 14-4 shows a sample cumulative flow diagram.

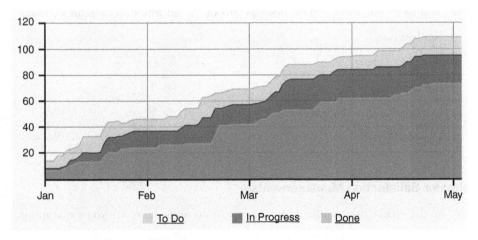

Figure 14-4 Cumulative Flow Diagram

Information Radiator

Primarily used on agile projects, the *information radiator* is a collection of charts, graphs, and reports showing the status of the project and status of the agile team to key stakeholders. Traditionally, information radiators were physical charts and graphs hung on the wall of a high-traffic area near to where the agile team members were co-located. As stakeholders walked past, they could quickly browse the information radiators and review project status.

The use of the information radiator reduces the need to have lengthy stakeholder status meetings, which most of the time are non-value-added work for technical teams. Instead, stakeholders can quickly assess the status by studying the charts and graphs on the information radiator. Of course, the stakeholders might have questions or need further clarification, in which case these questions are addressed to the team facilitator (or Scrum master) rather than the team. This approach ensures that the team facilitator is shielding the team from non-value-added work, allowing them to work on only value-added items. If stakeholders still have additional concerns, they can always be invited to any of the agile ceremonies to observe only.

These days, an increasing number of agile teams are working virtually rather than being co-located, so information radiators are usually located on shared drives and dashboards as appropriate.

EXAM TIP   If a new stakeholder approaches the team facilitator requesting regular status of the agile project, the team facilitator should first give the stakeholder access to the information radiator.

Some common charts that are included as part of the information radiator include

- Kanban board
- Burndown chart
- Burnup chart
- Cumulative flow diagram
- Velocity chart

Stakeholder Satisfaction Measurements

Stakeholder satisfaction can be measured in various ways. Here are some examples:

- *Net promoter score (NPS):* This measurement is generally used to gauge customer satisfaction of a product or service and the likelihood that they would recommend it to others. It is usually measured on a scale of –100 to +100, with a positive figure meaning the stakeholder is satisfied overall with the product or service. The exact number determines the levels of satisfaction (or dissatisfaction).

- **Team morale:** Simply observing team interaction can determine morale within the team. However, evaluations and surveys may also be used to identify the exact levels of team morale. These surveys and evaluations can determine whether the team member feels engaged, appreciated, or satisfied with their contribution to the project.

- *Mood chart:* Using this chart is a quick and easy way to track the mood and reaction of stakeholders. Commonly, emojis or icons are used to identify the levels of engagement and satisfaction, but other measures may be used, such as colors and numbers. Figure 14-5 shows a mood chart using emojis.

Figure 14-5   Mood Chart (Credit: Evgeniy_D/Shutterstock)

Business Value Measurements

You need to ensure the project is achieving the business value it was intended to, and doing so includes determining the business value at the start of the project. Some metrics used for business value measurements are as follows:

- *Benefit-cost ratio:* This metric is calculated as part of benefit-cost analysis usually to prioritize projects and determine which project to do next. Senior management will be more involved with this decision to determine the benefit of the investment. If the benefit is greater than the cost, the project should be considered, and the higher the benefit-cost ratio, the better. A benefit cost ratio is usually not performed during a project.

- *Return on investment* **(ROI) and internal rate of return (IRR):** ROI and IRR are other measurements usually taken to prioritize projects and are used to measure the financial return of the project. The higher the ROI or IRR, the higher the potential return.

- **Present value (PV), future value (FV), and *net present value* (NPV):** These measures take into consideration the time value of money and the higher the NPV, the better. Generally, a negative NPV figure indicates the project should not be accepted unless there are nonmonetary reasons, such as regulatory requirements or goodwill.

- **Opportunity cost:** This metric measures the business value given up by choosing one opportunity over another. For example, say project A will yield $50,000, and project B will yield $70,000. If you decide to choose project B because it yields the higher return over project A, the opportunity cost is $50,000 because that is the return that you have forgone.

For the PMP exam, you should be aware of these terms, but it is highly unlikely that you will be asked to calculate any of these figures.

Other Performance Tracking Tools and Artifacts

Project managers, senior stakeholders, and project teams use many other measurements to measure performance of a project. Some additional performance tracking tools and measurements include the following:

- **Gantt chart:** This tool is used on predictive projects to show the schedule and timelines of project activities. It was discussed in Chapter 7, "Project Schedule."

- **Milestone chart:** This tool is used on predictive projects to show the schedule of significant points on a project. It was discussed in Chapter 7.

- **Product roadmap:** This tool is used on adaptive projects to show the high-level start and end of agile products. It was discussed in Chapter 7.

- ***Throughput:*** Used primarily in agile, throughput shows the number of items being completed in a fixed time frame.

- ***Cycle time:*** Used in agile, cycle time is a measurement that shows how long a particular task takes from start to finish.

- ***Velocity:*** Used in agile, velocity shows how many story points have been completed in a sprint and is shown on a velocity chart.

- **Work performance reports:** Examples of work performance reports include the following:

  - ***Status reports:*** These reports show where the project currently stands.

- *Progress reports*: These reports show what has been accomplished since the previous update.

- *Forecasts*: These reports show projections based on historical data and trends, such as estimate to complete (ETC), to complete performance index (TCPI), variance at completion (VAC), and estimate at completion (EAC). They are covered in more detail in the following section.

- **Earned value reports:** These reports show the value of the work completed compared to the work planned. Earned value management concepts are next.

- **Variance reports:** These reports show the difference between planned and actual results.

- **Quality reports:** These charts, graphs, and reports are based on quality measures and metrics collected.

Earned Value Management (EVM)

To determine the financial and schedule measures of a project, you can use many methodologies and approaches in different situations. There are many ways of valuing a project, and different industries use different cost management methodologies and budget conventions to determine the performance of the project.

One such method, and the method that PMI has chosen to adopt, is known as earned value management (EVM), also referred to as earned value analysis (EVA).

The whole principle behind EVM is that values are calculated from a monetary perspective—even the schedule. So, in an EVM environment, you do not say, "The project is three weeks behind schedule." Instead, you say, "We are $100,000 worth of work behind schedule."

The way the formulas are constructed, even the schedule is converted into a monetary value, and that can be a little confusing initially if you are not used to EVM. Three formulas are indices (CPI, SPI, TCPI), but apart from these three, the rest are based on monetary values.

Here, we discuss the EVM terms and formulas. It is important for you understand what the terms mean rather than blindly memorizing the formulas. Of course, you need to know the formulas too because formulas will not be provided to you in the exam, but when you understand the terms, the formulas become much more straightforward to understand.

Let's use the following scenario:

> **You are 5 weeks into a 10-week project costing $100,000. You are 40 percent complete and have spent $60,000 so far.**

Table 14-2 outlines four fundamental EVM variables.

Table 14-2   Four Fundamental EVM Variables

Acronym	Terminology	Explanation
PV	*Planned value*	At this point, how much work you should have completed.
		If you're 5 weeks into a 10-week project costing $100,000, you should be 50 percent complete. So, PV = $50,000.
		For the exam, assume planned value will be spread across the project linearly.
EV	*Earned value*	At this point, how much work you have accomplished.
		If you are 40 percent complete, you have earned/produced $40,000 worth of work. EV = $40,000.
AC	*Actual cost*	How much has the project cost you to date?
		You've spent $60,000 so far (given in the question). AC = $60,000
BAC	*Budget at completion*	The original baseline budget for the project.
		$100,000 in this case, given in the question.

Table 14-3 details the formulas for schedule variance (SV) and cost variance (CV).

Table 14-3   Schedule Variance and Cost Variance

Terminology	Formula	Explanation
Schedule variance	SV = EV – PV *PV = 5/10 × $100,000 = $50,000* *EV = 40% × $100,000 = $40,000* *SV = $40,000 – $50,000 = –$10,000*	How much ahead of schedule or behind schedule you are right now. Positive = ahead of schedule. Negative = behind schedule. *In this case you are $10,000 worth of work behind schedule.*
Cost variance	CV = EV – AC *EV = 40% × $100,000 = $40,000* *AC = $60,000 (given in the question)* *CV = $40,000 – $60,000 = –$20,000*	How much over budget or under budget you are right now. Positive = under budget. Negative = over budget. *In this case you have overspent by $20,000. You are over budget by $20,000 based on the amount of work done.*

Table 14-4 details two important indexes: the cost performance index (CPI) and schedule performance index (SPI).

Key Topic

Table 14-4 Cost Performance Index (CPI) and Schedule Performance Index (SPI)

Terminology	Formula	Explanation
Cost performance index (CPI)	$CPI = \dfrac{EV}{AC}$	Rate of expenditure of funds (that is, for each dollar spent, how much have you earned).
	EV = $40,000	Less than 1 = bad.
	AC = $60,000	Greater than 1 = good.
	$CPI = \dfrac{\$40K}{\$60K} = 0.67$	*In this case, for every dollar that you have spent, your team has only performed 67 cents worth of work. Thus, you are over budget.*
Schedule performance index (SPI)	$SPI = \dfrac{EV}{PV}$	Rate of performance of work achieved so far.
	EV = $40,000	Less than 1 = bad.
	PV = $50,000	Greater than 1 = good.
	$SPI = \dfrac{\$40K}{\$50K} = 0.8$	*In this case the team has worked at a rate of 80 percent, so you are behind schedule.*

Table 14-5 shows four estimate at completion (EAC) formulas. EAC is also known as the forecasted budget.

Table 14-5 Estimate at Completion (EAC)

Terminology	Formula	When Used
Estimate at completion (EAC) (1)	EAC = AC + Bottom-up ETC	New estimate is required.
		Original estimate is flawed.
Estimate at completion (2)	EAC = AC + (BAC − EV)	Future spending will be at **budgeted** rate.
		Variances are atypical.
		Variances will not continue.
Estimate at completion (3)	$EAC = \dfrac{BAC}{CPI}$	Spending continues at **current** rate.
		Current CPI will continue.
		Variances are typical.
		Variances will continue.
Estimate at completion (4)	$EAC = AC + \left(\dfrac{BAC - EV}{CPI \times SPI} \right)$	Poor cost performance and there's a need to hit a firm completion date.

Using the example, Table 14-6 shows how to calculate EAC_2 and EAC_3.

Table 14-6   Examples using EAC_2 and EAC_3

Terminology	Formula	When Used
Estimate at completion (2)	$EAC = AC + (BAC - EV)$ $AC = \$60K$ $BAC = \$100K$ $EV = \$40K$ $EAC = \$40K + (100K - 60K) =$ $\$120,000$	Future spending will be at **budgeted** rate. Variances are atypical. Variances will not continue. *In this case, as long as you don't go any further over budget, the project will finish at $120,000.*
Estimate at completion (3)	$EAC = \dfrac{BAC}{CPI}$ $BAC = \$100K$ $CPI = 0.67$ $EAC = \$100K/0.67 = \$150,000$	Spending continues at **current** rate. Current CPI will continue. Variances are typical. Variances will continue. *In this case, if you continue working at the same rate, then the project will finish at $150,000.*

Table 14-7 shows two additional variables: estimate to complete (ETC) and variance at completion (VAC).

Table 14-7   Estimate to Complete (ETC) and Variance at Completion (VAC)

Terminology	Formula	Explanation
Estimate to complete (ETC)	$ETC = EAC - AC$ $EAC = \$120,000$ $AC = \$60,000$ $ETC = \$120,000 - \$60,000$ $= \$60,000$	Funding required to complete the project from now until the end. *This example uses EAC_2 and it means that you need to spend $60,000 to finish the project.*
Variance at completion (VAC)	$VAC = BAC - EAC$ $BAC = \$100,000$ $EAC = \$120,000$ $VAC = \$100,000 - \$120,000$ $= -\$20,000$	How much over/under budget you expect to be by the end of the project. *In this example, you will be $20,000 over budget by the end of the project.*

Table 14-8 describes the to complete performance index (TCPI), which is the rate of cost efficiency you need to achieve to meet the budget.

Table 14-8 To Complete Performance Index (TCPI)

Acronym	Terminology	Explanation
TCPI	*To complete performance index*	The rate of cost efficiency you need to achieve to meet the budget. $$\frac{\text{work remaining}}{\text{budget remaining}}$$ *If you have $100,000 worth of work left to do and $50,000 left in the budget, then* $$\frac{\$100K}{\$50K} = 2 \ \ (or \ 200\%)$$ *If you have $50,000 worth of work left to do and $100,000 left in the budget, then* $$\frac{\$50K}{\$100K} = 0.5 \ (or \ 50\%)$$

Table 14-9 outlines two TCPI formulas you need to know for the exam.

Table 14-9 TCPI Formulas

Terminology	Formula	When Used
To complete performance index (1)	$TCPI = \dfrac{(BAC - EV)}{(BAC - AC)}$ *BAC = $100,000* *EV = $40,000* *AC = $60,000* **TCPI = ($100K − 40K) / ($100K − 60K) = 1.5**	The rate of cost efficiency needed to achieve the original budget. Use when original budget is achievable.
To complete performance index (2)	$TCPI = \dfrac{(BAC - EV)}{(EAC - AC)}$ *BAC = $100,000; EAC = $120,000* *EV = $40,000* *AC = $60,000* **TCPI = ($100K − 40K) / ($120K − 60K) = 1**	The rate of cost efficiency needed to achieve the forecasted budget. Use when original budget is not achievable.

Sample Exercise for EVM

Scenario:

You are remodeling a small office building. Renovations include upgrading the bathroom, replacing carpet in the halls, and upgrading the lighting on 10 floors. Each floor is expected to take one week and cost $60,000.

The project is four weeks in, costs are $280,000 to date, and 4.5 floors have been completed.

Assume future performance will be typical of the past.

Answer:

Table 14-10 provides the solution for this scenario.

Table 14-10   EVM Exercise Solution

	Formula/Calculation	Answer
BAC	10 floors × $60,000	$600,000
PV	4 weeks × $60,000	$240,000
AC	$280,000 (given)	$280,000
EV	4.5 floors finished × $60,000	$270,000
CV	(EV – AC) $270,000 – $280,000	–$10,000
CPI	(EV/AC) $270,000/$280,000	.96
SV	(EV – PV) $270,000 – $240,000	$30,000
SPI	(EV/PV) $270,000/$240,000	1.12
EAC	(BAC/CPI) $600,000/.96	$625,000
ETC	(EAC – AC) $625,000 – $280,000	$345,000
VAC	(BAC – EAC) $600,000 – $625,000	–$25,000
TCPI	(BAC – EV)/(BAC – AC) ($600K – $270K)/($600K – $280K)	1.03

Exam Preparation Tasks

As mentioned in the section "How to Use This Book" in the Introduction, you have a couple of choices for exam preparation: the exercises here, Chapter 17, "Final Preparation," and the exam simulation questions on the Pearson Test Prep practice test software.

Review All Key Topics

Review the most important topics in this chapter, noted with the Key Topic icon in the outer margin of the page. Table 14-11 lists a reference of these key topics and the page numbers on which each is found.

Table 14-11 Key Topics for Chapter 14

Key Topic Element	Description	Page Number
Paragraph	SMART	467
Paragraph	Work Performance Data, Information and Report	468
Section	Kanban Board	470
Section	Information Radiator	474
Table 14-2	Four Fundamental EVM Variables	478
Table 14-3	Schedule Variance and Cost Variance	478
Table 14-4	Cost Performance Index (CPI) and Schedule Performance Index (SPI)	479

Define Key Terms

Define the following key terms from this chapter and check your answers in the glossary:

SMART, work performance data, work performance information, work performance report, Kanban board, burndown chart, burnup chart, cumulative flow diagram, information radiator, net promoter score, mood chart, benefit cost ratio, return on investment, net present value, throughput, cycle time, velocity, status report, progress report, forecast, planned value (PV), earned value (EV), actual cost (AC), budget at completion (BAC), schedule variance (SV), cost variance (CV), cost performance index (CPI), schedule performance index (SPI), estimate at completion (EAC), estimate to complete (ETC), variance at completion (VAC), to complete performance index (TCPI)

Review Questions

1. A project manager diligently measured progress of a project by taking many performance measurements. These measures were promptly documented and filed away. The project went over budget and behind schedule, which came as a surprise to key stakeholders. However, the project manager showed them the performance measures that were taken, so this shouldn't have been a surprise to anyone. What advice would you give to this project manager?

   a. The project manager should have saved these files in a more accessible location so that all the key stakeholders could have had visibility to the status.

   b. These measures should have been communicated to key stakeholders as they became available.

   c. The key stakeholders should have been more involved in decision-making during the project.

   d. The project manager should have reached out to the team earlier to discuss ways of improving their performance.

2. Which of the following are common project KPIs? (Choose all that apply.)

   a. SPI

   b. CPI

   c. Number of tasks complete

   d. Number of defects

   e. Planned hours versus actual hours

3. Which of the following would be work performance information?

   a. Burnup chart.

   b. You have spent $80,000 on this deliverable.

   c. Information radiator.

   d. You are 5 percent behind schedule.

4. A project manager collected metrics such as CPI, SPI, CV, number of defects, and number of tasks done and is now converting and formatting these metrics into charts and graphs. What is the project manager doing?

   a. Developing work performance reports

   b. Creating the information radiator

   c. Developing work performance information

   d. Determining the team's performance

5. Which of the following tools do you use to gauge stakeholder satisfaction?

    a. Velocity

    b. Return on investment

    c. Net promoter score

    d. Actual cost versus planned cost

6. Your project has a CPI of 1.09 and SPI of 1.06. You have a CV of $34,300 and an SV of $29,200. Your clients have a strict deadline and are cost sensitive. Even at this stage of the project, they are concerned about these results and are asking you to find ways of getting back in line with the project management plan. What advice should you give your clients?

    a. Your project is under budget and ahead of schedule, so the clients have nothing to worry about at this stage. You should inform them of this misunderstanding.

    b. Because you are over budget and behind schedule, you should immediately look for ways to increase efficiencies.

    c. Explain to your clients that you will collect all work performance information and explain these concerning results to them.

    d. Explain to your clients that you will engage the team and finds ways to work more efficiently going forward.

7. Your project has a BAC of $45,000; AC of $23,450; CPI of 1.09; and SPI of 0.93. What do these numbers tell you about the project?

    a. You are under budget but ahead of schedule.

    b. You are under budget but behind schedule.

    c. You are over budget but ahead of schedule.

    d. You are over budget and behind schedule.

8. You have been delivering system functionality in increments to your organization, and key stakeholders want a report that details the user's satisfaction of the system so far. You are trying to determine the best approach for this and will decide on which of the following tools?

    a. Mood chart

    b. Benefit cost ratio

    c. Return on investment

    d. Net promoter score

9. You have the following metrics on your project so far: PV = $63,000; EV = $61,000; AC = 62,000. Which of the following is true?

   a. You are over budget and ahead of schedule.

   b. You are under budget and ahead of schedule.

   c. You are over budget and behind schedule.

   d. You are under budget and behind schedule.

10. Match the performance tracking tools and charts to the descriptions.

1. Burndown chart	a. Shows how long a task takes from start to finish.
2. Velocity chart	b. Shows the high-level start and end of agile products.
3. Kanban board	c. Shows the tasks that have not started, work in progress, and tasks that are complete.
4. Information radiator	d. Shows how much work remains to be completed based on the definition of done.
5. Product roadmap	e. Shows stakeholder satisfaction based on emojis.
6. Net promoter score	f. Provides a collection of charts, graphs, and reports showing the status of the agile team and project.
7. Present value	g. Shows the work that has been accomplished since the previous update.
8. Cycle time	h. Shows how many story points have been completed in a sprint.
9. Mood chart	i. Gauges customer satisfaction based on a scale of −100 to +100.
10. Progress report	j. Considers the time value of money.

This chapter covers the steps and procedures required to close a project, phase, or iteration of a project.

- **Reasons for Project Closure:** Review the various ways projects might need to be closed.

- **Closing Activities:** Review the common activities required for closing projects.

- **Transition Readiness:** Review plans for transitioning the project deliverables to ongoing operations.

## CHAPTER 15

Closing a Project

In this chapter, we discuss closing a project, phase, or iteration and the steps required for closing. We discuss the principles related to the *PMBOK® Guide*, Sixth Edition, the *PMBOK® Guide*, Seventh Edition, and the Exam Content Outline (ECO).

This chapter addresses the following objectives from the PMP Exam Content Outline:

Domain	Task #	Exam Objective
People	Task 3	Support team performance
People	Task 9	Collaborate with stakeholders
People	Task 10	Build shared understanding
Process	Task 1	Execute project with the urgency required to deliver business value
Process	Task 2	Manage communications
Process	Task 4	Engage stakeholders
Process	Task 9	Integrate project planning activities
Process	Task 12	Manage project artifacts
Process	Task 16	Ensure knowledge transfer for project continuity
Process	Task 17	Plan and manage project/phase closure or transitions
Business Environment	Task 2	Evaluate and deliver project benefits and value

"Do I Know This Already?" Quiz

The "Do I Know This Already?" quiz allows you to assess whether you should read this entire chapter thoroughly or jump to the "Exam Preparation Tasks" section. If you are in doubt about your answers to these questions or your own assessment of your knowledge of the topics, read the entire chapter. Table 15-1 lists the major headings in this chapter and their corresponding "Do I Know This Already?" quiz questions. You can find the answers in Appendix A, "Answers to the 'Do I Know This Already?' Quizzes and Review Questions."

Table 15-1 "Do I Know This Already?" Section-to-Question Mapping

Foundation Topics Section	Questions
Reasons for Project Closure	1–2
Closing Activities	3–4
Transition Readiness	5–6

CAUTION The goal of self-assessment is to gauge your mastery of the topics in this chapter. If you do not know the answer to a question or are only partially sure of the answer, you should mark that question as wrong for purposes of the self-assessment. Giving yourself credit for an answer you correctly guess skews your self-assessment results and might provide you with a false sense of security.

1. When should the project manager prepare the final project report?

   a. After the customer has accepted the final deliverable.

   b. After the project manager has been informed that the project has been canceled.

   c. After the project manager has been informed that your organization no longer needs the project deliverable.

   d. All of these answers are correct.

   e. None of these answers are correct.

2. Which of the following are not appropriate reasons for canceling a project? (Choose two.)

   a. A merger with another company impacts the entire organization.

   b. The customer requests a significant number of additional requirements.

   c. The organization no longer needs the deliverable.

   d. Adequate funding is no longer available.

   e. The project is placed on indefinite hold.

   f. Material prices have significantly increased, resulting in the project costs doubling the original cost baseline.

3. All the following can occur as part of closing a project, or a phase, or an iteration, except which one?

   a. Validation of scope

   b. Iteration retrospective

    c. Update to lessons learned

    d. Archiving of documents

4. You are in a meeting with your team members, and some key stakeholders are observing. The team is discussing what went well and what can be improved. They also briefly discuss the next two-week iteration. What meeting are you attending?

    a. Lessons learned meeting

    b. Project closeout meeting

    c. Iteration review

    d. Sprint retrospective

5. After the customer has accepted the final deliverable, what should the project manager ensure happens before transferring to ongoing operations?

    a. Quality control

    b. Transition readiness

    c. Validation of scope

    d. Definition of done

6. Which of the following is not included in the transition plan?

    a. Procedures for knowledge transfer

    b. Transition readiness

    c. Procedures for customer acceptance

    d. End-user training

Foundation Topics

Closing a project, in theory, sounds straightforward. To many, it's simply a case of "deliver the final product (or service) and let's move on to the next project!" If only it could be as simple as that.

There are many reasons for closing out a project, and different projects and life cycles handle closure steps differently. Moreover, closing can refer to closing a phase, an iteration, a release, or the whole project, and each is handled differently. However, they have some common principles between them.

The *PMBOK® Guide*, Sixth Edition, covers the closing steps in the Closing process group, more specifically in the Close Project or Phase process.

The *PMBOK® Guide*, Seventh Edition, does not have a separate performance domain for closing but rather addresses closing principles across several chapters.

Reasons for Project Closure

The *PMBOK® Guide*, Sixth Edition, steps for closing are detailed in the Close Project or Phase process of the Closing process group. Another name for Close Project or Phase is *administrative closure*. The key benefits of administrative closure are

- Information regarding the phase or project is archived.
- The planned work is completed.
- Team resources are released.

However, before we discuss the steps involved in closing, let's talk about why a project might be closed.

There are various reasons why a project might be closed. The most common reason—and the best reason for closing a project—is that the deliverable has been met. The team has successfully completed the product or service, it has been accepted by the customer, and it has been transitioned to production, ongoing operations, or go-live. Naturally, that is what all project managers and project teams strive to achieve. In fact, meeting the deliverable is one of the success factors of a project.

However, a project might need to end for other reasons. It might be canceled (also known as a premature or forced closure).

A project might be canceled for many reasons, such as the following:

- The deliverable has become obsolete or is no longer needed.

- The reason for doing the project is no longer valid.

- The organization no longer needs the product or service.

- Resources have moved to another higher-priority project.

- Financing is no longer available.

- Significant risks have been identified, rendering the project unfeasible.

- Regulatory changes deem the project unfeasible.

- A merger or acquisition requires the project to close.

- Changes in senior management may change project priorities.

- Other economic and external changes may impact the organization, causing the project to close.

- The project is on hold until further notice.

Let's add a point regarding the last bullet (the project is on hold until further notice). For PMI's purposes, a project that is on indefinite hold should be officially closed and the closing steps followed. The project can always be reopened at a later date if needed.

Many organizations use a ***phase gate*** approach to determine whether to continue or cancel a project. In this approach, at various points along the project, usually at the end of major defined phases of the project, senior decision makers or the steering committee determine whether to continue or cancel the project. Figure 15-1 shows a simple phase gate approach.

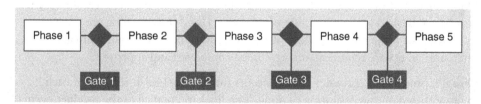

Figure 15-1   Phase Gate

In this example, at the end of Phase 1, the project has reached the first gate (Gate 1). At this stage, analyses and discussions are made on whether to continue the project. If the organization decides to continue, the project moves on to Phase 2. At the end of Phase 2, the project has reached Gate 2. Again, senior decision makers analyze and discuss the future of this project. If they determine that the project is no longer feasible, the project is canceled. This is known as the ***kill point***.

The term *phase gate* has several synonyms, such as the following:

- Governance gate

- Tollgate

- Phase end

- Stage gate

The kill point is specifically the point when the project is canceled.

Phase gate approaches are commonly used in research and development projects and government projects, among others.

The approach to closing also varies by life cycle. A predictive project might have several phases and a one-time delivery of the final product to the customer. The project manager needs to perform steps to close out each phase and also close out the entire project.

Iterative and incremental life cycles require closing each iteration and increment, respectively. These activities are led by the project manager.

Agile projects require the closure of each sprint and the release, which is led by the entire agile team.

 ## Closing Activities

Before a project, phase, iteration, or release can be closed, the project manager and team must get the acceptance from the customer.

On predictive projects, key stakeholders accept deliverables based on the acceptance criteria established at the beginning of the project, and these criteria are documented in the project management plan. The requirements traceability matrix is often used to ensure requirements have been completed and approved.

On agile projects, the product owner accepts the deliverables at the end of each iteration based on the definition of done. The final acceptance of the product occurs prior to the release. This step must be done prior to the closing steps and performed as part of the Validate Scope process.

Although closing steps can vary by organization, they are generally included in the project management plan. Some common activities performed during closure are as follows:

- Transitioning the deliverables to ongoing operations, production, or the next phase of the project.

- Ensuring appropriate costs are charged to the project.

- Ensuring any vendor contracts are closed (vendors have been paid and procurement is closed).

- Ensuring contracts are archived.

- Collecting project records.

- Ensuring all documents are up to date and appropriately signed off, if applicable. Any components of the project management plan including baselines might need to be updated for the final time.

- Preparing the final project report (discussed at the end of this section).

- Auditing successes and failures and updating lessons learned.

- Managing knowledge transfer to the ongoing operations or production team if it's the end of the project, or the appropriate project team if it's the end of the phase.

- Archiving all project documentation; they will now become organization process assets (OPA).

- Communicating to appropriate stakeholders that the project is now closed.

- Measuring stakeholder satisfaction.

- Reallocating any physical resources.

- Releasing team resources.

These activities are not listed in any specific order and do not represent an exhaustive list. Generally, however, releasing the team resources would normally be the last step because the project manager needs these resources to perform these closing activities.

It is also important to understand that the project manager must perform these closing activities regardless of how a project has ended. Even if the project is canceled for any reason, these closing activities must still be followed.

Key Artifacts of Closing

In addition to various project document updates (which are artifacts for all project processes), two key artifacts are involved in closing:

- *Transition plan*: This plan is also known as the implementation plan and rollout plan. It is discussed later in this chapter.

- *Final report*: This report provides a summary of the project performance and includes these elements:

- Summary-level descriptions of the project or phase

- Scope objectives, criteria used to evaluate the scope, and evidence that the completion criteria were met

- Quality objectives, criteria used to evaluate quality, and reasons for quality variances

- Cost objectives, including acceptable cost ranges and actual costs

- Schedule objectives, including whether results achieved the planned benefits

- Validation information, including approvals for the final product, service, or result

- A summary of how the final product, service, or result achieved the business needs

- A summary of risks and issues and how they were addressed

It's also worth noting that one of the key outputs of closing is the final product, service, or result transition, which refers to the handover of the deliverable to a different group or organization. This new group or organization could be the ongoing operations or support team if this is the end of the project, or it could be a different project team if it's the end of the phase.

 ## Transition Readiness

Before the final deliverable can be moved to ongoing operations, production, or go-live, the project manager must plan this transition. Just like any project activity, the handover to ongoing operations needs to be adequately planned for a smooth transition.

For example, after you have a built a new machine to replace two existing machines in a manufacturing plant, you can't immediately go ahead and replace that machine without a plan. The whole production line needs to stop, end users and their supervisors need training, operating procedures and guideline documents need to be created, and the machine needs to be tested after installation and before production resumes. All this activity needs a proper plan.

Failure to adequately plan this transition can lead to failure in delivery of the product, and it would be unfortunate to have a project go smoothly up to this point only to fail at transition.

The project manager and team need to determine the readiness of the organization, end users, and other stakeholders to accept the new deliverable and start the transition. They need to determine what processes are affected, which teams are affected, who needs training, when that training will take place, how that training is to occur, who will provide the training, where the transition and training are to be documented, and so on.

This plan is documented in the transition plan (also known as the implementation plan and the rollout plan) and includes the procedures for the following:

- **Transition readiness:** This step determines whether the organization is ready to accept this new product, deliverable, increment, or service.

- **Knowledge transfer:** This process educates the ongoing operations team or the customer on the use of the product or service and things to watch out for when operating the deliverable.

- **End-user/customer training:** This task ensures that the customer and end users know how to use the product or service.

- **Communication:** This procedure provides communication protocols regarding the use of the product or service, including any escalation procedures for support and maintenance.

- **Post-implementation support** (also known as *DevOps* or *hypercare*): This procedure documents how to support the new product or service.

NOTE   DevOps refers to a method or shared approach for a smooth delivery by improving communication and collaboration between the development and operations teams.

One could argue, "Shouldn't we have this in place already?" or "Shouldn't this have been planned at the beginning of the project?"

Possibly, but not necessarily. Remember the term *progressive elaboration*. Plans are created and updated as and when necessary. Often on a project (even predictive projects) you do not know how to transition to go-live or operations until after the deliverable has been built and tested.

NOTE   The steps, activities, and principles discussed in this chapter refer to predictive projects and refer to both closing a project or a phase of the project. Depending on the size and nature of the project, the assessment of transition readiness might be needed when moving from one phase to the next, especially if the next phase will be performed by a different team. The new team will need to understand what has been created so far.

On predictive projects, a project closeout meeting may be scheduled with the customer to obtain final acceptance of the delivered scope.

On adaptive (agile) projects, the transition of the product increment for each iteration is handed to the product owner, and the close of each sprint or iteration occurs during the sprint retrospective ceremony where the agile team discusses lessons learned. They discuss what went well, what went badly, and what can be improved. This discussion should not be an opportunity to point fingers but should be a productive meeting to improve processes, procedures, and team performance for future sprints. The sprint retrospective meeting usually ends with a brief discussion about the next sprint. Often, other key stakeholders attend this meeting too.

Hybrid projects tailor the transition based on the project and situation, but generally transition and handover happen incrementally to the customer.

Benefits Realization

Effective transition of deliverables increases the likelihood of success and ***benefits realization***. The timeline of when the project benefits are achieved depends on the life cycle and nature of the project. On adaptive projects, benefits may be realized at the end of each sprint. On predictive projects, they are realized after the product has moved to production or ongoing operations. The benefits might be realized immediately, or it might take some time (months or even years).

For example, if you are developing a new product that is expected to increase sales by $200 million a year, reaching that goal and realizing the benefit could take several years. In contrast, a process improvement project might yield the benefit immediately.

Benefits realization and the procedures for achieving the benefits are documented in the ***benefits management plan***, which is initially developed with the benefits owner prior to project initiation (along with the business case). The benefits management plan is updated at the closing of the project and reviewed during the transition to ongoing support.

After the product is delivered to the customer, continued improvements are often needed to gain the full realization of benefits:

- On predictive projects, any such improvements or modifications might be a new project.

- On adaptive projects, any improvements or modifications might be planned for a future sprint.

- On hybrid projects, such procedures need to be tailored, depending on the methodology and approach used.

During the transition process to ongoing support, the project team is responsible for delivering the product or service that will provide the benefit to the customer organization. Additionally, the team does the following:

- Provides planned performance data

- Collaborates with business owners to determine business realization metrics

- Analyzes any remaining risks that may affect the realization of benefits

- Provides any technical information needed for using the product or service

On predictive projects, the customer ensures that benefits are being realized and adopts any improvements and modifications to sustain the realization of benefits. The customer also does the following:

- Compares actual performance to plan (including any key performance indicators [KPIs])

- Identifies risks affecting the delivered benefits

- Identifies any processes and tools needed to ensure continued benefits realization

On adaptive projects, the product owner works with the customer to identify any improvements or upgrades needed. The product owner also does the following:

- Collaborates with the team to determine suitable metrics to measure performance

- Identifies and monitors risks

Throughout the transition process, the *benefits owner* works with the project manager and team to ensure that the planned benefits are realized as appropriate. They ensure measurement metrics are created and analyzed, and they report the realized benefits to management.

On a predictive project, the benefits owner could be the sponsor, operations manager, or a business analyst.

On adaptive projects, the product owner has this responsibility.

Exam Preparation Tasks

As mentioned in the section "How to Use This Book" in the Introduction, you have a couple of choices for exam preparation: the exercises here, Chapter 17, "Final Preparation," and the exam simulation questions on the Pearson Test Prep practice test software.

Review All Key Topics

Review the most important topics in this chapter, noted with the Key Topic icon in the outer margin of the page. Table 15-2 lists a reference of these key topics and the page numbers on which each is found.

Table 15-2   Key Topics for Chapter 15

Key Topic Element	Description	Page Number
Paragraph	Administrative closure	492
Paragraph	Phase gate	493
Section	Closing Activities	494
Section	Transition Readiness	496
Section	Benefits Realization	498

Define Key Terms

Define the following key terms from this chapter and check your answers in the glossary:

administrative closure, phase gate, kill point, transition plan, final report, DevOps, hypercare, benefits realization, benefits management plan, benefits owner

Review Questions

1. The project team has completed the third phase of the project, and the project manager is in a meeting with other key stakeholders to review the project and discuss its future. Due to several external factors and major risks, they decided to cancel the project. This review and the subsequent decisions are best referred to as what?

    a. Stage gate and phase gate

    b. Termination gate and phase end

    c. Go-live and kill point

    d. Phase gate and kill point

2. Which of the following are benefits of the administrative closure process? (Choose two.)

    a. Project information is archived.

    b. Team members are released to pursue new endeavors.

    c. The deliverables are accepted.

    d. Milestones have been achieved.

    e. The product successfully moves to ongoing operations.

3. The final project report contains all of the following information except which one?

    a. A summary of the how the final product achieved the business need

    b. A summary of risks and issues and how they were addressed

    c. A summary-level description of the project or phase

    d. A summary and official authorization for the project to begin

4. You are in the process of administrative closure and have collected project records, ensured vendor contracts are closed, and prepared the final report. What should you do next?

    a. Archive project documents

    b. Get formal acceptance from the customer

    c. Validate scope

    d. Verify the product acceptance criteria have been met and close out the project

5. Your organization has recently moved to an adaptive project environment. You are coaching the team and advising key stakeholders who have no prior agile experience. They are trying to understand the closing process in agile. How would you advise them?

    a. Explain that the closeout happens during project delivery at the end of the project.

    b. Explain that the closeout occurs at the end of each sprint during the sprint review meeting.

    c. Explain that the closeout occurs during the sprint retrospective.

    d. Explain that the closeout occurs when key stakeholders have approved the deliverable.

6. Your software development project is reaching its end. This is a completely new system that is replacing the old legacy system, and no one in the organization has ever used this new system before. You are demonstrating the final system capabilities to key stakeholders before you go live, and they are very impressed with what they are seeing. They agree that the system is ready to go live. What should you do next?

    a. Ensure the organization is ready to go live.

    b. Move the system to go live as soon as possible and sunset the old system.

    c. Start archiving project documents.

    d. Update lessons learned.

In this chapter, we cover two additional topics that you need to know for the exam; these topics span across all the PMP domains, knowledge areas, and process groups. Here we cover the following topics:

- **Tailoring:** Learn the approach to tailoring the project management processes.

- **Organizational Change Management:** Examine changes to an organization due to internal and external environmental factors.

## CHAPTER 16

More Things to Know

Two topics are relevant to many chapters of this book, and there is no clear defining chapter to which they belong. In this chapter, we discuss tailoring and organizational change management. We discuss the principles related to the *PMBOK® Guide*, Sixth Edition, the *PMBOK® Guide*, Seventh Edition, and the Exam Content Outline (ECO).

Tailoring and organization change management are relevant to all the tasks of the PMP Exam Content Outline:

Domain	Task #	Exam Objective
People	Task 1	Manage conflict
People	Task 2	Lead a team
People	Task 3	Support team performance
People	Task 4	Empower team members and stakeholders
People	Task 5	Ensure team members/stakeholders are adequately trained
People	Task 6	Build a team
People	Task 7	Address and remove impediments, obstacles, and blockers for the team
People	Task 8	Negotiate project agreements
People	Task 9	Collaborate with stakeholders
People	Task 10	Build shared understanding
People	Task 11	Engage and support virtual teams
People	Task 12	Define team ground rules
People	Task 13	Mentor relevant stakeholders
People	Task 14	Promote team performance through the application of emotional intelligence
Process	Task 1	Execute projects with the urgency required to deliver business value
Process	Task 2	Manage communications

Domain	Task #	Exam Objective
Process	Task 3	Assess and manage risks
Process	Task 4	Engage stakeholders
Process	Task 5	Plan and manage budget and resources
Process	Task 6	Plan and manage schedule
Process	Task 7	Plan and manage quality of products/deliverables
Process	Task 8	Plan and manage scope
Process	Task 9	Integrate project planning activities
Process	Task 10	Manage project changes
Process	Task 11	Plan and manage procurement
Process	Task 12	Manage project artifacts
Process	Task 13	Determine appropriate project methodology/methods and practices
Process	Task 14	Establish project governance structure
Process	Task 15	Manage project issues
Process	Task 16	Ensure knowledge transfer for project continuity
Process	Task 17	Plan and manage project/phase closure or transitions
Business Environment	Task 1	Plan and manage project compliance
Business Environment	Task 2	Evaluate and deliver project benefits and value
Business Environment	Task 3	Evaluate and address external business environment changes for impact on scope
Business Environment	Task 4	Support organizational change

"Do I Know This Already?" Quiz

The "Do I Know This Already?" quiz allows you to assess whether you should read this entire chapter thoroughly or jump to the "Exam Preparation Tasks" section. If you are in doubt about your answers to these questions or your own assessment of your knowledge of the topics, read the entire chapter. Table 16-1 lists the major headings in this chapter and their corresponding "Do I Know This Already?" quiz questions. You can find the answers in Appendix A, "Answers to the 'Do I Know This Already?' Quizzes and Review Questions."

Table 16-1   "Do I Know This Already?" Section-to-Question Mapping

Foundation Topics Section	Questions
Tailoring	1–2
Organizational Change Management	3–4

CAUTION   The goal of self-assessment is to gauge your mastery of the topics in this chapter. If you do not know the answer to a question or are only partially sure of the answer, you should mark that question as wrong for purposes of the self-assessment. Giving yourself credit for an answer you correctly guess skews your self-assessment results and might provide you with a false sense of security.

1. Which of the following are benefits of tailoring the project management approach?

   a. Increased commitment from team members

   b. More efficient use of resources

   c. Customer-oriented focus

   d. All of these answers are correct.

   e. None of these answers are correct.

2. Which of the following is not a tailoring process step?

   a. Making continuous improvements

   b. Following the ADKAR Model

   c. Selecting the initial development approach

   d. Tailoring for the organization

3. You are managing a project to implement a business change to your organization. In doing so, you are documenting the plan for knowledge transfer, training, and readiness activities required to implement the business change. Which document are you updating?

   a. Change management plan

   b. Change control plan

   c. Project management plan

   d. Rollout plan

4. Which of the following are steps in the ADKAR Model? (Choose three.)

   a. Reinforcement

   b. Adjourning

   c. Desire

   d. Denial

   e. Accept

   f. Knowledge

Foundation Topics

Tailoring

PMI defines *tailoring* as the "adaptation of the project management approach, governance, and processes to make them more suitable for the given environment and work at hand."

Let's examine what this definition means! There are many project management methodologies and many ways of managing a project. Every project is unique, so the project manager and project team must apply and adjust tools, techniques, processes, and artifacts according to the situation. Project managers must adapt their leadership style, and team members then must adjust their ways of working appropriately. This process is known as *tailoring*, which occurs throughout the project. Adapting to the unique objectives, stakeholders, and the environment contributes to project success by maximizing value, managing constraints, and improving performance.

Tailoring involves understanding the project context, goals, and operating environment, and balancing competing demands of the project and the project environment. You need to tailor to better suit the organization, stakeholders, and environmental factors. Many factors impact the type and level of tailoring you should perform, such as size and duration of the project, criticality of the project, location, stakeholder demands, and team members' experience.

Following are some of the benefits of tailoring:

- Increased commitment from team members
- Customer-oriented focus
- More efficient use of resources

What to Tailor?

In the sections that follow, we discuss what you need to tailor on a project.

Life Cycle and Development Approach

Determining the life cycle approach—whether to use a predictive, iterative, incremental, adaptive, or hybrid life cycle—is an example of tailoring. If this is a predictive project, the project manager plans the phases and the length of each phase. Some phases might have multiple iterations, and some phases might be operated using an adaptive approach. For example, an office building construction and relocation project that involves relocating employees and computer equipment and updating new software requires a hybrid approach that could include a predictive life cycle for construction, an incremental life cycle for relocation, and an agile life cycle for the software upgrade. The project manager needs to tailor the procedures, processes, and artifacts accordingly.

Leadership Styles

As discussed in Chapter 9, "Managing Resources and the Team," there are many types of leaders and many characteristics of leaders. Project managers need to adjust their leadership style based on the situation, team, stakeholders, project life cycle, environmental factors, and the needs of the project. Consequently, you need to adjust your leadership style to manage conflict, lead your team, and perform processes more efficiently. Here are some factors to consider:

- **Team's experience:** Teams with more experience on the specific project might be more self-managing and require less leadership than inexperienced teams. If the project is new to the organization, generally more oversight and a more directive leadership style are usually needed.

- **Maturity of individual team members:** Team members who are well experienced and mature in a technical field might need less supervision and oversight than inexperienced team members.

- **Organization's governance structure:** Is the organization structure very much "top-down," where senior management staff is heavily involved in project decisions, or are the teams given autonomy to do what they need to? The structure can affect the project manager's leadership style.

- **Organizational culture:** The culture within an organization can determine the project manager's leadership style because the style determines the procedures that need to be followed, templates to use, senior management approvals needed, and so on.

- **Geographical location:** Project managers need to tailor their leadership style based on where the project is being conducted and adjust to factors such as availability of resources and external cultures of the location.

- **Distributed teams:** It is very common to have project teams geographically disbursed and working virtually, which can cause challenges to communication and collaboration.

This list is not exhaustive but provides a few factors to consider.

Process Tailoring

Tailoring project processes can aid in process improvement and help identify bottlenecks and inefficiencies. For example, you could use lean production methods using tools such as value stream mapping and lessons learned (or retrospectives in agile) for process improvement.

Tailoring processes for the life cycle and development approach used can include the processes that need to be modified, removed, or added, blended, or aligned. Blended means that you are mixing various elements of different processes; aligned means there are standard definitions or terminology and approaches on large projects with many project teams.

Engagement

It is the project manager's responsibility to engage and collaborate with stakeholders and team members and to support team performance. However, everyone is an individual, so engagement styles vary with leadership style. Some examples of engagement tailoring might include

- **People:** Evaluating capabilities and skill sets of team members to determine their project assignment can determine their engagement and motivation. For example, a project with a tight deadline will be better served employing experienced team members rather than inexperienced. Alternatively, team members might need to attend training to improve their skill sets.

- **Empowerment:** This refers to determining the responsibilities, authorities, and decision-making capabilities bestowed on team members. Depending on the situation, some team members have a high degree of authority to make decisions, whereas some have low. For example, on agile projects, the team has the authority to make decisions, but on predictive projects, the team might not have that level of authority.

- **Integration:** Project teams and stakeholders can come from many different departments and organizations, so you need to integrate and tailor communication and engagement among all contributors to achieve project success.

Tools, Methods, and Artifacts

Selecting the right machine and tools for the appropriate work is a type of tailoring, and the project manager and project team determine the appropriate tools and techniques to use. Likewise, tailoring project artifacts and templates ensures efficient use of these documents.

Way of Working (WoW)

The way of working (also known as WoW) determines how the team will work together and includes the types of management approaches and team relationships that may evolve.

Performance Domains

All the performance domains we have discussed in this book are tailored according to the situation and project. Following are some examples:

- **Stakeholders:** The number of stakeholders, location, internal and external environment, and technology may determine the collaboration of stakeholders.

- **Project team:** Physical location, diversity, experience, employee versus contractor, and special needs or training are factors to tailor leadership of your team.

- **Development approach and life cycle:** As discussed in this chapter, you need to determine and tailor the appropriate life cycle for the project.

- **Planning:** Plans are impacted by internal and external factors and must be progressively elaborated throughout the project and adjusted accordingly.

- **Project work:** Information needs to be collected throughout the project to determine the performance. What information is collected; how it is collected; and how it is recorded, transmitted, and communicated are tailored for the project. For example, are you having regular status meetings or sending out status emails or using information radiators?

- **Delivery:** You might need to tailor how value is to be delivered. For example, are you delivering value each sprint, increment, or end of the project?

- **Uncertainty:** Risks are a major constraint on the project, and the stakeholders' risk appetite and tolerance could determine the tailoring approach.

- **Measurement:** You need to tailor how value is measured and how the project is monitored and controlled based on the situation. How work performance data is captured and converted to work performance information varies based on the situation. Likewise, how the information is reported and when will differ and will need to be tailored (such as charts, reports, and graphs).

The Tailoring Process

Prior to any tailoring, you need to understand the project environment. The tailoring process involves the following steps:

Step 1.   Select the initial development approach.

Step 2.   Tailor for the organization.

Step 3.   Tailor for the project.

Step 4.   Make continuous improvements.

Let's look at each of these steps.

Step 1: Select the Initial Development Approach

The project manager, project team, and other subject matter experts apply their knowledge of the product, delivery cadence, and other factors to determine the best methodology and development approach for the project. They might employ the use of information tools, such as suitability filters, to determine the validity of the tailored approach.

Step 2: Tailor for the Organization

Per PMI, tailoring for the organization involves adding, removing, and reconfiguring elements of the development approach to make it more suitable for the organization. The level of tailoring depends on the situation. For example, a small project that impacts one small department may not need as much oversight as a large safety-critical project impacting groups of external customers. Such projects require additional processes for approval, preventive actions, and issue resolution. The Project Management Office (PMO) or Value Delivery Office (VDO) might be involved in reviewing and approving tailored delivery approaches.

Step 3: Tailor for the Project

The project processes, tools, and artifacts need to be tailored due to many factors, such as

- Compliance, industry, and technology available

- Time frame and budget

- Project team size, location, and experience

- Location and availability of the customer
- Organizational and external cultures

Step 4: Make Continuous Improvements

It is important to understand that tailoring is not a one-time process but is performed continuously throughout the project to ensure you are producing the deliverable in the most efficient way. Preventive actions and continuous improvement are effective tools for proactive decision-making and help keep the team engaged throughout the project. Such team engagement can also lead to innovation and improvement instead of settling for the status quo.

Organizational Change Management

How an organization manages change is a key factor for business success. The external business environment is constantly changing, and not adapting to change or not responding rapidly enough can have far-reaching consequences for organizations. We have seen many examples of business failures over the years because management failed to adequately respond to change. Companies such as Blockbuster, Kodak, and Nokia once used to be market leaders in their industry, but they either went out of business or have a much lower market share because they were unable to respond to the changing business environment.

How do organizations adjust and respond to change? By doing projects, of course!

By the very definition, a project is a change. It is creating something unique, something different to what you had before (remember the definition of a project is "a temporary endeavor to create a unique product, service, or result"). Organizations create projects and embrace change as a strategy to balance investment and risk, be more flexible, and ensure maximum ROI. They embrace change as a strategic business activity, and PMOs build and sustain alignment between projects and the organization.

Organizational changes are needed for many different reasons. The following are just a few common examples of the reasons for organizational change:

- Changes in customers' needs
- PESTLE, TECOP, and VUCA factors (see Chapter 13, "Uncertainty")
- The adoption of new technology
- Mergers and acquisitions

- Changes in management

- A private company becoming public

- The adoption of a new business model

- Competition

- External and internal environmental changes (also referred to as enterprise environmental factors, or EEFs)

However, just like any project, organizational change must also be planned, addressed, and properly controlled throughout the life cycle. Generally, organizational changes might be unpopular with employees and possibly be met with resistance. Organization culture is therefore a key factor in the planning of these projects. Whether employees embrace the change or resist the change can determine its ultimate success or failure. For example, for a brand-new startup company, constant change is going to be inevitable while the company finds its place in the market. In such companies, employees should expect and embrace change. By contrast, a large established company where the average tenure of employees can be counted in decades might experience pushback when trying to implement major changes to the organization.

Plan for Change

Planning for the change transformation is key. Instead of making one huge change that is often unsustainable, it is much more efficient to make small incremental changes that are easier handle, are more likely to be accepted, and allow for increased employee buy-in. Just as in any project, every action needs to be properly planned and executed for success. Often this plan is documented in the *rollout plan* and includes knowledge transfer, training, and readiness activities required to implement the business change. An organizational change project is planned, executed, and monitored and controlled just like any project. The tools, artifacts, and processes we have discussed in this book would be relevant for a change management project too. Any of the life cycles previously discussed (predictive, adaptive, iterative, incremental, or hybrid) would also apply to change management projects.

NOTE Per PMI, the rollout plan is not included as a component of the project management plan.

As a project manager, you need to define how the change will be communicated and accepted and how employees will be trained. In addition, you might include attitudinal surveys to gauge how people are feeling about the change and plan information sharing sessions to ensure people are familiar with the new process. Often, people resist change due to the uncertainties associated with the change. We have already stated many times that communication, engagement, and collaboration are keys to a successful project—no more so than a project that requires an organizational change.

As a project manager managing your team through organizational changes, you should coach, mentor, and support your teams through knowledge transfer and regular information sharing. You should keep knowledge current and improve processes. You also need to avoid forcing any changes and alienating people because change can breed conflict.

PMI created a ***Brightline® Initiative*** to support executives who need to know how to bridge the gap between strategy and execution. It also offers resources on change management relevant to project managers and teams who work in environments undergoing change transformation. The Brightline® Initiative consists of five building blocks directed toward the leaders of an organizational transformation; these building blocks consist of the following:

- A ***North Star statement*** articulates the vision and strategic objectives of the transformation and needs to be concise.

- Leaders need to understand customer insights and global megatrends (like PESTLE but customer focused). They also need to understand what is impacting the business and driving the change.

- Leaders need to use an adaptable cross-functional transformation operating system employing rapid response teams and savvy project professionals who can execute a transformation strategy to empower the change (not a hierarchical top-down approach from senior management).

- Leaders need to use volunteer champions from inside the organization to drive the transformation (not external consultants).

- They also need to aim for inside-out employee transformation (similar to ADKAR).

It is highly unlikely you will get any detailed questions on this initiative. Just know it exists.

Change Models

Many organizational change management models focus on addressing how the organization will transition from the current to the future desired state. In the sections that follow, we describe a few of the common models. Although you don't need to memorize all the aspects of these models, you should have a basic understanding.

Managing Change in Organizations: A Practice Guide

Managing Change in Organizations: A Practice Guide is an iterative model based on several change management models; it is focused on many feedback loops for optimum success. The basic framework is as follows:

- **Formulate change:** Help people understand the rationale for the change.

- **Plan change:** Determine the work required to successfully implement the change.

- **Implement change:** Execute the plan, demonstrate the capabilities, ensure positive impact, and make necessary improvements.

- **Manage transition:** Consider how to address any needs related to the change that might surface when the future state is achieved.

- **Sustain change:** Ensure the new capabilities continue and processes cease.

ADKAR® Model

The *ADKAR® Model* focuses on five sequential steps an individual must achieve when adapting to change:

Step 1. **Awareness:** In this step people identify the need for change.

Step 2. **Desire:** When people know why the change is necessary, there needs to be a desire to support the change.

Step 3. **Knowledge:** People need to understand the new processes, systems, and any new roles and responsibilities through training and education.

Step 4. **Ability:** This step refers to hands-on practice to demonstrate new skills and behaviors.

Step 5. **Reinforcement:** This step supports the sustainment of the change and can include rewards, recognition, feedback, and measurement.

Additional Change Models

The models described in the following sections are not necessarily needed for the PMP exam; however, they are mentioned in the *PMBOK® Guide*, Seventh Edition, and summarized here.

Kotter's 8-Step Model

Kotter's 8-Step Model is a top-down approach starting with senior management of the organization and is promoted down through the management layers to employees. The steps are as follows:

Step 1.   **Create urgency:** Identify the reasons for the change, including any opportunities and threats that drive the change.

Step 2.   **Form a powerful coalition:** Identify change leaders who can influence the change.

Step 3.   **Create a vision for change:** Create a vision statement to identify values guiding the change.

Step 4.   **Communicate the vision:** Communicate this vision through the organization.

Step 5.   **Remove obstacles:** Address and remove issues as appropriate.

Step 6.   **Create short-term wins:** Identify quick and easy successes to build momentum and support for the change.

Step 7.   **Build on the change:** Incorporate continued improvement.

Step 8.   **Anchor the changes on corporate culture:** Ensure the change becomes ingrained into the corporate culture.

Virginia Satir Model

The *Virginia Satir Model* addresses how people experience and cope with change and the purpose is to help team members understand their feelings, enabling them to navigate the change more efficiently. The components are as follows:

- **Late status quo:** Everything feels familiar, and people are comfortable with the current processes and procedures. People are in their comfort zone.

- **The foreign element:** The change is new, and people may resist adopting the change. They may ignore it or dismiss the relevance of the new change.

- **Chaos:** People are unfamiliar and may not be comfortable with the change. Their performance may drop, and they may feel anxious. Yet some will embrace the change and feel excited.

- **The transforming idea:** People begin to see a way out of the chaos as they get comfortable with the change.

- **Practice and integration:** People implement the change into their day-to-day work.

- **New status quo:** This new environment becomes their new norm.

Transition Model

The *Transition Model* identifies three stages of transition in an attempt to provide an understanding of what occurs to individuals psychologically when an organizational change takes place.

- **Ending, losing, and letting go:** Change is introduced and often associated with fear, anger, uncertainty, denial, and resistance.

- **The neutral zone:** As the change is happening, some people might feel frustration, resentment, confusion, and anxiety, leading to reduced performance. However, some people may embrace the change and be more creative and innovative.

- **The new beginning:** People accept and embrace the change as they get used to it.

Summary of the Roles on a Project

Throughout this book, in various places we have mentioned several roles found in predictive and agile projects that you need to know for the PMP® exam. Here we have summarized these roles for quick access:

- **Stakeholder:** Any individual, group, or organization that is positively or negatively impacted by the project or can have a positive or negative influence on the project.

- **Sponsor:** Provides funding for the project; signs, publishes, and issues the project charter. Can be an individual, group of individuals, senior management, the PMO, or an external organization.

- **Project team:** Everyone involved on the project who are performing the work of the project or making decisions about it.

- **Project management team (project leadership team):** Key stakeholders that make strategic decisions about the project. They are a subset of the project team and are sometimes referred to as the steering committee.

- **Project manager:** Accountable for the project. Collaborates with stakeholders to drive results and is responsible for meeting stakeholders' expectations and leading the team. On a predictive project they are "large and in charge."

- **Functional manager:** Provides resources for the project (team members). The project manager often needs to negotiate resources with the functional manager. The functional manager often has no direct role on a project other than providing team members.

- **Business analyst:** Focuses on and defines the collection of requirements. Possesses knowledge of the business environment and customer and works to ensure value delivery. Often bridges the gap between the business and technical teams. The business analyst defines what the deliverable will be, whereas the project manager defines how to achieve it.

The following roles are specific to agile projects:

- **Team facilitator (servant leader, scrum master):** Encourages collaboration between agile team members. Removes impediments and ensures that the team has the tools to complete the work. Facilitates rather than manages. Hosts the daily standup meeting and often serves as the agile coach.

- **Product owner:** Represents the business (customer). Prioritizes user stories to create the product backlog and approves items delivered during the sprint review.

- **Agile team:** Is self-organizing and includes all the roles needed on the team, including developers, testers, business analysts, and designers. Possesses cross-functional proficiencies with T-shaped skills.

Exam Preparation Tasks

As mentioned in the section "How to Use This Book" in the Introduction, you have a couple of choices for exam preparation: the exercises here, Chapter 17, "Final Preparation," and the exam simulation questions on the Pearson Test Prep software online.

Review All Key Topics

Review the most important topics in this chapter, noted with the Key Topic icon in the outer margin of the page. Table 16-2 lists a reference of these key topics and the page numbers on which each is found.

Table 16-2 Key Topics for Chapter 16

Key Topic Element	Description	Page Number
Section	Life Cycle and Development Approach	509
Section	Leadership Styles	510
Section	Process Tailoring	511
Section	Engagement	511
Section	Performance Domains	512
Section	Plan for Change	515
Section	ADKAR Model	517

Define Key Terms

Define the following key terms from this chapter and check your answers in the glossary:

tailoring, rollout plan, Brightline® Initiative, North Star statement, *Managing Change in Organizations: A Practice Guide*, ADKAR® Model, Kotter's 8-Step Model, Virginia Satir Model, Transition Model

Review Questions

1. You are a well-experienced project manager who has successfully managed many projects in the past. You are now managing a project in a foreign country that you have never been to before, and the culture is different to what you are used to. Due to these cultural differences, some team members have not been responsive to some of your requests. What should you do?

   a. Adjust your leadership style according to the culture.

   b. Escalate the issue to the team members' functional manager.

   c. Set up a meeting with each of the team members in question, demanding an explanation of why they are not responding to you.

   d. Continue following up with them until you get a response.

2. Who is responsible for tailoring project processes and procedures?

   a. The project manager

   b. The team

   c. The project manager and the team

   d. The project manager, team, and sponsor

3. Which of the following is not included in the rollout plan?

   a. Knowledge transfer

   b. Transition readiness

   c. Procedures for customer acceptance of the deliverable

   d. End-user training

4. Which of the following would least likely result in an organizational change management project?

   a. Merger and acquisition

   b. The adoption of a new business model

   c. Systems upgrade

   d. A private company going public

## CHAPTER 17

Final Preparation

Now that you've read this book, answered the DIKTA questions, and done the quiz questions at the end of each chapter, how do you go about preparing for the final exam?

First, understand that technique is the key to passing the exam. The PMP exam does not just test your knowledge of the subject matter. It also tests the application of your knowledge to the ambiguous and challenging situations the PMP exam throws at you! There are many different writing styles employed in the exam questions, and with them, many different styles of questions. The exam mixes topics together, and you might need to think outside the box to choose the best out of the option choices. You must therefore take the practice exams that come with this book and consistently score in the upper 70 to 80 percent range to be confident of your readiness to take the real exam.

This chapter covers the information that is necessary to pass the exam; however, most people need more preparation than simply reading the first 16 chapters of this book. This chapter, along with the Introduction, suggests activities and a study plan to help you complete your preparation for the exam.

Exam Technique

The purpose of this section is to give you some basic tips and pointers on how to approach PMP exam questions.

Please understand that this list is not exhaustive; there are many new tricks and curveballs that PMI can introduce in exam questions. However, by understanding these basic approaches, you will be able to apply these skills to any kind of situation that PMI throws at you on the real exam. You must practice the following skills by taking the practice exams.

1. Read the last sentence first.

2. Learn to pick out key words and phrases.

3. Pick the best option.

4. Eliminate bad options.

5. Recognize when only one option addresses the question.

6. Understand predictive versus agile.

7. Understand real-world terminology versus PMI terminology.

8. Use the correct terminology in the right context.

9. Understand the purpose of all documents.

10. Follow all PMI processes.

11. Be aware of other considerations.

1. Read the Last Sentence First

You might come across some bait-and-switch questions where the scenario is irrelevant to the question. Always start by reading the last sentence first because the last sentence usually is the question. You can answer some questions by simply reading the last sentence and looking at the option choices. If the scenario is irrelevant, reading the scenario before the question can sometimes cloud your judgment.

Even when the scenario is relevant, some irrelevant information might be given. By focusing on the last sentence first, you ensure an understanding of the question initially. This approach then makes it easier to pick out key words and phrases and eliminate distractors and irrelevant information.

2. Learn to Pick Out Key Words and Phrases

Sometimes an entire question can hinge on one key word or phrase. It is important you be able to pick out these key words and phrases. Sometimes the key word or phrase could be in the question (the last sentence). Sometimes the key word or phrase could be in the scenario, or sometimes in one of the option choices. Sometimes those key words or phrases could be things like *first, last, always, never, not, least likely,* or *most likely.* If you miss these words or read them incorrectly, that can change the entire context of the question. Always be careful of these types of words and phrases.

3. Pick the Best Option

Many times, there is no clear-cut definitive answer. In these situations, you have to learn to pick the best option. Sometimes the best option might include all the other options (for example, options A, C, and D are all included in B). Sometimes the best option is the more detailed answer. Many times, the correct choice can depend on a key word or phrase. Look for options that

- Engage the team.

- Collaborate with stakeholders.

- Are proactive rather than reactive approaches.

If the question asks what the project manager should do next, look for options that

- Update a document.

- Communicate with stakeholders.

- Engage the stakeholder or team.

- Analyze or investigate the situation.

- Identify the root cause of a problem.

4. Eliminate Bad Options

Sometimes the process of elimination can be challenging when picking out the best option. Eliminate options that have a negative tone to them, such as finger-pointing, or suggesting a person or team is at fault. Project managers need to be proactive, so any reactive approaches are generally incorrect.

Eliminate any nonsubstantive options—the ones that don't really have any meaning, such as "a good-quality process is really important" or "the PM has a calm, collective management style." There's no real functional implication of these terms, and such option choices are generally incorrect.

5. Recognize When Only One Option Addresses the Question

Sometimes picking the best option is as simple as realizing that only one of the options actually addresses the question. Although the other options might be true statements, if they don't address the question, they are not the correct answer.

6. Understand Predictive Versus Agile

It is very important to be able to distinguish between predictive and agile because questions might mix the option choices.

- In agile there is no real project manager per se, but the actual question might refer to the agile project manager. In this case, you assume that person to be the team facilitator, the Scrum master, or the agile practitioner. Any of these terms may be used.

- The project manager in a predictive environment is large and in charge and is accountable for all that transpires during the project. The team facilitator of an agile project is a servant leader.

- The team facilitator of an agile project does not delegate or assign tasks to the team. The project manager on a predictive project does. Make sure you can distinguish this difference when eliminating option choices.

- If you are stuck on an agile question, thinking of the Agile Manifesto can help in picking the best option.

7. Understand Real-World Terminology Versus PMI Terminology

Always be cognizant of the fact that the correct answer will use PMI terminology rather than terms you may use in the real world. For example, in reality, you might hire a project assistant, but there is no such role mentioned in the *PMBOK® Guide* or any other PMP exam material authorized by PMI. You can eliminate such real-world terms.

8. Use the Correct Terminology in the Right Context

In addition to ensuring you are not confusing real-world terms with PMI terms, you also need to ensure you are using the terms correctly. For example, in risk management, you *share* a positive risk (you do not share a negative risk), and you *transfer* a negative risk (you do not transfer a positive risk). If you see a scenario that describes a negative risk, you know *share*, or any of the other positive risk response strategies, is not a correct approach. Using the right terminology in the right context can help eliminate incorrect option choices.

9. Understand the Purpose of All Documents

We have discussed many documents and artifacts in this book. Make sure you understand the purpose of each of those documents because you may get some confusing questions around them. For example, a team charter documents the team's values and agreements, whereas the project charter is the authorization for the project to begin. Any document that is labeled a management plan always documents procedures and how to perform that particular area of the project.

Ensure you understand the purpose of all PMI documents.

Conversely, watch out for made-up terms and documents. For example, there is no PMI document called a dispute management plan. Always watch out for made-up terms!

10. Follow All PMI Processes

In reality, no project will ever utilize every single process and best practice that PMI advocates. Remember, PMI is simply setting a common standard that organizations pick and choose in the real world. For the purpose of the PMP exam, you should assume that all procedures and processes need to be followed. For example, if a project charter has not been written and you are halfway through the project, you work with the sponsor to write the project charter. If the WBS has not been created and you are nearing the end of the project, you still create the WBS.

11. Be Aware of Other Considerations

Other factors to be cognizant of when determining the correct option choice include the following:

- Documents are updated regularly.

- Project managers are proactively communicating with stakeholders and team members.

- Changes go through a formal change control process on predictive projects.

- If the project has not been baselined, you don't need to go through the change control process. After the project management plan has been baselined, any changes from that point need to be properly controlled via the change control process (for predictive projects).

- Agile allows for change. Any changes are entered into the product backlog and reprioritized.

- A register refers to current project documentation (an artifact), whereas a repository (such as the lessons learned repository) is historical information and refers to an organizational process asset (OPA).

- If the question regards a predictive project, and there is no indication about the type of organizational structure, assume you are in a strong matrix organization where the project manager is large and in charge. If it is an agile question, the team facilitator is a servant leader, but no such assumption about the type of organization can be made.

Study Plan and Tips

This section provides some standard advice on how to best prepare for the PMP exam. Although some of these tips do not apply to everyone, this section gives you a good, general idea of how you can save time and reduce the stress of preparing for and taking the actual PMP exam. Everyone has a unique style of studying, so you should tailor this approach to do what best works for you.

- If you enjoy studying as part of a group, try to form or join a study group. There are many PMP study groups online and in local areas that you can search for on the Internet.

- If you have a copy of the *PMBOK® Guide*, Sixth Edition, the *PMBOK® Guide*, Seventh Edition, or access to *Process Groups: A Practice Guide*, use them as a reference only rather than study material. The PMP exam is not based off any *PMBOK® Guide*, so try to refrain from using them for extensive studying. You may download the *PMBOK® Guide*, Sixth Edition, and the *PMBOK® Guide*, Seventh Edition, for free from the PMI.org website if you are a member of PMI.

- Develop a system and time frame for your studying. Set milestones and dates for completion of the chapters and review of this book. The downloadable study planner included on the companion website for this book will help you achieve this goal.

- Spread out your reading and studying over time. Because this is complex material, it is not easy to comprehend in a short period of time. Too much reading in a short time period can be overwhelming and lead to exhaustion and frustration.

- Do not try to cram all of your studying over one evening or one weekend! There is a lot of material, and you need to learn to apply these materials to the questions.

- Don't let your real-life, on-the-job project management experiences interfere with your study behaviors. Remember: You must pass the exam according to PMI principles and standards, not your perspective based on your industry and past experiences. This conflict can sometimes be difficult to overcome, especially for seasoned practitioners of project management.

- Read all the chapters of this book and successfully answer all the DIKTA questions and the end-of-chapter quizzes. Make sure you read and understand the explanations to the questions.

- If you feel you are weak in any chapter, make a second pass at that chapter.

- Review the key topics listed in the table at the end of each chapter or just flip the pages looking for key topics.

- Complete tables from memory. Instead of just rereading an important table of information, you will find some tables in the book have been turned into memory tables, an interactive exercise found on the companion website.

Memory tables repeat the table, but with parts of the table content removed. You can then fill in the table content to exercise your memory, and click to check your work.

■ Take a full 230-minute practice exam available with this publication. The Pearson Test Prep software provides a bank of unique exam-realistic questions available only with this book. The Introduction contains the detailed instructions on how to access the Pearson Test Prep software. This database of questions was created specifically for this book and is available to you either online or as an offline Windows application. As covered in the Introduction, you can choose to take the exams in one of three modes: Study Mode, Practice Exam Mode, or Flash Card Mode.

■ As you are taking any of the practice exams, pay special attention to exam techniques and strategies mentioned earlier in this chapter and practice those strategies and techniques.

■ After you have finished the practice exam, review every single question again, including the ones you got correct. Pay special attention to the explanations to ensure you understand why the correct option is correct and why the other options are incorrect.

■ For any areas that you are weak, study that chapter from the book again.

■ Take another 230-minute practice exam.

■ Repeat until you are consistently scoring in the upper 70 to 80 percent range. Repetitive exam taking has frequently been the best method to identify knowledge deficiencies and areas to concentrate on future studies.

For additional practice and explanation of topics, you may download the *PMP Certification Complete Video Course and Practice Test* available from O'Reilly media at https://tinyurl.com/PMP-CVC.

Answers to the "Do I Know This Already?" Quizzes and Review Questions

Chapter 2

"Do I Know This Already?" Quiz

1. **Answer B is correct.** It correctly highlights the two most important attributes of a project per PMI. Answers A and D are common best practices but do not speak to describing a project. Answer C is incorrect because it does not speak to a unique product, and the second part, like Answers A and D, do not describe a project.

2. **Answer C is correct.** It correctly states the first part of the PMI definition of project management. Answer A seems as though it could be correct and is an example of the trickiness that can be found on the PMP exam, but this is not part of the official definition. Answer B is incorrect because it is too narrow. Answer D is incorrect because it is also too narrow and is not always the correct approach.

3. **Answer D is correct.** It correctly lists three of the common eight functions associated with projects. Answers A, B, and C correctly list two of the eight common functions, but each has one that is not correct. For Answer A, it is *produce earned value analysis reports*. This function may be needed on certain projects, but it is not a common high-level function. For Answer B, it is *generate detailed schedules*. This function may be needed on a given project, but it is too specific and is not always applicable. For Answer C, it is *agile development*. This function would be part of the "perform work and contribute insights" function, and agile development is not always appropriate to meet the project goals.

4. **Answer B is correct.** It correctly identifies the three primary skill areas per PMI, and it combines terms from both the former and current PMI Talent Triangle. The other answers all look as though they could be correct, but each one is missing at least one of the three primary skill areas. For Answer A, it is business acumen, and communication is a part of leadership. For Answer C, it again is business acumen, and the items listed are

too specific and are subskills of either technical project management or leadership. For Answer D, *schedule development* and *facilitating meetings* are too specific and are subskills of technical project management and leadership, respectively.

5. Answer B is correct. A project is used to create, update, or improve a product. Answer A is incorrect because there are differences. Answer C is incorrect because it describes the purpose of the product and does not speak to the relationship with a project. Answer D is incorrect because although projects are part of program and portfolio management, a product may or may not be. This depends on how an organization implements product management.

6. Answer D is the best answer. Scope, schedule, and resources are the traditional three project constraints. Answer A is incorrect because *documentation* is not considered a project constraint. Answer B is incorrect because *executive sponsorship* is not considered an official project constraint, although it may be an example of a *risk* constraint. Answer C is incorrect because *PMO oversight* is not an official project constraint.

7. Answer D is the best answer. This answer best summarizes the difference in the roles on hybrid agile projects. Answer A is incorrect because the roles are distinct and have different focus areas. Answer B is incorrect because the *PM and Scrum master roles* are not interchangeable, even though it is common to see organizations try to fill both roles with the same person. Answer C is incorrect for similar reasons.

8. Answer A is the best answer. The three principles listed are among the Twelve Project Management Principles. Answer B is incorrect because *always prioritize schedule and budget over any other stakeholder concerns* is not considered a project management principle. Answer C is incorrect because *customize status reports for each stakeholder group* is not considered a project management principle. Answer D is incorrect because *address high-risk items first in the project work plan* is not considered a project management principle.

9. Answer C is the correct answer. Each of the five project management process groups is listed here. The other options are incorrect because they do not list all five correct process groups. Answer A is incorrect because *development, testing, and deployment* are not project management process groups, although they may be project phases. Answer B is incorrect because *implementation* is not a process group, and this option is missing the initiating process group. Answer D is incorrect because *business case development* is not a project management process group; it is missing the initiating process group, and the controlling process group is missing the monitoring component.

10. Answer B is the best answer. Each one of the three project management knowledge areas listed is a member of the official group of 10. The other options are incorrect because they have one option that is not an official project management knowledge area. Answer A is incorrect because *status report management* is not an official project management knowledge area. Answer C is incorrect because *issue management* is not an official project management knowledge area. Answer D is incorrect because *team management* is not an official project management knowledge area.

11. Answer C is the best answer. Each one of the three items listed is a performance domain of project management. The other options are incorrect because they have one option that is not an official project management performance domain. Answer A is incorrect because *integration management* is not a performance domain, but it is a knowledge area. Answer B is incorrect because *closing* is not a performance domain, but it is a process group. Answer D is incorrect because *leadership* is not a performance domain, but it is a core project manager skill needed across all performance domains.

12. Answer B is the best answer. As the project matures, all plans and projections become more accurate, and the levels of risk and uncertainty decrease. The other options are incorrect because they are referencing later stages of the project life cycle.

13. Answer D is the best answer. This is the official definition of a System for Value Delivery from PMI. Answer A is incorrect because it is more than a project management system; it is an organizational approach. Answer B is incorrect because it is more than a financial management approach focused on single projects. Answer C is incorrect because it excludes portfolios, programs, and operations, and it is not only focused on customer satisfaction.

14. Answer C is the best answer. This answer provides the best description of how all three are related. Answer A is incorrect because although the breadth of scope is generally larger from portfolio to project, this does not describe the relationship among the three. Answer B is incorrect because portfolio management is more than the financial management of the programs and projects within an organization, and it does not describe the relationship among them. Answer D is incorrect; a portfolio can consist of programs, projects, and operations.

15. Answer A is the best answer. These are the three general organizational structures per PMI. Answer B is incorrect because although hierarchical and team-oriented are features of the functional and project-oriented structures, that is not what they are called, and the matrix type is missing from this list. Answer C is incorrect because hierarchical is a feature of functional, and balanced

matrix is one of the subtypes of the matrix structure type. Answer D is incorrect because decentralized and centralized are features of project-oriented and functional structures, respectively, and the matrix type is not accounted for.

16. Answer C is the best answer. These are all process, data, or governance system resources that comprise the OPA. Answer A is incorrect because *organizational culture* and *infrastructure* are not considered OPA, but they are environmental factors. Answer B is incorrect because *market conditions* are an external factor and not considered part of OPA. Answer D is incorrect because *regulatory environment* is an external factor and not part of OPA.

17. Answer B is the best answer. These are the three PMO structures per PMI, depending on the amount of influence and control the PMO has over projects. Answer A is incorrect because *monitoring* and *executing* are project management process groups. Answer C is not a bad incorrect answer because the options do describe a key differentiator between the three types, but those are not official type names. Answer D is incorrect because *functional* is an organizational structure type, and *integrated* is not one of the types.

18. Answer D is the best answer. These are four of the stakeholder groups that a project has. Answer A is incorrect because the stakeholders are more than just the customers and end users. Answer B is close, but *competitor organizations* are not considered to be a project stakeholder group. Answer C is incorrect for the same reason Answer A was incorrect. This option is just describing the customers and end users.

Review Questions

1. Answer B is correct. Company policies are part of the organizational process assets (OPAs) because they are documents relating to the organization. The other options are all enterprise environmental factors (EEFs).

2. Answer D is correct. Standard operating procedures for your organization are part of the organizational process assets because they are documents relating to your organization. Any documents that impact your organization as a whole would be an OPA. Answer B is incorrect because current project documents are generally not considered an OPA until they are archived and become historical information. Answers A and C are incorrect because both *regulatory requirements* and *corporate culture* are EEFs.

3. Answer D is the best answer. All the choices given are technically correct; however, the best option would be the one that includes all the other options, which is quality, resources, schedule, and budget. The other two major constraints are scope and risk.

4. Answer B is the correct response. A project coordinator has limited authority to make decisions on the project. The fact that you have the authority to delegate tasks to team members implies that you have limited authority.

Thus, the other options are incorrect. If you had full authority, you would be the project manager. If you had no authority, then you would be a project expeditor. A team facilitator collaborates with the team to ensure they have the appropriate tools to perform the work

5. Answer C is correct. In a functional organization, the project manager has the least support and the least ability to control project resources. Answers A and D are incorrect because in a balanced matrix organization or project coordinator situation, the project manager would be empowered with more control over resources or would be able to leverage senior management to influence resource assignments. Answer B is incorrect because *tight matrix* deals with the colocation of project team members within a matrix organization and is not relevant to this question.

6. Answer D is correct. This statement accurately summarizes the goals of all projects. Technical leadership is not the most important element of effective project management. Therefore, answer A is incorrect. Answer B is incorrect because a project needs leadership at multiple levels and via multiple roles. Regardless of the size of the project, the project manager is expected to be the project leader. Therefore, answer C is incorrect.

7. Answer B is the best answer. This is a great example of where you are looking for the best response. Effective leadership, negotiation, and communication skills are important to the other three situations too, but the project team leadership aspect is where these skills are essential and where they will have the greatest impact on project success. Therefore, Answers A, C, and D are incorrect.

8. Answer C is correct. The project management processes should be executed for each project life cycle phase and/or iteration. Answer A is incorrect because the project management processes are used to manage the progress of the project life cycle, and project life cycle phases are not normally associated with controlling and executing processes, for example. Answer B is incorrect because it is the opposite of the correct choice. Answer D is incorrect because a relationship can exist between the initiating, planning, and closing processes and traditional project life cycle phases (such as concept, analysis, and closure).

9. Answer D is the best response. As explained in this question, recurring security vulnerability assessments with no end date cannot be considered a project. Projects must have time boundaries. Answer A is incorrect because the project product does not have to be directly related to an organization's System for Value Delivery. Answer B is incorrect because a security vulnerability assessment does create at least one product—the vulnerability assessment report. Answer C is incorrect because the lack of a specific start date in the question description would not automatically disqualify the assessment as a project.

10. Answer A is correct. In a balanced matrix, the project manager and functional manager work together to meet the needs of the department and the project. Answers B and C are incorrect because the functional manager has greater authority and would likely handle problems directly in a functional or weak matrix structure. Answer D is incorrect because the project manager would handle such issues directly in a project-oriented organization.

11. Answer C is the best option. On traditional prescriptive projects, stakeholder influence is greatest at the beginning of a project. When the initial objectives are being developed, the stakeholders have a lot of input. After the main project parameters are agreed upon, the project manager and project team start working on those objectives, and the stakeholder involvement decreases. Answer B is incorrect because the project manager, not the stakeholders, directs project activities. Answers A and D are incorrect because they do not accurately reflect stakeholder involvement on traditional projects.

12. Answer B is correct. The question states that training is not meeting the schedule, and the result is that the training is not getting people properly trained. This means both schedule and quality are suffering. Of all the solutions, Answer B provides the best description of the effects on your project. Answer A is incorrect because it does not mention the impact on project quality. Answer C is incorrect for several reasons. The problem might be the responsibility of the organization that supplied the trainers, but the responsibility for the impact on the project is the project manager's. Answer C also ignores the quality issue. Answer D is incorrect because it implies that the project manager padded the schedule. This is not an ethical practice. Your estimates should be realistic. If you expect such problems to occur, you should address them in the beginning of the project, along with appropriate recovery methods. By padding the schedule, you hide a real risk to the project.

Chapter 3

"Do I Know This Already?" Quiz

1. Answer D is correct. It correctly highlights why these aspects are important to project success per PMI. Answer A is true, but it is not the best choice from the possible answers. Answer B is incorrect because, although the development approach may influence the skills needed on the project, it certainly does not determine project duration. Answer C is incorrect because the exact opposite is closer to the truth.

2. Answer C is correct. It correctly states the relationship between the two and the factor of including all the work of the project. Answer A is incorrect because there is a difference. Answer B is incorrect but mostly true regarding development life cycle models; it is common to modify them per the needs of a

given project and is not the best answer option. Answer D is incorrect because it not accurate.

3. Answer B is correct. It correctly applies the definition per PMI. Answer A is incorrect because it describes the development approach. Answer C is incorrect because it describes a product life cycle. Answer D is incorrect because it references the project management process groups.

4. Answer B is correct. It correctly states the definition per PMI. Answer A is incorrect because it applies to all industries, not just the music industry. Answer C is incorrect because, although this may occur, it is not the proper definition and does not address the delivery of target deliverables. Answer D is incorrect because it has nothing to do with the verbal communication skills of the project manager. Answer E is incorrect because it is not about the number or duration of development iterations, although a project may need to use an agile or iterative approach to meet the delivery cadence requirements.

5. Answer D is correct because it states the primary difference between the two approaches. Answer A is incorrect because both approaches can be used for both physical and digital products, although iterative development is much easier with digital products. Answer B is incorrect because neither product improvement nor process improvement is a defining feature of these development approaches. Answer C is incorrect because there is a difference between the two, as previously indicated; often the terms are incorrectly used interchangeably in the real world because both approaches are often used simultaneously, especially on adaptive/agile projects.

6. Answer D is the best answer. Iterative and incremental development approaches, constant feedback loops, and a process that expects changes are common features of adaptive/agile development approaches. Answer A is incorrect because this is just a list of project phases most associated with predictive development approaches. Answer B is incorrect because *top-down management* is not considered a feature of adaptive/agile approaches. Answer C is incorrect because *focus on perfect product* is not a trait of adaptive approaches. The focus is on delivering a minimum viable product after each iteration.

7. Answer D is the best answer. This answer best summarizes all the variable groups that must be considered when selecting the best development approach. Answer A is incorrect because the project schedule is determined after the development approach and project life cycle are determined. Answer B is not the best answer. The factors listed are valid ones, but there are many others too. Answer C is incorrect because *desires of the project team* is not a primary consideration. The skills and experience of the project team with the development approach options are factors. Answer E is incorrect because different development approaches can be used within the same project.

8. Answer A is the best answer. The nature of the high risks will help determine which approach should be used. If the risks need to be mitigated through intensive analysis, detailed planning, rigorous testing, and documentation, a more predictive approach may be needed. If the risks are more focused on the feasibility of the product solution or on market/stakeholder acceptance, a more adaptive/hybrid approach may be best. Answers B, C, and D are incorrect because they state the option is always the best option.

9. Answer C is the correct answer. The type and nature of the deliverable determine which development approach options are available. From the development approach, the delivery cadence options are determined. After the development approach and delivery cadence are determined, the subsequent project phases and overall project life cycle can be finalized. The other options are incorrect because they do not list the relationship in the proper order.

10. Answers B and D are correct because both accurately describe the relationship between the two performance domains. Answer A is incorrect because *development approach selection* is a key aspect of initial project planning. Answer C is incorrect for the same reason.

Review Questions

1. Answer B is correct. An organization's performance management system is not a primary consideration for selecting the development approach. The other options are valid primary considerations.

2. Answers C and D are correct. Answer C describes a hybrid life cycle using a combination of predictive and agile approaches. Answer D describes an incremental approach. Answer A is incorrect because it describes an adaptive approach. Answer B is incorrect because it describes a predictive approach.

3. Answers A and D are correct. Answer A describes a predictive project life cycle. Answer D describes a hybrid project life cycle using an iterative development approach. Answer B is incorrect because it lists the project management process groups. Answer C is incorrect because it describes a product life cycle.

4. Answer C is the correct response. Given the nature of the deliverables involved, the need to manage the change aspects involved, and the culture maturity level in using pure adaptive approaches, it is most likely each deliverable will be developed and/or deployed using a hybrid approach with aspects of incremental and/or iterative methods. Answer A is incorrect due to the organizational maturity level. Answer B is incorrect because many, if not all, of these deliverables will benefit from elements of incremental and/or iterative development approaches to better manage stakeholder expectations, manage the change aspects, and coordinate deployments. Answer D is incorrect because the mobile application is most likely to benefit from adaptive

approaches, and the legacy application is most likely to use a predictive approach since there are fewer unknowns with this application.

5. Answer C is correct. Four aspects of agile/adaptive development approaches are tight collaboration within the team and between the business and the technical team, the approach expects and welcomes changes, the focus is on delivering work product frequently in two- to four-week intervals, and the teams are self-organizing. Answer A is incorrect because strong project management style and minimal business involvement are not defining characteristics. Answer B is incorrect because *focus on maximum product value* is not a defining characteristic. Actually, the focus is on delivering the minimum viable product each iteration. Answer D is incorrect because the schedule is not the highest priority in an agile approach.

6. Answer D is correct. While the goal of each sprint is to deliver a more valuable working product, the results of the sprint can be rejected or deemed not ready for production by the stakeholders. The other answers are incorrect because they all represent accurate characteristics of Scrum agile development approaches.

7. Answer B is the correct answer because it is an incremental development approach that involves developing and deploying the product in pieces. The other answers are incorrect because they are true statements about iterative and incremental development.

8. Answer C is correct. This is the name of the delivery cadence option that indicates multiple deliveries on a fixed schedule. Answer A is incorrect because it is the name of the delivery cadence option for delivering the product anytime and as frequently as needed. Answer B is incorrect because, although it would be an example of a periodic delivery cadence, a periodic cadence does not have to be monthly. Answer D is incorrect because iterative is a development approach and not a delivery cadence.

9. Answer D is the best response. Requirements certainty, ease of change, and safety and regulatory requirements are all valid deliverable variables when evaluating the best development approach to use. Answer A is incorrect because *organizational structure* is not a deliverable variable. Answer B is incorrect because *expected ROI* is not a typical variable when selecting a development approach, and certainly not a deliverable-based one. Answer C is incorrect because *the expected duration of the product life cycle* is not a variable when selecting a development approach.

10. Answer A is correct. A project life cycle can contain multiple development approaches and delivery cadences. These aspects are deliverable based, not project life cycle based. The remaining answers are incorrect because they are all valid statements.

Chapter 4

"Do I Know This Already?" Quiz

1. Answer D is correct. The project manager could potentially interact with any stakeholder on the project when performing project processes. Even though all the options are technically correct answers, they are all included in answer D.

2. Answer C is correct. The team's ground rules are found in the team charter (not project charter). The project charter is the formal authorization for the project to begin, and it contains high-level requirements, the scope, the business justification for doing the project, and any identified resources.

3. Answers A and D are correct. The purpose of the project charter is to authorize the project to begin and ensure stakeholders are on the same page regarding the purpose and scope of the project and its deliverables. It does not contain any detailed information about the budget, schedule, or deliverables. A detailed plan has not been performed at this stage, so no baselines have been established.

4. Answer C is correct. The project management plan is usually signed off by the project manager, sponsor, key stakeholders of the project leadership team, and key team members. However, during planning, a determination is made as to who will sign off on the project management plan. The term *all stakeholders* includes end users and vendors supplying raw materials, who do not sign off on the project management plan.

5. Answer B is correct. Being near the end of a sprint implies this is an agile project, so you don't need to go through the change control process. Nor do you decline. You simply add the requirement (user story) to the product backlog, and then the product owner will reprioritize.

6. Answer D is correct. The project management plan has not been approved yet and is therefore not baselined; it has been completed and sent to the key stakeholders for their approval. If a missing activity is identified at this stage, you can simply add it into the plan. After the approval has been given and a missing item found, the PM would need to go through the change control.

7. Answer B is correct. The metrics provided in the scenario are raw data, which is work performance data. Work performance information would be the interpretation of those results (such as "we are behind schedule or over budget"). There is no such term as *work performance figures*. A report is the representation of the information.

8. Answers A, C, and D are correct. Business value is the net quantifiable benefit of the business endeavor and can be tangible or intangible. A deadline or budget is not considered business value but is a project constraint. Answers A, C, and D are the benefits that may be attained after the project is over. Note that Answer D is an intangible benefit.

9. Answer B is correct. Of the options given, the next thing to do is perform an impact analysis. Although the scenario states that it's a quick and easy fix, there is no definition of what that actually means. An impact always involves quantified values (such as $3,000 or two weeks or one extra resource). Simply saying *major* fix or *minor* fix is not an impact.

10. Answer D is correct. The key is the word *version*. Because team members refer to different versions of the documents, you do not have a very good configuration management system in place. Change control is for managing changes to the deliverables (not updates to documents). Assigning one team member to update documents is not the most efficient use of resources. Although the file management system option sounds promising, the best, more detailed answer is configuration management.

Review Questions

1. Answer A is correct. The project manager is solely responsible for ensuring that all knowledge area processes and tasks of projects are being performed at the appropriate time. Whereas the tasks of other knowledge areas may be delegated to team members, the processes of integration can be performed only by the project manager because the PM brings all of these processes together as a unified whole.

2. Answer B is correct. Regardless of the urgency of the situation, you should always have a signed project charter before you can begin any work on the project. Thus, the correct approach is to wait until you have a signed project charter from the sponsor before proceeding.

3. Answers C and E are correct. Requirements documentation and the risk register are not components of the project management plan. The project management plan is made up of many documents classified as subsidiary plans, baselines, and additional components.

4. Answer C is correct. In agile, there is no baseline (no scope baseline or schedule baseline or cost baseline). Agile uses relative estimating, creates a product backlog, and uses a product roadmap. All the other options are agile artifacts.

5. Answer D is correct. Work performance information compares the actual results with the plan to interpret the results. In this case, knowing that you are 10 percent over budget means that you have compared the actual cost so far with the planned budget (or cost baseline). All the other options are work performance data because they are actual results or raw observations.

6. Answer A is correct. The scenario describes a hybrid approach, and each product increment is known as a minimum business increment. Each iteration

(sprint) delivers the smallest increment that will deliver value to the customer (one of the principles behind Agile).

7. Answer B is correct. Explicit knowledge is knowledge that is easily codified and tangible (reports, graphs, charts, pictures, and so on). Tacit knowledge is based on your experience and beliefs.

8. Answer B is correct. The correct PMI approach is to perform an impact analysis. In this situation, the scenario simply states that the problem is a *quick and easy fix* without delving into the definition of *quick and easy*. Without such metrics, you must always perform an impact analysis before submitting to the CCB for approval.

9. Answer D is correct. The scenario describes the team members looking at different versions of the code, so they failed to implement a configuration management system. Configuration management refers to accessing the latest version. This would not be updated in the communication management plan and is not necessarily a communication breakdown, eliminating Answers B and C.

10. Answer D is correct. All of these answer options would be correct, but the best option here is Answer D because it is inclusive of all the other options. The whole purpose of change control is to prevent unnecessary changes to the project. The project manager does this by performing the tasks mentioned in the other options.

Chapter 5

"Do I Know This Already?" Quiz

1. All of these responses would be considered stakeholders on your project. A stakeholder is any individual, group, or organization that is impacted by a project or can influence a project.

2. Answer B is correct. The question refers to the salience model and the stakeholder grid. In the salience model, the definitive stakeholders are the intersection of all three variables (power, legitimacy, and urgency), and so of the options given, that is the best answer. In the power and interest grid, the highest priority stakeholders would be the stakeholders who have high power and high interest. In the power and influence grid, it would be the stakeholders who have high power and high influence.

3. Answer B is correct. You have just identified a new stakeholder, so you update the stakeholder register. After updating the stakeholder register, you perform the other options.

4. Answer A is correct. On the power and interest grid, the status of a stakeholder who is low power but high interest would be "keep informed."

5. Answer C is correct. Stakeholders are identified throughout the project.

6. Answer A is correct. You never stop identifying stakeholders on your project while the project is still open. You can only stop identifying them after the project is officially closed. Even when you start the closing process, you may identify new end users, for example, thus making Answer B incorrect. Answer C is incorrect because you never know whether you have identified all stakeholders until the project is officially closed. Senior stakeholders should never tell you to stop identifying stakeholders; it is up to the project manager to ensure all stakeholders have been identified throughout the project.

7. Answer A is correct. Stakeholders' current and desired engagement levels are documented in the stakeholder engagement assessment matrix, and this is the document you will be reviewing here. The stakeholder management plan documents how to engage and collaborate with stakeholders. The stakeholder register documents all stakeholders and stakeholder groups. The resource calendar documents availability of resources on the project.

8. Answer B is correct. The key phrase in the question is *approach and strategy*, which implies you are looking for procedures to engage and collaborate with stakeholders. These strategies will be documented in the stakeholder engagement plan, which is a subsidiary document that makes up the project management plan (remember that any subsidiary plan documents procedures for the project). Answer A is incorrect because the stakeholder engagement assessment matrix documents the engagement levels of stakeholders (not how to collaborate with them). The salience model and the power and interest grid are classification models used to prioritize stakeholders.

9. Answer A is correct. Although they all look like decent options, the best answer is A because you need to communicate with stakeholders as necessary. Hosting weekly status meetings will be ineffective if stakeholders need information daily. Hosting daily status meetings will be inefficient if stakeholders need information weekly. Remember to always choose the best option because the perfect option will not always be there.

10. Answer D is correct. You should always choose the most proactive approach that will engage stakeholders the most. In this situation, although the stakeholders will benefit from the project, they are still resistant, so you need to find out why they are resistant and try to make them understand the goals and benefits of the project. The goals will be documented in the project charter and the benefits in the benefits management plan. Answer A is incorrect because *avoid giving them too much information* and *pushback* imply a negative tone; you need to engage and collaborate. Answer B sounds promising because

you do want to engage them as early as possible, but not every stakeholder will have a role and responsibility on a project (end users, for example, are stakeholders but may not be involved on the project). Answer C is incorrect here because, although you would update the stakeholder register and engagement assessment matrix, the question asks about the approach to handling this situation, not which artifacts to update.

Review Questions

1. Answer B is correct. You always want to engage the stakeholder, and of the options given, the best way is to involve them early and throughout the project. Never choose an option that tries to isolate key stakeholders or treat them in a negative manner. You always want to engage and collaborate.

2. Answer C is correct. Of the options given, the technical expert is least likely to be a stakeholder. You just refer to them for advice; there is nothing in the scenario that suggests they have anything to do with the project. A building inspector is a stakeholder because their decisions can impact the project. A vendor supplying you with raw materials is always a stakeholder, even if you did business with them once. If they delay the raw materials, then that can impact your project. End users are using your product, so they are stakeholders on the system's implementation project.

3. Answer C is correct. Any stakeholders who are outside of the organization would always be an outward influence. Upward relates to stakeholders who are hierarchically above you in the organization, downward relates to stakeholders hierarchically below you, and sideward relates to peer stakeholders within the organization.

4. Answer D is correct. Because this person is no longer a stakeholder, the first thing to do is update the stakeholder register to identify them as a non-stakeholder, which is a classification on the salience model. There is nothing in the scenario to suggest that the person leaving could be a risk for the project (do not make assumptions that are not there, which is very easy to do). You may notify your team, but the question asks what you should do "next." The next thing to do is to update the stakeholder register.

5. Answers A, C, and E are correct. Check sheet and statistical sampling are tools used in quality management (check sheet identifies quality issues and statistical sampling is used to test a representative sample of the population). All the other options could be used for identifying stakeholders.

6. Answer B is correct. Stakeholder engagement levels are documented in the stakeholder engagement matrix. In this case the question mentions "unaware" and "supportive," which are engagement levels. The stakeholder engagement

plan documents how you are going to engage your stakeholders. Salience models and power and interest grids show classifications of stakeholders.

7. Answer A is correct. The question describes the salience model, and the intersection of all three variables (power, legitimacy, and urgency) refers to a definitive stakeholder.

8. Answer C is correct. C means "current level of engagement," and D means "desired level of engagement." If C and D are in different columns, it means stakeholders' current engagement level is not the same as desired. Because there is a difference, this indicates that you need to take action to engage the stakeholders accordingly.

9. Answer C is correct. You will choose whichever option will engage the stakeholder, and in this case, it is reviewing the benefits of the project charter. If you continue writing the project charter, that is ignoring senior management, which is a reactive approach. You need to choose the most proactive approach. You also do not need to automatically comply with senior management's request because they are not the experts. It is up to you to collaborate with senior management to make decisions that are best for the project.

10. Answer A is correct. Stakeholder A is unaware of the project, but you want this person to be supportive, so your highest priority will be to determine why they are unaware and reach out to them so that they can become aware and supportive of your project. Stakeholders C and D both have "current" and "desired" status in the same box, meaning that they are at the engagement level you want them to be, so you don't need to spend a huge amount of effort in trying to engage them because they are already supportive. Stakeholder B, although neutral, would still be a stakeholder to reach out to, but they would not be your highest priority.

Chapter 6

"Do I Know This Already?" Quiz

1. Answers A, B, C, D, E (all of these answers) are correct. All of these options can lead to project failures related to scope.

2. Answer B is correct. The question asks about procedures (*determine the next steps*). Scope procedures are documented in the scope management plan. The other documents also need to be updated, but the question does not ask what needs to be updated.

3. Answers A and D are correct. Of the given options, only interviewing and observation are tools you can use for collecting requirements. An Ishikawa diagram is used to get to a root cause of an issue. A Pareto chart is used to show

critical issues in descending order of frequency. Backlog grooming is an agile activity that reprioritizes the product backlog.

4. Answer B is correct. Of the option choices, the best option is to update the scope statement because finishing a month earlier is a change to the schedule constraint. The other options do not document the schedule constraints. The scope management plan documents any changes to the procedures for developing the scope. The product backlog is a prioritized list of user stories, and the traceability matrix traces the requirements throughout the entire project lifecycle.

5. Answer D is correct. The scope baseline is made up of the scope statement, the WBS, and the WBS dictionary. It does not include tasks or activities, which is why the other options are incorrect.

6. Answer B is correct. The WBS does not contain the details of any work packages. Instead, these details (such as dependencies between work packages) are shown in the WBS dictionary. The other options are true statements.

7. Answer C is correct. Validate Scope is the process of accepting the deliverable, which is performed by the customer. The customer tests and verifies before accepting. The team's testing of the deliverable is known as control quality.

8. Answer D is correct. Ensuring that scope changes go through the proper change control process is Control Scope, an important role of the project manager. Although it is vital to engage stakeholders throughout the project, the scenario itself does not describe stakeholder engagement, making Answer A incorrect. Scope creep is the uncontrolled expansion of work, whereas the scenario describes that you are controlling the expansion, making Answer B incorrect. The customer validates the scope, not the project manager, making Answer C incorrect.

9. Answer B is correct. User stories should be small and independent. If the user stories are large, they should be broken down to smaller user stories. You do not reassign user stories or assign additional team members because the team members themselves determine the tasks that they will work on in agile.

10. Answer D is correct. User stories should be of the form: "As a *<Role>*, I want *<Functionality>*, so that *<Business benefit>*," and the only option that fits this template is Answer D. The travel agent option is missing the business benefit, so it needs to be broken down further. The four-bedroom house option is a scope, not a user story. The blue wall option is a requirement on a predictive project rather than a user story for agile projects.

Review Questions

1. Answer C is correct. Because the customer didn't request this additional functionality, and because this was not in the original scope of the project, this

change would be considered gold-plating and should have gone through the change control process.

2. Answer D is correct. The scenario describes a new procedure that has been identified for collecting requirements, so the first thing to do is to update the requirements management plan. Only after that would you reach out to the managers to introduce yourself and collect any additional requirements (which would need to go through a change control process if not part of the original scope of the project). After you have identified who they are, you would update the stakeholder register (the scenario does not say that you have identified the managers, only that there is a new procedure).

3. Answer B is correct. The requirements traceability matrix traces the requirements throughout the project lifecycle. In this case because the activities do not tie back to any requirements, this implies a lack of requirements traceability matrix. The original PM may well have created a detailed set of requirements, but the activities did not tie back to the requirements (making Answer A incorrect). The WBS does not contain activities (making Answer C incorrect). A change control process may well have been in place, but it might not have been followed (making Answer D incorrect).

4. Answer D is correct. The scope statement is a detailed description of the project's deliverables and the work required to create those deliverables. It includes the scope description, acceptance criteria, deliverables, inclusions, exclusions, constraints, assumptions, and requirements, which will be more informative to the senior manager than the other options give. The business case is too high level. The WBS shows the work that needs to be done but does not include assumptions, constraints, acceptance criteria, and so on. The scope management plan documents how to develop the scope.

5. Answers A and C are correct. The scope baseline is made of the WBS, WBS dictionary, and the scope statement. The work package is part of the WBS, so is included on the scope baseline. Tasks and requirements are not part of the scope baseline. The scope baseline is used to create tasks and activities. Requirements are needed to create the scope the baseline.

6. Answer A is correct. There is a lot of information in the scenario, so you have to pick the appropriate information carefully. The customer's observation and testing of the deliverable are validating scope. The team's testing is quality control, making both C and D incorrect. The impact has already been done by the team lead (they've found the root cause, and it will take 15 hours to fix), so you will not need to do an impact analysis; you can just submit the change request.

7. Answer D is correct. Validate Scope is the process of accepting the deliverable, which is performed by the customer. The team's testing is quality control. In

the scenario, because the project manager is performing an impact analysis and submitting a change request, the PM is controlling the scope of the project by performing change control. All the other options have one or two correct statements, but then the other statements are incorrect, which makes the whole option choice incorrect. Only Answer D has three correct statements, making it the best answer.

8. Answer B is correct. The definition of done is determined collaboratively by the team and product owner, not delegated by the team facilitator, and is determined at the beginning of the release, not during sprint planning.

9. Answer C is correct. The Iteration Review meeting is the product owner's acceptance or rejection of the deliverable. Because the product owner represents the customer, this ceremony is closely related to the Validate Scope process, which is the predictive project's customer acceptance of the deliverable. The Retrospective is more closely related to Closing.

10. Answers B and D are correct. Of the preceding, the agile prioritization tools are Paired Comparison and the 100-point method. T-shirt Sizing and Planning Poker are estimation techniques, and Roman Voting is for reaching a consensus.

Chapter 7

"Do I Know This Already?" Quiz

1. Answer D is correct. The scenario describes a procedure for developing the schedule, and any procedure regarding the schedule is documented in the schedule management plan. The project schedule is the planned schedule for the project, and the schedule baseline is the approved schedule. The work performance information tells you how much ahead of schedule or behind schedule you are.

2. Answers A and D are correct. An activity uses verbs (action words), whereas work packages use nouns. *Order* and *check* are both action words in this context (you are performing something). Master bedroom, electrical rewiring, and plumbing work are work packages; they don't tell you the details of what work is involved to accomplish, just that work needs to be done. Each of those three will be broken down into activities.

3. Answer C is correct. You have to wait until the machine is fully installed before you can test, so this is a mandatory dependency. The relationship would have been a finish to start (not start to finish as given in the option here). With discretionary, you can change the relationships, and external dependencies are outside of the project team's control.

4. Answer A is correct. Because one person has to start clearing snow before the other person can start putting down rock salt, this is a start-to-start

relationship. In a finish to start, you finish one activity before you start the next activity; in this case, it might make logical sense because, in reality, you finish clearing the snow before starting to put down rock salt, but you have to think in terms of what the question is stating. The question states you have to start one activity before you finish the other. In a start to finish, one activity must start before the other can finish, and in a finish to finish, one activity has to finish before the other can finish.

5. Answer C is correct. Although the scenario states that you are developing a website, it is tempting to assume that this would be an agile project and choose T-shirt or relative estimating. Here, you are simply comparing the current project to a prior project, which is analogous estimating.

6. Answer A is correct. The answer is given in the question. An *expected activity duration* is the PERT. The optimistic and pessimistic values are irrelevant and are distractors. If you incorrectly assume the "most likely" figure to be 26, you would calculate a PERT of 31.5, which is incorrect. Always understand the formulae and understand what the terms mean so that you don't inadvertently make the wrong calculation.

7. Answer D is correct. Resource smoothing is a resource optimization technique in which you cannot go behind schedule. One common way is to move resources from noncritical to critical path activities. Resource leveling is adjusting the start and end dates of activities based on availability of resources, which can cause schedule slippage.

8. Answer A is correct. The customer has taken two weeks away from you, so that means you have a negative float of two weeks. A project float would be if the customer said you could finish two weeks later. A positive float would be if you are ahead of schedule.

9. Answers B and C are correct. On-demand scheduling and iterative schedule with a backlog are tools used in agile. The other options are for predictive.

10. Answer B is correct. Although the question sounds a little vague, you may get such vague questions on the real exam. You have to recognize that because the question refers to an agile project, only agile terms in the option choices are relevant. Answers A, C, and D are all predictive terms.

Review Questions

1. Answer B is correct. The key phrase here is *how to move forward*. Schedule management procedures are documented in the schedule management plan. If this were an agile project, you might consult the team; however, the scenario states *tight deadline*, which rules out agile. At some point, you might update

the risk register and do an impact analysis, but the question refers to *how to move forward*, which is the management plan.

2. Answer C is correct. The lowest level of the WBS is the work package, and it does not contain activities, so the junior PM is correct. It is true that there are different ways of creating the WBS, but it should never contain activities. Activities are in a separate document called the activities list.

3. Answer B is correct. Because you *must* disconnect the gas lines before you can remove the cooktops, that is a mandatory dependency, also known as hard logic. A mandatory dependency (or hard logic) is due to physical limitations. Discretionary dependency means you can move activities around based on your needs. Preferred is a type of discretionary dependency that depends on your preferences. Internal dependencies are internal to the team.

4. Answer D is correct. Initially, you had a finish-to-start relationship (finish configuration before starting testing). But now you have decided to do them in parallel, so this is now a start-to-start relationship (start configuration before starting testing). You cannot change a mandatory dependency to discretionary or vice versa (hard logic is mandatory; soft logic is discretionary).

5. Answer D is correct. Because this is a predictive project, you can rule out T-shirt Sizing (the scenario tells you that you are delivering the final product on a deadline). Because there are uncertainties, this implies you need to calculate optimistic, most likely, and pessimistic, which is three-point estimating.

6. Answer C is correct. Team members are not utilized at their most optimum level, so you should use a resource optimization technique to smooth out the amount of work. Resource leveling is specifically adjusting the start and end dates based on availability of resources, and this can extend the schedule (you cannot go behind schedule here, so that would rule out Answer A). Resource smoothing means you can make resource adjustments within the amount of float without going behind schedule, which makes C the correct answer. There is no evidence to state that there any low-performing team members, ruling out Answer B.

7. Answer A is correct. Project float is how long a project can be delayed without impacting the customer's deadline. Here, the deadline is 85 days, and the critical path is 55 days. So the project can be delayed by 30 days (85 – 55) without impacting the deadline, which is project float. The other numbers given are irrelevant to the question.

8. Answer C is correct. If the customer has decided to crash the schedule, it means that the additional cost is not a major concern to them. You also have their buy-in because they were the ones who made the decision, and there is no reason why the change control board would not approve it (the customer may even be part of the CCB). Your biggest concern now is finding these additional resources to perform the work.

9. Answer D is correct. Pulling the work from a queue refers to on-demand scheduling. Iterative scheduling with a backlog is used in agile but is a way of prioritizing user stories for a sprint (not creating a queue). The critical path method is a way of developing a predictive schedule. Resource leveling is adjusting the start and end dates of activities based on resource constraints.

10. Answer B is correct. Spikes are used when further investigation of user stories is needed. You do not need to adjust sprints (there is no schedule that you need to extend). Although the team facilitator ensures that the team has the tools to perform, that option does not answer the question.

Chapter 8

"Do I Know This Already?" Quiz

1. Answer D is correct. Providing new formulae refers to a new procedure, so you would update the cost management plan. You use the new formulae to calculate the cost baseline and cost estimate. There is no document called the formula register for PMP purposes.

2. Answer A is correct. The best classification is a direct cost. You could argue that it could be a fixed cost if you know exactly the amount of raw materials you need or a variable cost if you don't. However, in either case, it is still a direct cost because it is directly attributable to your project.

3. Answer A is correct. Any costs that are shared by other teams, business units, or other areas of the organization are considered indirect costs. These are costs that would be incurred by the organization regardless of the project, such as benefits for employees. The other options are all direct costs, expenses incurred to do the project.

4. Answer D is correct. The most detailed estimating technique is bottom-up estimating where you do a detailed analysis of your activities, but this is also time consuming and the most expensive approach.

5. Answer C is correct. A ROM estimate is –25% to +75%.

   25% * $200,000 = $50,000

   75% * $200,000 = $150,000

   Therefore, the ROM range is

   $200,000 – $50,000 = $150,000

   $200,000 + $150,000 = $350,000

6. Answer A is correct. Because this estimate is *time consuming, accurate,* and *detailed,* these keywords imply a bottom-up estimate. Analogous is a high-level

estimate using historical information. Parametric uses a single parameter and extrapolates results base on repetitive units of work. Planning Poker is a relative estimate (not detailed).

7. Answer D is correct. Because you previously identified that this risk could occur, it is a known risk (known unknown), so you would have set money aside in contingency reserves. Management reserves are the responsibility of management and are for unforeseen circumstances (unknown unknowns). The fact that the risk is beyond the control of the vendor is completely irrelevant.

8. Answer C is correct. In this case, because you know the number of gallons of paint per room (two) and how many rooms there are (100), you can extrapolate how many gallons of paint are required altogether and therefore how much the total materials (in this case, paint) will cost. Plus, you know the labor rate and can calculate the cost of labor. Parametric estimating is extrapolating results based on repetitive units of work and is basically = Quantity * Rate. T-shirt Sizing is a relative estimate for user stories, which is not the case here. Analogous estimating is comparing to a prior project, and PERT estimating uses optimistic, pessimistic, and most likely based on risks identified (which are not mentioned here).

9. Answer C is correct. Funding limit reconciliation is reconciling the amount of work that needs to be completed within an amount of time, with the funding limits imposed by senior management. In this case, you have estimated $930,000 of work, but management can afford $310,000 per quarter. You therefore need to plan the work to meet this funding limit. Cost aggregation is estimating the costs rolling through each layer of the WBS. Notice that the question does not ask what document needs to be updated, so you can immediately eliminate all options that mention any documents (project budget and cost baseline).

10. Answer C is correct. Comparing actual results to the plan is a monitoring and controlling process, and the best answer from the options provided is controlling costs. Cost aggregation is a planning process for determining the budget by adding up all the individual component costs of the project. Estimating costs is the process of calculating these individual costs. Reserve analysis is the process of calculating the contingency reserves.

Review Questions

1. Answer D is correct. Direct costs are costs that must be incurred to do the project and are incurred only as a result of the project. In this case, travel expenses relate only to this project and so are a direct cost. All other costs are indirect costs because they are shared by other teams and other areas of the organization.

2. Answer D is correct. How to manage any costing procedures is documented in the cost management plan. Based on the scenario, you review all the documents given in the option choices. However, the key word in the question is *how*, which asks about cost management procedures (negative cost variances), and they are documented in the cost management plan.

3. Answer C is correct. The scenario describes procedures for cost management that are documented in the cost management plan. Because the question asks what document you are reviewing, you can immediately eliminate Answer B because funding limit reconciliation is not a document; it is something you do (and therefore a tool). Code of accounts is the unique numbering system of the WBS, and the budget forecasts option refers to EAC.

4. Answer D is correct. The best tool to use in this case is parametric estimating, which involves using a statistical relationship to extrapolate results. In this case, if it takes three hours to paint one room, 250 rooms should take $3 \times 250 = 750$ hours of work. You can estimate the cost of one and therefore the cost of the project. Analogous estimating is using historical information based on a prior similar project. In this scenario, although you are using historical experience, the fact that you are extrapolating by multiplying the units of work implies that parametric is a better answer. Bottom-up is a detailed analysis, and Planning Poker is used for agile projects.

5. Answer B is correct. Because this is a kickoff meeting, the best you can do is a rough order of magnitude, which is a range of –25% to +75%. The kickoff meeting implies that you do not have any detailed information, so the estimates are very high level at this stage. Relative estimating is used in agile projects, but this is a predictive project because the deadline is fixed.

6. Answer D is correct. Notice the bait and switch! The scenario is irrelevant to the question. The question simply asks about the most accurate cost estimate, which is bottom-up estimating. Always train yourself to read the last sentence first in case you get questions of this nature.

7. Answers A, B, and D are correct. Management reserves are not part of the cost baseline but are included in the overall project budget (making C and E incorrect). Answer F is simply a red herring.

8. Answer B is correct. The fact that you are on your third sprint implies that this is an agile project, and agile projects do not set baselines (which also rules out Answer C). You do not automatically comply with senior management's request (you have to engage and collaborate to ensure they understand the correct procedures), making Answer A incorrect. Although you could argue that the cost management plan will document procedures for cost management, because there is no baseline in agile, you need to explain this to senior management (making B the best answer).

9. Answer B is correct. You are finalizing the cost, which implies you are working on the cost baseline, and this includes work packages, activities, control accounts, and contingency reserves. The project budget includes management reserves, which is beyond your authority as the PM. You may be utilizing cost aggregation to achieve this, but cost aggregation is not a document; it is a tool. The work packages and control accounts are shown on the WBS, but they do not show costs.

10. Answer B is correct. The question asks for a tool, which rules out project budget and cost baseline (because they are documents). Cost aggregation sums up all the cost estimates of activities and work packages to create the cost baseline (including contingency reserves).

Chapter 9

"Do I Know This Already?" Quiz

1. Answer D is correct because it correctly lists the three processes from the resource management section of the *PMBOK® Guide*, Sixth Edition, that describe the planning for and acquisition of project resources. Answer A is incorrect because, although procuring resources is a part of acquire resources, it does not cover resources that are assigned internally and thus is incomplete. Answer B is incorrect because the planning for resource management process is missing, and budgeting for resources is an integrated overlapping activity with project cost management and not a resource management–specific process. Answer C is incorrect because interview resources is not an official process step. Interviewing candidates is a part of acquiring resources, but it does not cover the complete activity scope.

2. Answer B is correct because the resource management plan is not focused on identifying the complete list of all team members and physical resources needed for the project. This artifact is focused on defining how the resources will be managed throughout the project. Answer A is incorrect because this response defines a project organization chart and this is typically included. Answers C and D are incorrect because they are also key elements of a resource management plan.

3. Answer D is correct. It correctly highlights three of the characteristics of high-performing teams. Answer A may be true, but this could also be true on dysfunctional teams and is not the best choice from the possible answers. Answer B might be true but does not guarantee a high-performing team. Answer C is true for high-performing teams, but it is too narrow in its focus. Individuals on high-performing teams have clarity on all project aspects (from project vision to their own assignments), and they take ownership of all project outcomes, not just their own assignments.

4. Answer C is correct. It correctly states the four original stages of the Tuckman Ladder model. Answer A is incorrect because it refers to four of the seven steps of the Drexler/Sibbet team performance model. Answer B is incorrect because the items mentioned may be elements of the team development process; they do not reflect a common term to describe any popular team development model. Answer D is incorrect because the order of the stages is incorrect.

5. Answer B is correct. It correctly lists three management principles that help maximize team performance. Answer A is incorrect because you do not want to involve the team in every decision. This would take them away from their primary focus and would be too disruptive to productivity. Answer C is incorrect because you want to celebrate wins along the way, not save them until the end. This can be a boost to team motivation and to the team culture. Answer D is incorrect because you do not want to force team members to work on their weaknesses. As a rule, you want to leverage each person's strengths, and if they want to improve on weaknesses, then work with them to find opportunities to do so.

6. Answer B is correct. It correctly lists three management techniques that can improve team performance. Answer A is incorrect because a Theory X management mindset is not recommended for complex, challenging project work or for knowledge workers. Answer C is incorrect because, although using agile approaches might be appropriate, they do not necessarily lead automatically to better team performance. Answer D is incorrect because you want to have a purpose for holding a team meeting out of respect for team members' time and their work productivity.

7. Answer D is correct because it states the four leadership skills components as noted in the *PMBOK® Guide*, Seventh Edition. Answer A is incorrect because conflict management, decision-making, and emotional intelligence are considered interpersonal skills per PMI, so the list is missing motivation, critical thinking, and establishing vision. Answer B is incorrect because servant leadership and public speaking are not considered to be two of the four components. Also, servant leadership is more of a type or style of leadership. Answer C is not the best choice because salesmanship and charisma are not explicitly listed as four of the leadership skill components, and emotional intelligence and decision-making are part of the interpersonal skills component.

8. Answer D correctly lists the four regarded aspects of emotional intelligence. Answer A is incorrect because the aspects of self-awareness and social skill are not accounted for. Having self-control and thinking before acting are aspects of self-control. Reading body language and other nonverbal cues and having empathy are aspects of social awareness. Answer B is incorrect because possessing social media skills is not part of emotional intelligence. Answer C is

incorrect because the aspects of self-awareness and self-management are not accounted for. Recognizing other people's feelings and having empathy are examples of social awareness. Building rapport is an aspect of social skill.

9. Answer C is the best answer because it describes one of the benefits of making project decisions with the team. Answer A is incorrect because this is what you want to avoid when making decisions with the team. Answer B is incorrect because it is not a benefit and the project manager is still accountable for the project outcomes. Answer D is incorrect because the opposite is actually true. Group decisions do take more time than unilateral decisions.

10. Answer A is the best answer because it lists the four recommended approaches to conflict management per the *PMBOK® Guide*, Seventh Edition. Answer B is incorrect because you don't always want to take a compromising approach. Answer C is incorrect because you don't always want to assume any conflict will just go away on its own. Answer D is incorrect because you want to focus on the issue, not on the people involved.

11. Answer C is the correct answer. Per the *PMBOK® Guide*, Seventh Edition, the four variables listed can impact the project leadership style needed. Answer A is incorrect because use of agile approaches is not considered a factor for tailoring the leadership style; the reason is that agile approaches tend to dictate the leadership style as part of the approach. Answer B is not the best choice, although the variables listed seem reasonable. Answer D is incorrect for the same reason that Answer A is incorrect.

12. Answer B is correct because this is a key first step to understanding the situation. Answer A is incorrect because, although it is true the rest of the team is watching, it is more important that the situation is handled fairly and balances the person's situation with the overall performance of the team. Answers C and D are not the best choices because these would not be the first steps to take.

Review Questions

1. Answer C is correct. This response addresses most aspects of emotional intelligence. Answer A is a part of emotional intelligence, but the question content does not speak to this aspect. Answer B is incorrect because motivation entails understanding what the primary motivators for each member of the team are and then applying this understanding to get the best performance from each individual. Answer D is a result of emotional intelligence. Answer E is incorrect because, although emotional intelligence is a foundation skill for all people-to-people interactions, including coaching, the question content does not describe coaching.

2. Answer C is correct. Storming is the stage of the Tuckman Ladder model where initial conflicts can emerge among the team members. The other answer options are other stages of the Tuckman Ladder model but not the correct ones for this question.

3. Answers B and C are correct. Both are positive steps the project manager can take to improve the productivity of the team. Answer A is not the best answer because the project manager can often facilitate resolution to an issue much faster, and the project manager wants to anticipate potential issues and take action to prevent or mitigate them from occurring. Answer D is not the best answer because the project manager is often better positioned to accomplish this (from experience), and ideally, if the team member is doing this, the effort is delaying their ability to start work and/or taking them away from their primary tasks. Answer E is incorrect because this is a nonproductive action item and causes context switching if the team member is focused on something else when they are asked.

4. Answer E is the best response. Although there may be some value in assigning a challenging work task to a new team member right away, this is not always the best course of action, Answers A through D are all recommended action items to help a team member be productive as soon as possible.

5. Answers A through D are all examples of demonstrating leadership by the project manager. Answer E is incorrect because the action is prioritizing the process management aspect over the leadership of the project team.

6. Answers B through E are all correct and illustrate leadership actions by other members of the project team. Answer A is incorrect because this is not an example of leadership by the technical leader. One of the ways a technical leader can provide leadership is by identifying potential risks as soon as possible.

7. Answers A, B, D, and E are the correct choices because each does provide a reason for the value of critical thinking in a project environment. Answer C is incorrect because in most cases the opposite would be true. To apply critical thinking to decisions generally requires more time and the participation of others in the process.

8. Answers B, C, and E are the best answers. Confronting/problem-solving and collaborating are definitely approaches used by high-performing teams because there is a high degree of trust and collaboration on the team, and the working relationships are highly valued. Compromising can be used as well, because the team members are of relatively equal power status. Answer A is not the best answer because this approach is normally employed when the parties are not of equal relative power of authority. Answer D is not the best answer because this would not be common on a high-performing team.

9. Answers A, B, C, E, and G are correct answers. Each of them is an effective method to help earn the respect of those team members and stakeholders you are leading. Answer D is not the best answer because this is the opposite of what you want to do and can lead to disillusionment among the team members. This does not mean you can't continue to inspire them with the project vision, but not at the expense of dealing with the realities of the current situation. Answer F is not the best answer because this is also the opposite of what you want to do and can lead to a loss of respect from the team.

10. Answers A, B, C, E, and G are the best responses. Each answer is an illustration of a servant leadership mindset. Answer D is not the best response because a servant leader accepts responsibility for all project outcomes. This does not mean that they do not provide opportunities for team members to take on more responsibility and grow, but they do not abdicate final responsibility. Answer F is not the best response because a servant leadership mindset solicits input and feedback from others when making decisions whenever possible, especially ones that will impact the project.

11. Answer D is the best response because it focuses on how the project resources will be managed and the effort level required, and this is the primary value of planning resource management. Answer A is not correct because this step gets into actually identifying the resources needed for the project and is not focused on how project resources should be managed. Answer B is not the best response because it is not the primary value of the process, but this is a common outcome of the process. Answer C is not the best response because like Answer B it is not the primary value, but it is a key benefit of proper resource management planning.

12. Answers B, C, and D are the best responses. Each is an example of a preassignment tool that can be used to assess and evaluate potential candidates for project team roles. Answer A is not the best response because resource requirements identify the type and quantity of resources needed for the project. Answer E is not the best response because the training plan defines the training needs for the team that has been formed. Answer F is not the best response because the team charter defines the values, agreements, and operating guidelines for the working team.

Chapter 10

"Do I Know This Already?" Quiz

1. Answer A is correct. Interactive means that people can talk as they need to, and video conferencing is normally considered interactive. You could argue that in some situations it could be formal verbal; however, you have to choose the best

answer. Video conferencing is not always formal verbal, but it is always interactive, which is why that is a better answer. A pull communication is one-way communication (such as voicemails, memos), and a tight matrix means team members are co-located.

2. Answer A is correct. Communication constraints between stakeholders are always documented in the communication management plan. The team charter may document communication procedures and constraints for an individual team, but for the entire project, these items would be documented in the communication management plan.

3. Answer C is correct. The best answer is feedback according to the sender-receiver model. You could argue that it would also be interactive, but the fact that someone is repeating a message means that they are engaged in interactive communication, which is a communication type. The physical act of repeating the message is giving feedback to the other person.

4. Answer B is correct. Communication procedures between stakeholders are always documented in the communication management plan, and that is what you would refer to first. You may follow up with stakeholders afterward, but the question asks what you would do first. Answer D is very wrong! You should not be communicating all information to all stakeholders; you should be communicating relevant information to relevant stakeholders.

5. Answer C is correct. Taking notes is always informal written, even if the meeting is formal. All the other options are formal written documents.

6. Answer C is correct. The key in the question is that it states "initially." You always want to choose the most proactive approach, the most engaging approach, or the most collaborative approach. In this case, first find out the reason for the decreased performance and encourage the team member to increase their performance. Initially, you should have an information conversation with them to find out why their performance is lacking.

7. Answer D is correct. The communication formula is: $n(n - 1) / 2$

   Because you are managing 15 people initially, there are 16 people altogether on your team; thus,

   Initially: $16 * 15 / 2 = 120$

   Add 2 more people: $18 * 17 / 2 = 153$

   Channels increased: $153 - 120 = 33$

8. Answer A is correct. It is the sender's responsibility to ensure the receiver has received and understood the message. You should have followed up to ensure that all the stakeholders attending the meeting had received the report.

9. Answer A is correct. Another term for tight matrix is *colocation*, which is where osmotic communication will work best. Osmotic communication means that you are subconsciously absorbing surrounding conversation even though you are not part of the conversation nor eavesdropping. This type of communication is not possible in a virtual environment. A face-to-face conversation is direct communication (not osmotic).

10. Answer C is correct. The Kanban board (a.k.a. task board) shows the work that has not started, the work that is in progress, and the work that has been completed. The chart that shows what work has been accomplished is the burn up chart. The burn down chart shows what work remains outstanding.

Review Questions

1. Answer B is correct. You have identified a new communication procedure because you now need to update the stakeholder weekly via email. You first update the communication management plan, which documents the communication requirements needs for each stakeholder, among other things. The scenario implies that this is not an agile project, so the options mentioning team facilitator and information radiator are invalid. You may update the team, but only after documenting in the communication management plan.

2. Answer B is correct. According to the sender-receiver model, it is the sender's responsibility to ensure that the receiver has received and understood the message. The sender initially encodes the message (not decodes) when sending the message. The sender decodes the message only after receiving feedback.

3. Answer A is correct. This is an example of noise in the sender-receiver model. Noise is anything that can interfere with or cause misinterpretations. There is no evidence to suggest these team members have a lack of communication skills or lack of communication styles assessment. Nor are they intolerant of one another.

4. Answers C and D are correct. The 5 Cs are **C**orrect grammar and spelling, **C**oncise expression and elimination of excess words, **C**lear purpose and expression directed to the needs of the reader, **C**oherent logical flow of ideas, and **C**ontrolling flow of words and ideas

5. Answer C is correct. The communication methods are interactive, push, and pull. Saving information in a central repository is a pull communication, where people can retrieve the information they need.

6. Answer C is correct. David provided *all* information to *all* stakeholders. Instead, he should have provided only the relevant information to the appropriate stakeholders. In this scenario, the stakeholders are confused because

they have an overload of information, much of which might not pertain to them.

7. Answer B is correct. The key is the word *initially*. You want to engage and collaborate with stakeholders, so initially you want to find out what the problem is and work with the team member. If this behavior continues, you can escalate to formal written.

8. Answers B and E are correct. Active listening provides feedback to the sender, and effective communication means providing the information in a timely manner, both of which are enhancers of communication. Noise is a barrier to communication. Formal verbal and pull communication are neither enhancers nor barriers; they are types of communications used.

9. Answer D is correct. The most effective way to ensure someone has understood the message is to ask them to repeat the message back to you, which is active listening. Sending an email does not ensure that the person has understood. The scenario states you are on the phone, so you can't see body language. Simply asking Cathy to confirm does not ensure she understood everything.

10. Answer A is correct. First, you should recognize that this is an agile project due to the fact that you are a team facilitator. In agile, the best way to keep key stakeholders apprised of the latest project status is via the information radiator. You can invite them to the daily standup meetings if you want, but that is not the primary method of keeping stakeholders informed. The email distribution list is a distractor. There is no weekly status meeting in agile.

Chapter 11

"Do I Know This Already?" Quiz

1. Answer A is correct. Fixing the process or machinery is a corrective action. Fixing a nonconforming deliverable is a defect repair. A preventive action is to prevent an issue from occurring in the first place. A corrective action would be a cost of nonconformance, not the cost of conformance.

2. Answer D is correct. Quality refers to whether the product meets requirements, not whether it works. A product that works but does not meet requirements is a defect, rendering Answer A incorrect. A machine that is being used to test the product but fails is a corrective action. Seven consecutive data points below the mean would be out of control, but here the word *consecutive* is missing. You may have found seven data points below the mean, but there may be some above the mean in between these seven.

3. Answer B is correct. When the product reaches the customer and the customer finds a defect, that is an external failure cost. Recalls occur after the product has reached the customer, so this would be an external failure cost. Internal

failure costs are issues found before the product is delivered to the customer. An appraisal cost refers to costs associated with the inspection and testing of the product and process. Cost of conformance refers to costs associated with preventing failures.

4. Answer B is correct. A new procedure has been identified and agreed to (in this case, the quality standards), so the next thing is for you to update the project management plan. After that, you can notify the team or the sponsor, but first you need to update the document. A kickoff meeting would be held at the beginning of the testing phase to initiate the phase.

5. Answer B is correct. A quality audit is a structured independent review to ensure project activities comply with processes, policies, and procedures, which is what the other group is doing here. The team, by testing the product, is performing quality control, but then by ensuring they are following procedures, they are performing quality assurance. Notice that the question asks what *tool* is being employed here. Although Answer C (quality assurance) sounds promising, the *best* answer would be B (audit) because quality assurance is a process, and audit is the tool employed by the process. Always watch out for such situations where more than one option choice looks good. Statistical sampling is testing a representative sample of the population.

6. Answer A is correct. The scenario asks about getting to the root cause of an issue, and the best tool for that is an Ishikawa diagram (also known as a fishbone diagram and cause-and-effect diagram). A Pareto chart is used to identify the 20 percent of problems that cause 80 percent of the issues. Statistical sampling is testing a representative sample of the population. A scatter diagram shows the correlation between two variables.

7. Answer C is correct. The scenario describes the 80:20 rule, which is that 80 percent of issues are a result of 20 percent of the causes. An Ishikawa diagram is used to identify root causes. Statistical sampling is testing a representative sample of the population. Scatter diagrams are used to show a correlation between two variables.

8. Answer B is correct. One data point above the upper control limit would be out of control. Seven data points above the mean would be acceptable, but seven *consecutive* data points above the mean would not (notice the word *consecutive* is missing from this option). One data point above the lower control limit is within statistical control (one data point below the lower control limit is not). Common cause variance is within statistical control.

9. Answer C is correct. Kaizen means "continuous improvement." The primary function of a sprint retrospective is that of a lessons learned meeting to determine what went well and what the team can improve on, which is a continuous improvement method. Backlog grooming is reprioritizing user stories, and the

sprint review is demoing the product to the product owner. The daily stand-ups provide a status to the team and team facilitator. Although any of those ceremonies may identify success and failures, the retrospective is where these success and failures will be discussed and acted upon.

10. Answer D is correct. Juran promoted "fitness for use," and Crosby promoted "zero defects." The 80:20 rule is Pareto. The 14 points of TQM was developed by Deming.

Review Questions

1. Answer D is correct. Replacing a machine is a corrective action because the machine is part of the process. Fixing the defects would be a defect repair or rework. A preventive action would be if you identified that part of the machine was about to cause problems before any defects occurred and you replaced that part.

2. Answer D is correct. The quality goals and objectives are documented in the quality management plan, so that is what you should review. The project charter may have some high-level information about quality standards but does not contain the quality goals and objectives. The question states "goals and objectives for the project," so you wouldn't review OPA because that is for the organizations. You don't reach out to the team because you, as the PM, need to ensure the team is following the quality standards.

3. Answer B is correct. This is an external failure cost because the product has reached the customer, and the customer has found the issue. An internal failure cost is defects that the team discovers and fixes before delivering to the customer. This would also be known as rework.

4. Answer D is correct. The team should first follow the guidance in the quality management plan because it documents procedures regarding quality management—in this case, the tolerance levels. There it states whether you need to follow industry standards or the organization's standards. They would not reach out to the PMO.

5. Answer A is correct. Reviewing documentation to ensure the team is following procedures is a quality audit and generally performed by an independent team. Quality control is testing the product to ensure it meets requirements and standards (which is also verifying deliverables). Managing quality does refer to the process, but this is the responsibility of the project manager. An audit is a tool for managing quality.

6. Answer A is correct. Because the UCL is 400 and the data point is at 375, it is within statistical control. But because the USL is at 280 (below the data point), it does not meet the customer's requirements.

7. Answer C is correct. Be careful of such "bait-and-switch" questions where the scenario is irrelevant to the question. In this case, the question specifically asks for the tool to test a representative sample of the population, which is statistical sampling. The scenario describes the Ishikawa diagram but is irrelevant to the question. Always focus on the last sentence, which is the call of the question.

8. Answer A is correct. One of the main goals of the retrospective is lessons learned, which is a type of continuous improvement process

9. Answer D is correct. *Precise* means that data points are grouped together. *Accurate* means the data points are on the mean. One data point above the upper control limit is out of control (neither accurate nor precise). Although seven consecutive data points violate the rule of seven, it is the first part of Answer A that is incorrect, rendering the whole option choice incorrect.

10. Answers:

    1: C

    2: A

    3: D

    4: B

    1 and 2: Grade refers to the number and types of features a product has, whereas quality refers to whether the product meets the customer's requirements. An 8 mega-pixel camera is a lower grade than a 10-megapixel camera (but both are good quality if they do what they are supposed to do—meet the customer's requirements). If the customer requested 24-inch monitors and you delivered 20-inch monitors, you did not meet their requirements and that would be poor quality.

    3: Appraisal cost is any kind of testing. Because D mentions testing, it is an appraisal cost.

    4: When you deliver a product and the customer finds defects, that is an external failure cost. Answer B states that the customer called with an issue, which means it has been delivered, so this would be an external failure cost.

Chapter 12

"Do I Know This Already?" Quiz

1. Answer C is correct. In centralized contracting, there is one procurement department to conduct all procurement activities for the organization. The disadvantage is that there is no dedicated procurement resource for your project; you can be assigned any procurement personnel every time you reach out to them. The other options are thus incorrect because they would be advantages to centralized contracting

2. Answer B is correct. Determining whether to perform the work in-house or to outsource the work is referred to as a make-or-buy analysis. Conduct procurement starts after you have decided to outsource the work and are reaching out to vendors. Likewise, procurement strategy begins after you have decided that you will outsource the work and will now plan the steps for outsourcing the work. Cost benefit analysis is used to make decisions on a project and would be a type of make-or-buy analysis. Although Answer A could technically be a good option, Answer B is better because it incorporates all factors used to determine whether to outsource.

3. Answer C is correct. Choosing a vendor because the organization has a preference for that vendor would be single source contracting. In sole source contracting, there is only one vendor. A make-or-buy analysis is the process of determining whether the work will be outsourced. A proposal evaluation would come into play if a decision had been made to solicit the best offer from multiple vendors.

4. Answer D is correct. Because this is a standard design available from several suppliers, you just want to know how much each supplier will charge you, so the RFQ is the best one to use. An RFP is used when you need to understand the requirements first before giving a quote. RFI is used for general information. FP-EPA is a type of contract, not a bid document.

5. Answer C is correct. A letter of intent (LOI) is not a legal document, so banks generally do not give you a loan on that basis. For all the other options, there is no evidence from the scenario that any of those situations would apply.

6. Answer B is correct. If you are meeting with potential sellers at the same time, it is most likely a bidders' conference. The mention of agile is irrelevant to the question, so the two agile ceremonies listed are incorrect. This is not a stakeholder's status meeting because there is no status to discuss.

7. Answer D is correct. One of the tools to find vendors is to advertise the opportunity so that vendors could reach you to find out more. An RFP is a document you send out to receive proposals after you have identified the vendor. A proposal evaluation is what you do after you have received all the bids. The procedures for finding vendors could be documented on the procurement management plan, but specifically the question asks what tool you would utilize, and of the options given, the best answer is advertising.

8. Answer B is correct. Termination for convenience is a right offered only to the buyer, not the seller. The other options are true statements.

9. Answer D is correct. Procedures for handling disputes with the vendor are documented in the contract itself, so that is what you should review initially. This procedure is not documented in the procurement management plan.

Answers B and C are not the best answers because they would refer to the contract first as well.

10. Answer A is correct. In an FFP, the seller has all the risk of the contract because they will have to cover the cost of price increases and using more resources. The buyer will be concerned that the seller might try to cut costs by, for example, using poorer quality materials than they had originally planned (an example of bait and switch). The other options are all concerns of the vendor in an FFP contract.

Review Questions

1. Answer B is correct. The key in the scenario is that senior management are risk averse. This implies you want a contract with the least risk to you (as the buyer), which will be FFP.

2. Answer C is correct. An RFP is used where the seller needs to understand the needs and expectations of the customer before they can give a quote. A custom solution means that you need to give the seller your requirements before they can give you a quote. All the other options use an RFQ.

3. Answer A is correct. Senior management tells you what type of vendor would prequalify for the project, so this is known as source selection criteria. It is true that this could be considered a requirement from the senior stakeholders, but the best answer would be source selection criteria because it is the more detailed option.

4. Answer D is correct. CPPC means Cost Plus Percentage of Cost. You will reimburse the seller for their cost and pay a certain agreed-upon percentage on top of the cost. In this case the seller has no incentive to control cost, so that will be your biggest area of concern. It is true that the vendor might have access to proprietary information, but that is true for any contract. There is no evidence from the scenario that they will have access to any proprietary information, so you cannot make that assumption.

5. Answer A is correct. RFQ is the best option because you need multiple products of the same dimension and spec. You use an RFP where you need to understand the needs and expectations of the customer before you can provide a quote. An FFP is a type of contract, which is not asked about here.

6. Answer A is correct. Because you are not in privity with the subcontractors, they are within their right not to respond to you. You should discuss any issues with your vendor that you are in privity with. You cannot take legal action against the subcontractors, and because you have not brought up the issue with the vendor, it is inadvisable to take legal action against them at this stage.

7. Answers B and E are correct. Force majeure refers to an "act of God," which is a negative and sudden event that you are not in control of; it cannot be

predicted or avoided. Natural disasters and rioting fall into this category. Poor economic conditions and recession can be predicted months in advance. Material price increases do not warrant nonperformance of work. If prices have increased, they must be paid for by the buyer or seller (depending on the contract).

8. Answer D is correct. The delay in this situation is due the inaction of the buyer, so this is a constructive change. If the delay had been for any other reason (such as raw materials not being available), that could have been a contract modification. You wouldn't terminate the contract due your team's inaction. This is not a risk; it's an issue.

9. Answer C is correct. Administrative changes are simple nonsubstantive changes that do not require a lot of effort.

10. Answers:

    1: b

    2: c

    3: a

    4: d

    1: Only the firm fixed price contract tells you definitively what the final cost is going to be. The other types of contracts involve ranges and uncertainties.

    2: If the parameters are uncertain, cost reimbursable contracts are best (for PMI purposes). The only cost reimbursable contract shown in the option choices is CPFF.

    3: T&M contracts are used for short-term staff augmentation projects, which is what Answer A describes.

    4: To reduce the risk to your organization, the best contract type is a fixed price (the seller has all the risk), but because there is an adjustment for inflation, this would make it an FPEPA contract.

Chapter 13

"Do I Know This Already?" Quiz

1. Answer D is correct because it correctly states the difference between threats and opportunity risks. Answer A is partially true; they both need to be managed, but there is a difference on potential impact to project objectives. Answer B might be true for certain opportunities, but escalation can also be needed for some threat risks. Answer C is not true because only threats have a potential negative impact on project objectives.

2. Answer C is correct. It correctly states the difference between the three terms. Answer A is incorrect because there are differences between the three terms, even though they are often used interchangeably incorrectly. Answer B is

incorrect because risk threshold and risk tolerance do not mean the same thing. Answer D is incorrect because risk appetite is more of a general attitude measure, whereas risk tolerance defines a specific impact range on a project objective. In addition, risk threshold does not define the impact level where the risk would be avoided.

3. Answers B and D are correct. Both statements are true about the risk management plan. Answer A is incorrect because this statement defines the risk register. Answer C is incorrect because the last part of the statement is incorrect. The risk management plan does not list any risks that have been identified. It is focused on the methodology to be used to manage and control project risks.

4. Answer B is correct because it correctly states both artifacts are used by each risk management process. Answers A, C, and D are all incorrect because all indicate that one or more of the artifacts are used in only some risk management processes.

5. Answer D is correct because it lists the three common acronyms used to describe common sources of project risks. PESTLE represents political, economic, social, technical, legal, and environmental. TECOP represents technical, environmental, commercial, operational, and political. VUCA represents volatility, uncertainty, complexity, and ambiguity. Answers A and B are incorrect because those options are not common acronyms for sources of project risks. Answer C is not the best choice because it is missing one of the three common acronyms used to describe common sources of project risks.

6. Answer D is correct because it properly states the goal of qualitative risk analysis. Answer A is not the best choice because it states one of the key activities of qualitative risk analysis, but this is not the primary goal. Answer B is not the best choice because it does not state the primary goal and is not required for every project. Answer C is incorrect because this action is part of the risk response planning.

7. Answer C is correct because each option is an example of a quantitative risk analysis tool. Answer A is incorrect because a probability and impact matrix is used in qualitative risk analysis, and a SWOT analysis is a source of risk identification. Answer B is incorrect because only expected monetary value is a quantitative risk analysis tool. Answer D is incorrect because risk breakdown structures are a tool used in risk identification.

8. Answer A is the correct answer because it lists the five response options for threats per both the *PMBOK® Guide*, Sixth Edition, and *PMBOK® Guide*, Seventh Edition. Answer B is incorrect because this is the response options for opportunities. Answer C is incorrect because these are three response options for dealing with general uncertainty. Answer D is incorrect because these are three response options for addressing ambiguity.

9. Answer C is correct because it is the definition of secondary risk. Answer A is incorrect because secondary risk is not related to the priority of the risk. Answer B is not the best choice because this is the definition of residual risk. Answer D is incorrect because it is defined by the original list of identified risks.

10. Answer B is correct because this is the primary objective of risk response implementation. Answers A, C, D, and E are all incorrect because each one is an objective of the risk monitoring process.

Review Questions

1. Answer C is correct. Risk avoidance is the act of eliminating the threat risk entirely. Answers A, B, D, and E are all incorrect because they are the other four threat risk response options.

2. Answer C is correct because both strategies require effort by the project team to either reduce the probability the risk will occur (risk mitigation) or to eliminate the risk entirely (risk avoidance). Answer A is incorrect because risk acceptance involves taking no action. Answers B and D are incorrect because risk escalation is the act of assigning the risk to someone with higher authority than the project team.

3. Answer B is correct per the Stacey complexity model. Answer A is not correct because this would be the recommendation for a project that falls into the Simple range. Answer C is not the best answer because it is not referenced by the model, but it may be appropriate. Answers D and E are not the best answers because they are not considered official project approaches but rather are elements of either an adaptive or hybrid project approach.

4. Answer E is the best response because determining the impact on the project's critical path is one of the primary reasons to leverage simulation tools based on Monte Carlo analysis. Answer A is incorrect because decision trees are used to decide between alternative options. Answer B is incorrect because a tornado sensitivity diagram is used to determine which sources of risk or uncertainty have the greatest potential impact on project objectives. Answer C is incorrect because influence diagrams are graphical tools that show all the factors that lead to a given outcome and the relationship among those factors. Answer D is incorrect because a probability and impact matrix is used to prioritize and rank individual project risks.

5. Answers A, B, and D are correct because they are all reasons for organizations to not leverage quantitative risk analysis. Answer C is incorrect because project responsibility and accountability are not impacted by the use of quantitative risk analysis. Answer E is not the best choice because quantitative risk analysis is used in other industries besides financial.

6. Answer D is the best choice because each factor is from the list described in *PMBOK® Guide*, Sixth Edition. Answer A is not the best choice because political and economic are associated sources of project risk. Answer B is not the best choice because social impact is associated with sources of project risk. Answer C is not the best choice because resource availability is a common risk and not a risk evaluation factor. Answer E is not the best choice because technical is associated with sources of project risk.

7. Answer A is the correct choice because risk exploitation is the act of making sure a risk opportunity definitely happens. Answers B–E are incorrect because they are all different risk threat or opportunity response strategies that do not involve making sure an opportunity risk definitely happens.

8. Answer C is correct because Risk C has the highest risk score of 5.4. This question is an example of qualitative risk analysis using probability and impact values, where the risk score is the product of probability * impact. For the four risks listed, the scores would be Risk A = 4.5 (.50 * 9), Risk B = 4.8 (.60 * 8), Risk C = 5.4 (.90 * 6), and Risk D = 3 (.30 * 10).

9. Answer D is correct because effect-based risk classification is defined by classifying risks by their impact on project constraints. Answer A is incorrect because source-based is defined by classifying risks based on their source type. Answers B and C are incorrect because these risk types could both be classified by scope, schedule, cost, or quality. Answer E is not the best choice because the project objectives are not necessarily the same as the project constraints, and this term usually is not used for risk classification.

10. Answer A is the best response. The scenario in the question defines a risk-tolerant level of risk appetite. Answer B is not the best choice because risk-seeking is defined as an organization that welcomes risks and uncertainty. Answer C is not the best choice because risk-neutral is defined as an organization that will take risks for a short period of time when there is a clear trade-off between risk and reward. Answers D and F are not the best choices because these are not risk appetite classifications. Answer E is not correct because risk-adverse is defined as an organization that is uncomfortable with uncertainty.

Chapter 14

"Do I Know This Already?" Quiz

1. Answers B and C are correct. Per the *PMBOK® Guide*, Seventh Edition, the two types of indicators are leading indicators and lagging indicators. The others listed are made-up terms.

2. Answer B is correct. Performance measures are taken to determine the health of a project. An impact analysis determines the implications of the cost, schedule, and other constraints on a project. Options A, C, and D are all reasons for performance measures.

3. Answer C is correct. SMART stands for specific, measurable (or meaningful), achievable (or agreed or attainable), realistic (or reasonable or relevant), time-bound (or timely). Analytical is not one of the variations of SMART.

4. Answer D is correct. The chart that shows the information described is the Kanban board. You could argue that the information radiator can be used to show this information also because often the information radiator includes the Kanban board. That assessment may be true. However, the information radiator does not always have to include the Kanban board. Another major distractor here is option C. The cumulative flow diagram shows the number of tasks that are in progress, that have not started, or that are complete. It does not show the actual tasks, which is what the scenario refers to. The burnup chart shows how many story points have been accomplished to date.

5. Answer C is correct. The burnup chart shows the number of user stories or story points that have been accomplished by an agile team. The burndown chart shows the work remaining. You could argue that the information radiator can be used to show this information also because often the information radiator includes the burnup chart and other charts that could describe the scenario. However, the information radiator does not always have to include these charts. It is up to the team facilitator to determine which charts and graphs to include in the information radiator. The cycle time shows how long a task takes from start to finish.

6. Answers B and E are correct. An Ishikawa diagram is used for root cause analysis of issues, and the Pareto chart is used to show critical issues in descending order of frequency. All the other options are used for performance tracking on a project.

7. Answer D is correct. Gantt charts are used on predictive projects and generally not used in agile (although they may be used in some hybrid projects). All the other options are common charts found on an information radiator.

8. Answer C is correct. CPI is the cost performance index and shows the current level of cost efficiency you have achieved so far. TCPI (to complete performance index) shows the cost efficiency you need to achieve going forward. SPI is the rate of performance of the scheduled work. CV is the cost variance and the difference between what you should have spent and what you have actually spent based on the work complete.

9. Answer D is correct. If the CPI and SPI are 1, then you have worked at the planned rate for both cost and schedule, so you are on budget and on schedule.

A negative SV and CV means that you are over budget and behind schedule, respectively, making option A incorrect. If CPI and SPI are greater than 1, then it means you have worked at a rate better than expected, so you are under budget and ahead of schedule, making B incorrect. If BAC is less than EAC, then it means you are going to be over budget, making C incorrect.

10. Answer C is correct. If you have a negative SV, it means you are behind schedule (not over budget). Based on the question, it shows that you are $2,000 worth of work behind schedule (or a week behind schedule because $2,000 = 1 week). However, you don't know what week you are in or how long the project is, so you cannot determine the metrics given in B and D.

Review Questions

1. Answer B is correct. There is no point in taking measures and filing them away. You need to analyze those results and engage key stakeholders to make appropriate decisions. There is nothing in the scenario that shows that these files were not accessible to key stakeholders, and it is up to the project manager to engage stakeholders in decision-making, making A and C incorrect. You cannot assume that poor team performance led to these results because many factors could have caused these results, making D incorrect.

2. Answers A, B, C, D, E are correct. All of these options are examples of KPIs.

3. Answer D is correct. Work performance information is comparing the plan with the actual results to interpret the variance. To know that you are 5 percent behind schedule, you would have compared the plan schedule with the actual schedule. The burnup chart and information radiator are examples of work performance reports. Option B is work performance data.

4. Answer A is correct. Charts and graphs refer to a work performance report, so by creating these tools, the project manager is developing the work performance reports. The information radiator is a type of work performance report, but there is no evidence from the scenario that this is an agile project; therefore, this option would not apply. The metrics that the project manager is collecting are work performance information, but the formatting to charts and graphs refers to work performance reports. These are analyzed and discussed to assess the performance of the project and the team.

5. Answer C is correct. Net promoter score (NPS) is used to determine stakeholder satisfaction. Velocity determines how many story points an agile team can complete in a sprint. Return on investment shows the financial return a project may produce or has produced. Actual cost versus planned cost is used to determine whether you are on budget. Options B and D may lead to stakeholder satisfaction, but the actual measure is NPS.

6. **Answer A is correct.** Because CPI and SPI are greater than 1, it means you are ahead of schedule and under budget. So the clients have nothing to worry about at this stage. The CV and SV figures are irrelevant in this question. All the other options assume that the project is doing badly, which is not the case.

7. **Answer B is correct.** The BAC and AC are irrelevant in this question. Because CPI is greater than 1, you are under budget. Because SPI is less than 1, you are behind schedule.

8. **Answer D is correct.** The net promoter score (NPS) is the best tool to measure stakeholder satisfaction. You create an evaluation, and based on their selections, an NPS is calculated. A mood chart is used to track mood and reaction at any given point and is not appropriate here. The benefit cost ratio and return on investment do not capture the stakeholder satisfaction but are financial measures.

9. **Answer C is correct.** A PV of $63,000 means you should have done $63,000 worth of work at this point. However, EV is $61,000, meaning you have only done $61,000 worth of work at this point, so you are behind schedule. In doing $61,000 worth of work, you should have spent $61,000, but you have actually spent $62,000 (AC), so you are over budget.

10. **Answers:**

    1. D

    2. H

    3. C

    4. F

    5. B

    6. I

    7. J

    8. A

    9. E

    10. G

    Refer to the "Performance Tracking Tools and Artifacts" section for an explanation of the definitions.

Chapter 15

"Do I Know This Already?" Quiz

1. **Answer D is correct.** All the options are reasons for project closure, which involves preparing the final project report as one of the steps.

2. Answers B and F are correct. Common reasons for canceling a project are identified in options A, C, D, and E. If a customer requests additional requirements, even a significant number, the request must go through the change control process. If there are significant cost increases, they, too, must go through the change control process, and the project is re-baselined if necessary.

3. Answer A is correct. Although no answer seems to be a good answer, option A is the best one because scope validation must occur before you can start the closing steps. Scope validation is the customer's acceptance of the deliverable, and on predictive projects, this process occurs as part of the Validate Scope process in monitoring and controlling (on agile projects, it occurs in the iteration review meeting). All other options occur as part of closing.

4. Answer D is correct. The scenario describes a sprint retrospective because the team is discussing lessons learned and the next sprint. The fact that the scenario mentions "next two-week iteration" implies this is an agile project. Otherwise, option A could be correct if this were a predictive project. This is not the end of the project, making B incorrect. The iteration review is the meeting where the product owner approves or rejects the deliverables, making C incorrect.

5. Answer B is correct. The project manager needs to ensure the organization is ready to accept the deliverable and plan accordingly. Quality control should already have been completed, and the fact that the customer has accepted the deliverable means that scope validation is also complete. Definition of done is part of the acceptance criteria on agile projects.

6. Answer C is correct. Procedures for customer acceptance are in the scope management plan because this refers to the Validate Scope process. All the other options are included in the transition plan (a.k.a. the implementation plan and rollout plan).

Review Questions

1. Answer D is correct. *Stage gate* and *phase gate* are synonyms, making option A incorrect. There is no term *termination gate*, making B incorrect. Because the project has been canceled, there is no go-live for this project, making C incorrect.

2. Answers A and B are correct. According to PMI, options A and B are benefits of this process, along with planned work being complete. The deliverables are accepted prior to closing (Validate Scope), and the deliverable must be accepted before the team can close, making option C incorrect. Options D and E are incorrect because milestones are not always achieved, and the product

does not always successfully move to operations/go-live (the project may be canceled).

3. Answer D is correct. Option D describes the project charter, which is not part of the final report. All other options are included in the final report.

4. Answer A is correct. Although there is no chronological order of the closing activities, what you have to recognize here is that all the other options in the question need to occur before the closing process can even start. Options B and C are the same thing: Validate scope is the customer's acceptance, which must be obtained before any of the tasks in the scenario are even performed. Likewise, verifying the product has met its acceptance criteria refers to quality control, which should be complete before the customer's acceptance.

5. Answer C is correct. On an agile project, the closeout occurs at the end of each sprint during the sprint retrospective. The sprint review is the precursor to the retrospective, where the product owner approves or rejects the deliverable (making B incorrect). Option A is incorrect because it describes a predictive project. Option C is incorrect because key stakeholders do not approve the deliverable; the product owner approves it during the sprint review.

6. Answer A is correct. Although the other options look good, you must first follow the transition readiness steps to ensure that the organization is ready to accept this new system before going ahead and replacing the old system in the live environment. End users need training; they also need adequate support documents and support personnel. You must plan for the transition before you can perform any of the other option choices.

Chapter 16

"Do I Know This Already?" Quiz

1. Answer D is correct. All the options are benefits of tailoring the project management approach.

2. Answer B is correct. ADKAR is an organizational change model. The other three steps are tailoring process steps, along with tailoring for the project.

3. Answer D is correct. The document described in the question is the rollout plan because the scenario describes an organizational change management project. Option A is incorrect because the change management plan documents procedures regarding change control of a project (not organizational change management). There is no document called the change control plan,

making B incorrect. The project management plan (option C) includes all the subsidiary plans, baselines, and additional components, but specifically what is described here is the rollout plan.

4. Answers A, C, and F are correct. ADKAR stands for Awareness, Desire, Knowledge, Ability, Reinforcement. Adjourning is a stage in the Tuckman Model, denial is part of the Transition Model, and accept is a risk response strategy.

Review Questions

1. Answer A is correct. Because you are in a foreign country, you should tailor your leadership style according to local culture and customs. The same leadership style does not work in every situation; a good leader adjusts leadership style accordingly.

2. Answer C is correct. The project manager and the team are responsible for tailoring processes according to the situation. The sponsor provides funding for the project but is not responsible for the day-to-day work of a project.

3. Answer C is correct. procedures for customer acceptance are in the scope management plan. All the other options are included in the rollout plan.

4. Answer C is correct. Systems upgrade projects are not changes to the organization and so would not necessarily be organizational changes. Although it could be argued that many org changes require a systems upgrade (which is true), a systems upgrade by itself is not an org change. All the other options specifically lead to organizational changes.

Project Management Professional (PMP) Cert Guide Exam Updates

Over time, reader feedback allows Pearson to gauge which topics give our readers the most problems when taking the exams. To assist readers with those topics, the authors create new materials clarifying and expanding on those troublesome exam topics. As mentioned in the Introduction, the additional content about the exam is contained in a PDF on this book's companion website, at http://www.pearsonitcertification.com/title/9780137918935.

This appendix is intended to provide you with updated information if PMI makes minor modifications to the exam upon which this book is based. When PMI releases an entirely new exam, the changes are usually too extensive to provide in a simple updated appendix. In those cases, you might need to consult the new edition of the book for the updated content. This appendix attempts to fill the void that occurs with any print book. In particular, this appendix does the following:

- Mentions technical items that might not have been mentioned elsewhere in the book

- Covers new topics if PMI adds new content to the exam over time

- Provides a way to get up-to-the-minute current information about content for the exam

Always Get the Latest at the Book's Product Page

You are reading the version of this appendix that was available when your book was printed. However, given that the main purpose of this appendix is to be a living, changing document, it is important that you look for the latest version online at the book's companion website. To do so, follow these steps:

Step 1. Browse to www.pearsonitcertification.com/title/9780137918935.

Step 2. Click the **Updates** tab.

Step 3.   If there is a new Appendix B document on the page, download the latest Appendix B document.

> **NOTE**   The downloaded document has a version number. Comparing the version of the print Appendix B (Version 1.0) with the latest online version of this appendix, you should do the following:
>
> - **Same version:** Ignore the PDF that you downloaded from the companion website.
> - **Website has a later version:** Ignore this Appendix B in your book and read only the latest version that you downloaded from the companion website.

Technical Content

The current Version 1.0 of this appendix does not contain additional technical coverage.

Glossary of Key Terms

A

accuracy   The state when data points are on or close to the mean.

active listening   The process of providing feedback to the sender.

actual cost (AC)   The amount of money spent so far.

adaptive development approach   A development approach using both iterative and incremental approaches based on the values and principles from the Agile Manifesto.

ADKAR® Model   An organizational change management model that focuses on five sequential steps an individual must achieve when adapting to change.

administrative closure   The process of closing a project or phase (a.k.a. Close Project or Phase).

ambiguity   A state of being unclear, having difficulty in identifying the cause of events, or having multiple options to choose from.

B

baselines   The approved versions of a plan. A component of the project management plan.

benefit cost ratio   The ratio between expected cost and expected benefits.

benefits management plan   A plan that documents the process for achieving and sustaining the value of the project.

benefits owner   The accountable person to monitor, record, and report realized benefits.

benefits realization   The point where the value of the project is achieved.

bidders' conference   A meeting arranged by the buyer with all potential sellers.

Brightline® Initiative   A PMI model to support executives who need to know how to bridge the gap between strategy and execution.

budget at completion (BAC)   Also known as cost baseline, BAC is the original baseline budget for the project.

burndown chart   A chart that shows the work the agile team has remaining.

burnup chart   A chart that shows the work the agile team has accomplished.

business case   The documented economic feasibility study to establish the validity of the benefit.

business documents   Business case and benefits management plan.

business value   The net quantifiable benefit derived from the business endeavor.

C

cadence   The rhythm of activities conducted throughout the project.

complexity   A characteristic of a program or project or its environment that is difficult to manage due to system behavior, human behavior, and ambiguous nature.

configuration management   Version control.

conflict management   The set of techniques required to identify and resolve conflict in the workplace.

contingency reserve   Money set aside for known risks.

control account   A management point where scope, budget, and schedule are compared to earned value for performance measurement.

control chart   A tool to show whether a process is stable and predictable.

corrective action   An intentional activity that realigns the work with the project management plan.

cost aggregation   The process of adding up individual costs to determine the budget for the project.

cost management plan   A plan that documents procedures for managing cost.

cost of conformance   Money spent to avoid failures.

cost of nonconformance   Money spent due to failures.

cost performance index (CPI)   The cost efficiency you have achieved to date.

cost reimbursable contract   An arrangement in which the seller is reimbursed for all expenses.

cost variance (CV)   How much you have overspent or underspent based on the amount of work you have done so far.

crashing   Adding additional resources.

critical path   The longest path through a network representing the earliest completion for the project.

critical thinking   The objective analysis and evaluation of an issue to form a judgment.

cumulative flow diagram   A chart that shows the number of work items that have not started, are in progress, and are complete.

cycle time   A measurement that shows how long a particular task takes from start to finish.

D

decomposition   The technique of dividing the project into smaller manageable components.

defect repair   An intentional activity to modify a nonconforming product to ensure it meets requirements. Also referred to as *rework*.

definitive estimate   A range of –5% to +10%.

deliverable   Any unique and verifiable product, result, or service that is required to complete a phase, process, or project.

delivery cadence   The timing and frequency of project deliverables.

development approach   A method to create and evolve the product, service, or result during the project life cycle.

DevOps   A method or shared approach for a smooth delivery by improving communication and collaboration between the development and operations teams.

direct costs   Costs directly attributable to the project.

E

earned value (EV)   The amount of work that has been completed at a point in time (from a monetary perspective).

effective communication   The act of providing the right information to the right stakeholders at the right time, via the correct medium, addressing the audience.

efficient communication   The act of providing only the information needed in the shortest possible time.

emotional intelligence   The ability to identify, assess, and manage the personal emotions of oneself and other people, as well as the collective emotions of groups of people.

enterprise environmental factors (EEFs)   Conditions, not under project team control, that influence, constrain, or direct the project.

estimate at completion (EAC)   The forecasted budget for the project.

estimate to complete (ETC)   Funding required to complete the project from now until the end.

explicit knowledge   Knowledge that is tangible and easily codified.

F

fast-tracking   Converting sequential activities to parallel activities.

final report   The key artifact summarizing the project performance.

fixed costs   Costs that are fixed regardless of usage.

fixed price contract   An arrangement in which the seller provides the entire work at one fixed cost to the buyer.

forecasts   Projections based on historical data and trends, such as estimate to complete (ETC), to complete performance index (TCPI), variance at completion (VAC), and estimate at completion (EAC).

free float   The amount of time an activity can be delayed without delaying the early start of any subsequent activity.

funding limit reconciliation   The process of reconciling the work that needs to be performed with funding limits imposed by senior management.

G–J

gold-plating   A process similar to scope creep, but initiated by the project team rather than the customer.

grade   A category assigned to deliverables having the same functional use but different technical characteristics.

hybrid development approach   A development approach using some aspects of incremental and/or iterative approaches along with some aspects of predictive development approaches.

hypercare   Post-implementation support.

incremental development approach   A development approach in which the deliverable is produced successively, adding functionality until the deliverable contains the necessary and sufficient capability to be considered complete.

indirect costs   Costs shared among teams and departments.

information radiator   A collection of charts and graphs showing the status of the agile team and the status of the agile project.

interactive communication   A type of communication in which anyone can talk at any time.

interest   The level and frequency of information the stakeholder needs about your project.

interpersonal skills   Skills used to establish and maintain relationships with other people.

Ishikawa diagram   A tool to identify the root cause of an issue. Also known as a cause-and-effect diagram, a fishbone diagram, or a why-why diagram.

iterative development approach   A development approach in which the deliverable is produced by starting from an initial simplified (low fidelity) implementation and then progressively elaborating on the solution until it contains all the features, details, and/or correctness to be considered complete (high fidelity).

K–L

Kanban board   A chart that shows work that has started, is in progress, and is complete. Also known as the task board and Scrum board.

kill point   The point where the project is cancelled.

Kotter's 8-Step Model   A top-down organizational change management approach.

lag   An imposed delay due to the nature of the work or other factors impacting the project.

leads   The amount of time successor activities can be adjusted so they can start earlier.

legitimacy   The level of involvement that a stakeholder has on a project.

M

make or buy analysis   A process used to determine whether to outsource the work or perform it in-house.

management reserve   Money set aside for unknown risks.

Managing Change in Organizations: A Practice Guide   An iterative model based on several change management models that is focused on many feedback loops for optimum success.

minimum business increment (MBI)   The smallest amount of value that can be added that benefits the business.

minimum viable product (MVP)   The smallest collection of features for a product to be considered functional.

mood chart   A visual used to track the mood and reaction of stakeholders using emojis and icons.

motivation   The reason or reasons one has for acting or behaving in a particular way.

N

negotiation   An acceptable agreement reached between two or more parties.

net present value   The difference between the present value of inflows of capital and the present value of outflows.

net promoter score   A number used to gauge customer satisfaction.

North Star statement   A declaration that articulates the vision and strategic objectives of the transformation.

O

opportunity   A positive risk. An uncertain event or condition that, if it occurs, has a positive effect on one or more project objectives.

organizational process assets (OPAs)   Plans, processes, policies, procedures, or knowledge bases specific to and used by the performing organization.

osmotic communication   The act of absorbing the information around you without any direct communication.

outcome   An end result or consequence of a process or project. It can include outputs, artifacts, benefits, and value delivered.

P

Pareto chart   A histogram showing issues in descending order of frequency.

phase gate   The point where a determination is made whether to continue a project (a.k.a. stage gate, governance gate, toll gate, phase end).

planned value (PV)   The amount of work that should have been completed at a point in time (from a monetary perspective).

portfolio   A group of projects, programs, subsidiary programs, and operations managed together to achieve strategic objectives.

power   The level of authority a stakeholder has on a project.

precedence diagramming method   A method to sequence activities and create the schedule. Also known as *activity on node*.

precision   A state that occurs when data points are clustered together (little scatter).

predictive development approach   A development approach that leverages a traditional waterfall sequential phased approach that results in a single delivery of the deliverable at the end of the project.

preventive action   An intentional activity that ensures future performance of the work aligns with the project management plan deliverables, assumptions, constraints, and requirements.

principles of project management   Foundational statements to guide the behavior of the people involved with a project.

privity   The contractual obligations between the buyer and seller.

product   A quantifiable component or result generated from the project.

product backlog   A prioritized list of user stories.

product roadmap   A tool used in Agile to show a high-level timeline of the product deliverables.

program   A group of related projects and activities that are managed in a coordinated manner to obtain benefits not available from managing them individually.

progress report   A report that shows what has been accomplished since the previous update.

project   A temporary endeavor to produce a unique product, service, or result.

project activity   The amount of time a project can be delayed without impacting an externally imposed deadline.

project charter   The formal authorization for the project to begin.

project life cycle   The series of phases that a project passes through from start to completion. It includes all the work for the project, not just the development approach.

project management   The application of knowledge, skills, tools, and techniques to project activities to meet project requirements.

project management knowledge areas   Identified areas of project management defined by knowledge requirements and described in terms of component processes, practices, inputs, outputs, tools, and techniques.

Project Management Office (PMO)   A management structure that standardizes the project-related governance processes and facilitates the sharing of resources, methodologies, tools, and techniques.

project management plan   The document that describes how the project will be executed, monitored, and controlled and is composed of the subsidiary plans, baselines, and additional components.

project management process groups   Logical groupings of project management inputs, tools, techniques, and outputs. The groups are Initiating, Planning, Executing, Monitoring and Controlling, and Closing.

project management team   The members of the project team directly involved in project management activities.

project manager   The person assigned by the performing organization to lead the team that is responsible for accomplishing the project objectives.

project performance domains   Groups of related activities that are critical for the effective delivery of project outcomes.

project phase   A collection of logically related project activities that culminate in the completion of one or more deliverables.

project team   The set of individuals performing the work to achieve the objectives of the project.

pull communication   Information saved in a central repository that can be retrieved at the stakeholders' leisure.

push communication   One-way communication to a specific audience.

Q

quality   The degree to which a set of inherent characteristics fulfills requirements.

quality assurance   The act of verifying the project process.

quality audit   The structured independent review of the quality management process.

quality control   The act of testing the product.

R

regulation   Rules imposed by a government body.

requirements documentation   Records that document what is to be delivered on the project.

resource leveling   Adjusting start and end dates based on availability of resources.

resource management plan   The component of the project management plan that provides guidance on how project resources should be categorized, identified, allocated, managed, and released.

resource smoothing   Making schedule adjustments within the amount of total float and free float.

return on investment   A measure of the amount of financial return to the cost.

risk   An uncertain event or condition that, if it occurs, has a positive or negative effect on one or more project objectives.

risk acceptance   A risk response strategy whereby the project team decides to acknowledge the risk and not take any action unless the risk event occurs.

risk appetite   The degree of uncertainty an organization or individual is willing to accept in anticipation of a reward or benefit.

risk avoidance   A risk response strategy whereby the project team acts to eliminate the threat or protect the project from its impact.

risk breakdown structure   A hierarchical representation of potential sources of risk.

risk categorization   Organization of the project risk sources by the project area affected, or other useful category, to determine the project areas most exposed to the effects of uncertainty.

risk category   A group of potential causes of risk. Often used in the risk breakdown structure.

risk enhancement   A risk response strategy whereby the project team acts to increase the probability of occurrence or impact of an opportunity.

risk escalation   A risk response strategy whereby the project team acknowledges that the risk is outside its sphere of influence and shifts the ownership of the risk to a higher level of the organization where it is more effectively managed.

risk exploitation   A risk response strategy whereby the project team acts to ensure that an opportunity occurs.

risk exposure   An aggregate measure of the potential impact of all risks at any given point in time in a project, program, or portfolio.

risk management plan   A component of the project, program, or portfolio plan that describes how risk management activities will be structured and performed.

risk mitigation   A risk response strategy whereby the project team acts to decrease the probability of occurrence or impact of a threat.

risk register   A repository in which outputs of the risk management processes are recorded.

risk report   A project document that summarizes information on individual project risks and the level of overall project risk at any point in time on the project.

risk review   The process of analyzing the effectiveness of risk responses in dealing with individual project risks and overall project risk and of identifying new risks.

risk sharing   A risk response strategy whereby the project team allocates ownership of an opportunity to a third party who is best able to capture the benefit of that opportunity.

risk threshold   The measure of acceptable variation around a project objective that reflects the risk appetite of the organization and stakeholders. Below this level, the organization will accept the risk; above it, it will not be accepted.

risk tolerance   The maximum potential impact of a risk that the stakeholder or organization is willing to accept for a given risk.

risk transference   A risk response strategy whereby the project team shifts the impact of a threat and ownership of the response to a third party.

rollout plan   A plan that documents the organizational change management plan, which includes knowledge transfer, training, and readiness activities required to implement the business change.

rough order of magnitude   A range of –25% to +75%.

rule of seven (rule of 7)   Seven consecutive datapoints above or below the mean that signifies the process has gone out of control.

S

salience model   A type of classification model based on stakeholders' levels of power, legitimacy, and urgency, shown as a Venn diagram.

scatter diagram   A tool that shows a correlation between two variables.

schedule performance index (SPI)   The rate of performance of the work achieved to date.

schedule variance (SV)   How much ahead of schedule or behind schedule you are at a point in time (expressed in a monetary form).

scope baseline   An artifact that contains the scope statement, WBS, and WBS dictionary.

scope creep   The uncontrolled expansion of work without adjustment to the time, budget, or resources.

scope statement   A detailed description of the product scope and project scope that will include major deliverables, assumptions, constraints, and requirements.

servant leadership   The practice of leading the team by focusing on understanding and addressing the needs and development of team members to enable the highest possible team performance.

single source   A preferred vendor.

SMART   Specific, Measurable, Achievable, Relevant, Time-bound.

sole source   The only vendor that can provide the good or service.

source selection analysis   An analysis to determine the minimum attributes the potential must possess to be considered.

stakeholder   An individual, group, or organization that may affect, be affected by, or perceive itself to be affected by a decision, activity, or outcome of a project, program, or portfolio.

stakeholder engagement assessment matrix   A document that shows the current and desired engagement levels of stakeholders.

stakeholder engagement plan   A plan that identifies the strategies and actions required to engage and collaborate with stakeholders.

stakeholder grid   A type of classification model that a project manager may use to prioritize stakeholders and determine the management approach to stakeholders based on their levels of power, interest, influence, or impact on the project.

stakeholder register   An artifact documenting stakeholders' contact information, position/title, power, and influence, among others.

standard   Best practice.

status report   A document that shows where the project currently stands.

subsidiary management plans   Plans that document procedures and processes of the project. A component of the project management plan.

System for Value Delivery   A collection of strategic business activities aimed at building, sustaining, and/or advancing an organization. Portfolios, programs, projects, products, and operations can all be part of an organization's system for value delivery.

T

tacit knowledge   Knowledge that is intangible and personal, based on beliefs, thought processes, insights, and experiences.

tailoring   The adaption of the project management approach, governance, and processes to make them more suitable for the given environment and work at hand.

team charter   An artifact that documents the values, agreements, and operating guidelines for the project team.

threat   A negative risk. An uncertain event or condition that, if it occurs, has a negative effect on one or more project objectives.

throughput   The number of items being completed in a fixed time frame.

time and material (T&M) contract   An arrangement in which the seller is paid for their time and reimbursed for materials.

to complete performance index (TCPI)   The rate of cost efficiency you need to achieve to meet the budget.

total float   The amount of time an activity can be delayed without delaying the end date.

Transition Model A type of model that identifies three stages of transition in an attempt to provide an understanding of what occurs to individuals psychologically when an organizational change takes place.

transition plan A plan for moving the deliverable to ongoing operations or go-live (a.k.a. implementation plan or rollout plan).

U

uncertainty A lack of understanding and awareness of issues, events, paths to follow, or solutions to pursue.

urgency How quickly stakeholders need immediate attention or regular information about the project.

user story An agile requirement.

V

validate scope The process of formalizing the acceptance of the deliverable.

value The worth, importance, or usefulness of something. Different stakeholders perceive value in different ways.

variable costs Costs that vary with usage.

variance at completion (VAC) How much over or under budget you expect to be by the end of the project.

velocity A measurement of how many story points have been completed in a sprint and shown on a velocity chart.

Virginia Satir Model A type of model that addresses how people experience and cope with organizational change.

volatility The possibility for rapid and unpredictable change.

W–Z

work breakdown structure A hierarchical decomposition of the total scope of work to be carried out by the team to accomplish the project objectives.

work package The lowest level of the WBS.

work performance data (WPD) Raw observations, actual results.

work performance information (WPI) An interpretation of the work performance data.

work performance report (WPR) A representation or summary of the work performance information.

Index